*Eugene O'Neill Remembered*

AMERICAN WRITERS REMEMBERED
Jackson R. Bryer, Series Editor

# Eugene O'Neill Remembered

Edited by

BRENDA MURPHY
and
GEORGE MONTEIRO

THE UNIVERSITY OF ALABAMA PRESS
Tuscaloosa

The University of Alabama Press
Tuscaloosa, Alabama 35487-0380
uapress.ua.edu



Hardcover edition published 2016.
Paperback edition published 2022.
eBook edition published 2016.



Typeface: Garamond

Cover image: Eugene O'Neill in his Provincetown Players days; Library of Congress, Reproduction Number: LC-B7901-36
Cover design: Michele Myatt Quinn

Paperback ISBN: 978-0-8173-6045-0

A previous edition of this book has been cataloged by the Library of Congress.
ISBN: 978-0-8173-1931-1 (cloth)
E-ISBN: 978-0-8173-9064-8

*To Dante and Aldo Morelli and Dhruv Iyer Monteiro*

# Contents


Acknowledgments xi

Chronology xiii

Introduction 1

PART 1. NEW LONDON, SCHOOL, AND WANDERING (1888–1913) 7

1. George C. Tyler 9
2. Warren H. Hastings and Richard F. Weeks 11
3. Kathleen Jenkins Pitt-Smith 18
4. William Lee 20
5. Pierre Loving 22
6. Mabel Haynes 25
7. Clayton Hamilton 28
8. Irvin S. Cobb 31
9. Frederick P. Latimer 33
10. Arthur B. McGinley 36
11. Robert A. Woodworth 39

PART 2. CAMBRIDGE, PROVINCETOWN, AND GREENWICH VILLAGE (1914–1917) 43

12. Beatrice Ashe Maher 45
13. John V. A. Weaver 47
14. Susan Glaspell 51
15. Mary Heaton Vorse 53
16. Hutchins Hapgood 56
17. Harry Kemp 59
18. Adele Nathan 66
19. Dorothy Day 70
20. William Carlos Williams 74

PART 3. PROVINCETOWN PLAYHOUSE, PEAKED HILL BAR, RIDGEFIELD, BROADWAY (1918–1927) 77
21. Hazel Hawthorne Werner 79
22. Juliet Throckmorton 84
23. Manuel Zora 88
24. Edmund Wilson 89
25. Charles O'Brien Kennedy 92
26. Agnes Boulton 94
27. Jasper Deeter 102
28. Stark Young 104
29. Malcolm Cowley 110
30. Hart Crane 118
31. Harold De Polo 121
32. Brooks Atkinson 130
33. Calvin Hoffman 132

PART 4. EUROPE, GEORGIA, THE THEATRE GUILD, CALIFORNIA (1928–1937) 141
34. Louis Fladger 143
35. John Lardner 144
36. Bennett Cerf 146
37. Lawrence Langner 150
38. Brooks Atkinson 158
39. Rouben Mamoulian 161
40. Theresa Helburn 165
41. George Jean Nathan 187
42. Maxine Edie Benedict 198

PART 5. CALIFORNIA AND NEW YORK (1938–1948) 201
43. Carlotta Monterey O'Neill 203
44. Marcella Markham 211
45. Ingrid Bergman 212
46. Sean O'Casey 215
47. Karl Schriftgiesser 220
48. S. J. Woolf 224
49. Max Gordon 229
50. Herbert J. Stoeckel 231

51. Saxe Commins 237
52. Bennett Cerf 249
53. Paul Crabtree 252
54. Mary Welch 257

PART 6. MARBLEHEAD AND BOSTON (1948–1953) 263
55. Saxe Commins 265
56. Carlotta Monterey O'Neill 276
57. Bennett Cerf 281
58. Earle F. Johnson 283
59. Frederic B. Mayo, MD 287
60. Sallie Coughlin 290
61. Russel Crouse 295
62. Carl Van Vechten 303

List of Reminiscences 307
Additional Reminiscences 311
Biographical Sketches of Important Names 313
Permissions 317
Notes 321
Works Cited 351
Index 359

Illustrations follow page 177.

# Acknowledgments

A volume like this incurs many debts for its authors. We are particularly grateful to Julie Cyzewski for her expert and dedicated research assistance in the project's early stages. Libraries and librarians were equally essential to our work, particularly the Interlibrary Loan division of the University of Connecticut Libraries, Benjamin Panciera of the Department of Special Collections, Charles E. Shain Library at Connecticut College, and the staffs of the Beinecke Rare Book and Manuscript Library at Yale University and the Billy Rose Theatre Division, New York Public Library for the Performing Arts. We are grateful to the many individuals who were helpful to us in securing manuscripts or permission to publish them. We would particularly like to thank Michael Burlingame, Timothy Crouse, Michele Slung, Louis Peck, Celia Irvine, Deborah Hobson, Carol LaDuke, Anna Avellar, Scott Kovarovics, James T. MacIlveen, Samuel Ceccarelli, Barbara Andreasson, Wendy Cooper, Bill and Kent Brewer, Claudia Andreasen Fetzer, Daniel Sullivan, Erica Varela, Camille Apodaca, Susan Areson, Angel Diggs, and Diana Pesek. We are grateful to Robert Dowling for his thoughtful comments on the manuscript and to Daniel Waterman and Jackson R. Bryer for their editorial oversight.

# Chronology of Eugene Gladstone O'Neill

| | |
|---|---|
| 1888 | Eugene O'Neill is born in New York on October 16, 1888, the third son of James O'Neill, a famous actor, and Mary Ellen (Ella) Quinlan O'Neill, preceded by James Jr., born in 1878, and Edmund Burke, who was born in 1883 and died in 1885. Ella becomes addicted to morphine after Eugene's birth. |
| 1895 | Eugene O'Neill is enrolled at St. Aloysius, a boarding school in Riverdale, New York. |
| 1902 | Begins his attendance at Betts Academy, a boarding school in Stamford, Connecticut. |
| 1906 | Enters Princeton University in the fall but is dismissed in spring 1907 and does not return. |
| 1909 | Has a romance with Kathleen Jenkins and marries her when she becomes pregnant. Before the child (Eugene Gladstone O'Neill Jr.) is born (on May 4, 1910), O'Neill leaves for San Francisco and then goes on to Honduras. |
| 1910 | Works temporarily as stage manager with his father's company on tour but soon sails for Buenos Aires, arriving on August 4. Stays eight months. |
| 1911 | Returns to New York as ordinary seaman on the freighter *Ikala*. Visits Kathleen and his son once and lives in a waterfront flophouse run by "Jimmy the Priest" (James Condon). Sails to London and returns to Jimmy the Priest's. Is divorced by Kathleen. |
| 1912 | Attempts suicide by taking an overdose of the barbiturate Veronal at Jimmy the Priest's. Returns to New London, where he works as a reporter on the *New London Telegraph*. In November, O'Neill is diagnosed with tuberculosis and enters Fairfield County State Sanatorium in Shelton, Connecticut, but stays only two days. |

On December 24 he enters Gaylord Farm, a private sanatorium in Wallingford, Connecticut.

1913 O'Neill writes his first plays: *The Web*, *Thirst*, *Recklessness*, and *Warnings*. His tuberculosis arrested, he returns to New London on June 3.

1914 Has a romance with Beatrice Ashe. Enrolls as special student in George Pierce Baker's playwriting workshop at Harvard University. James O'Neill pays for his year at Harvard and the publication of his *Thirst, and Other One-Act Plays*. Ella O'Neill overcomes her addiction.

1915 Eugene O'Neill goes to New York and stays at the Garden Hotel, drinking heavily at the hotel saloon and at The Golden Swan ("Hell Hole"). Meets Terry Carlin, an anarchist drifter and alcoholic.

1916 Goes with Carlin to Provincetown, Massachusetts, where the first production of an O'Neill play, *Bound East for Cardiff*, takes place on July 28, followed by *Thirst* in August. Associates with Provincetown Players, including George Cram Cook, Susan Glaspell, John Reed, Hutchins Hapgood, Neith Boyce, Wilbur Daniel Steele, and Saxe Commins. They produce *Before Breakfast* on December 1. He begins an affair with Louise Bryant, which continues even after she marries John Reed later in the year.

1917 In New York's Greenwich Village, Provincetown Players premiere his plays *Fog*, *The Sniper*, *The Long Voyage Home*, and *Ile*, on, respectively, January 5, February 16, November 2, and November 30. Washington Square Players open *In the Zone* on October 31. O'Neill publishes "Tomorrow," a short story, in *Seven Arts* magazine. He meets the journalist Dorothy Day and the magazine-fiction writer Agnes Boulton.

1918 On April 12 O'Neill marries Agnes Boulton. *The Rope* premieres at the Provincetown Playhouse on April 26, *Where the Cross Is Made* on November 22, and *The Moon of the Caribbees* on December 20. *Beyond the Horizon* is optioned for Broadway.

1919 Son Shane Rudraighe O'Neill is born on October 30. *The Moon of the Caribbees and Six Other Plays of the*

*Sea*, published by Boni & Liveright, is well received by reviewers. O'Neill begins a friendship with the critic George Jean Nathan. In May he moves to Provincetown, where he takes up residence in Peaked Hill Bar, a former Coast Guard life-saving station. *Chris Christophersen* is optioned for Broadway. *The Dreamy Kid*, with an all-black cast, is produced by the Provincetown Players, opening on October 31.

1920 *Beyond the Horizon*, opening on February 2, wins the Pulitzer Prize for drama in June. James O'Neill, the playwright's father, dies on August 10. *Exorcism* opens on March 26, *Gold* on June 1, and *Diff'rent* on December 27. O'Neill revises *Chris Christophersen*, retitled *Chris*, the Broadway production of which had closed in Philadelphia in February, into *"Anna Christie."*[1] Provincetown Players stage *The Emperor Jones* on November 1 and *Diff'rent* on December 27. *The Emperor Jones* moves to Broadway with the black actor Charles Gilpin in the lead.

1921 O'Neill meets critic Kenneth Macgowan and designer Robert Edmond Jones. O'Neill's protest of the New York Drama League's decision not to invite Gilpin to its annual awards dinner results in the reversal of that decision. *Gold*, a longer version of *Where the Cross Is Made*, opens on Broadway on June 1 but lasts for only thirteen performances. O'Neill visits with his son Eugene for the first time since his infancy. *"Anna Christie"* opens a successful run on Broadway on November 2. *The Straw* opens on November 19.

1922 O'Neill's mother dies on February 28. *The First Man* opens on March 4. The Provincetown Players produce *The Hairy Ape*, opening the production on March 9, moving it to Broadway in April. *"Anna Christie"* is awarded the Pulitzer Prize. In the fall O'Neill and his family move to a fifteen-room house in Ridgefield, Connecticut, bought for $32,000.

1923 Receives Gold Medal from National Institute of Arts and Letters. *"Anna Christie"* opens in London. Brother Jamie dies on November 8. With Kenneth Macgowan and Robert Edmond Jones, O'Neill takes control of the inactive Provincetown Players; out of this emerges the Experimental Theatre, Inc.

1924 *Welded* opens March 17 but has a disappointingly short run. *The Ancient Mariner*, a dramatic adaptation of Coleridge's poem, opens at the Provincetown Playhouse on April 6. *All God's Chillun Got Wings*, amid controversy over the scene in which the white actress Mary Blair kisses the hand of the black actor Paul Robeson, opens at the Provincetown Playhouse on May 15. *Desire Under the Elms* opens November 11 at the Greenwich Village Theatre. O'Neill family goes to Bermuda on November 29.

1925 *Desire Under the Elms* moves to Broadway. Later banned in Boston and England. Daughter Oona is born in Bermuda on May 14. Returns to Ridgefield in October. *The Fountain* opens at the Greenwich Village Theatre on December 10.

1926 O'Neill stops drinking after psychoanalytic treatment with Dr. G. V. Hamilton. *The Great God Brown* opens on January 23 and has a successful run. O'Neill returns to Bermuda in late February and buys Spithead, a two-hundred-year-old-house on the water. In June receives an honorary doctorate from Yale University. On vacation in Maine is reacquainted with the actress Carlotta Monterey (she had played the role of Mildred in *The Hairy Ape* on Broadway) and begins an affair. Returns to Spithead in November.

1927 Finishes first draft of *Strange Interlude* in February. Boni & Liveright publishes *Marco Millions* in April and a revised *Lazarus Laughed* in November. *Marco Millions* and *Strange Interlude* optioned by Theatre Guild. Marriage deteriorates as affair with Carlotta intensifies.

1928 *Marco Millions* opens on January 9. *Strange Interlude* opens on January 30, eventually running for 426 performances. When published, *Strange Interlude* sells more than 100,000 copies over the next three years. Accompanied by Carlotta, O'Neill leaves for Europe on February 10. In March rents a villa in southern France.

Receives Pulitzer Prize for *Strange Interlude*. Leaves with Carlotta for China on October 5.

1929 On January 1 Carlotta leaves O'Neill in Ceylon after they quarrel, but they are reunited in Egypt two weeks later. While O'Neill is away from New York, the Theatre Guild production of *Dynamo* opens on February 11; it is badly received by the reviewers. The author of the novel *The Temple of Pallas-Athene*, Gladys Lewis (writing as "Georges Lewys"), sues O'Neill, charging that *Strange Interlude* is plagiarized from her privately published novel. Moves to Château du Plessis (which they often abbreviated as "Le Plessis" among themselves and in their writings) in St. Antoine-du-Rocher, near Tours, in early June. On July 2 Agnes is granted a divorce in Reno, Nevada. O'Neill marries Carlotta on July 22.

1930 Writes the first four drafts of *Mourning Becomes Electra*. The second movie version of *"Anna Christie,"* starring Greta Garbo in her first talking role, is released. In May attends performances of *All God's Chillun Got Wings* and *Desire Under the Elms* by the experimental Soviet theater company Kamerny.

1931 In February–March completes the fifth and sixth drafts of *Mourning Becomes Electra*; mails the typescript to the Theatre Guild on April 7. Judge John W. Woolsey decides against Gladys Lewis in the *Strange Interlude* plagiarism case. On May 19 Ralph Barton, Carlotta's second husband, commits suicide. In June O'Neill rents house on Long Island. On October 26 *Mourning Becomes Electra* opens; it runs for 150 performances. In November, O'Neill and Carlotta go to Sea Island, Georgia.

1932 In May, O'Neill and Carlotta return to Sea Island, staying in a rented cottage while awaiting completion of the house they call Casa Genotta. On September 1, O'Neill begins *Ah, Wilderness!* Completes a first draft in four weeks.

1933 Sells film rights to *The Emperor Jones* for $30,000. Released later in the year, the film stars Paul Robeson and Dudley Digges. With the bankruptcy of his publisher, Liveright, Inc., signs with Random House after Bennett Cerf visits him on Sea Island. Becomes friends with Russel Crouse, publicist for the Theatre Guild. On October 2 *Ah, Wilderness!* opens on Broadway and runs for nearly three hundred performances. O'Neill sells screen rights for $37,500.

1934 On January 8 *Days Without End* (his so-called Catholic play) opens in New York and runs for only fifty-seven performances. The play is staged in Ireland by the Abbey Theatre later in the year. In October, O'Neill meets the Irish playwright Sean O'Casey in New York. O'Neill consults doctors, who tell him he risks a "nervous breakdown."

1935 Plans his never-finished cycle of plays, "A Tale of Possessors Self-Dispossessed," about several generations of an American family from the early nineteenth century forward. In November begins writing *A Touch of the Poet*.

1936 On November 12 awarded the Nobel Prize for Literature. Moves to San Francisco after a brief stay in Seattle.

1937 The O'Neills sell Casa Genotta at Sea Island, Georgia, and on December 30 move to Tao House, which they have built in Danville, east of San Francisco Bay.

1938 Starts *More Stately Mansions*. Eugene Jr., now teaching at Yale University, coedits with Whitney Oates *Complete Greek Drama*.

1939 In January revises *More Stately Mansions*. Rewrites *A Touch of the Poet*. Begins writing *The Iceman Cometh* and composes scenario for the play he is then calling *Long Day's Journey*.

1940 His tremor, present since childhood, worsens. Begins to write *Long Day's Journey Into Night*, finishing a first draft at the end of September. On December 17 the Dalmatian nicknamed "Blemie" dies, and O'Neill writes "The Last Will and Testament of Silverdene Emblem O'Neill" in tribute to his favorite among all his dogs.

1941 During March, O'Neill works on *Long Day's Journey Into Night*. In April he writes the one-act *Hughie*. He begins *A Moon for the Misbegotten* in October and works on it for the rest of the year. His tremor is misdiagnosed as Parkinson's disease.

1942 O'Neill completes the first draft of *A Moon for the Misbegotten* in January. In November he finishes revising *A Touch of the Poet.*

1943 Finishes *A Moon for the Misbegotten*, which turns out to be his last complete play. His daughter, Oona, seeks reconciliation unsuccessfully with O'Neill after her marriage to Charlie Chaplin on June 16. O'Neill sells film rights to *The Hairy Ape* for $30,000.

1944 In February, Tao House is sold, and the O'Neills move to a San Francisco hotel. Revises *A Moon for the Misbegotten* and *A Touch of the Poet.* At times he is now entirely incapacitated by tremors.

1945 In October the O'Neills move to the Hotel Barclay in New York. Eugene deposits copy of *Long Day's Journey Into Night* with Random House, his publisher, with instructions that the play may be published twenty-five years after his death but never staged.

1946 In New York for rehearsals of Theatre Guild production of *The Iceman Cometh*, directed by Eddie Dowling. Opens on October 9 to mixed reviews.

1947 In New York for rehearsals of *A Moon for the Misbegotten*, which is produced on the road in several midwestern cities but does not make it to New York. The Guild's planned production of *A Touch of the Poet* is postponed at O'Neill's request.

1948 In January, O'Neill is hospitalized in New York with a broken left arm sustained eleven days after Carlotta left him following a quarrel; they are reconciled. In the autumn moves to the shorefront house in Marblehead, Massachusetts, that he and Carlotta have purchased. His son Shane is convicted of heroin possession and is imprisoned after O'Neill refuses to post bail. His tremor worsens, making walking difficult.

1949 Worsening tremor in hands makes it impossible to write.

1950 On September 25 Eugene Jr. commits suicide.

1951 On February 3, after a quarrel with Carlotta, O'Neill goes outside, breaks his right leg when he slips in the snow, and is left there for nearly an hour until the arrival of Dr. Frederic Mayo, who takes him to Salem Hospital. On February 6 Carlotta is admitted to a psychiatric hospital. O'Neill is moved to Doctors' Hospital in New York through the efforts of his friends. After consideration once again of separation and divorce, the O'Neills reconcile and move to what turns out to be the playwright's final home, a suite at the Shelton Hotel in Boston. Communication with his surviving children and most of his friends is cut off.

1952 Destroys manuscripts pertaining to his unfinished cycle plays. Random House publishes *A Moon for the Misbegotten*. O'Neill makes Carlotta the sole literary executor of his writings, published and unpublished.

1953 On November 27 Eugene O'Neill dies of pneumonia at the Hotel Shelton. He is buried on December 2 at Forest Hills Cemetery in Boston.

1956 Through Carlotta's efforts, and contrary to O'Neill's stated wish, *Long Day's Journey Into Night* is produced, first in Stockholm in February, and then, after several other European productions, in New York in November. It is published by Yale University Press.

*Eugene O'Neill Remembered*

# Introduction

The life of Eugene O'Neill has long been shrouded in myth. After the extended series of interviews with Barrett H. Clark that resulted in *Eugene O'Neill: The Man and His Plays* (1926), the first book about its subject, O'Neill rarely gave personal interviews and was not forthcoming about the details of his life. He also abetted, with anecdotes and allusions, some of the misconceptions about his youth, such as the story that he was expelled from Princeton for throwing a rock or a beer bottle through Woodrow Wilson's window, and exaggerated the amount of time he had spent at sea. The myth of the hard-drinking, tormented playwright with a tragic view of life was further extended when *Long Day's Journey Into Night* was produced in 1956, three years after his death instead of the twenty-five he had stipulated. The play's autobiographical elements were immediately recognized, and he was identified by critics as the inspiration for Edmund, the innocent younger brother who was victimized by his mother's morphine addiction, his father's parsimony, and his brother's jealousy and corrupting influence.

The myth of the tragic O'Neill was solidified in Croswell Bowen's biography, *The Curse of the Misbegotten: A Tale of the House of O'Neill* (1959), written "with the assistance of Shane O'Neill," O'Neill's second son. With Bowen's account as background, in the public mind O'Neill became the center of an American tragedy of classical Greek proportions. The drug addiction and alcoholism of his parents was seen to produce a dysfunctional family dynamic that repeated itself in his own and his brother Jamie's lives, and in the lives of his children. Eugene Jr. was an alcoholic who killed himself; Shane was a heroin addict who also killed himself. Oona married the fifty-four-year-old Charlie Chaplin when she was eighteen and had eight children with him. Although she was long thought to be the one O'Neill immune to the curse, Oona was revealed by her biographer to suffer from alcoholism as well. O'Neill himself was finally able to stop drinking, most of the time, in 1926, as his mother had stopped taking morphine in 1914, but he developed a degenerative brain disease, long erroneously thought to have been Parkinson's, and he found himself, with devastating tragic irony, physically unable to write, and trapped in a severely dysfunctional relationship with his third wife, Carlotta, for the last years of his life. He saw little of his children and had nothing to do with Oona after her marriage. His will disinherited his two surviving children, Shane and Oona.

The outline of the tragic narrative is still very much alive in contemporary accounts of O'Neill's life that dominate the public imagination, such as Ric Burns's *Eugene O'Neill: A Documentary Film* (2006). There have also been several excellent biographies that represent his life from a more informed and judicious perspective, particularly Louis Sheaffer's two-volume Pulitzer Prize–winning biography, *O'Neill: Son and Playwright* (1968) and *O'Neill: Son and Artist* (1973). Arthur and Barbara Gelb worked for many years on their biography, *O'Neill* (1962), publishing an "enlarged edition" (1973) and an additional volume about O'Neill's early life, *O'Neill: Life with Monte Cristo* (2000). From a psychoanalytic point of view, Stephen Black has contributed *Eugene O'Neill: Beyond Mourning and Tragedy* (1999), which specifically seeks to penetrate beyond the myth to the man himself. Most recently, Robert Dowling has written *Eugene O'Neill: A Life in Four Acts* (2014).

The aim of this collection differs from the aim of the biographer, which is essentially to construct a single narrative of a life that conveys the biographer's interpretation of the subject. This often requires sifting through many versions of an event or a motive to choose the one that best fits a narrative that is as accurate and consistent as the biographer can make it in the context of the biographer's overall account of the person. This collection does not provide a consistent narrative or point of view, and it unabashedly presents impressions rather than "the truth." Its purpose is to present O'Neill as others saw him and described him in their first-person accounts, which are as varied as the tellers themselves. Many of the impressions in the more than sixty chapters that make up the collection conflict with and contradict one another. The end result, we hope, is a composite portrait, more cubist than realist, but, in reflecting the many perspectives trained on O'Neill, a revealing one. A good example is the layered accounts of the events on February 5, 1951, when O'Neill, lightly dressed, left the house he shared with his third wife, Carlotta, in Marblehead, Massachusetts, during an argument, fell in the snow, broke his leg, and was left lying there by Carlotta for almost an hour before the family physician, Dr. Frederic Mayo, arrived and rescued him. Rather than trying to present the "truth" of the incident, this volume offers the direct accounts by Carlotta and Dr. Mayo; the accounts of O'Neill's friend and editor, Saxe Commins, and his nurse, Sallie Coughlin, who heard the story of that night directly from O'Neill; and the second-hand account of O'Neill's publisher, Bennett Cerf. Like all narratives, these accounts reflect the varied perspectives and agendas of the tellers. Readers have the opportunity to weigh the versions against one another.

The basic facts of O'Neill's life are by now well established, and the reader can review them in the chronology and headnotes to the six parts of this volume. O'Neill received the Nobel Prize for Literature in 1936, largely on the strength of *Strange Interlude* and *Mourning Becomes Electra*, but his reputation declined during the 1940s. With José Quintero's successful Off-Broadway revival of *The Iceman Cometh* and his Broadway production of *Long Day's Journey Into Night* in 1956, along with the play's publication, thanks to Carlotta O'Neill's disregard for his ban on producing it or publishing it for twenty-five years, O'Neill's reputation was completely revived in the 1950s. He is now recognized, with Tennessee Williams and Arthur Miller, as one of the three most significant playwrights the United States has produced.

The chapters in this book are first-person accounts of O'Neill at every stage of his life, from George Tyler's memories of the screaming infant Eugene to Sallie Coughlin's interview about nursing him after the Marblehead incident. The chapters include memoirs, letters, diary and journal entries, interviews, and newspaper and magazine articles. Particularly interesting are the previously unpublished memoirs by Hazel Hawthorne Werner, who knew Eugene and his second wife, Agnes, in Provincetown, and Calvin Hoffman, who spent time with O'Neill in the late 1920s; the transcript of Seymour Peck's interview with Carlotta in 1956; and the diary entries and interview of Russel Crouse, who facilitated the reconciliation of Eugene and Carlotta twice after major battles, in 1948 and 1951. Also appearing for the first time in their complete state are the notes of O'Neill biographer Louis Sheaffer from his interviews with O'Neill's first wife, Kathleen Jenkins Pitt-Smith; Mabel Haynes, a nurse who cared for Ella O'Neill during her addiction; Beatrice Ashe Maher, O'Neill's New London girlfriend; Provincetown character Manuel Zora; *Marco Millions* director Rouben Mamoulian; Paul Crabtree, who originated the role of Don Parritt in *The Iceman Cometh*; and Salem nurse Sallie Coughlin.

The aim in selecting the chapters has been to achieve a balance among several types of sources: 1) well-known friends and associates of O'Neill, such as Susan Glaspell, Hutchins Hapgood, Dorothy Day, William Carlos Williams, Edmund Wilson, Mary Heaton Vorse, Stark Young, Malcolm Cowley, Hart Crane, Bennett Cerf, Sean O'Casey, Russel Crouse, Ingrid Bergman, and Carl Van Vechten; 2) people whose names might not be household words but who played an important part in his personal or professional life, such as his wives, Kathleen Jenkins, Agnes Boulton, and Carlotta Monterey; the Theatre Guild producers and directors Lawrence Langner, Theresa Helburn, and Rouben Mamoulian; and his close friends George Jean Nathan and Saxe Commins; and 3) people who may have encountered O'Neill only briefly but who provide an unusual or revealing perspective on him, such as his college friends Warren Hastings and Richard Weeks; the stagehand William Lee, who saw him act with his father; his colleagues at the *New London Telegraph* Frederick Latimer, Art McGinley, and Robert Woodworth; his classmate in George Pierce Baker's playwriting workshop John Weaver; his friend and fishing companion Harold De Polo; the young actors Paul Crabtree, Mary Welch, and Marcella Markham, who encountered him in the 1940s; and his doctor and nurse from the 1950s.

From this wide variety of observers, a number of common threads come up again and again in reminiscences of O'Neill. One is the power of his eyes. Ingrid Bergman said, "They were the most beautiful eyes I have seen in my whole life. They were like wells; you fell into them. You had the feeling that he looked straight through you."[1] S. J. Woolf, who drew O'Neill's portrait while he interviewed him, wrote, "What one remembers best is his mournful eyes that look oddly like those in portraits of Poe. Like Poe, too, he looks as if he were surrounded by an aura of mysterious sorrow."[2] Another thread is the masklike quality of his face in repose, rather like the faces of the Mannons in *Mourning Becomes Electra*, and the startling change that was wrought by his sudden smiles. In an image that is eerily and perhaps intentionally reminiscent of *The Great God Brown*, reporter Herbert Stoeckel wrote: "Throughout the interview it seemed as if he were wearing a tragic mask of concentrated sorrow. Then, without warning, he flashed an ear-to-ear smile, as if another mask had been suddenly superimposed. Then, instantaneously, this fleeting mask of comedy disappeared, and the mask of tragedy was donned again. One was shocked by the swift transition."[3] Stark Young, who knew O'Neill when he was a young man in Greenwich Village, wrote that he had "a handsome face on which for the moment there was a certain shade of brutality, which seemed to change immediately into a kind of delicate and fierce withdrawal—or shall I say a proud shadow?—and also a kind of covered entreaty. The mouth was both sensuous and hard; but when he smiled the effect was boyish and fresh—a stretch of white teeth—curiously candid and shy at the same time—the sudden engaging air of a child. As was usual in his case I felt vaguely an emotion of pity and defense. Though there was nothing particularly to defend him against, I wanted to defend him, to take his part."[4]

The most marked characteristic in his personality seems to have been his shyness, which intensified as he grew older, so that when it was combined with Carlotta's mania for privacy, he became a virtual recluse in his later years. Juliet Throckmorton, who knew him in Provincetown, remarked that he "always seemed baffled by conversational trivialities and small talk. His shyness was marked."[5] The other side of this was his perseverating, his apparent inability to stop once he started talking about a subject that interested him. Several people describe experiences that were similar to the one recounted by Edmund Wilson: "Once started talking, it seemed O'Neill could never stop. What was striking was that he quite lost connection with anything that was said by me or Mary [Blair Wilson]. He did not answer questions or seem to recognize that we were there at all. He disregarded all our hints. We got up and crossed the room; we made remarks which with anyone else would have brought the session to a close. But his talk was an unbroken monologue."[6]

Although he was by nature self-involved, withdrawn and shy, O'Neill inspired intense loyalty in his friends and associates throughout his lifetime. He was often spoken of as kind and generous, and he was indeed often free with his money, particularly to early friends and associates from his Greenwich Village days. He also inspired great respect for his dedication to his work. But many people remarked on his love of the six-day bicycle races and his knowledge of burlesque from the 1910s. What's more, many of his friends appreciated his sense of humor. Several years after his death, George Jean Nathan was so tired of hearing about the tragic, haunted O'Neill that he felt compelled to report that "as O'Neill's long-time friend and confidant, I must divulge the news that he was in fact no such chronic sour ball. While scarcely a man given to large mirth, he nonetheless viewed life as something to tickle the sardonic passing fancy. [. . .] Those who have been led to think of O'Neill as a brooding pessimist may find it disturbing to learn that he liked nothing better than to sit by the television set, watch a prize fight, and—however stimulating it might be—manufacture disparaging comments on it."[7] But he also said that, in their many years of friendship, he had heard O'Neill laugh out loud only once. O'Neill was a complicated man, with many inner complexities and contradictions. A number of these emerge from the accounts in this volume, which in our view enrich the composite portrait of O'Neill that it constructs.

In arranging the chapters in the volume, we have divided them into six parts that represent major phases in O'Neill's life. Within each part, chapters are arranged chronologically in relation to the time they describe. We have annotated the chapters to identify people or allusions that may be obscure to the reader and have supplied brief biographies of important figures in his life. Except for corrections of minor typographical or spelling errors, the chapters appear as they do in their original state. Bracketed material, including ellipses, is added by us; unbracketed ellipses appear in the original. Notes, including birth and death dates when we have been able to find them, identify individuals at first mention and additionally when their identification is key to understanding a particular text. Significant factual errors are also pointed out in the notes.

# I
# New London, School, and Wandering (1888–1913)

Eugene O'Neill was born in a hotel in New York, the city where his father James O'Neill, a well-known actor-manager, was performing. As a small child, Eugene was often brought along on tour with his father's company. The first reminiscences record O'Neill's early life in the theater and in New London, Connecticut, where the family had established the only permanent home they ever had, a summer cottage that James named Monte Cristo, after his most famous and most lucrative role. Eugene's mother, Ella, became addicted to morphine as a result of complications after his birth, and he was sent to boarding school at the age of seven, attending several schools before he enrolled at Princeton University in 1906. He left Princeton at the end of his freshman year, suspended because of poor grades and poor attendance, and never returned. After working briefly at a job obtained for him by his father, he lived in New York on a small allowance, drinking heavily. In 1909 he married Kathleen Jenkins, who had become pregnant. Disapproving of the match, his father got a job for him on a prospecting expedition in Honduras that was being subsidized by a mining-stock company in which he had invested. O'Neill contracted malaria and returned to the United States. After working briefly for his father's touring company, he went to sea for a few months and then began living in a flophouse in New York. Kathleen bore a son and named him Eugene O'Neill Jr. O'Neill visited him as an infant only once (though they reconnected when the boy was eleven). He and Kathleen divorced, and, after attempting suicide, he went to live in New London, where his father got him a position on a local newspaper, the *New London Telegraph*, to which he contributed verse as well as news. Diagnosed with tuberculosis in 1912, he went first to the state sanatorium in Shelton, Connecticut, and then to Gaylord Farm, a private sanatorium in Wallingford, where his disease was arrested, and he began writing plays.

In the selections included from this early period of his life, Eugene O'Neill is remembered by George Tyler as a baby, by William Lee as a very bad young actor, and by Warren Hastings and Richard Weeks as an enthusiastic drinker and indifferent Princeton student; Pierre Loving describes him as a barroom critic; Frederick Latimer, Art McGinley, and Robert Woodworth remember him as a rather clueless cub reporter, and Clayton Hamilton as an ambitious young writer. Mabel Haynes recalls what it was like to be called as a nurse to the New London house during Ella's addiction, and Irvin Cobb remembers James O'Neill's pride in his young son's early writing.

# 1 / George C. Tyler

George C. Tyler (1868–1946) was a very active Broadway producer from 1902 until 1935. Among his producing credits were popular comedies such as *Dulcy* (1921) and *Merton of the Movies* (1922) by George S. Kaufman (1889–1961) and Marc Connolly (1890–1980), as well as serious plays like *The Plough and the Stars* (1927) by Sean O'Casey (1880–1964), and revivals of *Macbeth* (1928) and *Magda* (1902). His 1920 production of O'Neill's *Chris Christophersen*, retitled *Chris*, which was intended for Broadway, closed out of town in Philadelphia before it reached New York. He did produce O'Neill's *The Straw* at the Greenwich Village Theatre in 1921.

Source: George C. Tyler in collaboration with J. C. Furnas, *Whatever Goes Up* (Indianapolis: Bobbs-Merrill, 1934), 90–92.

In connection with tricks I've missed, it's funny now to look back and think of the bright way I behaved when James O'Neill used to bring me round plays that his young son Gene had written and ask me to tell him what I thought of them. That was years later when I was sitting on top of the world considering George Bernard Shaw a promising newcomer. O'Neill and I were very close friends, of course, but I didn't see any particular reason to suppose that Gene should be taken seriously. I figured it was just run-of-mine paternal pride that made his father bring me these scripts of his. So I'd take them in and forget about them for a while—maybe read a little, but I wouldn't take oath I did that often, and I'm certain that I can't remember at all what they were like—and then I'd give them back to his father with the customary polite remarks about how Gene undoubtedly showed signs of talent, and deserved encouragement, but needed more development and had better wait a while. He seems to have got plenty of development since then, all right.

After all, though, I was still thinking of Gene as the baby in arms who traveled with Mrs. O'Neill when she'd be sent on ahead of the company to rest from the hardships of one-night stands, and I'd scramble round and do things for her and see she was comfortable, like the polite young man I was. One night in Chicago I was routed out of bed by a hurry-call from Mrs. O'Neill—Gene was dying, it seemed, and something had to be done about it at once. So I got into some clothes and went in and had a look at him—he was sort of black in the face and gasping and raising Cain—he looked to me like a pretty sick baby all right. I went hotfoot for the house-doctor. And of course he was out. There was nothing for it but to dive out into one of those fine, cold, windy nights they have in Chicago—I was wearing nothing much but a pair of pants and an overcoat—and dig up a doctor. When I found one, he huddled on a similar costume and we came galloping back to the hotel like the last act of an old melodrama—and then it turned out that the baby only had a routine case of colic. So you can understand that I did have some excuse for not taking Gene's playwriting as seriously as I might have. When you've assisted at walking the floor with fifteen pounds of howling infant at four in the morning, it's hard to come round to thinking of that howling infant as genius in the making.

# 2 / Warren H. Hastings and Richard F. Weeks

Warren H. Hastings (1888–?) spent his career working for the advertising agency Folkard and Lawrence, representing British mills in the woolen industry. He retired to Princeton, where he wrote the following piece with Richard F. Weeks (1888–1971), who was retired and living in California after a career of practicing customs law in New York. They were friends and classmates of Eugene O'Neill's during their freshman year at Princeton, the academic year of 1906–1907. They published their account of his college year in the hope that it would clarify the many inaccuracies or wrong impressions that had appeared in previous accounts of O'Neill's year at Princeton.

Source: Warren H. Hastings and Richard F. Weeks, "Episodes of Eugene O'Neill's Undergraduate Days at Princeton," *Princeton University Library Chronicle* 29 (Spring 1968): 208–15.

Eugene O'Neill never had much to say about his family. He assumed we knew that his father was James O'Neill, the famous actor who played the Count in *The Count of Monte-Cristo* for many years. He did mention his mother as being an accomplished pianist and an elder brother Jamie, for whom he had a regard which reflected extreme admiration.

He was then barely eighteen years of age, tall, slender, broad-shouldered, but flat-chested and somewhat tubercular in appearance. He had long arms which he used to gesture dramatically and large hands with artistic fingers which he may have inherited from his mother. His theatrical gestures and oratorical discourses, no doubt, came to him from his father. One might describe him as handsome—certainly striking in mien—black hair; high, broad forehead and dark brown eyes, keen and inquisitive; finely chiseled nose. His otherwise attractive features were detracted from by an angular chin with a very thick lower lip and a cruel sensuous mouth drooping at the corners, conveying the sense of inward cynicism.

He was slow of speech unless animated by his subject. He spoke well in a modulated, low-toned voice, somewhat hesitatingly. He was shy, self-conscious;

he often smiled, but was a bit sardonic and cynical. He was sarcastic and often foul-mouthed. Sometimes he became blasphemous, defying God and standing on a chair theatrically proclaiming with outstretched arms, "If there be a God, let Him strike me dead!" His classmates shuddered at the shock of such a diatribe, yet they realized that it was only for dramatic effect. He was inclined to deliver himself of his views in like exaggerated manner. He definitely was not an atheist. He had spoken of his mother and father as being devout Catholics and said that he himself had been brought up in that faith and had attended a Catholic school. His background refuted any such notion of atheism. His views on religion seemed nevertheless those of an agnostic. If anyone spoke disparagingly of Catholicism he would spring furiously to its defense.

Eugene O'Neill, as an undergraduate, was what is called today a "loner." His acquaintance with his class was extremely limited. The Class of 1910 consisted, at the beginning, of something less than 350 members. Probably less than fifty knew he existed and of this number not more than eight, whose friendship he seemed to relish and enjoy, knew him intimately. It is probably true that this group befriended him partly because of sympathy for a lonely soul, partly because of his unusual attitude towards the world which intrigued them, and perhaps because he was an interesting companion—especially when a drink or two would loosen his tongue. As a matter of fact, his fare was "hard liquor," which was a shock since the undergraduate custom of the era was beer and light wine; only "bums" drank the other "stuff." He was an inveterate cigarette smoker. He could be amusing, but he was not a particularly good storyteller. His topics of conversation were apt to be morbid. He spoke affectionately of his brother Jamie, who undoubtedly exercised a bad influence over him, and Gene would regale his friends with accounts of Jamie's dissipations.

O'Neill roomed on the campus in University Hall, which many years prior had been an old hotel at the corner of Nassau St. and University Place. Holder Hall has now replaced it. His room was No. 30, one flight up, on the campus side. The dining hall for the Freshman Class, called "The Commons," was in this building and was where he dined. Rooming and dining in the one building and leaving it only to go to classes made him all the more a recluse. Even other occupants of University Hall had no recollection of him. He admitted to an occasional lone walk about the countryside. He took no part in athletics, nor in any extra-curricular activities such as *The Daily Princetonian* or other publications; nor even in the theatre about which he had a lot of knowledge from traveling with his family on his father's tour of the country acting on the stage.

In the dining hall in "The Commons" he kept aloof mainly because of an intense shyness. He would not drift into a group to dine. He was not gregarious. The small group of friends he had tried to get him to join an eating club.

Various congenial groups would get together to form eating clubs designated by a certain color of hat. The Freshmen were allowed, by tradition, to wear these hats after February 22. Prior to that date every Freshman wore a traditional black cap known as a "beanie." This was about the only thing this non-conformist would conform to, this, and the plain black tie, which Freshmen had to wear, and a black "slicker" raincoat on wet days. (Of course, he observed obligatory chapel attendance and went to classes.) It should be added, he was always well-dressed and neat in appearance.

This small group of friends finally persuaded Gene to join one of these Freshman eating clubs. However, there were obstacles to overcome. The majority of the clubs had only the slightest awareness of O'Neill; consequently, not knowing him, they simply "black-balled" him. This annoyed his friends. Tom Welch, one of this group who liked Gene, was president of the "White Hat" club and a popular football player in the class. When Gene's name was again put up, Tom picked for his "ballot counters" those who were friendly to Gene. They "fixed" that situation and he was accepted without a protest from those who knew they had cast a negative vote.

For the first half of the college year little is known about O'Neill among this small group of friends. It must be assumed that he did try to gain academic knowledge during that period because there is no record of any escapades and he did pass his mid-year examinations or a sufficient number of them to permit him to continue in college. There were signs of continued effort, with lapses, after mid-year. It was during the second half of the college year that his friends really begin to know him.

It cannot be said that his year at Princeton was fruitless. He did not squander his time. He may have lacked interest in his prescribed courses and subjects, but he did an extensive amount of reading on his own and in his own room. His particularly close friends, after their own study period for the next day's assignment, would drift around to O'Neill's room about 3 or 4 o'clock in the afternoon. He would always be found reading. Most of these friends roomed on University Place just a step away from "The Commons." He was a diligent reader of, to name a few, Shakespeare, Bernard Shaw, Kipling, Byron, Oscar Wilde, Smollett, and such poets as Keats, Swinburne, Shelley, and Poe. He obtained his books from the University Library by "swiping" them surreptitiously and had them "sneaked" back into the Library by a classmate. He was ever a non-conformist, and library rules irked him.

His preceptor in English was the popular Duncan Spaeth,[1] who used to needle him a bit to get him to talk. Spaeth seemed to have recognized an unusual personality with latent talent and possible genius. He did arouse Gene's interest in Chaucer and tried to bring out further interest in other authors, but it was not easy because of Gene's innate shyness among others in the preceptorial group. He could not stomach his English lecturer, Professor Henry van Dyke,[2] who was prone to stress Milton's *Paradise Lost* and books and poems of that nature which were definitely not to O'Neill's tastes or disposition. He also detested van Dyke's sermons of a Sunday which he was obliged to listen to, or, more accurately, "doze to."

O'Neill was interested in books of his own choosing which he must have devoured because he delighted his friends with quotations of many passages from Shakespeare and verses from the poets mentioned. He tried versifying himself, which, he confessed, was not good. One of these pieces, which revealed his bent of thought, was (as now recalled):

Cheeks that have known no rouge,
Lips that have known no booze,
What care I for thee?
Come with me on a souse,
A long and lasting carouse,
And I'll adore thee.

This amused his listeners, and, although they considered it somewhat crude and uncouth, it gave them an insight into his attitude toward life. Besides his distaste for the poetry of van Dyke for being too saintly, he hated mathematics, especially conic sections, for being a waste of his time. O'Neill flunked the subject and said he would have no part of it.

Of all his readings from which he quoted he seemed to his friends to prefer the morbid and the tragic. He was of a restless pessimistic nature. A classmate would argue with him why it was, if given the choice between gazing at the beauty of a vase of roses or at a stinking garbage pail, he preferred the latter. His only reply was, "Both are nature." The questioner was obliged to form his own conclusions. Yet in all his arguments and discussions, always friendly, he seemed to his listeners to be striving for an answer to something he knew not what—a meaning to life? He had a compassion for the "beat" in body and spirit.

He had a pessimistic attitude toward the chastity of the female species. He would shock his friends by declaiming that "There is not such a thing as a virgin after the age of fourteen." His friends' reaction was readily understandable. It was the era of chaperones when a student inviting a girl to a football game was usually accompanied by a young married friend of either or both—as aptly expressed by one of the Class, "twice the expense but half the fun." This attitude towards unchastity was formulated by his introduction to a life of drinking and unvirtuous women by his older brother Jamie, whom Gene termed "wild" and "worldly." He would describe his adventuring with Jamie in the "Tenderloin" district in the Thirties west of Broadway in New York. He spoke of drinking with his brother in a dive known as the "Haymarket," frequented, he said, by prostitutes and unsavory characters.[3] To prove his statements he took two of his classmates on a tour of that neighborhood to point out to them the whorehouses, which, in that day, went under the polite name of "fancy houses." His companions later described this trip and admitted to a reluctance to enter one of the houses so that an interior description cannot be given here and O'Neill never volunteered to do so.

In spite of his skepticism on the virginity of women, he did consort with a girl of good character in Trenton to whose defense he came when his classmates questioned her morals to tease Gene. He would expatiate in high dudgeon upon "harpies" who bandy gossip about girls. He would become quite heated over this as he evidently was fond of her, respected her, and visited her often.

It was not until the later part of his college career that O'Neill started to neglect his classwork and skip an occasional class assignment. He went into more extensive drinking. He was, in truth, never found drunk in his room nor did he have liquor in his room except once which will be noted. He was always found reading; but, strange to his friends, never writing, hence he was not a "time-waster" or a general "hell-raiser" as legend proposes.

What "hell-raising"—or, to use a better term, "drinking bouts"—there was were weekend affairs with him, either trips to New York or Trenton or local bouts on Nassau Street in Princeton in a bar known as "Doc" Boyce's. This place was frequented by Freshmen as one of the few places on Nassau Street tradition allowed them—the Nassau Inn and the Princeton Inn were forbidden grounds for Freshmen by tradition and the latter Inn was for upperclassmen only. There was also a shabby saloon of small dimensions in a poorer section of Princeton on lower Alexander Street patronized mainly by the town's laboring element. It was a "dump" of a place that O'Neill had discovered, and it appealed to him as a place to go of a Saturday night. He would sometimes go to Trenton and drink at one of the tables or at the bar at the old Sterling Hotel. One of these Saturday night visits led to an adventure.

It was after the final examination period that two of his classmates, to celebrate the end of the college year, went with O'Neill to Trenton. They imbibed too long; ignoring the time, they missed the last trolley to Princeton. They went to the Penn Station and found they could catch a New York-bound train, which stopped at Princeton Junction but which did not make connection with Princeton. They, therefore, were obliged to walk to Princeton, which they did by way of the railroad tracks. Along the roadbed approaching Princeton Station was a high embankment sloping down to a row of unpretentious houses that paralleled the track and backed up to the embankment a short distance from its bottom. As they were staggering along the railroad ties, a dog started to bark furiously at them from the back porch of one of the houses. This annoyed O'Neill's sense of dignity so much that he started hurling roadbed stones at the dog. His aim not being too accurate, a stone broke a window. In the meanwhile O'Neill dashed down the embankment. The dog had not ceased to bark which exasperated him all the more. He commenced hurling porch furniture at the dog, and broke a chair. The owner of the house, having been awakened by breaking glass, the barking dog and the furniture being tossed about, came rushing out and put an end to the fracas. Somehow, none of the trio seemed to know by what means the owner obtained their names and reported them to the University authorities. This brought them to the Dean's office.

The outcome was a three-week suspension from college. As there remained only a few days left of the college year, the suspension would not become effective until the opening of the new term in September. This definitely refutes the legend that O'Neill was expelled from Princeton. One legend has it that he was expelled for throwing stones through President Woodrow Wilson's study in '79 Hall. That is not true. Another legend has it that he was expelled for throwing a beer bottle through the window of Prospect, the residence of the President of Princeton. This also is false; neither episode occurred. It is unknown how these fabrications came about. O'Neill denied these false rumors to classmates in after years.

Gene often spoke about a book entitled *Wormwood* written by Marie Corelli.[4] He said he loved the book for its devotion to horrible tales. It evidently interested him so much he decided to try out a bottle of absinthe to experience its effects. Some time prior to his rock-throwing episode O'Neill made the attempt. The sale and possession of absinthe was prohibited by federal law. Being a nonconformist was one more reason for his decision to drink it. He himself never revealed to his classmates how or where he obtained a quart of the absinthe. He had met a likable and amusing character by the name of Louis Holladay,[5] who was neither a student at the University nor a resident of Princeton. Holladay lived in Greenwich Village in New York. He appealed to O'Neill as an enjoyable drinking companion, and Gene invited him to spend a weekend at Princeton. Holladay later confessed to having brought the absinthe with him.

The setting of this drinking orgy was O'Neill's room in University Hall. This room was fairly large with a very large window. Beside this study was a small bedroom containing an iron cot, a high chest of drawers and a commode with washbowl, pitcher and slop jar. His study was equipped with unpretentious furniture: a round table, and two or three chairs of the kitchen variety. On one entire side-wall hung a huge fisherman's net with a number of cork floats attached to it. It was not learned from Holladay what time of day the experiment started. It was around 4 o'clock in the afternoon when Holladay, in great agitation, hunted up O'Neill's particular friends and brought them to Gene's room.

O'Neill had gone berserk. The room was found in a shambles with O'Neill glassy-eyed and still in a frenzy so great that it took three to pin him to the floor when he shortly collapsed and was put to bed. As the scene began to formulate, he had hurled a none too sturdy chair through the big glass window. The chair lay shattered by the window evidently broken by the window frame or casing. Retrieving a chair leg, he had gone to his bedroom and smashed his washbowl, pitcher and jar. He had pulled out every drawer of his bureau and tossed their contents about the room. Amongst the contents was a revolver. This, Holladay said, Gene had pointed at him, pulling the trigger. By good fortune it was not loaded. The room reeked of absinthe which was sickening. Fortunately this episode never leaked to the University, but was kept a secret by those who witnessed the disorderly aftermath.

O'Neill did not return to Princeton the following year to continue his college career. He was never expelled, but was automatically dropped by the University from its rolls. He never bothered to take a single final examination. He dropped out of college of his own volition and, to anyone's knowledge, never came back to Princeton in after years. A few years before his death the writers visited Gene in New York and it amused him to recall some of these episodes.

In spite of these deviations from conventional behavior there is much to be said for O'Neill. When he came to Princeton he was only seventeen and unaccustomed to many things. To his intimate friends there was no question but that there was a streak of genius in him, almost a touch of madness. He could thank his brother Jamie for not having many scruples or too much conscience. A great deal of emphasis could be placed on his adoration of Jamie, who encouraged Gene in doing everything he, Jamie, wanted to do himself, were it drinking or going off on wild escapades. Gene was far from being mature even though "worldly wise."

# 3 / Kathleen Jenkins Pitt-Smith

Kathleen Jenkins (1888–1982) was the daughter of Katie Shaw Camblos and Charles E. Jenkins. She met and fell in love with Eugene O'Neill when they were both twenty years old. In October 1909, after Kathleen became pregnant, they were married in New Jersey but never lived together. O'Neill's father, James, sent him off on a prospecting expedition in Honduras, and he saw his son Eugene Jr. only once before the boy was eleven years old. Kathleen divorced O'Neill in 1912 and married George Pitt-Smith in 1915. They lived in Douglaston, Queens, New York, and Kathleen did editorial work on a newspaper.

Louis Sheaffer (1912–1993) is the pen name of Louis Slung. He is best known for his authoritative two-volume biography of O'Neill, *O'Neill: Son and Playwright* (1968) and *O'Neill: Son and Artist* (1973), which won the Pulitzer Prize. He was born and brought up in Louisville, Kentucky, and attended the University of North Carolina. He served as reporter, theater critic, and film critic for the *Brooklyn Daily Eagle* between 1934 and 1955. It was while working as a press agent for *The Iceman Cometh* and *Long Day's Journey Into Night* in 1956 that he first became interested in writing about O'Neill. The research collection he amassed is now housed in the Charles E. Shain Library, Connecticut College, where it remains a rich source of primary and secondary materials about O'Neill.

Source: "Kathleen Pitt-Smith 7/13/62." Louis Sheaffer interview. Louis Sheaffer Collection of Eugene O'Neill Materials, Department of Special Collections, Charles E. Shain Library, Connecticut College, New London.

[Kathleen's] father was formerly commodore of the Larchmont Yacht Club in Westchester when he married her mother and had just become associated with Tiffany's [Tiffany & Company]. Her parents lived in Chicago a few years, when she [was] a small girl, and returned to Larchmont, had been there about two years when her mother left Jenkins . . . Her maternal grandfather was a member of Stock Exchange's predecessor when her mother, Kate Camblos, was a small girl, and remained until two years before his death, when he resigned because of age. Kate's father, Henry Camblos.

Denies that she was the social butterfly indicated by G[el]b.[6]

She had no idea [O'Neill] was being sent out of country by his father to get him away from Kathleen, doesn't believe J[ames] O['Neill] had any idea their romance had become serious. (Apparently E[ugene] O['Neill] wasn't truthful with her but told her that the Honduras trip had been planned even before he met her but had had to be postponed for some reason [ )] . . . Marriage was casually discussed between them but Kathleen at first didn't take this seriously as he was not working, had no income other than allowance, small, from his father.

Eugene Jr. around a year old when EO phoned Kathleen out of the blue, said he'd like to call on her, came either that night or following one. Her mother there, pleasant to him. Wouldn't say what they talked about ("nothing happened from it, so what's the use of mentioning it") but says that he didn't disclose the reason for his visit, why he'd called and asked to see her. During evening either he asked to see the baby or she suggested it, and he fell in with the idea. Baby was sleeping in next room but waked when she picked him up ("He was a beautiful baby—I know all mothers believe that but I've seen plenty of babies and he was unusual.") His face was all rosy and flushed, the way a baby is when he's been sleeping, and he behaved beautifully. He didn't burst out crying, anything like that, the way most babies will do if you suddenly wake them up and hand them to a stranger. He seemed to take to Mr. O'Neill, and I was very pleased about it. After a while he fell asleep again, in Mr. O'Neill's arms, and I put him back to bed. No, I can't remember what we talked about. It was all so long ago."

Junior was in his khaki military uniform the first time he called on his father, when 11. [. . .] EO was leaving for Provincetown when she phoned him to tell of Junior's bike accident, told her to get the best possible medical care and send the bills to him.

# 4 / William Lee

There are several accounts of O'Neill's stint as an actor with James O'Neill's company in 1912. This story is from the point of view of a stagehand who witnessed his performances as well as his interaction with his father backstage. The editors found no further information about William Lee.

Source: "O'Neill Bad Actor, Stage Hand Recalls," *Hartford Courant* 3 April 1929: 18.

What appears to be a new yarn, with Eugene O'Neill as its chief character, appeared recently in St. Louis, unearthed there by a gentleman traveling for the Theater [*sic*] Guild in the interests of the somewhat well-known drama, *Strange Interlude*, says the *New York Evening Post*. A local electrician, it seems, had vivid memories of O'Neill as a performer and, unimpressed by the man's present status, it appears that he exercised the prerogative of a critic and lambasted him thoroughly.

The author of *Strange Interlude* and *Dynamo* was branded as a very bad actor. This would be no shock to O'Neill; he has said many times that his bent was not toward acting, and that he was, while with his father, "probably the world's worst actor." This statement was made in reflective calm while *Strange Interlude* was being produced in New York about fifteen months ago. But the St. Louis electrician, whose name is William Lee, and whose post of duty is Loew's Theater there, carries the same impression, and it was largely his conversation which furnished the story.

It was in 1912 and the late James O'Neill, Eugene's father, was touring in *Monte Cristo*. Eugene was playing the jailer. He was an actor under sentence. He had to earn his own living in his father's company or shift for himself, and stage hands around the American Theater in St. Louis recalled that he was awkward and sullen. His shyness, noticeable even then, was mistaken by one of the scene shifters for stupidity, and it was his remark that he didn't see how a smart man like James O'Neill could have a son so dumb.

"When James O'Neill used to come to the Olympic in *Monte Cristo*," says

Mr. Lee, "we used to do a capacity business. He came about once every two years, and a grand job he did of that play. So that when we all noticed that one role was being badly played we wondered. It wasn't like James O'Neill to keep a bad actor in his troupe. This young fellow was quiet, too. He never had a word to say to nobody. He didn't mix up with the other actors offstage while waiting for his cue. He never said good evening to the doorman when he came in. Or anything.

"Then we found out he was James O'Neill's son.

"Young 'Gene and his father had a quarrel backstage one night. I remember O'Neill was in a rage and said to his son:

"'You never could act. You can't act. And you never will.'

"'What of it?' Eugene answered as he was led out."

How he came to take up acting at all is an interesting story.

He had, it seems, been expelled from Princeton and had been fired from a business office wherein he took a job at the termination of his collegiate career.[7] He went to sea as a common sailor. For a long time he knocked about bumming as best he could and living in water front saloons (those were the good old days). Angered because of his expulsion, James O'Neill would have nothing to do with his son.

Then one day in a sailors' boarding house in New York, 'Gene won a considerable sum of money. He had, it seems, been the lucky possessor of certain cards in various winning combinations, and, as often the case, he spent the winnings wildly—so wildly that when he woke up he was in a Pullman car pulling into New Orleans. He hadn't a cent in his pocket and struck out for the water front, hoping to grab a job on some outbound ship. On his way to the docks he saw posters advertising his father in *Monte Cristo*. James O'Neill was playing there and the prodigal went to him, asking for the price of a breakfast and a trip back to New York.

His father was unwilling to do this. Instead he offered him a job in the show at a salary and told 'Gene that he would not be given one cent more than he earned. Thus, for fifteen weeks the now famous playwright went through the motions of being an actor, a performance he did not repeat until *Bound East for Cardiff* was given its first presentation.[8] But that was years ago.

For years he remained to his father a ne'er-do-well. When he won the Pulitzer Prize for the first of three times,[9] his father had retired. Sitting around his club he was greatly impressed by his son's feat.

"Did you see," he would say, "about that son of mine? He won the Pulitzer Prize. I tell you, he's a great playwright."

# 5 / Pierre Loving

Pierre Loving (1893–?) was a writer, critic, and editor who wrote a biography of Baudelaire and a study of German theater, as well as novels, plays, and poetry. His play *The Stick-Up* (1922) was produced by the Provincetown Players. Here he tells of his first meeting with O'Neill in a bar in Greenwich Village. O'Neill borrowed his last name for the protagonist of *Days Without End* (1934).

Source: Pierre Loving, "Eugene O'Neill," *Bookman* August 1921: 511–13.

As we sauntered out of the Provincetown Playhouse after the performance of *The Emperor Jones* my friend, the vagrom poet who had traveled about the world as a common seaman in many ships, remarked:

> You know the Buenos Aires waterfront, that motley and populous marine thoroughfare, the Passo de Julio. I had just come from up-country, where I had been hired to boss a gang of Indians stringing a telegraph line across the pampas for a pioneer railroad company. My mates, both whites and redskins, were good fellows all, but I was weary of their crude talk, their oozy sentimentality, and their ribald jests picked up at many camps and ports. In this morose spirit I strolled into a noisy dingy sailors' tavern. The pot-bellied and exaggeratedly jovial Hollander who ran the place, apparently recognizing a Britisher, welcomed me with a broad, "How are you, matey?" Grateful to find myself back out of the wilds, I replied upon some wilful impulse with a line of verse from a contemporary poet. The quotation was apt. I've forgotten it now . . . but I had scarcely finished it when—imagine my amazement—a voice directly behind me, with a civilized stave in it, took it up and continued it. I slewed around and perceived a dark-haired young fellow, strong-shouldered, tanned, and with a black smudge of a mustache circumflexing a fine sensitive mouth. He was clad in something that resembled a compromise between shore and seagoing clothes.
>
> "You're from the States, aren't you?" I asked.

"Yes," he replied with what seemed a nostalgic grin.

"A sailor?"

"Ages ago I was one, or so it seems. I've been ashore here about six months."

I was quite beside myself. Taking a seat opposite him, I said: "Can you quote real poetry or . . . do you write it yourself? I've been aching to talk to someone human for weeks on end."

"You haven't been any worse off than I," he returned. "For months I've been feeling suicidal for lack of real talk."

After this introduction we picked out a table farthest removed from the rattle of the tin-canny piano and talked. How we talked! It was seven in the morning when we rose to leave the place. In the course of the conversation my new-found friend had said his name was O'Neill—Eugene O'Neill— and that his home was in New York.

Since that singular encounter (it was in 1911, I believe) Eugene O'Neill has written three long plays and numerous one-act pieces. He has been pronounced the finest American dramatist writing today. *Beyond the Horizon*, produced by Richard Bennett, has been hailed as a truly great play, while *The Emperor Jones* and *Diff'rent* drew large audiences to a Broadway theatre, having been dispatched uptown from the garage-like Provincetown Playhouse on Macdougal Street by a shrewd theatrical entrepreneur.

When my friend, the poet, had brought to a close the rare account of his first meeting with Eugene O'Neill, I retailed my own which came, I dare say, with something of the inutility of a stalemate or an anti-climax. My own first encounter with the author of *Beyond the Horizon* took place no remoter from where I now write than Sixth Avenue. Was it at Luke's (where John Masefield once tended bar) or at another well-known oasis now, alas! deserted since the passage of the Volstead act?[10]

This place used several years ago to be haunted by all sorts of odd characters living in the neighborhood: negroes who brought their banjos along, sailors, and I dare say gangmen of the district. Allured by its variety and richness of color, a handful of painters, novelists, and poets would gather about the shining deal tables of an evening to talk, wholly oblivious of the stone-blue spirals of dense smoke and stale fumes. One evening I dropped into the place with a well-known woman novelist. We had just been talking about several foreign dramatists whose works were not yet familiar to the American public. My companion interrupted her remarks long enough to present me to a group of persons seated about a round-topped table in one corner, whom we joined. We resumed our conversation and I was taken aback when one of the young men belonging to the group launched into a brilliant analysis of the dramatists whom the novelist and I had been leisurely discussing. He told us, I remember, that he had just read the newer men in their original tongue. This man was Eugene O'Neill.

I hold no special brief for the foregoing anecdote. Personally I far prefer that of the poet. I like the romantic touch, the thrill of plain circumstance in a true tale of two literary men, traveling incognito so to speak, coming across each other by pure accident in a strange seaport, with the unresting sea gurgling about the dock-piles almost at their very feet—both eager for intellectual friction, both salt-tanned and sea- or land-weary because they craved something imponderable to meet their needs. These two anecdotes, whatever their intrinsic value, may go some way toward drawing the veil from the mystery of personality that broods over the figure of Eugene O'Neill owing to his self-chosen retirement. He is not, as has been seen, an uncouth sailor nor yet, as one newspaper critic has broadly hinted, a sombre Malvolio[11] derelict with self-pity. He is, above all else, a highly sensitized being, swift and sharp in his responses to his environment, quick to absorb impressions of beauty and vividly abreast of the rumor of his own times.

# 6 / Mabel Haynes

Mabel Haynes was a nurse who cared for Ella Quinlan O'Neill (1857–1922) briefly in 1912 in New London when she was suffering one of her episodes of morphine addiction. This incident occurred at exactly the time when *Long Day's Journey Into Night* is set, and Haynes's description of the O'Neill family bears a striking resemblance to the play's Tyrone family. The editors found no further information about Mabel Haynes.

For information on Louis Sheaffer, see chapter 3.

Source: "Mrs. Mabel Haynes, nurse, 1912." Louis Sheaffer interview. Louis Sheaffer Collection of Eugene O'Neill Materials, Department of Special Collections, Charles E. Shain Library, Connecticut College, New London.

I knew immediately that it was not something I wanted to try and handle. That was not for me . . . . The difficulty I found was the quarreling going on downstairs between the father and the two boys . . . It was really pretty rough, and with the trouble with her upstairs, it was nothing I felt that I wanted to handle . . . They were all pretty much under the weather . . . quarreling and shouting at each other and in the state that they were in . . . Of course I didn't know the conversation but I felt the boys were doing the shouting at the father.

When I left there I was quite disturbed, I was quite upset really, and I can remember that I took a long walk before going back to the hospital. I got there between 4 and 5 in the afternoon . . . I rang the bell and someone called come in . . . The three men were sitting around a round table. There were glasses on it, and there was a bottle . . . One of them waved an arm, "Go on upstairs."

Whatever her disturbance was, she kept saying, "My son, my son, my son." I don't know whether it was about Eugene or whether it was about the one that she said something to me about that he had died . . . And then she rambled on and on, "My son, my son, my son, my son"—I guess I heard that a hundred times. All the time I was there the awful shouting was going on, and the only thing that disturbed me was I kept hoping that they wouldn't come upstairs . . .

She was in bed, she looked terrible, she looked—this is a horrible expression and I don't like to use it but it will give you the idea—she looked like a witch. She kept wringing her hands and wringing her hands. Once she got up out of bed and started to walk the floor. She said she was in pain . . .

(Haynes, chap she later married, worked for a pharmacy, Mrs. Downey, and once Mr. O'Neill dropped me and said that if his wife came in and wanted to get any kind of dope, to let him know.)

The impression is with me as I talk about it, that they were terribly upset that she had gone back to the addiction . . . I stayed there that night and left the next morning . . . She finally quieted down but it was hours and hours and hours. I think she wore herself out . . . They went on till three in the morning, all this controversy, whatever it was about . . . The boys were the ones who seemed to be doing the shouting at the father—but they were all doing plenty of it . . . I walked hours to get the thing off my mind . . . I had a time getting her back into bed. She kept walking back and forth, back and forth . . . I did see evidence of hypodermic marks . . . in the arm . . . I would say the marks were recent . . . The argument went on until 3 in the morning. What happened after that I don't know because I didn't want to go near them [ . . . ] "My son, my son, my son, my son," and kept wringing her hands. Then once she said "my baby son."

Furnishings were very plain. I wouldn't say it was my idea of luxury, far from it. I would call it very plain but adequate. . . . I was not impressed by [it as] a house for people of means to live in. In N[ew] L[ondon] everyone thought they were millionaires . . . No one around when she left in the morning . . . I don't know where they were. I'm sure if they'd come upstairs I would have heard them.

If the night could have been any worse, I don't know what it could have been. It was really a pretty horrible night. You have no idea of what that night did to me. It was a horror of horrors, as far as I was concerned. It just seemed so sad because senior O'Neill had quite a reputation for being an excellent actor, and I've always admired people who could do things. And I don't know, it was really a shame.

Mrs. O'Neill was a very gentle woman. My impression of her long before this happened was that she was very, very gentle, a sweet and very ladylike soul. But that night when I saw her at close range, she was more or less of a depressant. She was very sad, and when she'd wring her hands and say, "My son, My son," tears would come to her eyes. . . . She used to be driven around N[ew] L[ondon] in a car.

(Older son) was always in some kind of scrape. Jim O'Neill is on the rampage again, people used to say. It seemed strange that she would be the mother of someone like that.

I had the feeling they were upset about the mother.

He (Jamie) was always tight as a tick. He used to race thru New London in a car, and when you saw this car coming, you stepped aside.

[. . .]

The only time I got a close look at her, before this all happened, she was on Main St., near the Star drugstore. I remember looking closely at her because she was the mother of this character around town. She seemed to me very gentle and there were signs that she'd been very pretty.

# 7 / Clayton Hamilton

Clayton Hamilton (1881–1946) was a playwright and the author of many critical books about drama and fiction, including *The Theory of the Theatre* (1910) and the popular "*So You're Writing a Play!*" (1935). His plays *The Big Idea* (1914) and *A Friend Indeed* (1926) were produced on Broadway, but without much success. He taught at Columbia University and Barnard College. The excerpt below is from a series of lectures he gave at Columbia in the spring of 1924.

Source: Clayton Hamilton, *Conversations on Contemporary Drama* (New York: Macmillan, 1925), 199–200, 203–6, 208–9.

Eugene O'Neill's career is still in the crescent stage. I have forgotten his exact age at the moment, but he is under thirty-five[12] and is still in the process of growing up as a dramatist. Upon the basis of his past performances, we should be justified in hazarding a guess that his future work will probably be strangely different from anything that he has done thus far; for it seems to be his habit to startle his admirers by continually doing something unexpected. At the present time, it would be difficult for anyone to analyze his work with any hope of estimating its ultimate importance; and, in my own case, I must confess frankly that disinterested criticism is impeded by the fact that I have known the author personally since he was a boy in his teens.

Nine years ago this summer, Eugene O'Neill kept his bathing-suit in the little cottage on the beach in New London where I usually spend the summer, and used to come down every day to go in swimming with me. I had known him for several years before that, but I had never paid very much attention to him, because he was very shy and retiring and seldom had anything to say. If anybody at that time, which is only nine years ago, had suggested to Eugene O'Neill that I should be standing up this morning before three hundred people in Columbia University and solemnly discussing him as a dramatic artist, he would have been astounded; and I must admit that I myself would have been even more amazed. Nine years ago, he had never written a play; he had never even tried his hand at any kind of writing. Now, for the moment at least, he is generally regarded as the foremost of our playwrights and is the only American dramatist whose work is being seriously studied in Great Britain, France, and Germany. His rapid rise to fame is all the more remarkable because it has been achieved on critical grounds alone, without the impetus of any unusual success at the box-office. He first managed to attract attention by writing one-act plays for semi-professional companies operating little theatres for limited and special audiences; and, though his later and larger plays have been produced in the commercial theatre, none of them has made any considerable amount of money, with the single exception of "*Anna Christie.*" Yet his plays, as soon as they are published, are read eagerly throughout the country; and his work is praised with such unanimous enthusiasm by the press that he is already better known and more highly esteemed than any other American dramatist of the present or the past. Although I have been a fairly intimate witness of the various stages of his career, I am still amazed at its meteoric quality; and I don't think that this amazement arises merely from the fact that I happened to be one of those who "knew him when."

[. . .]

Eugene, as I have said, was very shy and uncommunicative. He had very large and dreamy eyes, which constituted the most conspicuous feature of his face. He looked like a lad who might amount to something; but, since his speech was rather hesitant and he never said very much, he was less impressive to listen to than to look at. His father finally decided that the only way to keep him out of trouble was to keep him poor; so he left Eugene throughout the winter in New London and gave him an allowance of eight dollars a week. That was enough to pay his board, and it was not enough to run away with. But Eugene needed pocket money for his drinks—because that was before the blow had fallen—and he managed to pick up a few dollars a week as a reporter for a New London newspaper.[13] This job was not exactly onerous, because nothing happens in New London in the winter; and, to occupy his ample leisure, he began to try his hand at writing one-act plays.

When I returned to New London the next summer, he confessed to me with great shyness that he had been trying to write some little pieces. He hesitated to ask me to read them, for fear of imposing upon me; but he did ask me if I wouldn't teach him technically how to write a one-act play, and I answered that the technical problem was less important than the primary problem of what to write about. I advised him to find out what aspect of life, if any, he was familiar with at first hand, what characters in life he had really observed. Now it happened that the life that he knew best was the life at sea, because he had so lately been a sailor; and I made the obvious suggestion that this might be a fortunate fact. There had been several novelists of the sea and poets of the sea—

Mr. Conrad and Mr. Kipling and Mr. Masefield,[14] for example—but there never yet had been a dramatist of the sea. The average playwright knew nothing whatsoever of the sea; and any one who really knew the sea and who could learn to say something about it in dramatic form would find a new field open to him.

Eugene wrote, as practice pieces, several one-act plays that dealt with the sea; and they showed an appreciable promise.[15] But then the problem was to get around his father. Eugene did not want to be put to work; he wanted to write plays; and he did not relish the idea of another winter in New London on eight dollars a week. So he asked me if I could not get the old gentleman to increase his allowance by advising Mr. O'Neill to send Eugene to Harvard to study with Professor Baker. Eugene allowed me to infer, with all due respect to Professor Baker, that his main idea was to get out of New London and that Harvard might be a good excuse; but his father was rather difficult to get around, because Mr. O'Neill had the ready argument that he had sent Eugene to college once before and that the boy had run away. I suggested that, since some of the one-act plays which Eugene had been trying to write were rather promising, it might be a good plan to send one or two of them to Professor Baker to find out what he thought about them. I wrote to Professor Baker; and Mr. O'Neill was finally persuaded to send Eugene to Harvard, although he still maintained that the boy would never amount to anything. Within a few months, Eugene O'Neill was recognized at Harvard as the best of all Professor Baker's pupils; and he took a long stride forward under the tutelage of that experienced technician and very able teacher.

[. . .]

Eugene O'Neill's earliest pieces were published at his father's expense by Richard Badger of Boston, and copies were sent out for review. In this entire country, that initial volume was reviewed by precisely one critic; and that one critic was myself.[16] It has long been out of print; and I believe that rare copies of it now sell at handsome prices, as the first published work of a noted author. But, as O'Neill's subsequent plays have been successively published, they have been widely read and have aroused nearly as much discussion in the literary columns of the press as they have received in the dramatic columns.

[. . .]

Mr. James O'Neill lived long enough to see *Beyond the Horizon* on the stage; and when that play was awarded the Pulitzer Prize, he came to see me, all aglow with pride. "My boy"—he said—"my boy Eugene; I always knew he had it in him! Remember how I always used to say that he would do something big some day. People told me he was wild and good-for-nothing; but I always knew he had it in him,— didn't I?"—So Eugene, at last, had managed to get around his father.

# 8 / Irvin S. Cobb

Irvin Shrewsbury Cobb (1876–1944) was an author, humorist, and columnist who once hosted the Academy Awards ceremony. He said that he wrote upward of sixty books, "some of which never should have been published in the first place." An enthusiastic clubman, he became acquainted with James O'Neill at the Lambs Club in New York. His memory of the chronology of events is shaky, but his account of James O'Neill's interest in promoting his son's work is borne out by others. The following is an excerpt from his autobiography.

Source: Irvin S. Cobb, *Exit Laughing* (New York: Garden City Publishing, 1942), 365–66.

For a third of a century James O'Neill played Monte Cristo up and down this country. He trod the boards stampingly, a heavy tragedian of the orotund school, all bombast and gesticulation. Upon his retirement he reverted to his proper and natural self, which would be another way of saying he was a simple, gracious, unassuming old gentleman. The few elocutionary flutings that he kept out of his former repertoire were as so many agreeable oddities to adorn his conversation. At the Lambs' Club I spent a good deal of time in his company. One afternoon he said to me, rather diffidently, "I wonder if I might ask a favor of you? My son Eugene—he's away now on a sea voyage—but at Harvard he studied under Professor Baker, and he has written some playlets—dramatic sketches, I suppose you might call them. Now I have read them and I confess I'm in doubt about their playability. I've brought them along with me—" he hauled some rather meager-looking folios out of his pocket—"and I'm taking the liberty of asking you to read them and give me your opinion on their possibilities. In strict confidence, of course. He knows nothing of this."

"I'll be glad to give you my opinion for what it might be worth, Mr. O'Neill," I said, "but why not submit them to some of the regular playwrights around here—this place crawls with 'em?"

"You are my friend," he said, "and you're a writer."

I tried to explain to him that as between writing stories and writing plays a wide gulf intervened—that in a way of speaking it was like the distinction between laying bricks and laying eggs; both laying operations, but different functional activities were involved. He insisted, and sat near by, sipping his cocktail while I read what the young man had written.

Before I turned the first page of the first script I could understand why this old-time melodramatic star, trained in the noisier mode of a vanished era, might be puzzled by the revolutionary technique of his junior. I read them through—there were four scripts. And then, stirred to my very marrows by the brute strength here expressed, I reread them.

"Mr. O'Neill," I said, then, "alongside some of the candy-store tripe that's being produced these days, this stuff is like a slab of fresh beef hacked with a cleaver on a butcher's block and slapped down on top of jelly beans and gum drops. This has got raw, crude life in it—blood and muscle and guts. Worked over into short-story form it might go—if you picked the magazines that would dare to print it. But as play material—well, I don't believe you'd ever find a manager to produce it or a critic who'd endorse it or a public that would go to see it."

"Exactly what I thought myself," he said, resignedly.

Included in the batch was a one-act play called *The Moon of the Caribbees* and one called *Bound East for Cardiff* and, unless my memory is wrong, the remaining two afterward were expanded into *The Emperor Jones* and *Anna Christie.*[17]

# 9 / Frederick P. Latimer

Frederick Palmer Latimer (1875–1940), known in New London as Judge Latimer, was born in Montville, Connecticut, and lived a colorful life, which included farming in Florida and meteorology, before he became a lawyer in 1902 and settled down to practice in New London, serving as judge of the town court for thirteen years as well as being a member of the Connecticut state house of representatives. In 1910 he bought the *New London Telegraph* and in 1911 obliged James O'Neill by giving his son Eugene a sort of internship as a cub reporter. After selling the *Telegraph* to the *Day* in 1913, he worked in government service as well as writing for the *New York Evening Mail* and the *Hartford Times* and sporadically practicing law in New London.

Source: Frederick P. Latimer, "Eugene Is beyond Us," *Day* [New London] 15 February 1928: 2.

Years ago in this city there was a very cunning and bashful little boy with brown shoes and a big flowing straw hat with a string under it and great dark eyes that seemed like they had been stolen from a frightened deer. That little boy has grown to be the most remarkable of living American writers. Perhaps if he continues to grow he may become the most remarkable of American writers living or dead. Certainly in that last wonderful drama of his, about how *Lazarus Laughed*, he touches heights indeed. [. . .] We feel much the same in the presence of this book that we would in the presence of the statue of Moses. It doesn't seem like the Eugene we used to know, who would grieve like a stricken collie if you so much as looked an unkind thought at him, could have done such a thing as Maurice Maeterlinck with all his beautiful mysticism could not do and the sentimental, egotistical Goethe would have spoiled in the attempt.[18] In many spots this play is crude and sputtery, but the power of it is simply terrible, terrific. It makes you gasp before you lay it down, forgetting who wrote it, not caring, but knowing that the words of it came out of the hidden well of inspiration itself.

It has been one of the proudest things about my own puny career that when

Eugene O'Neill was a cub-reporter, doing the police court and the Bank street fires, and scribbling funny verses about the old ferryboat or the statue on the parade; or when we sailed with him on the river or talked with him of moonlit nights or in the shadows of a smelly back room, and when he used often to make us choke with wrath at the queer wildness of his ideas, so different from those of other folks and hard to comprehend, we had sense enough to know in an instinctive way something of what sort of a soul the boy had and what a genius was burning in him. But it was only a dim, small notion we had, at that. When we realize what he is ripening into it makes us feel as humble as a mole. We scribble. He writes. It is a wonderful thing to be able to really write. Few can do it; not one in a million. We think, or think we think, but when Eugene disappears for weeks and months and then puts out a thought it is as if a mountain had been born and you are trying to glimpse a little of it while scrambling up the first foothill. We feel precisely as qualified to criticize or suggest anything helpful about a piece Eugene has done as we would to try and improve Rembrandt's Cavalier[19] with a sticky whitewash brush and a pigment of used crank-case oil. [. . .] He won't like this kind of adulation, being modest as a wild flower, but we hand it to him straight. And he's in Europe and won't see it.

Source: Barrett H. Clark, *Eugene O'Neill: The Man and His Plays* (1927; New York: Dover, 1946), 18–20.

Barrett H. Clark (1890–1953) was the author of many critical books and anthologies of literature, particularly drama, which include the often-reprinted *Representative One-Act Plays by British and Irish Authors* (1921) and *European Theories of the Drama* (1919) and his influential *History of Modern Drama* (1947). His book on O'Neill, based on extensive interviews with the playwright, was the first critical book about him, and the last to have such extensive access to his subject. It went through several editions between 1926 and 1947.

There in August O'Neill began work as a cub reporter on the *Telegraph.* He did regular reporting and contributed verse to a "colyum" once or twice a week for nearly six months. It has been said that his half year as a newspaperman was a period of unhappiness and depression, but he assures me that he was usually happy, interested in his work, and fortunate in most of his personal associations. His friendship with the boss, Frederick P. Latimer, who liked and believed in him, meant a great deal in those days. "He's the first one," O'Neill says, "who really thought I had something to say, and believed I could say it."

"As we used to talk together," the Judge told me in 1925 when I went up to

New London to see him, "and argue our different philosophies, I thought he was the most stubborn and irreconcilable social rebel I had ever met. We appreciated each other's sympathies, but to each, in the moralities and religious thought and political notions, the other was 'all wet.'"

"He was the cub reporter," he went on, "and the four things about him that impressed me at once were his modesty, his native gentlemanliness, his wonderful eyes, and his literary style. It was evidence at once that this was no ordinary boy, and I watched what he thought, wrote and did with extreme interest. From flashes in the quality of the stuff he gave the paper, and the poems and play-manuscripts he showed me, I was so struck that I told his father Eugene did not have merely talent, but a very high order of genius. I believe I am the first who ever made that prediction. My notion at the time was that he would eventually abandon the poetic medium and become a novelist. While I've not been surprised at his success as a dramatist, I still cling to my original opinion."

But what was O'Neill like in the New London days, I wondered?

"His health was precarious," the Judge answered, "so much so that he had to quit work and betake himself to the out-of-doors, where I was often with him, especially on the water. He's always been fond of that. He was at one time in love with a very sweet young lady quite opposed to his radical ways of looking at things, and they were in the throes of breaking apart.[20] He was adrift in mind and spirit, and the body was threatened. I was sorry for him, and sorry again because a good many of his local acquaintances were of a mildly Bohemian sort [. . .]. There was something in Eugene at that time—an innate nobility which inspires and drives a man against whatever hindrance to be himself, however Heaven or Hell conspires to rob him of that birthright.

"Emphatically he was 'different.' I thought it astonishing how keen was his wit, what a complete iconoclast he was, how richly he sympathized with the victims of man-made distress, how his imagination was running high as the festering skies above Ye Ancient Mariner;[21] his descriptions strong and his spirit hot to produce something worth while for the sake of its own value and in utter scorn of its commercial value or conventional fame.

"I wouldn't," he concluded, "call Eugene a misanthrope by any means, even if he certainly is no Will Rogers.[22] If he could only be in one of two places in a town—the church or the jail—I know where I would find him!"

# 10 / Arthur B. McGinley

Arthur B. McGinley (1890?–1974) was born in New London, Connecticut, and was a boyhood friend of O'Neill's. *Ah, Wilderness!* (1933) is said to be based on the McGinley family. McGinley worked with O'Neill on the *New London Telegraph*, and went on have a sixty-eight-year career in journalism, working in Providence, New York, and Boston before settling in Hartford, where he served for many years as sports editor and columnist for the *Hartford Times*. The Connecticut Sportswriters Alliance named the Arthur B. McGinley Award for Service to Profession and Community in his honor. He also led the fight to rename New London's Main Street after Eugene O'Neill in the face of opposition from the mayor.

Source: "Columnist Recalls Eugene O'Neill as Dreamy Reporter in New London," *New Haven Evening Register* 28 November 1953: 49.

Playwright Eugene G. O'Neill could say in all truth, "I was a newspaper man once myself." It was something more than 35 years ago that he joined the reportorial staff of the *New London Telegraph*, now defunct. I was a reporter on that newspaper when O'Neill rode up on his bicycle, dismounted and launched his brief career as a newspaperman.

In 40 years of newspaper work I have brushed shoulders with some unusual characters, but O'Neill was unique. He went gaily off on assignments on his bicycle but rarely returned with the story. He was living in a dream world of the plots of plays and would not be distracted by fires, burglaries and other items that make up the pattern of life in a small town.

O'Neill found keen amusement in some of the characters of New London. Like most seaports, the Whaling City spawned more colorful figures than the average town. O'Neill chose it for the locale of *Ah, Wilderness!*, and I could identify every character in the play, including myself and my brothers.

O'Neill's father, James O'Neill, a romantic actor and gifted interpreter of Shakespeare, met my father in New York when the senior O'Neill was a juvenile in Edwin Booth's company.[23] Years later when my father had moved back to New London and heard that the O'Neills were looking for a new house, he suggested that they come there too—Mr. and Mrs. O'Neill, Eugene and James Jr. The O'Neills moved into a fine house on the fringe of the exclusive Pequot Summer Colony.[24]

Many well-known men and women of the theater lived in New London or nearby: Richard Mansfield, Edmund Breese, Nance O'Neil, Tyrone Power, Mark Ellsworth and Frederick Debelleville.[25] Eugene's love for the theater, born of his being the son of one of the great actors of the day, no doubt was strengthened by their presence.

I was almost daily in his presence for many years. In 1916, when he left New London to spend the Summer in Provincetown, his father asked me to go along. "Eugene, I feel sure, has great talent and needs only to be where he can settle down to putting on paper the things that are in his mind. I fear life here is getting on his nerves. Last night he told me I was the worst actor on the American stage." He laughed. "He was kind enough to amend that. He said I was second—that Corse Payton is the worst actor."[26]

The literary colony in Provincetown was large. It included Theodore Dreiser, Susan Glaspell and her husband George Cram Cooke [*sic*], Wilbur Daniel Steele, Mary Heaton Vorse, Mrs. Max Eastman, Harry Kemp and many others.[27] O'Neill was unknown but they acclaimed him as a genius. I remember Helen Ware,[28] then a noted actress, stopping frequently to exclaim her delight as she read some of his plays at an informal evening gathering in one of the summer houses.

## Received Encouragement

It was in this period that O'Neill was encouraged by H. L. Mencken[29] and George Jean Nathan.[30] In the little theater of the Provincetown Players I saw many plays. Among those following the group with great interest was the late Heywood Broun,[31] still to be touched by fame.

O'Neill's interest in the theater was confined to writing plays. He had no wish to be an actor like his father. However, he was assistant manager of *The White Sister*, starring his father and Viola Allen,[32] and made a short tour in vaudeville playing with his father and brother in a condensed version of *The Count of Monte Cristo*.

The last time I saw him was when he invited me to New York for the opening of *Days Without End* nearly 20 years ago. This play was a fine piece of writing and superbly played, but failed to catch the fancy of theatergoers. O'Neill sent advance drafts to high Catholic clergymen. The night before the opening he read me some of the commendatory letters he had received from them.

He was a moody fellow, often brooding, but he had a keen sense of humor and in the company of intimates could be hilarious. He was intensely loyal to his friends and his ideals. In 1915 when he was at Provincetown a famous producer offered him $5,000 to write a play about submarine warfare. A $5 bill would have looked like the national debt to O'Neill then, but he answered, "that would be cheap theater, melodrama, claptrap, and I will have nothing to do with it."

The place posterity will allot to him only time will reveal, but it can be said for the record there never was a man of letters of greater fidelity.

# 11 / Robert A. Woodworth

Robert A. Woodworth (1881–1945) was a native of New London, Connecticut, and a reporter on the *New London Telegraph* and the *Day*, which bought the *Telegraph*, from 1900 until 1915, when he moved to Providence, Rhode Island, and went to work for the *Providence Journal-Bulletin*, where he remained for thirty years, retiring in 1945. During O'Neill's brief stint on the *Telegraph* in 1912, Woodworth was officially employed by the *Day*, although he may, like many New London reporters, have quietly worked for both newspapers at the same time. In any case, his account may be taken as a collective reminiscence among the reporters.

Source: Robert A. Woodworth, "The World's Worst Reporter," *Providence Journal* 6 December 1931: Sunday Magazine: 3.

Outside the circle of light shed by the long, conical shaped shade of the lamp above the City Editor's desk, in a far corner in the dark, glowed a cigarette. Below that, if you looked long and intently, there were white dabs on the black background of the dusty, dingy office wall. These were the corners of a collar. Once in a while the tiny embers of the cigarette end faded almost away. Then they came back again with brilliancy. Next the light moved as the smoker flicked off the ash.

Night after night for a week or more it was the same story. Smoke and dream. Smoke and dream!

"Hey, Mal! When is that guy going to get busy and do some work?" one of us asked the City Editor. "He sits in there and smokes, but he never turns in any copy. If he'd do something some of the rest of us wouldn't have to run our legs off, or, if he'd get another job somewhere, we'd get somebody else who would work."

"Mal" just laughed.

"Oh, he'll make a newspaper man some day, if he's crazy enough to stick to it, and then you'll all be sorry," the City Editor used to say.

One of us would come back at him with something like this: "Well that day is a helluva long way off."

And it still is!

He never made a newspaperman of himself. I, for one, predicted that he wouldn't and I was right. I've been right in two or three such matters. And my being right has been positively the most ludicrous feature of my newspaper career.

Sitting here and thinking over the scene of 25 years ago in a musty little morning newspaper office in New London, all I can do is wonder why my judgment on such matters turned out to be such a laughable thing.

The guy who sat and dreamed, and smoked and, then, dreamed some more—well that guy, who got on the nerves of the whole night crew while we sweated and cursed and worked for a pittance and prided ourselves that we were newspapermen—that guy was . . . Eugene O'Neill.

Yes, that youth was destined to become the premier of American playwrights. Of course it may seem strange that not even a flicker of genius was discernible to us at the time. What does seem strange is that the Gene O'Neill we saw as the office mope stands now with *Mourning Becomes Electra*, a *Strange Interlude*, *Hairy Ape*, *Emperor Jones*, *Desire Under the Elms* to his credit, and as far as any of the crowd can remember he never typed a thing in the late lamented *Morning Telegraph* office which savored of genius.

After a few nights of visiting church festivals and hammering at the outer doors of lodge rooms, O'Neill disappeared. We heard later that he had gone to Europe in the stoke-hold of a cattle ship.[33] We felt he had struck his level, and, we kept right on pouring our life blood into a "night sheet" which was so good that the public didn't appreciate it. Eventually, the owner had to give it away.[34]

[. . .]

An older brother of Eugene O'Neill was James Jr., who played in support of his father for several years, next to get into road companies and into stock. James Jr. frequently had luncheon at 3 A.M. in an all-night hashery up a side street, where there were mirrors at the ends of the horseshoe bar.

The newspaper crowd had a standing order for the counterman to telephone the office when O'Neill came in and then delay his order so we could get there to see him perform. As we munched sinkers and sipped coffee, it was our delight to look over the rims of the cups and watch "Young Jim" rehearsing. He practiced making facial expressions in the mirror, and his grimaces were so amusing that we sat out an hour at least of sleeping time to see him perform. "Young Jim" died soon after his brother Gene's bid for fame was made with his earliest plays.[35]

Anyone who knew the men-folk of the family would not wonder long where

Eugene O'Neill's penchant for stage craft was cultivated. He lived in the atmosphere of the theatre. We could not see ahead, of course, but looking back, we can see that with a father a born actor and a brother only slightly less talented, something theatrical had to happen to Eugene O'Neill.

[. . .]

Gene O'Neill might have been able to brag that he worked in the same newspaper office with us, except, as far as we can remember, he did not do any work.

# 2
# Cambridge, Provincetown, and Greenwich Village (1914–1917)

O'Neill spent the winter of 1913–1914 in New London and had a romance with Beatrice Ashe, a locally prominent singer. He left her there to attend the famed playwriting workshop of George Pierce Baker (1866–1935) at Harvard in 1914–1915. After this he lived in a New York hotel and began to frequent the seedy "Hell Hole" saloon, where he became acquainted with Terry Carlin, whom he accompanied to Provincetown, Massachusetts, in the summer of 1916, bringing the manuscripts of the plays he had been writing. There he met the Provincetown Players, a group of Greenwich Village artists and writers who were forming an "art theater" in opposition to the commercial values of the Broadway theater. Among the selections included here, Louis Sheaffer's interview notes record Beatrice Ashe's memories of the young O'Neill, and John Weaver's reminiscence describes his experiences with O'Neill in Cambridge. Susan Glaspell's account of O'Neill's first production with the Provincetown Players has become legendary. It is supplemented by the Provincetown memories of Mary Heaton Vorse, Hutchins Hapgood, Harry Kemp, and Adele Nathan. In the fall of 1916, the Provincetown Players moved their theater to Macdougal Street in Greenwich Village. O'Neill became their most-produced playwright and there met his future wife, the popular fiction writer Agnes Boulton. Dorothy Day, a close friend, describes O'Neill's Greenwich Village days, and poet and occasional actor William Carlos Williams remembers O'Neill's interaction with the latter's father, who had come to advise him during rehearsals at the Provincetown Playhouse.

# 12 / Beatrice Ashe Maher

Beatrice Ashe Maher (1896–1974) was born in Norwich, Connecticut, and lived most of her life in New London, where she became well-known for her singing. When she was in her teens, in 1914 and 1915, she was Eugene O'Neill's love interest. He proposed marriage to her and wrote to her often while he was studying with George Pierce Baker at Harvard. In 1969 she sold sixty letters and thirteen poems by O'Neill to the New York Public Library for $16,000. Some of the letters are collected in *Selected Letters of Eugene O'Neill*, edited by Travis Bogard and Jackson R. Bryer. She graduated from Connecticut College and married James E. Maher, who became a vice admiral in the navy, and they had two sons. She is buried in Arlington National Cemetery.
For information on Louis Sheaffer, see chapter 3.

Source: Louis Sheaffer interview, September 1962. Louis Sheaffer Collection of Eugene O'Neill Materials, Department of Special Collections, Charles E. Shain Library, Connecticut College, New London.

E[ugene] O['Neill] often told Bee of "Red" O'Neill, who cut off his hand and threw it up on the land, in order to be first—his right hand, too. . . .To give her an idea what the "O'Neills" were like.[1]

Liked Aubrey Beardsley illustrations for Wilde, tho apparently didn't take them seriously. Used to look at one of Salome holding John the Baptist's head, and laugh.[2]

Used to tell Bee there were three things he wanted: sable coat for her, reaching to her ankles; a silk bathing suit for her, and for himself a player piano.[3]

[. . .]

Eugene constantly urged Bee to lead her own life, do what she wanted to, to be a free, independent soul and fulfill herself, not allow her parents to control and direct her life, that her first and basic obligation was to be true to herself. Gradually she came to realize that he actually wasn't thinking of her following her own bend [*sic*] but adjusting her life to his desires, his ambition, his goal. While he seemed to get a kick out of write-ups in newspaper about her singing and praise of her voice, he also made light of her thoughts of a professional career. Without putting it into so many words, he would have expected her to subordinate her life to his. He scarcely envisioned her as a free, independent agent if she were to join her life with his. . .Was very possessive.

He kidded Bee that they might become a J Hartley Manners-Laurette Taylor combination.[4]

He had a sweet, gentle smile, the sort he should have had for children but didn't.

He resented even her girl friends, her making trips to Hartford to visit with Beatrice Hill.

Silent laugh.

[. . .]

Gene gave her a scarab bracelet, and "carried a wedding ring for two years hoping I'd change my mind."

Re so many of his poems extant from period she knew him. "They must really survive that some one sometime will recognize that sensitive, kind, patient, understanding man who asked so little of God . . . you [Sheaffer] are the only one who would believe there was such a man as the Eugene I knew and loved—but not enough.[5]

Bee and Gene met in early June, 1914. . . . "He never . . . sang, hummed or whistled . . . Gene loved a player piano and would grin with his eyes when he'd say, 'We're going to have one some day' . . . (he) loved a favorite of Caruso's[6] an Italian song (brought her a copy from New York) . . . Night after night have I sung it, half voice, lest the neighbors should recognize the fact that my beau was still about—And at the scandalous hour of eleven . . . He also asked for 'Songs of Araby'[7] and some current Chadwick."[8]

# 13 / John V. A. Weaver

John Van Alstyn Weaver (1893–1938) was a poet and novelist and had one successful play produced after he attended George Pierce Baker's Harvard workshop with Eugene O'Neill. *Love 'Em and Leave 'Em* (1926), on which he collaborated with George Abbott (1887–1995), was directed by Abbott and produced by Jed Harris (1900–1979). It ran for 152 performances on Broadway in 1926. Weaver married the actor Peggy Wood in 1934 and had one son.

Source: John V. A. Weaver, "I Knew Him When—," *New York Sunday World* 26 February 1926 (reprinted in *O'Neill and His Plays: Four Decades of Criticism*, ed. Oscar Cargill, N. Bryllion Fagin, and William J. Fisher [New York: New York UP, 1961], 26–29).

Of Baker's dozen for 1914–15 at the Harvard 47 Workshop,[9] I remember only three members by name. There was somebody called Massey,[10] who afterwards turned out a splendid little satire called *Plots and Playwrights*, I think; there was a scion of the Elkins-Widener[11] family, who matters in this narrative, since he was one of our own trio. And then there was Eugene O'Neill. He stuck out of that class like an oyster in a lunchroom stew.

The rest of us were decidedly awed by the grandeur of our ambitions. Learning to be playwrights! The name of Sheldon[12] gleamed brightly always before us; Frederick Ballard[13] seemed on the make; Cleves Kincaid [*sic*][14] was even then moulding his *Common Clay* into a meretricious but paying pattern; and a certain Lewis Beach[15] was present for a "super-year," already impressing us with the inviolability of scripts. What an atmosphere! What a tradition!

We others listened with scared respect to the professorial admonitions, urgings and objurgations. Not so the fierce-browed, sardonic young man at whose left I sat. These theoretical vaporings were to him simply so much asafetida.[16] While we sat open-mouthed and earnest, he would writhe and squirm in his chair, scowling and muttering in a mezzo-voce fearful imprecations and protests. This was, to me, delightful, fascinating anarchy. To have such a nerve as to pooh-pooh (that is a euphemism) this new gospel—and to get away with it—this O'Neill was a man indeed!

Of him, too, we were frightened. He kept so much to himself. He did not invite approach. For some weeks we let him alone. Then one day Dr. Baker read aloud a scenario by an aspirant. It was lugubrious, it was flamboyant, it was very, very earnest. Several of us gave timid suggestions. It came O'Neill's turn. He waited some moments. Finally he said, without a smile, "Cut it to twenty minutes, give it a couple of tunes and it's sure-fire burly-cue."

Looking at it now, this remark does not seem to have been startlingly witty or amusing. Falling into the academic stuffiness of our "little group" it broke, once and for all, the ice. We howled with laughter. Dr. Baker smiled. From that time until we parted in June there was a new ease, a refreshing relaxation in the meetings.

Going out of the class-room Elkins (the society man) and myself moved on O'Neill. His diffidence seemed to have gone. We repaired to one of the Shamrock bars which in the past made Boston a thing of joy. We drank ale. We continued drinking ale until four in the morning, feet on the rail, one hand in the free lunch. It was just one of those nights. Ribald tales, anecdotes of experience, theorizing about the drama—what the collegians used to call a "bull session." A bull session de luxe.

We piled finally into a decrepit hack. We fell into O'Neill's room some time about five. I had just purchased that day a copy of *Spoon River Anthology*.[17] When the dawn broke I was sitting on a trunk, Elkins sprawled across the bed, O'Neill reading in his powerful, melancholy bass, poem after poem from that disturbing collection. I was told of life on and about the stage, from infancy onward; how 'Gene's earliest delight was to make the canvas waves into which his father, the unforgettable Count of Monte Cristo, dived, emerging a moment after to announce that "The world is mine!" nightly and matinees during some thirty years; of tours with *The White Sister*, of pitcher-and-bowl-circuit caravansaries as Joseph, who withstood the charms of Potiphar's insistent spouse; of the exodus from Princeton, caused by the shying of a beer bottle through Prexy Wilson's dormer window;[18] of vagabondages, "wobbly" camps, long voyages as a stoker (vide *The Hairy Ape*[19]), riots, street fights and mad escapades in foreign ports; of hospitals and the will to live. And I read and listened to many a scenario, many a half-formed plot.

Elkins contributed vitally to these halcyon episodes. He was an amusing conversationalist and he was a generous host. There were numberless dinners at the Beacon Street mansion, where I, very callow and greatly impressed, and 'Gene, jocularly insolent, in a dirty brown flannel shirt, feasted amidst quiet elegance and flunkies. An incongruous sight, surely. Always, afterwards, we would go to some new show. Elkins would buy up a whole box, and once we were seated, tear up the rest of the tickets. He was a good scout. He knew what he wanted, and he could afford it. Why not?

Women were forever calling for 'Gene. There was something apparently irresistible in his strange combination of cruelty (around the mouth), intelligence (in his eyes) and sympathy (in his voice). I would not say that he was "good looking." But one girl told me she could not get his face out of her thoughts. He was hard-boiled and whimsical. He was brutal and tender, so I was told. From shop girl to "sassiety" queen, they all seemed to develop certain tendencies in his presence. What may have resulted, deponent sayeth not. About some things 'Gene was Sphinx-like. All I can report is the phenomena.

Meanwhile the course was proceeding. Over boiled beef and beer in Durgin and Parks,[20] or salami and red ink at the Roma, we three discussed our efforts. Suffice it to tell about Elkins and myself that he is still hopeful of presenting some day a deft but tenuous high comedy of the Four Hundred,[21] composed then, while I seemed to become more confused and less capable of creation as the days passed. But O'Neill, where he ever found the time for his output I can't imagine, but here is an incomplete list of his activities, as I remember them, for 1914–15:

Two of the one-acters in the Caribbean series, first drafts. A one-act play about a spy in the war then occurring—gruesome, devastating and wonderfully striking. A hasty draft of a full length play called at that time *The Second Engineer*, which formed, later, some of the basis for *Anna Christie*. A lovely little fantasy named *Abortion*, all about a doctor who took his Hippocratic oath seriously and refused to perform an illegal operation upon his own fiancée—something to make one's blood chill. And conversationally, a play about a man who was always hoping to get away from his environment, to go "beyond the horizon." This took four years to crystallize. There was also much discussion of a contemplated farce in which some Mexican General was to hire a movie company to stage a fake revolution for the films, the fake eventually turning into reality. This last has evidently been abandoned.[22]

All of us in the class were a little appalled at the savage radicalism of O'Neill. But we were all agreed that here was the One Best Bet. Even the most disapproving of our companions would say, "Well, I wonder how long it will be before he is the country's greatest playwright." We said it seriously, almost perfunctorily. Baker himself recognized the smouldering genius which was five years later to flame. He begged 'Gene to return for a second year. 'Gene wouldn't. No more academic stuff for him.

On a stifling May morning the three of us shook hands and scattered, Elkins to the Pacific Coast, I to a job selling canned fish in Chicago, O'Neill to wanderings, Provincetown, and fame. He hit 'em between the eyes, and he deserved it. *Beyond the Horizon*, *Anna Christie*, *The Emperor Jones*, *The Hairy Ape* and *Diff'rent*—yes, and that poignant, ill-fated *The Straw*. These will live.

Something has happened to O'Neill. I have seen him only twice since, and he is a stranger. Gone is the old swaggering zest, vanished is the charming swashbuckling. He looks tired and tortured. Probably it is my fault, but he finds little beyond monosyllables to say to me. Even his infuriated sense of humor seems to have lost all its edge.

I guess it is the fault of his sycophants, his village yes-men. No human could withstand, I suppose, the frightful adulation which has been his lot. His work looks bad, too, these days. I haven't seen *The Great God Brown*, but from what I hear, there is too much in it of this artificial, manufactured "Great God O'Neill." As for *Welded*, *All God's Chillun*, *Desire Under the Elms* and *The Fountain*—well, they have all the appearance, to me, of rungs down a ladder into sterility.

I'm sorry. One cannot help a little sadness over the spectacle of a high, exuberant spirit, becoming lacquered. I would like to hear, some day, that 'Gene had suddenly turned on some of his flatterers and socked a couple of jaws. I'd like to hear that he had vanished, full of hooch and hellishness, for parts unknown, beyond some new horizon, to touch the earth again and return plain 'Gene and not the deity of Washington Square.

I wish he'd go to see our *Love 'Em and Leave 'Em*, and sit with me over a flock of beers, and tear hell out of it.

But I guess he will not. We aren't high-brow enough, I'm sure, for this strange, literary O'Neill. We wouldn't be worth bothering about.

Things change.

# 14 / Susan Glaspell

Susan Keating Glaspell (1876–1948), from Davenport, Iowa, was a writer of fiction and plays. Already a well-known novelist when she went with her husband, George Cram Cook (1873–1924), to live in New York's Greenwich Village and spend summers in Provincetown, Massachusetts, she was one of the founders of the Provincetown Players in 1915, and a central figure in the group until she and Cook departed for Greece in 1922. Her association with the players resulted in several important plays, including *Trifles* (1916), *Inheritors* (1921), and *The Verge* (1921). She won the Pulitzer Prize for *Allison's House* (1930).

Source: Susan Glaspell, *The Road to the Temple* (New York: Frederick A. Stokes, 1927), 253–54.

Two Irishmen, one old and one young, had arrived and taken a shack just up the street. "Terry," I said to the one not young, "haven't you a play to read to us?"

"No," said Terry Carlin, "I don't write, I just think, and sometimes talk. But Mr. O'Neill has got a whole trunk full of plays," he smiled.

That didn't sound too promising, but I said: "Well, tell Mr. O'Neill to come to our house at eight o'clock to-night, and bring some of his plays."

So Gene took *Bound East for Cardiff* from his trunk, and Freddie Burt[23] read it to us, Gene staying out in the dining-room while the reading went on.

He was not left alone in the dining-room when the play had finished.

Then we knew what we were for. We began in faith, and perhaps it is true when you do that "all these things shall be added unto you."

I may see it through memories too emotional, but it seems to me I have never sat before a more moving production than our *Bound East for Cardiff*, when Eugene O'Neill was produced for the first time on any stage. Jig[24] was Yank. As he lay in his bunk dying, he talked of life as one who knew he must leave it.

The sea has been good to Eugene O'Neill. It was there for his opening. There was a fog, just as the script demanded, fog bell in the harbor. The tide was in, and it washed under us and around, spraying through the holes in the floor, giving us the rhythm and the flavor of the sea while the big dying sailor talked to his friend Drisc of the life he had always wanted deep in the land, where you'd never see a ship or smell the sea.

It is not merely figurative language to say the old wharf shook with applause.

# 15 / Mary Heaton Vorse

Mary Heaton Vorse (1874–1966), an heiress to a shipping fortune, was born in New York City and grew up in a twenty-four-room mansion in Amherst, Massachusetts. After traveling extensively as a child, she studied at the Art Students League in New York and married journalist Albert White Vorse (1866–1910) in 1898. The couple moved to Provincetown in 1906, and, after Albert Vorse's death, Mary married the radical journalist Joe O'Brien (?–1915). They were central figures in the artists' and writers' colony that Provincetown became, and they devoted themselves to writing and activism on behalf of suffrage and labor politics. They were founding members of the Provincetown Players, and it was their wharf that housed the Players' first home, the Wharf Theater, but after O'Brien's death, Mary Vorse spent most of her time in Greenwich Village working on the *Masses* magazine and the Women's Peace Party. She continued to write many newspaper and magazine articles about social issues such as child labor, infant mortality, and housing, as well as a number of books, including her Provincetown memoir, *Time and the Town*, until she died in Provincetown at the age of ninety-two.

Source: Mary Heaton Vorse, *Time and the Town: A Provincetown Chronicle* (New York: Dial, 1942), 120–22, 131.

Terry Carlin, an old anarchist whom all of us knew, took a shack on the water with a young fellow named Eugene O'Neill. Terry was a tall, beautiful old man, with gay blue eyes and a shock of iron-gray hair. He had fine, muscular workman's hands. I remember meeting him, looming out of the fog, in the back country, with him beautiful Mary Pyne, Harry Kemp's wife. Mary had on a gray cape and her red hair shone through the fog. Together they looked like a symbolic picture of Ireland.

Terry's young friend, Gene O'Neill, was dark and good-looking. He told us shyly that he had written some plays.

When Frederick Burt read *Bound East for Cardiff* at the Cooks', Gene went into the next room while the reading was going on, for his tough, hard-boiled pose covered extreme sensitiveness. There was no one there during that reading who did not recognize the quality of this play. Here was something new, the true feeling of the sea. O'Neill had spent a couple of years as a seaman in his young, turbulent days and he had brought back from the experience the Glencairn cycle.[25] Nothing that O'Neill did later had more truth than his early plays. From that moment he took his place as an important writer.

No one of us who heard that play reading will ever forget it, nor the reading of *Trifles* by Susan Glaspell, which took place at my house. Listening to the plays and giving them the instant recognition they deserved was a company of young people whom destiny had touched. Strange fates awaited them. Gene was to be America's greatest playwright and to withdraw completely from the world. Jack Reed[26] was to be buried under the Kremlin in Moscow, and Jig Cook was to die in Greece and be laid in his grave by the women of the village, a stone from the Parthenon for his head given by the Greek government.

[. . .]

Gene O'Neill, dark, handsome, silent, had no pose at all. He was himself at all times. You knew more about him when you saw him swim. He swam like a South Sea Islander. Yet this recluse who shunned people was afraid to be alone. The unfriendly universe pressed down on him in the dark and filled him with the forebodings of naked primitive man. He could write the epic of fear, *Emperor Jones*, because no one knew more of cosmic fear than Gene, fear of the unknown, fear of the dark and the universe. There was no such darkness as Gene's after a hangover. He would sit silent and suffering and in darkness. You could have taken the air he breathed and carved a statue of despair of it. No one has written a story of his life or his unending struggle with an empty universe.

And there was something else he knew—the cry of agony of the human spirit. The surrounding mystery and terror of life were always with him. Much of his best work came from the time when he was bumming around—when he was the companion of sailors and when he sat in the Hellhole with a bunch of bums. When he was young, he liked girls and drinking. He liked the people from the lower depths.

[. . .]

Provincetown did its share of witch-hunting at that time. Every stranger was under suspicion. Henry J. James in his fine book, *German Submarines in Yankee Waters*, tells of walking on the shore with his father carrying a lantern. They themselves belonged to the Shore Patrol, yet a patrol boat hurried in to find out to whom they were signaling. A sheet hung out of a window to dry would be considered a signal to the enemy and looked into.

Eugene O'Neill and a friend[27] came down in the very early spring of 1918 to write a play. Eugene was exempt from the draft because of tuberculosis. They would go out daily to walk on the dunes. Soon word spread through town that there were two men watching the coast defenses. O'Neill was arrested and it took him quite a while to prove his exemption and that he was the son of the great actor, James O'Neill, who lived in New London. He was then released, but a sleuth was kept upon his trail for weeks. He and the detective both lived at the Atlantic House and it was the detective's duty to read all of Gene's mail. They became great friends.

"Well," he would say cheerily at breakfast, "you got a letter from your mother, Gene, but your girl's forgot you today, but someone's sent you a knitted tie just the same."

# 16 / Hutchins Hapgood

Hutchins Hapgood (1869–1944), a self-styled philosophical anarchist, studied with William James at Harvard and became a journalist, social critic, and author of several influential books, including *An Anarchist Woman* (1909) and his memoir, *A Victorian in the Modern World* (1939). He was married to the fiction writer Neith Boyce (1872–1951), and the two had a long-lasting but strife-filled marriage, due mostly to his idea that marriage should be "open," allowing for sexual freedom for the husband, but not for the wife. The two collaborated on and acted in a marriage play called *Enemies* (1916) as one of the Provincetown group's first performances.

Source: Hutchins Hapgood, *A Victorian in the Modern World* (New York: Harcourt, Brace and Company, 1939), 396–98.

It was in this second summer [1916] of the Provincetown dramatic experiment that Eugene O'Neill appeared on the scene. He and Terry Carlin had been bumming around somewhere in New York, devoting themselves passionately to whisky and the life that accompanies it in the inner world; suddenly they left for Provincetown, and came to my house. The natural purpose was to borrow money from me, to the amount of ten dollars, which, it will probably amuse Gene to know, has never been repaid. But although Gene's pockets were at the moment empty of cash, he had in them a one-act play or two.

Gene came to a meeting of the little group at one of the houses, and sat on the floor, perfectly silent, listening intently—a striking figure, his young face gaunt and taut-mouthed, his eyes burning. After that meeting, he gave us the manuscript of *Bound East for Cardiff* to read. Neith took it to Jig and said, "We have got to do this play." Jig read it and agreed, but said, "I don't see how we can build that forecastle set in the fish-house."[28] But Jig loved problems; and he set to on this one and, within a day or so, he was building the set himself.

At the first performance of *Bound East for Cardiff* on the end of the wharf, Jig played the dying sailor, and the actual background of the sea and sound of the waves made this perhaps the best setting the play could have, certainly the most picturesque it ever had.

I think one or two other short plays of O'Neill's were produced before the Players went to New York—one about some castaways on a raft,[29] and perhaps others. Jig became very interested in the problem of setting O'Neill, and showed great energy and ingenuity in contriving these sets with the few resources of the little theatre.

And when, the next year, *The Emperor Jones* was produced in the little theatre, on MacDougal Street, made out of a bottling works,[30] Jig's genius expressed itself both in the setting and the realization of the inspiration behind the lines in some of the lighting effects, as also later in *The Hairy Ape*, in a most extraordinary way.

At this point I would like to record my, I think, well-based feeling that Eugene O'Neill might never have been heard of in the theatre, certainly not for long after this, had it not been for the work of George Cram Cook. Every writer needs a sympathetic background; that background was entirely absent from Broadway at the time and, as far as O'Neill's personality was concerned, it was absent everywhere. The man who felt O'Neill's personality vividly and who created, not only the social enthusiasm for it, but the definite mechanical body and setting, was George Cram Cook. His work was detailed, assiduous, inventive, lit up with constant enthusiasm, with a genuine propaganda which never ceased to be active.

[. . .]

At a somewhat later period, when Neith and the family had gone back to Dobbs Ferry, I was staying in our little house, the Pinehurst, at Provincetown, alone for a few days; and I invited Terry and O'Neill to stay with me. Terry produced a lot of very bad whisky, and later several of the toughest and lowest characters of the town, whom I had never met. You could always trust Terry to get to the bottom of things, in which he saw a significance that even I sometimes missed. Gene, Terry, and I had gotten to the genial stage in our drinking, when those—no, not bums, for bums are often very attractive—creatures appeared, and sat down with us around the table. Gene took one look at them and began to drink with great rapidity. Certainly within the hour he had drunk himself into a state of complete insensibility. It was clear enough to me, and also to Terry, for we afterwards compared notes. Whether consciously or not, O'Neill had acted in the spirit of self-preservation. He had a great and genuine sympathy and understanding for that type of human being, but he couldn't endure them. He couldn't possibly have sent them away. Had he done so he would have sinned against something very deep in him; on the other hand, his keen realization of the misery in them compelled him to try to escape, and the best escape was to "go out."

I managed to get rid of them, by some sort of diplomatic device, and then Terry and I put Gene to bed. That incident pointed, I think, to something sensitive, deep, and real in O'Neill's character. It seemed to have no relation to his purely theatrical side. It was no accident that he was the son of James O'Neill, who had created the role of Monte Cristo. Another instance of this more amusing and more superficial aspect of O'Neill was, according to Terry's account, one day when Gene and Terry were drinking: A very close friend of Gene's, a woman, was seen approaching; whereupon Gene arose and, with a haughty waft of his hand, occupying the center of the stage, he cried, "Back to the gutter, whence you came!"

I did not know O'Neill very intimately, though I knew him for a long time; but I always felt, both from my first impression and from his work, that his strong side was not that of humor. That little theatrical scene helps to explain it. I saw him smile humorously, so far as I recollect, only once. When he and Agnes, his wife, were living at the Life-saving Station across the Dunes, they had a little child, Shane, and an invaluable housekeeper on whose good offices they were very dependent.[31] Terry was visiting them at the time, as he often did for long periods. Gene loved Terry probably as much as he ever did any man; but one day—Gene told me this story himself—the housekeeper came to him and said, "Mr. O'Neill, either I or Terry must go." Gene knew that there had been friction between them for a long time, and he was expecting something startling, but when he heard her say, "Terry spat in the sink this morning," he knew that the end had come. It was then that Gene smiled; but Terry went.

Gene once remarked to me, "The only interesting thing is tragedy."

But, as I have indicated, his genius, as far as it had a dramatic expression, lacked perhaps the symbolic embodiment of tragedy, which like all poetry, lies in the phrase. So that although in his eyes his father appeared with all imperfections on his head, yet there was something quite close between them; and his father, of course, had great pride in his son's early success. When, in the MacDougal Street Theater, Gene's *Before Breakfast* was played, with the lovely Mary Pyne playing the only character on the stage, James O'Neill came down to see a rehearsal—a striking figure with fur-collared coat, gold-headed cane, and a diamond ring on his finger. He did not approve the diction or "business" of the actress; he began to show her how acting was done, how points were made, with the voice and gesture of Monte Cristo. When he went away, some of us spoke to him about Gene's gifts and promise, and he said benignly, "Yes, yes, I think the boy has something in him."

# 17 / Harry Kemp

Harry Kemp (1883–1960) was born in Youngstown, Ohio, and went to sea at the age of seventeen, traveling to Australia and China before coming back to the United States, where he rode the rails as a hobo before getting his degree at the University of Kansas. As an aspiring poet, he gravitated to Greenwich Village and Provincetown and became part of the Provincetown Players group, making his living as a journalist and fiction writer. He traveled a good deal throughout his life and often lived in a shack in Provincetown, becoming known as "the tramp poet" or "the poet of the dunes." His *Tramping on Life: An Autobiographical Narrative* (1922) made him a popular hero among bohemians of two generations.

Source: Harry Kemp, "O'Neill of Provincetown," *Brentano's Book Chat* May–June 1929: 45–47.

Finding the right environment, the surroundings that conduce to his best efforts, is one of the gravest problems of the creative artist.

The poet, the playwright, the painter, achieves his best work where he doesn't have to cope with the pull of a whole community against him, the hostility of the small town, the small mind.

Eventually the artist finds such a hostile environment too much for him. He's got to get away, to consort with his own kind, or he'll go entirely under. He's got to get away where he doesn't have mentally to bump into the invidious opinions of the local grocer, butcher, and village Klan, as regards his queerness, because he chooses to write or paint instead of being a go-getter.

This explains the wherefore of colonies where creative workers gather together in a group, to lend themselves strength and support for their work. It's a fine and normal instinct, and not a weakness, that sends the young poet, the young playwright, to Greenwich Village, to Provincetown, or some other Bohemian quarter, where he can find people of his own kind who do not think it somehow criminal or vicious to love beauty, and to try to bring a little more of it into the world. . . .

But then ensues the graver problem: the curse of the artist is too much sociability. Gathered with his own kind, in his own studios and restaurants—many and many a book and work of art is talked into air, not written down on paper, set down on canvas. Where one genius is killed off by the hostility of a stupid, commercial-minded community, ten are brought to nothing by finding it so pleasant to discuss what they are about to do, are at present at work upon. The unwary talent often does not learn until too late that talk is in itself a species of creation. . . .

This was my pitfall for years. I had a trunk full of incomplete manuscripts, at one time—never finished, because, over the wine glass, the coffee cup, and in the quiet of friendly studios and village restaurants, I talked my stuff when I should have been writing it. . . .

I began to get wise to myself when it was almost too late. I began to notice that this was the great vice of the artist—I saw others courting limbo by the same method.

I ran away to Provincetown, my first summer there, with the intention of putting all this destructive sociability behind me.

But there under the spell and power of a sociable Bohemian community, with the bright bay curling at the feet of our wharves and cottages and shacks, the great rowdy dunes just back of us—neither I nor many of the others put this vice of the artist behind us.

Frequently, tense and eager, we talked and debated till dawn put its face up at all the windows. And we walked home in the young daylight, dizzy with words.

That day, not a line would be written by me.

To confess the truth, in my heart I was beginning to look on myself as a great fake . . . which made me tell all the more of my greatness . . .

Then along came the young fellow who, by his quiet example, blazed a way for me; that I was not to gather strength to follow till several years after . . . a dark, brooding young man by the name of Eugene O'Neill.

O'Neill dropped down upon our group, in the company of an erect, Indian-built "old" man by the name of Terry Carline [*sic*], I put the quotes about the adjective because there never has been anything old about Terry despite his years.

O'Neill was unknown then. More unknown then than he's famed now.

O'Neill went to work like a navvy the same day he reached Provincetown.

His sole companion, this strange wise being we called "the Anarchist Philosopher," he went into practical seclusion in some rather bare rooms over the big blank building that fronted the bay, known as John Francis' General Store . . . he was seldom seen except when sitting in grave silence on the beach, looking out over the water. One was almost afraid to speak with him, because of his taciturnity. When you did speak, if he didn't want to talk, he'd simply rise and walk calmly away from you.

With many he won the reputation of being a grouch. But he wasn't a grouch.

At times he would talk, and talk brilliantly—when the time was ripe for talking; perhaps after he'd spent days at labour with the pen.

We were soon all of us set in awe of this dark grave young man.

He was writing plays. That was the rumour. Soon the rumour was substantiated, when he came up to a group of the newly formed Provincetown Players, and offered a one act sea-play of his. It's a fact some were instinctively jealous, I think I was among the number. But George Cram Cook, the founder and director of the Players, gave immediate voice to the opinion that here was a genius in the bud. And stuck to that opinion despite criticism which sometimes became violently adverse.

O'Neill was quite savage in his determination to find solitude. No early Christian martyr sought his hilltop remote from men, in order to be with his God, with greater zest than O'Neill, solitude to be alone with his work.

That late fall found me still in Provincetown, though I was half out of my skin with desire to return to the Village and the whirl of its winter's goings-on. But I was too broke to get back . . .

I lived in the same great frame building that O'Neill lived in. I had rooms right across from his—where he too stayed on; but from choice, not from necessity.

The building had been built for summer residence only—those upstairs rooms, at least, had been. It grew brisk and cold. The gales of the equinox came.

I sold a bunch of poems to a magazine, and was able to escape.

Day before I left, I chanced into O'Neill's rooms, on some valid pretext.

There I found Terry Carline [*sic*] sitting, reading a book, in his overcoat; O'Neill in a couple of sweaters, seated on a kitchen chair, his legs outstretched across an oilstove, his feet propped up on an opposite chair. He was writing. He stopped to hold his fingers over the radiation from the oilstove, while he dismissed me briefly and courteously.

To tell the truth, my awe over his conduct was mixed with a sort of pity. I had not yet arrived at the conviction that all genius is two-thirds hard work. I still believed that most great work was mainly inspiration. I was too much waiting around for the inspiration that never came. A fellow slaving at writing like that, must be somehow deluded. . . .

"What are you working at now, 'Gene?" I asked him, just to make conversation—a thing he hates most of all. If you have nothing to say, don't say it, seemed to be his guiding apothegm.

His answer to my question—fixing me steadfastly and penetratively with serious brown eyes—"I'm thinking of writing an epocal [*sic*] play . . . with a Chinese setting . . . in very many scenes—

"You see, in this play, there's a Chinaman, born a hundred times; and before each successive incarnation, he sees, next time he's doomed to a repetition of his former end—doomed to have his head chopped off—

"For a hundred re-births, Destiny allows him his choice of different situations in life, each time with the idea of not having his head cut off—

"And each time, from beggar to mandarin, there's the descending axe, and off pops that head!"

I'm sure now O'Neill was kidding me. . . .

I heard he stayed all winter in that summer-boarded place.

Several summers later, he took an even further move to get away from the elements that disturbed his work . . . as if he needed more solitude than that in the midst of which he had already insulated himself! . . .

There was a house on the edge of the ocean itself, that had previously been occupied as a coastguard station. The incessant battle between sand and waves had been going on in favour of the giant tugging ocean. After an especially hard winter, the house looked doomed to be washed away, by the next storm,

A mile further down a more modern station was erected, and the former one abandoned to what seemed its certain destruction.

Then, in its caprice, the ocean, instead of continuing the job, turned about, and began heaping up sand about the place. It was conserving it for the future playwright of the sea . . .

Three miles of toilsome sands rolling, undulating, scraped and scooped into slopes and hollows, a landscape like the moon's . . . that was the approach to O'Neill's house . . .

Three miles to the outside, as it was called, if you were fairly athletic, was not so bad; but it was the three miles back again, that gave pause to would-be visitors. For O'Neill's fame was growing . . .

It was not until this last summer that I realized the drastic step O'Neill had taken, to be alone with his work. O'Neill's control over himself, his austerity where his writing was concerned, had, in the meantime, become my admiration, the goal of my effort, too. . . .

I was an older man and should have known better without his example. But I hadn't known better. And there was his previous conduct standing out clear and fine, a polestar to steer mine by.

This summer when I landed in Provincetown, though I found myself yearning for the hurly-burly and whirl of pleasant companionship a vacation there affords, I set my face against returning to my favourite dock of the summer before . . . where the swimming was always excellent, the view, something better and more picturesque than anywhere along the Riviera . . . and where there was also plenty of distraction in various shapes: children and swimmers making the planks reverberate during the day; lovers whispering and murmuring up to midnight; cats and dogs disturbing the quiet stars till just before dawn: Then the bumping of boats, and fishermen discussing the prospects of the day's catch.

"Hell-on-Wheels" was what I had wished to put for a name, over the door of my shack on the dock. But its owner objected. . . .

This summer I rented a shack on the oceanside, not quite a mile down the beach from the house Eugene O'Neill had lived in. . . .

I had plenty of paper, a typewriter, a black cat for companionship. My food I fetched from town in a burlap sack. I can only compare trudging through the sand to walking in deep snow without snowshoes,

"You won't stick it out" a friend advised, "so better not waste your time trying." But I had a novel to write, I had a great example before me, and, for three months, I stuck. And, in sticking it out, my imagination widened, till it comprehended what O'Neill had experienced there.[. . .]

The house in which Eugene O'Neill wrote his greatest plays stands in a small crater of sand. You can nearly jump to its roof from the rear. Every Spring it is found half-up in sand that the winter has blown there. It has to be dug out again to make the doors free for entrance, like digging a house out of snowdrifts.

The front yard of the house is fifty miles of sheer beach, up and down; and straight out, an ocean that doesn't stop till it strikes the coast of Europe.

For his morning shower, O'Neill could almost literally tumble out of his bed, into a series of running breakers. Which he did in all weathers, to the consternation of the coast-guards, in their tower a mile below. . . .

There are two large long rooms in the house on the ground floor. In the outside room there stands a long table and many chairs. The dining room.

The inner room is long and bleak. Here it was that shipwrecked sailors were laid out, drowned . . . once or twice by the half dozen . . . impressionable people who stay in the house overnight say it bristles yet with the presence of the spirits of these, on occasions of weather, or when the Northern Lights search the dark sky everywhere, with eerie marching lights. . . .

In the upper part, are two or three bedrooms; I do not remember the number.

The observation tower, built on top of the second floor, is led up to by a sloping sort of affair, half-stairs, half-ladder.

There are windows here giving on all sides of space till space defeats itself with infinity.

From these windows you can see the sun come up, an enormous molten globe, the sun go down; its daily journey made pigmy by the vastness of the sky that dwarfs its arc of progress. The sun seems to open one door, like a little man in a very big house. He comes out of that door. Then he opens another door right next to the first door, and goes in again . . . after a few steps taken.

The sunrises are enormous, spraying the east with unimagined colours.

The sunsets are still more enormous. There isn't one that repeats on the other. And each one defeats the rainbow. And, when there are clouds, they march like cities moving, in whatever direction the wind blows. Out in the ocean a strange life goes on. Porpoises roll and sport. Herds of fish drive this way and that, sometimes frantic in their efforts to escape schools of dogfish that drive them up on the beach. Whales are often seen. Three several places [*sic*] along the beach, the huge whitened ribs and prolonged vertebrae of wrecks distinguish the endless wave-printed sand.

In the back, in the heart of the dune-country, there is a petrified forest buried. Bone-white sand-carved bits of wood and fragments of what were once greening branches work up through the sand.

The sea casts up curious shapes and forms of wood and what were the habitations of sea-creatures . . .

The observation-tower O'Neill made his workshop, his writing room.

On the trap-door leading up into it he firmly set his writing table. When he was up there no one else could come there.

From all the relics and shapes evicted from their sleep in the sand and in the depths of the ocean, O'Neill culled the strangest and weirdest. With them he stocked his tower.

They stand about his writing table in literal multitudes, expressive of the fancy of the playwright . . . bits of timber like arms upholding pointing hands . . . parts of drift that resemble human bodies and faces till you look steady and find they are only freaks and whimsies of tide and eroding sand and wind. They stand so close about there is hardly room to move.

They imprison your body. They set your imagination free.

*There* is the tick of eternity superceding the clocks of time; if you wish to measure your progress.

*There* are skies full of other systems and other worlds, if you care to voyage beyond this world.

But if, like O'Neill, you wish solitariness bitter and salutary, in which to appraise and measure the human values of the world you are in, there you can withdraw and find it!

Source: "O'Neill as an Actor Is Recalled by One Who Saw Him in '17," *New York Herald Tribune* 17 March 1929, sec. 7: 5.

The Provincetown production of O'Neill's *Before Breakfast*[32] awakened memories in at least one member of the audience, Harry Kemp. After the performance he talked of the first performance of *Before Breakfast*, in 1917.

"Gene O'Neill was great in his part." "What!" His audience jumped. The play calls for only one character and that [is] a woman. "He didn't play the part of Mrs. Rowland?"

"No, he was the hand that reached in from off-stage and he was the off-stage groan. You know the story of O'Neill's acting for his father, James O'Neill, in *The Count of Monte Cristo*? He played the part of a jailer but without enthusiasm. 'I am not satisfied with your performance, sir,' said the elder O'Neill. 'I am not satisfied with your play, sir,' came back the younger O'Neill.

"He played the Mate in *Bound for Cardiff* [*sic*], and gave a fine performance. He had just one line to say: 'Isn't this your watch, on deck, Driscoll?' but he said it with quiet brusqueness. The fact that he was sick with stage fright every evening seemed to improve his performance.

"Then he was the negro in *Thirst*. That was his biggest role, but he never cared for it. He was fonder of his part in *Before Breakfast*. In that play the artist husband of Mrs. Rowland is supposed to be shaving off-stage. He asked for a bowl of hot water and reaches through the door for it. The audience sees only the hand, which according to the script is long-fingered, sensitive, slender. Later a groan is heard. There's a part that calls for delicacy, restraint and finish. To coordinate the hand and the groan . . . Well, O'Neill did the hand and the groan, and a fine performance it was."

"What did you do in those early plays?" somebody asked.

"I acted. O'Neill could make anybody work for him. It was a joke to see him cast the plays. He'd go out and walk up and down the street in front of the theater, and if he saw somebody he wanted he got him. Artists, ironworkers, wealthy idlers, penniless strikers . . . that Irishman could kid them into anything."

"In what did you act?"

'Well, I used to have a small part for the first week of rehearsal; then they would take it away from me and rehearse me in another play for a week. I—er—I never got beyond the rehearsals."[33]

# 18 / Adele Nathan

Adele Gutman Nathan (1889–1986), a writer, director, and producer, was born and brought up in Baltimore. She graduated from Goucher College and was active in the theater throughout her life. Besides Baltimore's Vagabond Players, of which she was a founder, she also directed plays for twenty years for the Cellar Players of the Hudson Guild, did some film work, and was director of the Federal Theatre Project in New Jersey. Her major work, however, was as a writer and producer of historical pageants, including those for several cities and two world's fairs.

Source: Adele Nathan, "'Eugene G. O'Neill': 1916," *New York Times Magazine* 6 October 1946: 18.

TO THE EDITOR:

Readers of the Magazine's article, "Eugene O'Neill Returns After Twelve Years,"[34] who are now fighting to pay $25 for a single seat for *The Iceman Cometh*, may be interested to know that there was a time when Nobel Prize-winner O'Neill was glad to sell a whole play for considerably less than that amount.

It was the summer of 1916. The Little Theatre movement was epidemic in the United States, and Baltimore had caught it. We called our group the Vagabonds. Early in July we rented an old grocery store at Charles and Centre Streets, almost at the foot of the Washington Monument, and after three months of back-breaking toil converting it into a playhouse, we parted, exhausted, for a brief holiday. In a few weeks we would start rehearsals. The theatre was finished.

I took myself to an obscure little fishing village called Provincetown, at the tip of Cape Cod. A group of painters had their studios there, and it was an ideal place to "get away from it all."

But one worry about the Vagabonds went along with me as director of the theatre. There was a tremendous obstacle to our success; we had plenty of workers—stage-struck and otherwise— sufficient money and quite decent equipment. But like everybody else, we were short of good one-act plays.

There were some translations of one-acters by modern Europeans—Schnitzler, Molnár, Strindberg and Chekhov—and a few by "classics" like Molière and Oscar Wilde.[35] But except for a couple of Dreisers, a Mencken satire, and a thin little volume of Washington Square plays, there was practically nothing by Americans.[36] This left the Little Theatres—the Vagabonds among them—without much material from which to choose. We could do nothing but hope against hope that plays would be forthcoming.

In this mood I arrived at Provincetown. The news that a group of obscure newspaper people and magazine writers had built themselves a theatre on a broken-down wharf in the town and were writing and presenting their own plays to a meager audience did nothing to raise my hopes. However, the old fire horse in me demanded that I go where I smelled smoke, so go I did.

The "theatre" was not promising. The seats were mere benches and the curtain was almost transparent—but that evening I saw three uncommonly good one-act plays, the authors themselves serving for the most part as actors.[37]

At the end of the program I went backstage to meet the director. He was a good-looking man with a shock of white hair and his name was George Cram Cook. The upshot of our talk was that he invited me to come to his home the next day and meet the members of the group. (Mrs. Cook was a Western newspaper woman who wrote sporadically for the magazines under the name of Susan Glaspell.)

Next afternoon practically the entire group from the wharf was there to meet me. Each had at least one manuscript clutched in a hot little hand. I was introduced all round. The only name known to me was that of Max Eastman, the editor of a provocative magazine called *The Masses*. Among others were a writer of short stories, Wilbur Daniel Steele, a good-looking young model, Louise Bryant, and a fiery young reporter, John Reed.

The slim, bronzed young man who was the author of one of last night's plays was also there. I knew of him vaguely as the writer of a book of one-act melodramas which all of us at the Vagabonds had read eagerly and rejected unanimously.[38] They were pretty poor stuff.

The play of last night, however, was in a quite different vein. The scene was the fo'c'sle of a rusty merchant ship. One of the seamen was dying while the crew snored and groused and whistled and sang all about him. It was a gripping bit, and I wanted it.

But the young man had never made a copy of the play. Rehearsals had been conducted from a single working script, and that was in sad condition.

Everybody was visibly shaken by meeting with a director, especially a director ready to pay cold cash for one-acters. Evidently very few of them had seen real money lately. Even the scriptless author broke down and offered to make a clean copy of his play for me, only he said he was a very poor typist and it might take him quite a time.

A bargain was struck. I would take all three plays presented the night before in return for $15 each. I could take the finished ones along and count on my young man to deliver his before the week was out. A week passed. I was about to depart for home. At the eleventh hour he arrived with his clean copy. He certainly knew his limitations. He was not a good typist. He had made innumerable corrections in ink. The stage directions and offstage noises he had added almost illegibly in blue and red pencil. But he had taken good care to sign his name at the end—Eugene G. O'Neill. The title of the play was *Bound East for Cardiff*.

Back in Baltimore my acquisitions met with only mild rapture. *Trifles*, a stark little tragedy by Miss Glaspell, received unqualified acclaim, but *Suppressed Desires*, by the same author, which dealt in comedy vein with the new fad, psychoanalysis, was regarded as mildly amusing for the intelligentsia and too sophisticated for our town. Young O'Neill's play aroused practically no enthusiasm. I had to throw about a good deal of weight as our director to get it on the second bill.

After that came casting troubles. The play called for nine extras whose parts consisted mainly of walking in and out of the cabin door, climbing up into bunks and going noisily to sleep. Raymond Sovey and Carol Sax lay in the bunks and snored with a will. Robert Garland had two lines. Dr. Robert W. Wood, the discoverer of the ultra-violet ray, built a small foghorn and used it enthusiastically off-stage. [39]

The newspaper notices were negligible. *The Artist*, Mencken's satire on piano recitals,[40] got top billing.

But Eugene G. O'Neill had no reason to regret the time he had spent typing out that clean script. A short time later I received an envelope from *The Smart Set*, the delightful magazine which George Jean Nathan and H. L. Mencken were then editing. Inside the envelope was a set of galleys and at the top of the first page was written:

"Dear A. N.:

"The writer has asked me to send you these galley proofs. Maybe you can use them at the Vagabonds. They are a new one-acter by that young fellow whose work you like so much. We like it too."

H. L. M.

The one-acter was *The Long Voyage Home.*

A shrewd dealer in Americana once offered me a thousand dollars for the two items—the O'Neill typescript and the galley proofs—but I still have them. Just now, however, I am thinking seriously of parting with them. Perhaps Mr. O'Neill would like to exchange them for a pair of seats for the opening of *The Iceman Cometh.*

Adele Nathan
New York

# 19 / Dorothy Day

Dorothy Day (1897–1980) was born in Brooklyn and briefly attended the University of Illinois before she moved to Greenwich Village and began to work as a reporter for the socialist paper the *Call* and to write for the *Masses*. She had many occupations in her life, including working as a nurse and as a screenwriter. In the 1930s she converted to Catholicism, and in 1933 she and Peter Maurin founded the *Catholic Worker*, a left-leaning newspaper that became the center of a Catholic social justice movement. They also cofounded more than forty "houses of hospitality" for the homeless. At their meeting in November 2012, the United States Conference of Catholic Bishops voted unanimously to recommend her canonization, and in his speech to the United States Congress on September 24, 2015, Pope Francis said that "her social activism, her passion for justice and for the cause of the oppressed, were inspired by the Gospel, her faith, and the example of the saints."

Source: Dorothy Day, *The Long Loneliness: The Autobiography of Dorothy Day* (New York: Harper, 1952), 84.

The charm of my summer job on the older paper was gone. It was not the same, and I soon gave it up. It was more fun to hang around the Provincetown Playhouse where Eugene O'Neill and others of my friends had plays in rehearsal. After rehearsals, or after performances, the usual meeting place was the back room of a saloon on the corner of Fourth Street and Sixth Avenue, nicknamed Hell Hole by its customers. Here Eugene O'Neill, Terry Karlin [*sic*], an old Irish anarchist who had known the Haymarket martyrs, and whom Gene afterward supported till his death, Hypolite [*sic*] Havel,[41] who died a few months ago in the former anarchist colony at Stelton, New Jersey, Michael Gold,[42] and others, were my constant companions. No one ever wanted to go to bed, and no one ever wished to be alone. It was on these cold bitter evenings that I first heard "The Hound of Heaven," in an atmosphere of drink and smoke. Gene could recite all of Francis Thompson's poem, and would sit there, black and dour, his head sunk as he intoned, "And now my heart is as a broken fount, wherein tear drippings stagnate." The idea of this pursuit by the Hound of Heaven fascinated me. The recurrence of it, the inevitableness of the outcome made me feel that sooner or later I would have to pause in the mad rush of living and remember my first beginning and my last end. [. . .]

Virginia Gardner (1904–1992) was a journalist and Communist activist as well as the biographer of Louise Bryant. She worked for ten years for the *Chicago Tribune* before being fired for her union activities in 1940 and later wrote for a number of leftist publications, covering the Rosenberg trial in 1953 for the *Daily Worker*. She also wrote *The Rosenberg Story* (1954).

Source: Virginia Gardner, *"Friend and Lover": The Life of Louise Bryant* (New York: Horizon Press, 1982), 129.

O'Neill was in Provincetown, working on *Beyond the Horizon*, although it would be two more years before it was produced on Broadway, to wide acclaim. When [Louise] Bryant[43] wrote him a few days before she and [John] Reed sailed in August, he knew he had definitely lost her. He brooded over it unhappily and longed for companionship with a woman. He became interested in Dorothy Day, nineteen and beautiful, who wanted to be a writer. She never fell in love with O'Neill, but was spellbound by his genius, never tiring of sitting in the Hell Hole with him and hearing him recite poetry.

When O'Neill saw Agnes Boulton[44] in the Hell Hole waiting for Christine Ell,[45] he stared at her as if he were seeing a ghost, struck by her resemblance to Louise Bryant. Often Dorothy Day and O'Neill made a foursome with Boulton and Harold de Polo. Dorothy considered Boulton "much better-looking than Louise, with more chiseled features, but without Louise's brains and sophistication." But, shown photos of Louise, she saw "a surprising vulnerability about the eyes." It occurred to her, too, that as de Polo was married, Boulton was more sophisticated than she seemed.

Basically Dorothy Day mistrusted the kind of love that O'Neill could offer anyone. She had heard him dwell on the suffering he underwent at Louise's hands and remained unimpressed. "Gene fell in love with Louise first of all because Jack loved her," she said. "Gene needed a hopeless love, Jack was more in love with Louise than Gene was or ever could be. All Gene's experiences were 'copy' to him. So I watched the Agnes–Gene association and hoped she would not be too hurt."[46]

For information on Louis Sheaffer, see chapter 3.

Source: Louis Sheaffer, interviews with Dorothy Day, ca. 1957–58, Louis Sheaffer Collection of Eugene O'Neill Materials, Department of Special Collections, Charles E. Shain Library, Connecticut College, New London.

Eugene O'Neill and Dorothy Day went around together for a few months in the winter of 1917, from early December '17 to late January or early February '18. She met him through her friend Michael Gold, one of whose plays was being done at the Provincetown Players.[47]

> Dorothy: One of the fine things about Gene was that he took people seriously, more seriously than the rest of us did. He took Maxwell Bodenheim[48] seriously as a poet. He took Terry Carlin seriously. He took Hippolyte Havel seriously, and almost no one else did. Hipp would get up in the center of a room, when he'd been drinking, and whirl around in exuberance. He was in love with a lesbian named Rick Hornsby, an aerialist. He gave up his room to her when she was broke and slept outside in the hallway, on the floor. He'd say, "I'm her little doggie." We laughed at him, but not Gene. Gene would say: "This man has been in every prison in Europe. He's suffered." Gene was very responsive to people who suffered. We were revolutionaries and were supposed to sympathize with the unfortunate, and we did *en masse*, but we found Hipp a bit ridiculous. He was short, stocky, bald headed, had a little beard, wore glasses, talked with an accent. He was an anarchist.
>
> We in the Village looked on Gene as a genius . . . You couldn't feel he was a drunk, he wasn't a Village character, he was a writer and would put writing before anything—wife, children, anything.
>
> We all sat around and felt that Gene was a victim of unrequited love (for Louise Bryant) . . . There's a character in Gene's *Moon of the Caribbees* who lies around on deck and talks of his unrequited love . . . Everyone knew he was in love with Louise Bryant, something which is always attractive to other girls.

Dorothy didn't get the impression that O'Neill had a strong sex drive. He wasn't "really physically exciting" to her, because she felt that he couldn't really love anybody, she felt that he would devour you because he was devoured by all his talent, his all-consuming urge to write. At the same time, she considered him glamorous, the only glamorous one around.

Dorothy was engaged to Mike Gold during the time she saw a good deal of Eugene, but Gold thought she was frivolous, that she didn't take him seriously enough. He was jealous of her spending time with O'Neill.

O'Neill never got romantic with Dorothy, never even tried to kiss her. Apparently he liked her for her vitality, her companionship, her great admiration for his writings. Occasionally he'd suggest, almost in offhand fashion, that she sleep with him, but he wasn't perturbed when she rejected the idea. He wanted a sympathetic woman with him all the time. Shortly after she'd leave him to go to work, he'd phone urging her to rejoin him. Though he said to her a few times, "Don't you want to lose your virginity," she felt that he preferred their relationship as it was, an easy, relaxed companionship.

> Dorothy: "I was in love with his writings, while Agnes [Boulton] was in love with him.
>
> "Gene seemed to me a very dour, melancholy sort . . . He had a great sense of futility about everything . . . At the same time writing was a catharsis for him.
>
> "He was reading a great deal of poetry at the time, especially Baudelaire. He urged me to read Baudelaire, also Strindberg. He wanted people to face the tragedy of life, the fact that life is tragic. He was like a teacher. I remember him quoting from Baudelaire about 'the downward path that leads to salvation,' and the lines 'Cats that crouch on pianos and howl with hoarse sweet voices like women.'"[49]

But the poem he recited that made the strongest impression on her was Francis Thompson's "The Hound of Heaven." "I can see him now, reciting all of it by memory, his elbows resting on the table, chin cupped in hand, eyes looking inward and seeing none of us listening." . . . It seemed to Dorothy, perhaps because the lines struck her as true of O'Neill, that he gave special emphasis to: "My heart is like a broken fount for tears." It was after hearing him give "The Hound" that she began dropping in at St. Joseph's R. C. church in the Village. But this was not the first time that Dorothy was attracted to Catholicism. When she was around 12, her closest girl friend was Catholic and at that time she already thought of conversion.

As Dorothy recalls, O'Neill had a "monotonous, grating voice."

# 20 / William Carlos Williams

William Carlos Williams (1883–1963) was born in Rutherford, New Jersey. He received his MD from the University of Pennsylvania and returned to New Jersey, where he practiced medicine. He was also dedicated to the arts, primarily as a poet, and he became one of the most celebrated American modernists. He wrote several plays, including *Many Loves*, which had a successful production by the Living Theater in 1959. In 1916 he commuted nightly from New Jersey to Greenwich Village to act in Alfred Kreymborg's *Lima Beans* at the Provincetown Playhouse.

Source: William Carlos Williams letter to Louis Sheaffer, Louis Sheaffer Collection of Eugene O'Neill Materials, Department of Special Collections, Charles E. Shain Library, Connecticut College, New London.

William C. Williams M.D.
5 Ridge Road Rutherford, N. J.
April 19, 1957

Dear Mr. Sheaffer:

There is not much I can do to aid in your search for O'Neill material but what I have you are welcome to:

The Provincetown Players when they were on McDougel [*sic*] St. in New York 45 years ago were producing *Fog.*[50] Acting in a play *Lima Beans* by Alfred Kreymborg[51] with Mina Loy[52] and William Zorach[53] we had to wait sometimes until the earlier rehearsal was finished.

I was impressed there in the dark and empty theatre by what was going on before me. The shouts of the fog-bounders of the ship's crew before me were full of the tension which such a scene would invoke in the hands of a master young as he. It was vivid for me as I sat in the empty theatre waiting my turn.

But of equal interest to the play being sketched before me was the presence of an older man, an actor, who we were told was the author's father,

James O'Neill who was famous on the New York [stage] for his acting of the part of Monte Christo [*sic*]. We didn't know whether to laugh or keep a straight face when faced with this information but we had to acknowledge that the man had made a success of the role.

During the course of the rehearsal the father would often interrupt the course of the play and when he did the son would be closely attentive, god knows he had to be because the father made no bones about it but let himself be heard above the clatter that was supposed to be going on during the scene.

The old man and the son consulted together when there was some point they had to solve about the play itself or its presentation. The rival company that we represented would have to sit there while the father and son reiterated the details on which they were intent and then advanced to take charge. I never even so much as talked to O'Neill during the weeks of our rehearsals when he would leave the theatre still talking with his father.

Sincerely yours,
William Carlos Williams

# 3 Provincetown Playhouse, Peaked Hill Bar, Ridgefield, Broadway (1918–1927)

In 1918 Eugene O'Neill brought his bride, Agnes Boulton, to the house at Peaked Hill Bar on the Provincetown dunes that his father had bought them as a wedding present (see figure 7). She describes this in her memoir, as well as the good times and the bad in the O'Neills' relationship, including a detailed account of his drinking. Her account is supplemented by the memories of Hazel Hawthorne, a young woman who worked as a nanny in Provincetown and became Agnes's friend; Juliet Throckmorton, who visited them at Peaked Hill Bar; and Manuel Zora, a fisherman and village character who had his own view of O'Neill. In the early 1920s, *Beyond the Horizon* and *"Anna Christie"* gave O'Neill his first Broadway success and two Pulitzer Prizes, but he was still involved with the Provincetown Players and its successor, the Experimental Theatre, Inc., which was founded by O'Neill, Robert Edmond Jones, and Kenneth Macgowan in 1923. Edmund Wilson and Charles O'Brien Kennedy describe O'Neill in Greenwich Village and at the Provincetown Playhouse, and Jasper Deeter describes O'Neill's relationship with his brother Jamie.

In 1922, as O'Neill began to have success on Broadway, he and Agnes and their son, Shane, born in 1919, moved to a fifteen-room house in Ridgefield, Connecticut, where his daughter, Oona, was born in 1925. In the selections here, Stark Young, Malcolm Cowley, and Hart Crane remember a visit to the O'Neills' Connecticut estate, and Harold De Polo gives an unusual account of going fishing with Eugene and Agnes O'Neill. In 1926 the family moved to Bermuda. O'Neill's important relationship with the Theatre Guild began with the productions of *Marco Millions* and *Strange Interlude* in 1928. He took advantage of his trip to New York for the productions to see Carlotta Monterey, who was to become his third wife. Calvin Hoffman's memoir describes O'Neill's relationship with a young fan as he was in the process of separating from Agnes and departing for Europe with Carlotta.

# 21 / Hazel Hawthorne Werner

Hazel Hawthorne (1901–2000) was a poet and the author of two novels: *Salt House* (1934), based on the time she spent at Eugene and Agnes O'Neill's Peaked Hill Bar house when she rented it from O'Neill, and *Three Women* (1938). After her divorce from the artist Celian Ufford (1896–1982), she married Morris Robert Werner (1897–1981), an editor and the author of biographies of P. T. Barnum (1810–1891), William Jennings Bryan (1860–1925), and Horace Greeley (1811–1872). Dividing her time between Provincetown and Greenwich Village, Hawthorne became known in later years as the literary doyenne of Provincetown, and "the queen of the sand dunes" because of her devotion to preserving the solitary life of the writer in the famous shacks there, including her own.

Source: Hazel Hawthorne Werner, "Recollections," typescript, Louis Sheaffer Collection of Eugene O'Neill Materials, Department of Special Collections, Charles E. Shain Library, Connecticut College, New London.

I had no sooner come to Provincetown in the summer of 1918 than I realized that the O'Neills were the exciting people of the colony.

I was employed by Harvey and Harriet Gaul, the former an organist and teacher at Carnegie Tech and a composer. (I was to tend their children and help with housework.) This couple were within the orbit of the Players, chiefly through Mrs. Gaul's friendship with Susan Glaspell.

On my first evening in town I was instructed to go down to the shore for relaxation. I had already heard enough of Gene's glamour and importance as a playwright to want to know him. I went to the shore below the O'Neill apartment in the John Francis House. (Top floor, west.) The light of a full moon on the water was of secondary interest to the sounds of party gaiety from the lighted top floor.

Next day I told Mrs. Gaul where I had been and she said I was too young to be asked to the O'Neill parties; there was heavy drinking and Gene was sometimes ugly.

When Agnes [Boulton] passed on the street I found her most attractive: slender—lean, rather—as if not well nourished or as if very nervous—tanned, wearing a long scarlet cape.

After a poem of mine appeared in *The Masses*, which they all read in that group, the O'Neills took me up.[1] I think it was jealousy that prompted Mrs. Gaul, who like myself aspired to writing, to tell me one morning that the crowd had had "a good laugh" the night before over my verse. This made me hate O'Neill for a time but then he came to me on the beach one day and told me he liked the poem "all but the last four lines," and he talked as one professional to another which was being very kind to a young girl. I knew the last lines were insincere, tacked on for literary effect and that he was right not to like them.

I will interpolate here that in view of this kindness it was all the more surprising to me that years later when I sent him a copy of *Salt House*, with a note to make clear that it was about the old station he had lent me for use for about three years, I had from him no more than the coolest acknowledgement—one such as a secretary would write. When I spoke of this to Edmund Wilson he said that probably Carlotta hadn't even let him see the book.

Back to 1918. I was invited to tea sometimes in town. Gene went in and out of the room; he was restless, seemed often in a state of tension. Yet on the shore and in the water he was relaxed, especially in the water where he swam with suppleness. One of those who are well suspended in water and get maximum refreshment from it. Later, at Peaked Hill Bars, he would be idling by in the sea when I passed on shore, and would raise one arm in greeting with a flash of smile that I never saw when he was ashore.

On one of these occasions Agnes gave me a short story of hers to read; it might have been in *Ainslee's*. It was about a man who beat up his mistress because she concealed something from him; what she had concealed was baby clothes. You really should ask Agnes about this story as it has significance for that period in their lives.[2]

They brought *Dubliners*[3] to the shore to read, and talked of its importance.

We made a date, the three of us, to go to the Costume Ball. Agnes was excited as a schoolgirl going to a prom. The afternoon of the ball I went up the stairs to see if I could help with her costume. She bent over the rail before I reached the top floor and whispered that she couldn't go. No explanation, and I went right away knowing she was in some kind of trouble with Gene.

Sometimes she was beaten up, and used make-up to cover bruises.

Almost everyone in the group lunched or dined at Christine Ell's restaurant up a lane back of Mt. Pleasant Home. I never saw the O'Neills there, however. Not Gene and Agnes, that is. Jim O'Neill[4] was Christine's lover at the time. I discovered this for myself when I went back after lunch one day because I had left my bathing-suit. They were making love in the dining-room, on the table among the uncleared dishes. Jim was obviously an alcoholic, even to my untrained eye. He was jolly, flirtatious and a tease. He would sing out "Good morning, 'I, Mary Maclean'" [*sic*] when he saw me because of the ego of my *Masses* poem. That was the title of a confession book popular that season.[5] He called me 'Mary' all summer. Jim never gave me any trouble in an amative way as did some of the men in the colony. He clearly liked girls but my guess would be that he was enthralled with Christine.

These were all the direct contacts I had with the O'Neills until August, 1920. I was then married. My husband and I had walked down the coast from Maine. I had been certain as if I had seen a vision that there was somewhere along the shore a simple shack in a solitary place but we had found nothing of this description and now we were near the end of the search. As we came to Snail Road, then a narrow woods track going into the dune, Agnes and Gene were just walking out onto the highway. They said that Gene's father had died and they were going to the funeral.[6] They said we would find just what we were looking for at Peaked Hill and gave direction. Later, in August, we stopped in for tea at the "station." Shane[7] was let's see, about 9 months old. His nurse, a local woman, was also keeping house for them.[8] Agnes' sister, Cecil, and her admirer, Fiske (?) a painter, were visiting.[9]

Gene owned a horse and wagon for toting of supplies. Living had become easier, one could see. Physically, that is. I don't know whether it was quieter between them or not. I was shy of intrusion and saw them only casually on the beach after that.

In after years Harry Kemp[10] told me they used to go into town for "terrific" bouts of drinking. HK always exaggerates, you must remember, if you use his stories. He said that Gene would drag Agnes back through the moonlight by the hair.

[. . .]

Gene's contact with the [Coast Guard] station would have been in use of the telephone chiefly. One night, about 1928, Edmund Wilson, who was then living there, renting the old station from O'Neill, gave a party. Two of the guests, Norman Matson, then Susan Glaspell's husband, and Charles Kaeslau[11] [*sic*], went to the new station to telephone. When they came back they said they could well understand where Gene got the feeling of melodrama for his work—they had been impressed by the dramatic tension of the scene at the station, the skipper and crew sitting around the mess-room under a high, unshaded light. Someone else has commented that the Emperor Jones could well have been inspired by the night trips across the dunes and through the woods.

Harry Kemp, in trying to persuade me of the presence of spirits on the dunes cited Agnes's experience of seeing a file of Indians in the woods, and of seeing a coastguard come down the ladder that stood beside a bed in the crew's upstairs bedroom under the watch tower; this figure was in oilskins and the spectacle was in the middle of a storm night. He—it—went on down the companionway stairs to the kitchen below.

I'll write more of the station later.

In 1930, Harl Cook[12] and I wrote Gene to ask if we might buy the station. At the same time we warned him that it was in imminent danger of being undercut by the sea and said we couldn't afford, ourselves, to have it saved.

He wrote, after long delay, that something might be done if we wanted to buy it, that we should get in touch with Harry Weinberg (?) [*sic*] but he said nothing about its plight, didn't seem interested. Harry Weinberg was either his agent or his lawyer, and certainly a name for your list if you haven't it already.[13]

I passed by the station one night in January, 1931. The seaward end jutted at least ten feet out over space and the high water mark was under it. It looked so precarious that I didn't dare go in, though I had left a small crowbar behind a shutter in one of the sheds and could have pried off a shutter of the tower. I feared my weight alone, if I came downstairs into the kitchen, which was in that seaward end, would be enough to topple the house. At any rate, she slid down the bank the very next day.

The house stayed at the angle you've seen in Stiff's photographs until the big storm of March 4, 1931.[14] On that day the sea entered, spread the walls and the roof came down. The whole thing was awash and splintered into pieces "within ten minutes," according to the man on watch at the new station.

During the time the house lay on the bank townspeople rifled the place. Friends of O'Neill did not scruple to take souvenirs. I have a snapshot of John Dos Passos[15] and Norman Matson standing on the balcony of the tower. One comes across articles salvaged from the house in various homes in town, even now. O'Neill had Harry Weinberg put a plea in the paper for all these things to be held for him against the time he would come back to Provincetown to collect them.

Before the house went, he did intend to come back to town, but never did.

About 1926 I was staying there during the absence in New York of Edmund Wilson who had rented it that year. I kept getting telegrams signed "Bunny and Gene,"[16] with the message that they were on their way. Eventually Edmund arrived by himself, and said that Gene couldn't quite screw up his courage—or perhaps, his interest—to return.

[. . .]

Years later—1929 or 1930—I rented the Peaked Hill house from O'Neill in the early fall. He wrote that I need not pay rent, or pay whatever I could afford, and that if I wanted to stay the year round could have it for payment of the taxes. Terry Carlin would be there, he wrote, but there was room enough for all.

Apparently he wrote Terry that a woman with five children was arriving. I found no one in the house and signs of a precipitate departure. The Italian pottery bowls were dirty with dregs of berry wine, and in one pot was a mess of batter and sand eels.

[. . .]

My impression of the group around O'Neill in 1918 is of some wit and some talent but that the only extraordinary element was in the center and that center was O'Neill. Also, he was the only real worker (at his talent) in the group. Demuth[17] and Zorach excepted. The promiscuities and the experimental narcotics didn't interest him; his sins were not little ones but the savage ones of hard drinking and wife-beating. Except for the drinking-parties it's my impression he kept sternly isolated. He did not join the Beachcombers Club or the Art Association, and I never saw him at a cocktail party.

# 22 / Juliet Throckmorton

Juliet Brenon Throckmorton (1895–1979) was a stage and screen actor in the 1920s. She married Cleon Throckmorton, who became the chief designer for the Provincetown Players after rescuing the set of *The Emperor Jones* from the amateur efforts of the Players in 1920. In her later years she wrote about several of her Greenwich Village contemporaries for *Yankee Magazine*.

Source: Juliet Throckmorton, "As I Remember Eugene O'Neill," *Yankee Magazine* August 1968: 85, 93–95.

The man who stood in the reception room of the Red Inn at Provincetown, Massachusetts, was exceptionally tall. His light gray suit and soft white shirt emphasized the mahogany sunburn of his skin. The expression of his face, of his dark and piercing eyes, was sad, somber, even stern—but when he smiled, it became sympathetic and sweet. His manner was almost embarrassingly shy. This was Eugene O'Neill when I met him first in the early '20s. His mighty talent had burst like a hot sun on pale shores of mediocrity. He was 35 years old, and a score of his plays, short and full-length, had already been produced—among them *Anna Christie* and *The Emperor Jones*. Audiences and critics were dazzled. He was the man-of-the-hour.

But there was not the slightest trace of self-importance as he greeted Mary Blair[18] and me that summer night. Mary had created the leading role in his short play *Different* [*sic*]. Leaving New York for a holiday, she'd said to me, "Why don't you come up to Provincetown with me? I'll introduce you to Gene O'Neill—he has a home there." This had seemed to me an incredible prospect; but here he was, on the very first night of our visit, inviting us to come the next day to his house, Peaked Hill Bar, some miles out of Provincetown, across the dunes. He knew our time was limited and had made most careful arrangements for us. We were to drive to a certain point on the highway, and there, since a car could not mount the dunes, a little donkey cart and driver would meet us and take us to his door. He himself often walked the distance, but he thought, he said, it might be too much for us.

The following morning found us jogging along in this sweetly primitive conveyance until at last O'Neill's house came in sight. The long low yellow building, formerly a coast guard station, lay on the lonely shore, swept by sun and wind and looking out on the limitless sea. We lunched informally and delightfully at a refectory table in a sunny dining room. Outside, gulls wheeled and the ocean boomed softly. Present were O'Neill's wife, and a tiny boy in a white sailor suit, his son Shane.

I can remember most of the conversation. O'Neill then and always seemed baffled by conversational trivialities and small talk. His shyness was marked. But his was no one-track mind. His interest in all the arts was widespread. In speaking of painting, he was particularly enthusiastic about the art critiques of the American writer Thomas Craven.[19] He expressed interest in Scott Fitzgerald,[20] and had recently read and liked the German novel *The World's Illusion* by Jacob Wasserman [*sic*].[21] Of his own work, he said nothing, though he did remark naively that he hoped he'd be able to see *Anna Christie*, which had recently been filmed.[22]

Full of the enthusiasm that one has on first view of a tropic land, I told him of a recent visit to Bermuda. He was very interested and said he thought he'd go there in the coming winter. This indeed he did, eventually building a house at Spithead. He spoke of American schools, puzzled where to send his stepdaughter.[23] He asked where I had gone and, when I told him the convent's name, he said he thought he'd send the little girl there. This he, too, subsequently did. In fact, as I was to find out, he kept to his word in all matters. He drew from me that I had stage ambitions and was finding the going hard. He deplored the lack of theatre training in the young in America, and he offered generously and spontaneously to help me.

He had high hopes, he said, for the coming season at the New York Provincetown Theatre. A new group had been formed for it, headed by himself, Kenneth McGowan [*sic*], and Robert Edmund [*sic*] Jones, with Cleon Throckmorton, designer of the famous *Emperor Jones* sets, as technical director.[24] Elsewhere, he had expressed his credo for this theatre: "It should lay emphasis on building up a medium for achievement in acting that will make young actors want to grow up as a part of a whole, giving their acting a new, clean, fakeless group excellence, and group eloquence, that will be our own unique acting, our own thing, our own American theatre."[25] This was a subject on which he felt strongly, always.

He suggested that if I would ring him up in the fall, when the theatre was opening, he would do all he could to get me into it. When I tried to thank him, he merely smiled and said he hoped he could really help. We sat long over luncheon, and then swimming was suggested, but only O'Neill went in—and the rest of us sat on the shores watching his solitary figure plowing the waves with a powerful overhand stroke.

Dusk came on, and the little donkey wagon failed to return for us. Mary had an engagement in town. There was no telephone, and O'Neill suggested, hesitantly, that there was nothing for it but to walk back, guided by him. This we did. O'Neill fell into one of his dark moods and was silent for the most part, sometimes looking up at the now star-strewn sky with an almost tortured expression. What was he thinking of, I wondered. But he turned to us and smiled and made us sit down to rest for a bit; then we trudged on to the noisy highway where we said goodbye.

When the fall came, I read that O'Neill was in New York—but hesitated to ring him up. It was typical of him that he eventually called me, saying that he'd made an appointment for me with Robert Edmund Jones, who was directing a revival of *Patience*.[26] I saw Mr. Jones, and was promptly engaged for a small part and the understudy. *Patience* was given a polished jewel-like production. It was a huge success and ran for months. O'Neill was never in evidence at rehearsals, staying, when he did come, in the shade of the last row. But I remember very well Mary Blair telling me at this time of a young actress who had been tentatively cast for a part in a new O'Neill play. Ultimately, the Board decided against her. The girl burst into despairing tears. O'Neill, hearing about it, insisted the part be restored to her, remarking, hotly and indignantly, "As if writing of mine were worth a woman's tears!"

Shortly after this, he left for Bermuda and remained working there for a long period.

I saw him next at Redding, Connecticut, where I was visiting. The hostess was a friend of his, and he drove over from his house at Ridgefield to swim with us. He remembered he had promised me a copy of his favorite, *Beyond the Horizon*, but he also gave me an entire set of plays, each one of which he autographed. That evening, all the guests gathered round an ancient square piano, singing old songs—O'Neill joining in happily. It was the only time I ever saw him really gay.

Cleon Throckmorton and I were married that spring and were living at the Lafayette Hotel. One afternoon there came a quiet knock at the door. The visitor was O'Neill. "I had to wish you happiness," he said. He himself was going through much turmoil and anguish at the time. Not long after this, he remarried and sailed for France. When he returned, wrapped in a new happiness, he was rarely in New York. But invariably a little message came to us from him by way of his sons, Eugene or Shane, or some mutual friend.[27]

Just when the cruel disease that killed him first manifested itself, I do not know—but it was a long and dreadful business. The hands that had written so many burning lines to express his passionate and compassionate interest in mankind gradually became useless to him.[28] Here was a fate to wring the heart. He had always written his scripts in his own careful minute handwriting.

"God H'aint Easy," he'd written in his play *Desire Under the Elms*. "God H'aint Easy." Without the ministrations of his helpful wife,[29] this great and comparatively young man might well have despaired. But even as he became more and more helpless, he kept up his labors, slowly learning to dictate his work almost to the time of his death.[30] And up to that time, too, his messages, warm and remembering, still came to us.

The house at Peaked Hill Bar has long since been swept into the sea he loved so well. Like that sea, he was deep and restless. Restless, that is, to unleash the things that boiled within him. Did he perhaps know that he had not too much time?

Those who have said that O'Neill's plays lack universality because they are almost always tragic in theme, would, had they known him, realize that he wrote with a poet's intense pity for man so often cruelly trapped by life and circumstance; that he sought to understand and explain to us those aspects of human nature which are dark and terrible; that he was always acutely aware of the sufferings of others; and that he would have liked, in this world, to help and heal, before he, too, was taken far, far "Beyond the Horizon."

# 23 / Manuel Zora

Manuel Zora (1895–1979) was born in Olhão, Portugal, and immigrated to the United States in 1910, settling in Provincetown, where he became a fisherman, rumrunner, and local character. It was said that no man in Provincetown could handle a dory in the surf as well as Manny Zora. He also occasionally acted, sang Portuguese songs in concert, and gave lectures. Scott Corbett's book *The Sea Fox* (1956) features his legendary rum-running exploits.
For information on Louis Sheaffer, see chapter 3.

Source: Louis Sheaffer, Manuel Zora interview, Louis Sheaffer Collection of Eugene O'Neill Materials, Department of Special Collections, Charles E. Shain Library, Connecticut College, New London.

[O'Neill] wasn't really a nice person, but I felt he was damn close to a genius . . . When we first met, he felt I was good in my line as he is in his, we respected one another . . . I was posing as a sailor with oar, for Hawthorne's outdoor class[31] . . . O'Neill sat there waiting, liked my face, and suggested we have a few drinks.

He would get in arguments in a bar, when got to point of a fight, would get behind me, and say: "Go ahead, Manny." . . . I once warned him: "Someday I'm not going to do it and you'll have to fight for yourself." . . . sometimes it amused me, but other times I got annoyed . . . Generally get in fight with artist or writer he thought was phony, phoniness got him mad . . . arguments over literature . . . he was conceited, at least when drunk, knew his worth, but sober a gentle, quiet soul . . . Once he got talking boats, because he'd gone to sea, and I told him: "Look, you're a banana head, what do you know about boats? That's all right for the landlubbers, but to a seaman."

Eight drinks and he'd be pretty stewed . . . he wasn't really strong . . . Agnes would ask me to take care of him, and I'd lug him back to station . . . She really loved him . . . Fisherman trolled five or six miles out, where O'Neill would go in kayak.

# 24 / Edmund Wilson

Edmund Wilson (1895–1972) was a well-known writer and critic who wrote many books about American life and letters, as well as fiction and drama. He graduated from Princeton and served in World War I before entering into the literary and intellectual life of Greenwich Village and Provincetown. His first wife was Provincetown Players actor Mary Blair, who performed in his play *The Crime in the Whistler Room*, produced at the Provincetown Playhouse in 1924. He spent many summers in Provincetown, living at one time in O'Neill's house at Peaked Hill Bar.

Source: Edmund Wilson, *The Twenties: From Notebooks and Diaries of the Period*, ed. Leon Edel (New York: Farrar, Straus and Giroux, 1975), 110–12, 400.

Eugene O'Neill was still married to and living with his second wife, Agnes—to whom he referred as Aggie. I saw quite a lot of Agnes O'Neill because she was a friend of Mary Blair's. Her father was English, a painter, and she was an English type, sensible, practical, rather lacking in elegance but likable and with qualities that commanded respect. She had also some literary ability and wrote a book about her marriage.[32] O'Neill, on the other hand, in spite of an appealing boyish charm, was difficult to make contact with. I was grateful to him for persuading the Provincetown Players to produce my first play, *The Crime in the Whistler Room*, but I found conversation with him impossible. He was then completely on the wagon, and you were cautioned not to offer him anything to drink. But I got so bored with his nonresponsive silence that one night, having dinner with him in a Greenwich Village restaurant, I decided to prime him with some wine, which with no hesitation he accepted. For this I paid a heavy price. We talked about Greek tragedy, and I told him that in *Oedipus at Colonus* the crimes of Oedipus seemed to have been expiated when he was somehow miraculously removed by a supernatural agency. O'Neill said that he couldn't believe this: Sophocles would have had too much respect for human beings.[33] O'Neill had a peculiar point of view on the homosexual activities of the sailors he had known on shipboard. He thought that in degrading themselves by submitting to the demands of other sailors, they were always trying to atone for some wrong which was on their conscience. He was amusing about the old female performers—Trixie Friganza[34] and others like her—whom he had known in his early days. One of them had sat at his bedside and told him that if she hadn't been faithful to his brother, she would have come right into bed with him. Another had been warned by her friends that she would have to be very careful with the family of the groom of a pal who was having a proper wedding party at the Bellevue Stratford in Philadelphia. The friend restrained herself till the very last moment when the bride and groom were driving away in a taxi. She had collected several towels from the bathroom of the hotel and she threw them in at the window, with "I guess you'll need these!"

After dinner, we went on to my apartment at 3 Washington Square North, and, once started talking, it seemed O'Neill could never stop. What was striking was that he quite lost connection with anything that was said by me or Mary. He did not answer questions or seem to recognize that we were there at all. He disregarded all our hints. We got up and crossed the room; we made remarks which with anyone else would have brought the session to a close. But his talk was an unbroken monologue. And he drank up everything we had in the house: when a bottle was set before him, he simply poured out drinks for himself, not suggesting that we might care for any. If we said we ought to go to bed, he paid no attention to this. He told us at length about a rich man who lived near him in Connecticut. He had some tragic theory about him: he was frustrated, his conscience bothered him. O'Neill, there now being nothing more to drink, did not leave until four in the morning.

Mary Blair, having acted in *Diff'rent* and another O'Neill play, agreed to do *All God's Chillun*, in which she was to take the role of a white girl married to a Negro. The Negro was Paul Robeson, who had not long before graduated from Rutgers and had not yet a reputation as a singer. Mary got insulting letters, and somebody wrote to O'Neill he was so low that he'd have to take a stepladder to get up to a cockroach. As a result of all this, Mary came down with pleurisy, and the opening had to be postponed; but she went through with it, and O'Neill thereafter expressed a certain appreciation and exhibited a certain loyalty, telling one of his associates to remember *God's Chillun* and give her a part in one of his plays.

I do not much like O'Neill as a dramatist: he depends too much upon hatred; but I believe that *All God's Chillun* does have a certain advantage over some of the too smooth and easy films that deal with similar situations in that they show that racial antagonisms may rankle and break out after marriage. When O'Neill married again and went out to California,[35] he ceased to answer letters from any of his old friends. He had always been quite frank in his scorn for actors and seemed to feel that he had been unfair to his father, who had had a great success as Monte Cristo and no doubt was something of a ham. O'Neill himself had once acted with the elder O'Neill. He told me that *Ah, Wilderness!*, one of his very few amiable plays, had been a kind of attempt to make it up to his father; and I suppose that *Long Day's Journey* was something of an effort in the same direction. I did not share his admiration of Strindberg, in whose poison-spitting quarrels between man and woman he evidently took satisfaction and which to some extent in his own work he imitated.

[. . .]

Anecdote about O'Neill—had had such difficulty establishing contact with him—so thought him offish and, coming out to the beach one day, Harry [Kemp] decided to pass him by, simply saying, "Hello," and without any attempt to engage him in conversation—so he went on the beach and sat down and presently heard this pat-pat-pat like a big St. Bernard dog—O'Neill said, "You know, I'd have liked to be a prizefighter, too—but I got a blow once that loosened all my teeth."

# 25 / Charles O'Brien Kennedy

Charles O'Brien Kennedy (1879–1958) was born in Waltham, Massachusetts. He was an actor who performed with John and Lionel Barrymore, as well as a playwright, writer, and editor. He wrote several popular one-act plays while employed by Samuel French, as well as the plays *Boys Will Be Boys: A Comedy of the Soul of Man Under Prosperity* (1919) and *The Mighty Nimrod* (1931), both of which were produced on Broadway. He also edited *American Ballads: Naughty, Ribald, and Classic* (1952). He became friends with O'Neill as a young man with the Provincetown Players and directed *Diff'rent* in 1920. Their friendship lasted throughout O'Neill's lifetime.

Source: Charles O'Brien Kennedy, "Several Sides of Mr. O'Neill," *Call Board* June 1948: 7.

As the fame of Eugene O'Neill extends over all countries of the world, including the Scandinavian, we will not dwell on his playwriting accomplishments. Rather, your correspondent deems it a duty to history to induct the reader into the secret recesses of his friend's life when not engaged in dashing off masterpieces.

On the intellectual side; there was that visit devoted mainly to the appraisal of ball-players we admired. It was indeed a solemn moment when we both agreed that Jimmie Collins[36] was the greatest third baseman who ever played the game; a decision arrived at after deep thought and laborious research. It is merely cited here as an example of industry for the young.

Now for a darker side. After the last World's Series, Mr. O'Neill unblushingly avowed that he sided with the Yankees to win, which made your correspondent reach nervously for a book on Psychiatry. His merciful deduction was that perhaps as a young fellow Eugene played Brooklyn in his eminent father's company. (Now it comes out; he was once an actor.) Our conclusion was that the boy must have lost his way in his hurry to get out of Brooklyn and the recurring fright clouded his judgment on the World's Series. How else could he have rooted against the Beloved Bums?[37]

The session was vari-colored the day Mr. Thomas Mitchell[38] called on Mr.

O'Neill with your correspondent. The beginning of the conversation was sufficiently recondite to justify the correspondent's hope for mental stimulus. But the talk gradually veered toward farming, both gentlemen having been wealthy farm operators on our Western shores.[39] As for the modest third party, his only agricultural experience had been that of a menial, receiving fifty cents per day for Fourth of July money. The menial remained silent while the two landed gentry flaunted their knowledge of the care and upbringing of vegetables and livestock. It seems Mr. Mitchell once had a cow who could do anything but talk, although she could express herself in understandable pantomime as her kind master stroked her silken ear. Tears flooded the eyes of Mr. Mitchell and the menial. As for Mr. O'Neill, he lurked in ambush until he found an opening to brag about a rooster which had been the pride of his broad acres. It was a bellicose bird, named "Sugar Ray Robinson" after a prize-fighter.[40] The menial's ideality was tottering and at the end he feebly commented that Mr. O'Neill was on a higher plane of understanding with his rooster than Mr. Mitchell was with his cow. A tense moment ensued as Mr. Mitchell winced and his forelock flopped over his eye while he glared balefully at the menial. The offender held his breath in nervous anticipation.

The hostile spell was broken by the entrance of the beautiful and gracious Mrs. O'Neill bearing a Louis Quinze silver platter filled with delicious viands. For a moment your correspondent lapsed into cynicism. Supposing someone who had known these three men twenty-five years ago should walk in on this feast and observe them daintily sipping their coffee and nibbling at the chocolate cake? You know the disruption one of those "I knew them when" fellows can bring to a nice, refined party.

There is an old saying in Ireland: "'Tis a rare flavor that runs down a spoon from the hand of a woman." Mrs. O'Neill sat between the two rival farmers and her presence, plus her coffee and cake, brought an aura of peace and tranquility to the scene.

The foregoing is but a prelude to the darkest moment of all when your correspondent and Mr. Gene Buck[41] visited Mr. O'Neill at the hospital. During the trip uptown the correspondent felt uplifted at bringing these two minds together. Gradually his illusion withered and decayed as Mr. Buck proceeded to tell the ailing man of a fracas he once witnessed between some uncouth persons. The author of *The Hairy Ape* was instantly alerted into a state of rapture, his eye blazing with apostolic glee as he absorbed each gory detail. Mr. Buck was in rare form, using vivid gestures and terrifying nuances, like the blood-spattered messenger in an ancient Greek tragedy, while your timid correspondent wilted with pious horror. In all fairness, Mr. Buck's therapy proved effective, for shortly after Mr. O'Neill was discharged from the hospital as cured.

# 26 / Agnes Boulton

Agnes Boulton (1892–1968) was born in England, a daughter of painter Edward W. Boulton, and grew up in Philadelphia and New Jersey. She had enjoyed some success as a pulp fiction writer when she met Eugene O'Neill in 1917. They were married in 1918 and at first divided their time between Greenwich Village and Provincetown, where they lived first in John Francis's "flats," and then on the outer shore of Provincetown in Peaked Hill Bar, an isolated, abandoned life-saving station that had been renovated by Mabel Dodge (1879–1962) several years before (see figure 7). After O'Neill's Broadway success, beginning with *Beyond the Horizon* in 1920, they bought a large house in Ridgefield, Connecticut, and later moved to Bermuda. They had two children, Shane (1919–1977) and Oona (1925–1991). O'Neill left Boulton in 1928 to marry his third wife, Carlotta Monterey.

Source: Agnes Boulton, *Part of a Long Story: Eugene O'Neill as a Young Man in Love* (London: Peter Davies, 1958), 142–44, 287–92.

During the years that we were married, except for some sudden and rather dreadful outbursts of violence, and others of bitter nastiness and malevolence, I do not remember him as being affected by liquor in the usual way. He never raised his voice, he never staggered or walked into things, never "passed out." He never seemed to be what is called drunk, nor did I think of it that way or use that term to myself about him except on the occasions that I have mentioned, and then he appeared more like a madman than anything else—a strange being who was not the real Gene at all.

Rather he seemed to have entered another world where he greatly enjoyed himself for quite a while—until physical sickness and despair at last overcame him. His appearance changed after two or three drinks, his movements were slower than usual, but in some way he became intensified physically—or can I say more physically aware of himself?—thus giving the impression of a dark and increased vitality, and this vitality included a sardonic (and sometimes boyish) sense of humour.

Most often, with him, a period of drinking would start with what seemed to be an inability to face people *as he was*: after a few drinks he could face them (or a situation) as a somehow different person. But it seemed that in the country, at Peaked Hill, in Bermuda, or at Brook Farm near Ridgefield, Connecticut, where we lived for three or four years, it was never necessary for him to take a drink when people came to see us or even after they arrived. What I am speaking of seems connected with visits to the city, staying at hotels, going on trips from one place to another. He would never go to the desk and sign the register, but stood unobserved while I attended to it and to getting the rooms; and he would put off taking trips on a train or go about it in some unusual manner. Perhaps in the country, in a house of our own, he was like the fiddler crab, secure within its shell. . .

Sometimes he did drink in the country but almost always because of people coming there whom he associated with drinking, and who themselves liked to drink—Hart Crane, Louis Wolheim (who later stopped drinking when he fell in love with a fine woman),[42] perhaps Jimmy Light[43] or Harold de Polo—and this would almost always be when he had come to a stopping point in his work, for the two, for him, never went together.

But vice and love are not static; even the physical body goes through psychological changes reacting to environment, or emotion, to food, to cigarettes or drink. As these things occur I will tell about them. Alcoholism is properly considered a sickness now and it is true that Gene's drinking seemed to follow the pattern of a definite type of that sickness. There is much emphasis now on the escape angle or idea. Many people undoubtedly do drink to escape and it becomes a habit that they are not able to overcome—possibly because what they are escaping from is not worth a battle.

But there is another thing to consider, which is that the nervous system in people like Gene (I am speaking of when he was perfectly sober) seems to fail to come up to certain situations—does not, as it were, sufficiently stimulate the personality or the physical being itself. These situations are in the present—a funeral to be attended; a change of environment which will be boring when, instead, it should be enjoyed; the necessity of making a certain impression one way or the other—even the confusion of noise and movement of people, of traffic and crowds, which a less sensitive person would block out. Gene wanted to meet these situations, but there was no adequate response and he felt that a drink or so would give him response. Is that escape? I know that he wanted to meet the situation, not escape from it. It would work, but after the first day, or a certain number of drinks, that same nervous system behaved in such a way that his body became helplessly tortured and unstable without more drink—a sort of shaken, jelly-like protoplasm which stiffened into activity after a hair of the dog that bit it.

So alcohol, most of the time, seemed a needed prop to meet the situation, rather than an escape from it. He felt fine after the first drink. He talked for hours, laughed, and was gay if it was people or a party. If it was a boring trip, he enjoyed putting it off; or, if he took it, having the whole thing take on such a bizarre appearance that he enjoyed that too—if he had a drink. In more important things, alcohol enabled him to do what he wanted to do—not what was expected of him, or was the conventional thing to do.

It occurs to me now, as I write this, that in that empire of his that Gene talked about, where he had power over people and events and things, no situation would ever arise where he would be faced with the need of an adequate response to anything—for all would be under his control. There would never be any need of stimulating his personality or physical being because he would move everything around himself, like checkers on a board and a situation could never arise that he was not fully organised to meet. . . .

I do not really know the meaning of this personal world vision of his—it may seem later on to be something quite different but it does seem now that this may be a partly adequate explanation.

[. . .]

[After arriving at Peaked Hill Bar in the summer of 1919,] Gene and I unpacked, carried in, and arranged the contents of the boxes and bundles that had been piled outside the door. There were blankets and sheets to be taken upstairs, the bed to be made, clothes hung up and shoes unpacked. Gene carried in his books and arranged them on the shelves, took his dumbbells and what other equipment he had of that sort into another room that we had discovered next to the bathroom (which was downstairs).

He took off his clothes in there and came out barefooted in his bathing trunks. Every once in a while he would go to the window and look out at the sea. Then he would go back to work, helping me put things away in the kitchen, or carefully arranging what he wanted to keep in the table drawers in the big room.

After a while he began to get chilly, for the early June day was not too warm. So he collected wood and kindling, and we had a fire in the big fireplace. I lay on the wide blue couch, comfortable, and watched him.

That night we slept upstairs in a big white-enamelled iron bed, which was very cold at first, even the sheets chilly, listening to the sea and the slow rising of the wind, his arm around me and my head pillowed against his chest. I could hear his heart beating, and the sound of his heart and the sound of the sea were confused but peaceful as I drifted off to sleep.

It was there, that first summer at Peaked Hill, that Gene told me of how he first got himself into the writing of plays, trained himself, I was going to say, because in one sense it was that—a training of the senses. He wanted to write plays, that is understood. He may have even written a few of the earlier ones, which didn't amount to much. But he was undisciplined, he told me, not only in working habits, but in writing itself, what form to use and how. Then he began consciously to use a method which he kept up for over a year. He read nothing but plays, great plays, melodrama. . .

Before long he was thinking in dialogue, talking to himself in dialogue, and answering his own thoughts more or less aloud in his low voice, seeing life in scenes and acts—with the curtain going down, perhaps, as he went off to sleep.

There were always periods of working and not working with Gene, as with every other writer. Long periods of work, of course, depending sometimes on the length of the play. Nothing to stop him, no going to parties, no going out in the evenings or making trips away from the house. When a play was finished he relaxed, sometimes just swimming and lying in the sun, or seeing and talking to people he liked. It was harder in the winter, of course. Sometimes—but now I am remembering Peaked Hill—I think perhaps it was that first summer out there that he finally settled into the general routine that he followed faithfully when he was working as long as I knew him—long walks on country roads taking the place of sun and swimming, if we were where it was cold.

Every evening after dinner Gene sat down in the white Morris chair and, under the light of the tall Italian lamp, took his book and read until eleven. At midnight he would go to bed, and at Peaked Hill he seldom had trouble sleeping.

After breakfast, which he always ate silently, he was glum. He said some people were and some weren't; and he was one of the ones that were—so not to mind it. He told me that when we were first married. Sometimes I wonder when we did talk, but I know we talked a lot. He talked about his work with me before he wrote it, while he was writing it, and after it was finished.

Upstairs there were two long rooms, separated by a stairway, and they too had been given their seven coats of white paint so that they glowed luminously, even in the darkness. We slept in the room that looked out, through two small sand-glazed windows on either side of the chimney, on to the sand dunes behind the house, that first year in a white iron bed with a driftwood table beside it for Gene's cigarettes, the tall kerosene lamp and his book. Above us the beams of the ceilings, tied with iron cables, rose to the peak of the roof; and on windy nights we could lie there and listen to the sand beating with a sharp needlelike sound on the windows, and on the roof above us, and the sound of the sea. Gene had all he wanted there, me in his arms, the sound of the sea, and he would go to sleep at last, with my head on his shoulder.

The other room faced on the sea, so that the windows almost overhung it, above a narrow strip of sea grass which broke sharply into a cliff above where the ocean lay stretched out to the horizon. Here Gene had his driftwood desk, with several large drawers, and a grey weathered top on which he kept his manuscript neatly arranged. There was a captain's chair, a couch covered with dark blue denim, and a horror of a clothes-horse which he insisted on keeping there. Along the walls of this room he hung some old nets with weathered floats, and there were some pieces, too, of driftwood encrusted with barnacles. When the windows were closed the sanded glass shut the room off in a solitary and opaque light.

When he went up there to work, after breakfast, the door at the foot of the stairs was shut—the whole house was quiet and peaceful. At intervals a coast-guard would pass on his way along the shore, and sometimes he would come up and leave some mail.

Gene always read the mail eagerly. Sometimes his comments were extremely sarcastic; and although he wished to live with me in solitude, he kept a close and shrewd watch on the progress of his plays. But he never looked at the mail until after he was finished working. At one o'clock there would often be a cry of pleasure or relief, and the playwright would appear, sometimes with the dream still in his eyes, embrace me if he was happy about what he had finished that morning, or go to the larder to make a small sandwich if he was perplexed or troubled. Whichever it was it didn't last too long, for now was the time for his exercise. In good weather this was a run up the beach, his head thrown back, full of exuberance and joy, then a dive in the sea and a swim, from which he was apt to emerge a little cold and blue, ready to lie in the sun until lunch was ready. If it rained he would go into the back room and vigorously attack the punching bag for half an hour, then take a book and sit reading until we were ready to eat.

After lunch he always lay down and took a nap. Then he got up and went silently back to work alone and preoccupied, going over what he had written in the morning and often typing it out for the first draft. But soon he would be in the west room, punching vigorously at the bag again, wearing only his swimming trunks, and coming out with his brown lean body shining with sweat, ready for another plunge in the sea. It was that summer that Gene meditated most, and was most alone with and even sometimes absorbed into that reality which for him lay behind outer appearances—and which he was always, perhaps even later, seeking. In the warm peaceful afternoons we would walk along the beach, rousing little flocks of little sandpipers, who scattered as we approached; and sheltered by an old sand dune, Gene would remove his swimming trunks and lie naked in the sun (which warmed his closed eyes), his face turned upward, his eyes closed, at peace at last with the sun, the sea, and the earth. Sometimes he would get up and do a strange jungle dance, and then plunge, laughing, into the sea. This laugh—for it seems to me I saw it more than I heard it—was a half-pagan, half-ecstatic cry of himself to God.

I sat there, not too close, alone, too, with the dunes and the sky! But I think that I sometimes admitted a solitary sandpiper or a gull into my solitude and happiness; or looked wonderingly, at strange small tracks in the sand. Gene was beautiful that summer, tall and brown and tender and smiling, working all morning, lying for hours in the sun, absorbing life and courage and hope from the sea. . . . I too, felt strong and well and happy; full of a sort of creative joy and wellbeing, a physical at-oneness with life and nature, with the sea, the sand, the dunes and the ever-changing sky. The days went by; at night we walked along the edge of the vast friendly sea in the darkness, holding hands, our feet on the damp sand, in a mysterious world to which we both belonged.

Each day was the same and yet divinely different; we ate breakfast on a card table covered with a blue cloth, drinking coffee from the cups with the willow design, the morning sun slanting in across our faces, the gentle sound of the breakers outside. Whenever I fixed poached eggs I waited with silent joy for the moment when Gene would cut off the edge of the toast, and then solemnly put the entire egg and toast into his mouth. I never understood how he was able to do it. We made sandwiches for lunch, and with tea, always about five o'clock and always ready for it, devoured dozens of biscuits imported from England, for we were very hungry. We made strange concoctions, sometimes, for our evening meal, trying to think, as the end of each week came and we ran low on stores, what shipwrecked sailors would manage with. I remember Gene insisting once that we experiment with stewing a horseshoe crab with onions and marjoram; but at this I baulked and made curried duck eggs instead, with rice flavoured with marjoram, as he seemed to like this herb very much at that time. He decided that it was a prenatal craving on his part and seemed rather disappointed that I didn't crave marjoram too. Sometimes he would cross the dunes alone to town, and always when he left he would ask me if there wasn't something I craved, so he could bring it back to me, I would say no—only *him*! and he would laugh and say that I was easily satisfied; but when he returned, besides what we needed, he would always bring something special—preserved ginger in a little gray jar, or one of Mrs Avellar's famous blueberry pies.

Once, after a walk to town, he came back and very seriously inquired why I wasn't feeling sick at my stomach every morning. John Francis had told him how, when his wife was pregnant, he had morning sickness every day, just like his wife—and I'm almost positive that John Francis told him that when her labour pains began he, too, began getting cramps in his stomach. Gene began to wonder if this wasn't the way all husbands should be if they really loved their wives.

We grew quite fond of the large, prehistoric-looking horseshoe crabs—there were always two or three near the house or on the sand—and of the tiny sandpipers that ran in droves before us as we walked up the beach, rising in their flight and curving back to us again to pick up their food as the waves retreated, and even of the seagulls that screamed around the top of the house.

One day I was sitting on the sand, watching my husband's dark head as he swam further and further out to sea, going under the water and emerging again, when I saw another dark head swimming beside him. I thought I was seeing double at first; but as Gene began swimming nearer shore again, I saw I'd made no mistake. Then the second dark head disappeared; and a few minutes later Gene came through the surf and up the sand to where I was waiting, breathless and laughing. He told me he had been swimming underwater and when he came to the surface a beautiful sleek young seal was gazing at him with luminous friendly eyes. Not only that, she (we decided, of course, it was a she) swam along with him, under the water and on the surface of the sea, finally submerging as he came nearer the shore. For a few days after that his little seal remained off Peaked Hill Bar, waiting until he came out, when she would appear at his side, with the same curious, friendly gaze. Gene said he talked to her, and she seemed to understand; but something must have happened to her, or perhaps her husband came along and reproved her; for soon after that she left; we never saw her again.

Once a week, Gene carrying my red cape, we would walk into town in the early morning and return to Peaked Hill in the afternoon, with the big wagon and team of horses laden with food and necessities for the week. We saw our friends in town, stopped at Susan's house, talked with Hutch Hapgood, and if Mary Heaton Vorse was not working, stopped in there. Often we went to the Ballantines', where Stella would make a delicious lunch for us, evading little Ian's furious attacks as she cooked, and managing to talk to me and also listen to Teddy and Gene discussing the theatre.[44]

People were wonderful to us that summer. I think everyone realised how happy we were, and responded to it. Mary Vorse spoke later of how Gene had that look of security and sweetness that made him so lovable. As for me, she would look at my expanding red cape when she met me in town, and say that pregnancy was very becoming to me. Mary came out sometimes to see us, for she loved the dunes and the outside shore, and understood them better than anyone. I remember one night she kept us awake telling us the legend of a great white stallion who had once roamed the dunes and, when they tried to capture him, swam out among the breakers and disappeared.

Other people came out to see us, but not often, as it was a long walk; the coastguards were very friendly, brought our mail, and apparently worried about me when a storm came up and lashed the water against our house.

Source: Statement to Max Wylie, in William Davies King, *Another Part of a Long Story: Literary Traces of Eugene O'Neill and Agnes Boulton* (Ann Arbor: U of Michigan P, 2010), 110–11.

I suppose my greatest treasure was the portrait that Thomas Eakins[45] did of my father. Shane was perhaps two or three when this happened. He'd been quite ill and I'd taken him to the doctor. The waiting room was full, and we were there a long time. It was November and it was snowing. Shane and I came up the walk and Gene burst out the front door in a rage, full of his sea-faring profanity.

I'd had no chance to prepare supper but Gene's fury was so unprovoked, I knew he had to be drunk. I tried to ignore him and got something started on the stove, then went to put Shane to bed. Downstairs I heard the most awful clattering and banging, and a chair turned over. Then I heard the front door bang. Gene was in the front yard, rubbing something in the snow.

I was still upstairs when a horrifying thought struck me. I couldn't credit my own suspicion. I whirled down the stairs, looking up over the mantel. Father's portrait was not there. Gene was trying to smear off the face in the snow. I ran out but I was too late. The paint was so hard set it wouldn't smear, and on this fence post he was mercilessly shredding the canvas, banging it up and down till it was a mass of tattered ribbons.

Gene knew I loved this portrait more than anything we'd ever had in our home. Over the years scores of people had stopped by, asking if they might see the "Eakins." And it was often out on loan. Gene knew how to hurt me. He knew how to hurt everybody. I think he was hurting so much inside himself, that periodically he had to lash out. After such enormities, he was so contrite, he was embarrassing to be around.

Only once or twice in his life was he ever able to ask forgiveness, and these moments were even more torturing than the silences. If he hadn't had the plays in which to play out his principal hatreds, I feel very sure he'd have found his way to an asylum before he was thirty.

# 27 / Jasper Deeter

Jasper Deeter (1894–1972) was born in Mechanicsburg, Pennsylvania. After being expelled from Dickinson College, Deeter was inspired to try acting by one of James O'Neill's performances. A member of the Provincetown Players, he originated the role of Smithers in *The Emperor Jones* and became a lifetime friend of Eugene O'Neill. He is best known for founding the Hedgerow Theatre in Moylan-Rose Valley, Pennsylvania, near Philadelphia, where he served as director from 1923 until 1952, making it into the model for regional theaters in the United States.

Source: Dan Sullivan, "Friend of Eugene O'Neill Tells of Dramatist's Tie to Brother," *New York Times* 31 July 1967: 21.

Harrisburg, Pa., July 30—Jasper Deeter took the stage of the Harrisburg Community Theater last night to reminisce about an old friend named Eugene O'Neill.

Mr. Deeter, who will celebrate his 74th birthday tomorrow, is best known here as the founder and long-time director (1923–1959) [*sic*][46] of one of the country's first repertory theaters, Hedgerow, outside Philadelphia.

But before going home to Pennsylvania to start his own theater, Mr. Deeter was an actor in the troupe that produced O'Neill's first plays, the Provincetown Players.

He played the lead in O'Neill's autobiographical suicide-drama, *Exorcism*, later destroyed by the author,[47] and the part of Smithers, the cockney, in the first production of *The Emperor Jones*.

The two men kept up their acquaintance after O'Neill went on to grander, if not always greater, things on Broadway. When Hedgerow was down on its luck, the playwright allowed Mr. Deeter to stage his plays without paying royalties.

Mr. Deeter's program last night had a theme: the relationship between O'Neill and his flamboyant older brother, Jamie, whose spectacularly wasted life ended in 1923.

Mr. Deeter met both men in 1919 and wondered, until he realized that they were brothers, how two such dissimilar persons could be friends.

Jamie—named for his father, the famous actor, James O'Neill—was "congenial, cheerful, well-dressed and wearing a smile that would melt an iceberg," Mr. Deeter said.

"Gene's face was a mask, as if most of his energy came down from the brain instead of up from the belly. You remembered his eyes—instead of just looking at you they seemed to be sending rays through you.

"Gene wouldn't smile. Instead he had a sharp grin"—Mr. Deeter demonstrated with a wolfish one—"that would come and go."

"Jamie's voice had an Irish lilt to it; Gene's voice was tight, precise, all the consonants perfect. If he was at his ease with you, he spoke fluently enough. If he wasn't, the words would come with more effort."

Instead of analyzing the bond between the brothers, Mr. Deeter preferred to read scenes from two O'Neill plays that he felt demonstrated it.

In the first selection, from O'Neill's first Broadway play, *Beyond the Horizon* (1920), a sensitive young man tries to explain his longing for artistic beauty, and his cynical older brother declares that he is "nutty."

In the second, from the posthumous *Long Day's Journey Into Night*, a drunken older man confesses to his younger brother that, when the latter was ill, "the dead part of me hoped you wouldn't get well."

Reading the scripts with the aid of a magnifying glass, Mr. Deeter occasionally stepped out of character to comment on the scenes.

When the older brother in *Long Day's Journey* prefaced a drink with "Here's—hope!," Mr. Deeter drily observed: "the Irish have a peculiar way of using an optimistic expression to show their deepest despair."

In an interview after the performance, Mr. Deeter spoke of O'Neill's nervousness while watching rehearsals.

"He would sit there, tense, his jaw working like a man whose dentures don't fit. Then he'd be up and out of the theater and we might not see him for days. And he never came to opening nights."

Was O'Neill America's greatest playwright? Yes, Mr. Deeter said—because of his great "reach and his willingness to experiment."

Many of those experiments, however, were failures, Mr. Deeter said—particularly *Lazarus Laughed* ("a mess") and *Marco Millions*.

"He once asked me what I thought of *Strange Interlude*. I heartily disliked it; I thought it was full of fourth-rate psychology. I told him—'if you're going to go on thinking about life, you'd better start writing comedies.'

"Years later he came to me and announced that he had written a comedy. It was *Ah, Wilderness* and it's a lovely play."

# 28 / Stark Young

Stark Young (1881–1963) was born in Como, Mississippi, and was educated at the University of Mississippi and Columbia University. After sixteen years of university teaching, he moved to New York to become an editor of *Theatre Arts* and drama critic for the *New Republic*, a post he retained until 1947. He was one of the conservative group of literary critics known as the Southern Agrarians and in 1930 contributed to their critical manifesto *I'll Take My Stand*. He published four novels with southern themes, the best known being *So Red the Rose* (1934). He was also a playwright and had his play *The Saint* (1924) produced by the Experimental Theatre, Inc., under the "triumvirate" of O'Neill, Robert Edmond Jones, and Kenneth Macgowan.

Source: Stark Young, "Eugene O'Neill: Notes from a Critic's Diary," *Harper's Magazine* (June 1957): 66–71, 74.

## From My Journal

*September, 1923*

I was looking at Eugene O'Neill's face today while I sat there with him in the apartment on Grove Street that belonged to Eleanor Fitzgerald.[48] She was the manager and practical mind and inexhaustible friend of the Provincetown Playhouse, and had telephoned me that O'Neill had not been well and had asked her to tell me that he wished I would come and see him.

A handsome face on which for the moment there was a certain shade of brutality, which seemed to change immediately into a kind of delicate and fierce withdrawal—or shall I say a proud shadow?—and also a kind of covered entreaty. The mouth was both sensuous and hard; but when he smiled the effect was boyish and fresh—a stretch of white teeth—curiously candid and shy at the same time—the sudden engaging air of a child. As was usual in his case I felt vaguely an emotion of pity and defense. Though there was nothing particularly to defend him against, I wanted to defend him, to take his part.

I dwell on this for the simple reason that the more I have thought of the matter the more assured I am that some such similar feeling is behind what many of those who champion Eugene O'Neill's work bring to him. Among his plays at times the story limps, or the texture of the style is flat and barren, or the thought is creaking; but at the heart of it we sense a pressure, a spasm of desire and sanity or torment and madness that leaves us defending the play, swearing by the author, going to his aid with whatever glamor or common sense we can muster; and meanwhile with a half-subconscious admission, deep down in ourselves, that, even if, awkwardly, he can feel compassion where we feel only some tragic situation.

You heard of harsh times with him, violent even, especially when he was drinking.[49] As to this drinking of Eugene O'Neill's there were plainly earlier years when he seemed to have gone to it with a vengeance, and in these later years there had been scenes, ructions, ferocities not easy to forget; but it happened that I never saw him in the worst of such spells, and the time came presently when he was not drinking at all, strictly nothing.

I have sometimes on second thought wondered whether he was dramatic enough, shrewd enough as regards his own legend to let it stand his being a drunk, a wild drunk, just as he let stand the legend of a poor young artist, though he spent a good deal of money in his time. (His father had something of a fortune, and his brother, who was said to have died of drink, must have left him something.)

As to shrewdness, I remember once at dinner with Robert Edmond Jones, the leading stage designer of his time, that I said something in praise of shrewdness. Bobby went straight into a horror at the mere thought, a good Puritan conscience objecting. On a higher plane, if you like, it reminded me of the good man who said he was going to Boston to get drunk, and oh, how he dreaded it! But what I said was that to be shrewd did not mean that you had to be crooked; the highest use of shrewdness was, if you believed in something, to use the very best of your brains in its behalf. But that semi-dishonest Puritan morality of Bobby's refused to yield an inch. Later on I told Gene about this conversation—it had been a strangely long argument, futile on my part. All he said, drily, was, "If you want to know how shrewd Bobby is ask him to tell you how to put something over."

There was always a kind of sweetness or young quality in Eugene O'Neill's relation to me, though far back of it I could feel at times a core of resentment at the world as people live it, a touch even of hate. But this I got from the plays perhaps, rather than from himself directly. It belonged to some crisis in his mind or to some play he was working at rather than to his habitual temper.

A certain sense of helplessness had something to do with it, I thought. He had to summon his fiercer will, had to violate himself as it were, in order to create that effect of emotional power that the best remembered passages in his plays afford.

[. . .]

Eugene O'Neill made one of those remarks of his that go a long way, provided, that is, you spoke his language and were inside the subject. He spoke of James O'Neill, his father, who was a perennial favorite in *The Count of Monte Cristo*, which he played for something like twenty years for 6,000 performances, in New York and all over the country—and of how when he was a boy he used to go along on tour with his father and with the company. He said, "Here's just the difference: the actors those days would not have understood my play but they could act it; now they understand it but can't act it."

[. . .]

Eugene O'Neill when he means to be serious often drops into colorless writing, with no style, no vigor. But the limitations here are by no means solely his own; it was all, shall we say, a part of the literary scene.

When he writes: "Our life is to bear together our burden which is our goal—on and up! Above the world, beyond its vision—our meaning!"

or: "He is resolved into the thousand moods of beauty that make up happiness—color of the sunset, tomorrow's dawn, breath of the Great Trade Wind—" and so on—he suffers not only from second-rate taste but also from bad models, a bad dramatic climate.[50]

But whatever the result, the intention behind it and the dark center of it single out Eugene O'Neill from a great many writers in our theater, however adroit or smooth; and so whatever his faults and limitations he breaks your heart.

### *1923*

On the top floor of an old brownstone structure that has long harbored the Provincetown Playhouse, there is an odd room with a skylight, empty of everything but clothes-racks and a table. Some old costumes hang there and various bits and pieces left by those who come in and out of the theater. Today it was found that thieves had entered by the skylight and robbed the place. Eugene O'Neill had some books there, a sweater and silk muffler, and I had left an overcoat that had been made for me in Venice. I met Eugene O'Neill coming out of the door.

"Look here," he said, "the underworld is taking this art theater too seriously."

*1924*

Doris Keane[51] was persuaded by the two leaders at the Provincetown Playhouse, Robert Edmond Jones and Kenneth MacGowan [*sic*], to do O'Neill's new play, *Welded*. She was given to understand that I was to direct it.

She had returned from her London triumphs and often repeated tours in the provinces playing the great Cavallini, Edward Sheldon's singer in *Romance*, and was now settled in a luxurious New York apartment. Managers were eager to engage her for one play after another. Her choice of *Welded* was both high-minded and characteristic. Such a play could not hope to provide the glamor and exciting appeal that had kept *Romance* running for so many seasons in America and abroad. I have known people who had seen Doris Keane's *Romance* as many as eighty times, and found that all too little; and I have seen a trunkfull of letters to her, by every sort of devotee from a British admiral to soldiers in the field. And now and then some soldier dying far away willed her his helmet—one of these helmets was with the letters still in the trunk.

She took all of it in her stride, valued it, and then withdrew to her own life. At the same time she was eternally the prima donna. That did not come from any mere vanity or egotism entirely; it arose also from some brooding, solitary depth in her nature that was protected, shadowed, and illuminated within the private mysticism that she lived by, and that was based on Hindu thought and various associations with psychic experience and much reading of poetry.

Such things in her were not suspected by most of her audience or even by her friends. And if I have gone now into all this at some length it is to say that, except technically, she could not have been farther than she was from the heroine of *Welded* as written in this play that she had agreed to do.

She had an almost painful tenderness toward any suffering in human beings, but these two people in *Welded*, with their wrangling violence and what she would have taken as squabbling, belonged to another world from hers. She had a physical horror of a row and almost as much of bad taste in one's conduct.

[. . .]

At length after a week of rehearsals Doris Keane wanted to withdraw from the play. So far as she was concerned that was a wise conclusion; but Kenneth MacGowan [*sic*] and Bobby Jones persuaded her against it, not without appealing to her generous attitude toward their theater and toward Eugene O'Neill. Meanwhile she still insisted that when she first read the manuscript she had thought it was a scenario, not by any means the full play as it was to be given on the stage. This was not a perfect excuse, however, since she might have taken warning from various other plays of O'Neill's.

Her next remark was more to the point. What the play needed, she said, to come off convincingly was to be done by those young people downtown. They would take it all in good faith, and act it without any misgivings. She read one of the speeches. "Listen to this," she said, "could we imagine taking it seriously?

'Not for us the ordinary family rite, you'll remember! We swore to have a true sacrament—or nothing! Our marriage must be a consummation demanding and combining the best in each of us! Hard, difficult, guarded from the commonplace, kept sacred as the outward form of our inner harmony!'"[52]

This might well have been hopeless; but, as constantly happens under theater conditions, the rehearsals went on nevertheless. She was too fine an artist to disdain a script from a sincere creator, no matter what she thought of the quality displayed. And I knew that in her tender heart she discerned the torment that underlay the lines themselves, and sensed that the words were a misplaced travesty of some genuine feeling, the results of an uncertain taste and an uncertain sense of the banal, along with a semi-adolescent ambition toward the literary—ink perchance for blood.

But feeling is one thing, expression is another. What Eugene O'Neill said and what he felt were often two different matters. "*On est quelquefois aussi différent de soi-même que des autres*"— one is sometimes as different from oneself as from others. La Rochefoucauld never said anything truer.[53]

I knew that Gene's personal life in the period that *Welded* came out of had not been all smoothness, not between two such vivid temperaments as he and Agnes, his wife, for all the love between them, and I felt that this play was in the nature of a confession and a benediction. I can see them now at some of the rehearsals sitting side by side there in the third row and listening to every speech, good or bad, and taking it all as *bona fide* and their own. At least for love of them I could wish that the mild success the play had when it was produced had been greater.

[. . .]

## *1946*

I have been seeing the Old Vic production of *Oedipus Rex*, and it set me to thinking of Eugene O'Neill, not of the play so much as my association of it with him. I remember how we sat talking of it one day in my study, and how he expressed a depth of admiration for this Sophoclean tragedy that I had never heard him express for any other. I must say here that there was nothing involved in this interest that dealt with that well-worn cliché of the Oedipus complex; we both knew, of course, that that has been attached to the play by mere chance. The young Oedipus in an altercation with a stranger on the highway had killed him, and gone on to Thebes, where he married the queen, and years afterwards it turned out that the stranger was his father and his wife was therefore his own mother. It was the grandeur and completeness and the mounting power of *Oedipus Rex* that had so taken hold of Gene's imagination.

Thinking of all the hobos, drunks, prostitutes, saloons, brawls, and so on that figure so often in his plays, and of the general plainness of his words, you may well wonder at this response on Eugene O'Neill's part to this Greek classic. Thinking of some of the visual patterns in *Mourning Becomes Electra* and of the magnificent, inevitable movement toward its conclusion, and remembering here and elsewhere that brooding of his on the tragic lot of man, you may feel, perhaps, less wonder and surprise. He had never seen *Oedipus* performed, and I described for him as best I could something of what it had been like at the *Comédie Française* with the great Mounet Sully[54] in the part.

I tried to quote for him the lines that open Sophocles' play; but we do not know enough, alas, of how the Greek should really be spoken to make it convincing; and so I repeated Mounet Sully's opening speech, trying at least to keep the even emphases of the French. More than once afterwards he asked me to repeat it. I will not try to explain that, and we may let it go as part of a man's mystery.

# 29 / Malcolm Cowley

Malcolm Cowley (1898–1989) grew up in Pittsburgh and graduated from Harvard. He served in the American Field Service as an ambulance driver in World War I and, as an aspiring poet, was part of the expatriate circle of American writers in Paris, which he wrote about in his well-known memoir *Exile's Return* (1934). His best-known volume of poetry is *Blue Juniata* (1929). Most of his career was spent as a critic and an editor, and he is credited with reviving William Faulkner's reputation in 1946 with the *Viking Portable Faulkner*.

Source: Malcolm Cowley, "A Weekend with Eugene O'Neill," *Reporter* 5 September 1957: 33–36.

Back in the early 1920's, Eugene O'Neill was the animating spirit of a group that surrounded the Provincetown Players. His success as a dramatist had enabled the Players to move to New York and had kept their venture alive in bad seasons. It had kept me alive, too, during a hard year when I was paid ten dollars a week to be a black ghost in *The Emperor Jones* and a white ghost in a revival of *Where the Cross Is Made*;[55] I never aspired to play the part of any living person. Although I hadn't been eating much that year, I made a rather substantial wraith, even with streaks of aluminum paint over my ribs to make them look as if the flesh had rotted away. Then Gene stopped writing plays with ghosts in them and my stage career came to an end. It was a minor example of how his decisions affected all of us.

If The Provincetown Players drank at the Hell Hole—officially known as the Golden Swan—which stood at the southeast corner of Fourth Street and Sixth Avenue in Greenwich Village, that was also because of Gene. Before it became a speakeasy, the Hell Hole was a Raines Law hotel, which means that there were furnished rooms upstairs and that, in theory, it furnished meals to travelers. As legal proof of the theory, the same mummified sandwiches appeared Sunday after Sunday on the round tables in the back room. Not even the unfed stumblebums who slept there on winter nights would dust off the sandwiches and eat them. The Hell Hole before the first World War, when it stayed open all night, was one of the principal models that Gene copied for Harry Hope's saloon in *The Iceman Cometh*. It was the grubbiest drinking parlor west of the Bowery—the No Chance Saloon, Bedrock Bar, the End of the Line Café, the Bottom of the Sea Rathskeller, as Larry Slade calls it in the play. "Don't you notice the beautiful calm in the atmosphere?" he continues. "That's because it's the last harbor. No one here has to worry about where they're going next, because there is no farther they can go."

Larry Slade in life was Terry Carlin, a gaunt, benign Irishman who had retired from gainful occupation after a working career that lasted one day. It was a Saturday, Terry explained, and the gainful occupation was that of helping behind the bar, where he had slaved from noon to midnight in order to empty the till after the saloon was closed. But the proprietor emptied it first, and Terry, disillusioned, had sworn never to do another day's work in his life. He kept the oath and lived to be nearly eighty, on a chiefly liquid diet. During Prohibition he used to drink canned heat, strained through a not very clean blue bandanna—that is, till the afternoon when I heard him say dreamily, "I'll have to stop drinking wood alcohol. It's beginning to affect my eyesight." Terry was a mystic of sorts who had been a radical syndicalist in his early days and then a philosophical anarchist. He had also been a patron of the Hell Hole when anyone would buy him a drink, as Gene often did. At Provincetown in the summer of 1916, Terry had repaid the debt by introducing his desperately shy friend to the Players as a young man with a trunkful of unperformed plays.

Outside of a few drunken radicals or ex-radicals like Terry and Hippolyte Havel (Hugo Kalmar in *The Iceman Cometh*), the denizens of the Hell Hole were more practical than the characters in Gene's play. Some of the latter were invented and others were carried over from Jimmy the Priest's, a waterfront dive that had been one of Gene's earlier haunts. At the Hell Hole the regular patrons included sneak thieves and shoplifters, touts, a square-shooting Negro gambler down on his luck, and a few bedraggled prostitutes—until 1917, that is, when "us girls" were driven off the streets and saloonkeepers were told not to serve them. There was a famous West Side gang known as the Hudson Dusters. Not many of the anti-social characters at the Hell Hole had spunk enough to be gangsters, but Hudson Dusters—or simply Dusters—was what we always called them. Gene had been drinking with them since 1915, when he first lived in the Village. The Dusters pitied him, sometimes fed him when he was starving, and one of them offered to steal him an overcoat when he was shivering with cold. "Tell you what, Gene," said an amiable shoplifter. "You make a trip up Sixth Avenue right away. Go to any store, pick out any coat you like, and tell me where it hangs on the rack. I bring you the coat tomorrow."

Gene hadn't accepted the offer, but he liked to tell about it, and anyone could see that he was proud to be accepted by the Dusters as one of the crowd. He had earned a place there by his apprenticeship in raggedness and drunkenness and near starvation, as well as by his unfailing good manners. He felt—and perhaps the Dusters felt—that he was leagued with them in a sullen rebellion against property and propriety. To a lesser extent he was also leagued with the Greenwich Villagers, particularly if they were poor and eccentric and a little outside the law. I think that for him the world was divided into downtowners and uptowners, as for a later generation of rebels it would be divided into hipsters and squares. For some time after becoming a successful playwright, he entered the uptown world with trepidation and in disguise, almost like a scout in enemy country, fearful of being caught and condemned to death or forced to abandon his loyalties. He wouldn't even go to see his own plays when they were produced on Broadway. In the plays he depicted uptowners as hypocritical and sex-obsessed, and also as representatives of the paternal authority that he defied. He wanted to fling the truth about them into their smug faces. He wanted to show the uptowners, including his father, what he could do to enforce his dreams, but he didn't want to win them over; he wanted to impress and overawe, not persuade. In the back room of the Hell Hole, which was lighted by two flickering gas jets, with the corners of the room in darkness so that it looked like an expressionistic setting for *The Lower Depths*,[56] among the honest sneak thieves and panhandlers at the very end of the line, he was safe from his father's reproaches; he could take off his mask and be understood.

That was what I felt about O'Neill, but what did I really know about him? Today how much do I really remember? I had seen him perhaps a dozen times, in the street, in the back room of the Hell Hole, at the Provincetown Playhouse, and once in the cold-water flat of Spanish Willie Fernandez, a bootlegger and small-time politician who worshiped him. I had heard some of his stories about life on shipboard and in a tuberculosis sanitarium, but it seems to me now that I heard them from others, his good friends and mine. I know that he liked to sing chanteys, omitting the obscene stanzas, and that his favorites were "Whiskey for My Johnny" and "Blow the Man Down." When ordering another round of drinks, he might sing in a low voice,

Whiskey is the life of man,
(Whiskey—Johnny),
Oh, I drink whiskey when I ca-a-an
(Whiskey for my Johnny).

In humming the other chantey, he would pause to say that the slow rise and fall of the refrain, "Way-O, blow the man down," was like the movement of a ship on an ocean swell, and he would illustrate his meaning with a wave-like gesture of his right hand. But did I really see him make the gesture or was it someone else who made it in telling me about an evening spent with Gene? Often we fall into the illusion that the good friends of our friends are our good friends too. Searching through my mind, discarding the questionable pictures and the stories told by others, I find that most of what I truly remember about Gene is connected with a visit to the O'Neills' country house at the beginning of November, 1923, when the other guests were the poet Hart Crane, whom we had met that summer, and my first wife, Peggy Baird.[57] And what remains is not a continuous memory but a series of pictures, as if one's mind were a theater, and a spotlight, moved to illuminate one corner of the stage and then another while leaving the intervening spaces in blackness.

Hart Crane and I are climbing out of a nearly empty Harlem Division local at Purdy's Station on a Friday evening just after dark. Nobody else gets off the train. Gene's second wife, Agnes Boulton, had taken Peggy to the country earlier in the week, and now they are waiting for us on the dimly lighted platform. There are hugs, twitters, and Hart's boom of greeting. Shivering a little in the country air, I look up at the shadowy presence of big trees to the south of the station. Just north of it a sinister-looking bridge crosses the railway. A very bright electric bulb is burning at the top of the embankment, against a starless sky. A long flight of steps rises through shadows toward the single light. It is a stage setting by Robert Edmond Jones and makes me feel like a ghost again in one of Gene's early plays.

Carrying our bags, we struggle up the steps to where the O'Neills' new touring car is waiting under the light. The chauffeur, whose name is Vincent Bedini, drives us eastward by narrow roads lined with stone walls. From time to time, far back from the road, we catch glimpses of big houses among the trees, sailing past us like brilliantly lighted wooden ships. At some point we cross the Connecticut state line. . . .

The O'Neills have recently bought one of the big houses in Ridgefield, I think with part of a legacy from Gene's brother Jim, or Jamie, though there have also been big royalties from *Anna Christie* and smaller ones from *The Hairy Ape*. The house is an 1890-ish affair called Brook Farm by its former owners, with a wide tree-dotted lawn and more than forty acres of land. Gene meets us in the hallway and so does his new dog—an Irish wolfhound, we are informed, the color and texture of a coarse sand-paper and the size of a three-month-old calf. "He's extinct," I say, patting his head. "The *Encyclopaedia Britannica* tells us that Irish wolf-hounds are an extinct breed." Off-stage the telephone rings. With his hind paws slipping a little on the pale yellow hardwood floor, the dog rises to his full height, which is greater than mine, puts his forepaws on my shoulders, and looks down into my eyes. Enter Mrs. Fifine Clark, the housekeeper, known as "Gaga" by the family; she says there is another call from New York, from the Theatre Guild. "I'll take it," Gene murmurs. He comes back with a brief report, "I said no." There aren't any other guests and we sit down to an excellent dinner without being offered a drink. The door to the hallway is closed against Finn, the dog, who hasn't learned table manners. [. . .]

After luncheon on Saturday, Gene and I are alone in a window nook at the left rear of the enormous living room. Hart has disappeared, I don't know where, and the girls are in Agnes's bedroom exchanging confidences over glasses of whiskey and water, I suspect, but there is no liquor downstairs. Gene picks up a heavy green medical-looking book from the table beside us; it is one of Wilhelm Stekel's treatises on sexual aberrations—perhaps *The Disguises of Love*, which has recently been translated from the German.[58] There are enough case histories in the book, Gene says, to furnish plots to all the playwrights who ever lived. He turns the pages and shows me the clinical record of a mother who seduced her only son and drove him insane. Then he talks about the German Expressionists, Toller and Kaiser and Hasenclever,[59] whose plays he has read because they are said to resemble his own. Gene thinks their work is bold and interesting, but much too easy. The word "easy," which seems to be his strongest expression of disapproval, reminds him of *Anna Christie*. "I never liked it so well," he says, "as some of my other plays. In telling the story I deliberately employed all the Broadway tricks I had learned in my stage training. Using the same technique, and with my early experience as a background, I could turn out dozens of plays like *Anna Christie*, but I won't ever try. It would be too easy."

Nodding politely, I look down at the polished beech floor, with tiny eyes here and there in the wood. I think it is the handsomest floor I have ever seen. . . .

Gene has taken me upstairs to the room where he works, a big bedroom so meagerly furnished that it looks like an abbot's cell. (Croswell Bowen, who is writing one of the books about O'Neill, tells me there was a crucifix over the bed, but I don't remember seeing it.) There are no books or pictures in the room. Between the two north windows is a dark mahogany secretary with drawers at the bottom, a cabinet at the top, and a drop-leaf table for writing. There are no papers on the writing surface. Gene opens the doors of the cabinet and takes out two or three medium-sized bound ledgers; "I write in these," he says. Each ledger contains several plays. Opening one of them, he shows me the text of *The Emperor Jones*, written with a very fine pen, in characters so small that they are illegible without a reading glass. There are no blank lines, and the text of the whole play fills only three pages of the ledger—or is it five? I think of the Lord's Prayer engraved on the head of a pin.

Gene tells me he is writing a play about New England, but he doesn't want to discuss it until it is finished.[60] He is being extraordinarily kind to a shabby young man without a reputation. Partly that is because I am a friend of his friends, definitely not an uptowner, but there is something else involved—perhaps a need to explain himself to a new generation of writers, to a representative of the future by which he will be judged. I listen but do not respond, as I might well have done if he were French or English. In this country, as a result of the First World War, there has come to be a gulf between literary generations, besides that older gulf between fame and obscurity. Although Gene is only ten years older than I, he had come of age in a different world, and I feel we have very few admirations or even interests in common. Gene is trying to cross the two gulfs but, in my defensive pride and foolish reticence, I do nothing to help him. . . .

Rather late in a dry evening, Gene takes Hart and me down to the cellar, the only part of the house that seems to arouse his pride of ownership. He shows us the big coal furnace, with pipes radiating in all directions like the arms of an octopus. Standing under a bare electric light, he points to the cement floor and says that Vincent keeps it as clean as the living room. Vincent is a European who can't stand the way Americans let things go to waste. Last month he had gathered apples from the old orchard and made three barrels of cider. There they are—Gene points a finger into the shadows, where three fifty-gallon casks stand on a rack.

As a country boy I offer a disquisition on the virtues of hard cider, the wine of the Puritans, the interior sunlight of New England. "Let's broach a cask," Hart says. Gene demurs, but hesitantly; Vincent mightn't like it, he says, the cider is only three weeks old, and besides he doesn't know how a barrel should be tapped. Here I interrupt with my country knowledge. There is a spigot lying on the rack, I say, with a maul beside it. Cider doesn't have to ferment all winter; sometimes it tastes even better when the sugar hasn't quite worked out.

Gene goes upstairs to Gaga's kitchen and comes back with a white china pitcher and three glasses. By that time I have tapped a barrel, spilling more than a little cider on Vincent's clean floor. We stand with our full glasses under the bare electric light. "I can see the beaded bubbles winking at the brim,"[61] Hart says. Gene takes a sip of cider, holds it in his mouth apprehensively, gives his glass a gloomy look, then empties the glass in two deep nervous swallows. After a while we fill the pitcher again. When I go upstairs to bed, long after midnight, Gene is on his knees drawing another pitcher of cider, and Hart stands over him gesturing with a dead cigar as he declaims some lines composed that afternoon. . . . .

Soliloquy. I am lying awake while the clear gray morning light pours in through the bedroom windows. I am saying to myself that the O'Neills rattle around in this big country house like the last dried peas in a box—or better, like castaway sailors who have blundered into a deserted palace on the shore. But the sailors would laugh if they found wine in the cellar, where Gene hardly even smiles. . . . .

Peggy and I are running over the immense lawn in pursuit of the wolfhound. He mustn't be allowed to cross the road because, in spite of his amiable temper, the mere size of him terrifies the neighbors; he has developed a bad habit of killing chickens, and there have been threats that he would be shot. Finally he lets us catch him and lead him, or be dragged by him, back to the house. "The O'Neills—were kings in Ireland," I pant as we go. "It's like Gene—to buy—a dog of an extinct breed—the royal hunting dog of Irish kings—that kills the neighbors' chickens."

The big round table has been set for luncheon, with a plateful of hors d'oeuvres at each place. I look through the glass doors of the dining room and see the extinct dog walking gravely round the table, lowering, not raising, his head to empty each plate in turn. At luncheon Mrs. Clark gives soup to us instead. We are told at the last moment that Gene won't be down because he's working.

That evening we are in Woodstock, New York, sixty miles from Ridgefield as the crow flies. I know from one of Hart's published letters that we had been taken there in the O'Neills' touring car, which means that Vincent was at the wheel, but I don't remember by what roads, or how we crossed the Hudson, or anything that was said. A sort of curtain had fallen, to rise on another scene. My one intervening impression, a faint one, is that Agnes came along for the ride, then left rather hurriedly before dinner.

Now we are in a sort of eviscerated farmhouse, where ceilings and partitions have been ripped out to make an immensely high living room, with a balcony at one side and bedrooms opening out of it. There are six of us, all of an age except Niles Spencer's[62] kid sister, who is pretty and sixteen. We have organized a game of hide-and-seek and go storming in and out of doors, up and down the balcony stairs, in alternate troughs and crests of laughter—first laughter pushed down, as into the hollow of a wave, then laughter splashing over us in breakers, with Hart's voice booming above them. For the Ridgefield pilgrims, it is as if a thin but perceptible mist of constraint, of jokes not made and differences of opinion that mustn't be aired, had suddenly been laughed away. . . .

Hart stayed at the Woodstock farmhouse until after Christmas. Peggy and I went back to New York, where on Thursday of that week I wrote a letter to one of my literary friends. I told him briefly about the trip and said, "Eugene O'Neill, Mr. O'Neill the playwright, Gene . . . . speaks a language so different from ours that we seemed to converse from different worlds." So the trip had ended for me in a failure of communication that was largely my fault.

There was, however, a sequel. All that Sunday, instead of working Gene had kept on drawing pitchers of cider from the tapped barrel. While Agnes was away from Brook Farm he had called a taxi that took him to Purdy's, where he vanished. Agnes went to New York and spent a frantic week in search of him. Afraid of what the newspapers might say, she avoided the Bureau of Missing Persons; instead she made telephone calls to his friends and kept visiting his old haunts, including the Hell Hole.

On the last of her visits there, the proprietor confessed to her that Gene had sat in the back room and drunk himself into a coma. To avoid trouble with the police, he had been stashed away in the mysterious upstairs that none of us had seen, where Gene said that a crazy old woman wandered through the hallways, opening and closing doors. Agnes had him driven to Ridgefield, where in a few days he went back to work on *Desire Under the Elms*. That was not the last of his alcoholic misadventures, but his need to write plays proved stronger than his impulse toward self-destruction. A few years later, faced with the choice between writing and drinking, he stopped drinking for the rest of his life.

# 30 / Hart Crane

Harold Hart Crane (1899–1932) was born in Garretsville, Ohio, of a well-to-do family. He did not complete high school but went to New York and lived in Greenwich Village, working in advertising as a copywriter. In the 1920s he was considered by many critics to be the best poet of his generation. He got to know O'Neill in Greenwich Village and visited him at his house in Ridgefield. O'Neill agreed to write a preface for his first collection, *White Buildings* (1926), but withdrew. Crane's most important work is *The Bridge* (1930), which earned him many accolades. He committed suicide two years after its publication.

Source: Hart Crane, letters to Grace Crane, 1 November 1923; 3 February 1924; 30 July 1926; letter to Charlotte and Richard Rychtarik, 5 March 1924; letter to Waldo Frank, 3 July 1926. *The Letters of Hart Crane, 1916–1932*, ed. Brom Weber (Berkeley: U of California P, 1965), 155–56, 174, 177, 262–63, 270.

To Grace Crane,[63] November 1, 1923

Tomorrow afternoon I leave, stopping off for a couple of days at Ridgefield, Conn., as a guest of Eugene O'Neill (the author of *Anna Christie*, *Emperor Jones*, *Beyond the Horizon*, etc.). I met O'Neill at some friends last week end when he was in town. He likes my poetry very much and invited me to come to stay with him. He has a regular estate, I am told,—an establishment that is quite complete, and breakfast for guests is never served out of bed. If everything goes right they are to drive me up to Woodstock on Sunday,—about three hours through beautiful hills and foliage.

To Grace Crane, February 3, 1924

Tonight is the opening of a new play at the Provincetown Theatre,[64] and I am invited to attend with Sue [Jenkins],[65] who is the wife of James Light, the stage director. Through Light and O'Neill I know the whole crowd over there now, and it is very interesting to watch this most progressive theater in America in the details of its productions,—going behind scenes, watching rehearsals, etc. I have changed my opinions, or rather prejudices, about Claire Eames[66] since meeting her there and watching her work in two recent productions. She isn't at all stiff or pompous,—and as an artist she is very flexible and exact. O'Neill, by the way, recently told a mutual friend of ours that he thinks me the most important writer of all in the group of younger men with whom I am generally classed.

To Charlotte and Richard Rychtarik,[67] March 5, 1924

I have seen a great deal of Eugene O'Neill and his wife lately. They have been wonderfully kind to me, invited me out to their house in the country. O'Neill thinks my poetry is better than that of any other American writing today, and in many ways we seem to agree about things. I wish you could both see the charming play called *Fashion*[68] which they are running now at the Provincetown Theater. An old play written seriously in 1840 [*sic*], but the funniest thing in the world to see now. Such costumes and settings by Robert Edmond Jones! You may have seen in the papers what a terrible row is being stirred up all over the country by the prospect of acting O'Neill's new play, *All God's Chillun Got Wings*, in which a white woman marries a Negro. There will be some kind of mobbing or terrors on the first night, and I expect to be there with my cane for cudgeling the unruly! He is frightfully upset about it, and receives terrible threats and insults through the mail from the KU KLUX Klanners. This country is very immature as yet. Such actions prove that thoroughly.

To Waldo Frank,[69] July 3, 1926

I must thank you immediately for your wireless. The news is most welcome—and your affectionate haste in notifying me is not without results in piercing the miasmas of these tropics.

Also comes a letter from Sue [Jenkins]. It seems the news reached Patterson via Jimmy Light. I copy Sue's account of the circumstances given her by Jimmy, as having been so active an agent in the matter you probably will be interested. "The way it came about is not without interest. About a month ago Liveright, Jimmy and others were at Otto Kahn's[70] for a week-end. L. had the mss. with him at that time and on the boat coming back he said he had decided not to publish it—that he didn't care for the poems and so far as could see, nobody understood them. Then, a little over a week ago, Jimmy and O'Neill were in L.'s office on business and your mss. was on the table. Jimmy asked him if he had stuck to his decision and he said 'Yes.' Then Jimmy and Gene both told him they thought he would eventually be 'proud' of having published your first volume, so that even if he himself did not care for the poems, as a publisher he was failing to take advantage of an opportunity. So finally L. came around to his old position of saying that he would publish them if Gene would write a preface. (Previously L. had said that he did not want to publish the poems at all—preface or no preface.) Gene protested some, saying that while he liked the poems he wasn't at all sure he could tell why he liked them, that he was by no means a critic of poetry, and that L. was preparing a fine opportunity for him (O'Neill) to make a fool of himself. But finally it was decided that the preface would be written, L. phoned immediately to the printer and dictated the announcement. And I understand that the preface is already written and in L.'s hands."[71]

To Grace Crane, July 30, 1926

Meanwhile my other book, *White Buildings*, will have been published. It comes out sometime this fall. I have my contract and the $100. advance royalties mentioned in Grandma's letter. O'Neill finally backed out on the foreword, as I thought he would. He's enthusiastic about my work, I've never doubted that, but he didn't have the necessary nerve to write what his honesty demanded—a thorough and accurate appraisal of my work. He can't write criticism, never has tried even, and I foresaw the panic that this proposal on the part of our mutual publisher would precipitate in his bosom. [. . .] And (mum's the word on this!) I was very much touched to hear from Waldo, who knows all the inner workings on this, that Allen [Tate][72] offered his foreword under O'Neill's signature when he heard that O'Neill had backed out. Of course I wouldn't think of anything like that—so the foreword goes back to its own name. I'm very glad things have turned out this way. My umbrage toward Allen is erased by the fidelity of his action, and I'm glad to have so discriminating an estimate as he will write of me.

# 31 / Harold De Polo

Harold De Polo (1888–1960) was a popular writer who claimed to have written three thousand western and detective stories, as well as several novelettes. His acquaintance with O'Neill began in his Greenwich Village days when they were both hard drinkers. Dorothy Day (chapter 19) says that she and Eugene used to go out with De Polo and Agnes Boulton before Agnes became involved with Eugene. De Polo accompanied O'Neill to Provincetown in 1918. He remained friendly with both Agnes and Eugene during their marriage, and like them he later moved to Bermuda. When Eugene married Carlotta Monterey, his friendship with De Polo, as with most of his friends from early days, dropped off.

Source: Harold De Polo, "Meet Eugene O'Neill—Fisherman," *Outdoor America* May 1928: 5-8.

SAY, kid. What kind of a bird is this austere and mysterious Eugene O'Neill guy, anyway?" My old pal Bob Davis[73] put this one up to me, some five or six years back, when I'd dropped into his so-called editorial sanctum to extract a check for a yarn.

"Bob," I told him, "he ain't—I mean he ain't mysterious. He's just so unbelievably natural and incapable of lamping you and lying that all the intellectual girls and boys have built up this myth about his being a human puzzle. Honest, he's so unaffected that it's too good to be true; he's the most regular guy, every way, that I—"

"A bass caster, eh? Why didn't you say so in the begin— . . . Oh, well, it always *did* take you a long time to get into the story."

I had to duck, at that—on the first count, anyway. Tears probably came to my orbs and did the proverbial coursing down my cheeks, and I guess my voice was husky as I replied:

"Bob, he's young yet; he'll learn in time; he just doesn't know. Don't hold it against him—he's never had the kick of slapping out a plug and feeling a bronze-back sock it; he's never seen one of the red-eyes break night water and make that inward rush on his tail; he's never gripped a bamboo wand or—"

I said much more, I guess—very much more—for although Bob Davis may be almost a passable editor, he is and was and always will be one of the few lads who thoroughly understands the wooing and winning of small mouth black bass. What's more, he isn't unwilling to talk about 'em, being joyously amenable to discarding any typed masterpiece he happens to be perusing in order to listen to a tale anent the greatest fighters that ever flipped a fin. I gave him plenty, that day, I suppose, while I stood up and made excuses for Gene—and I think Bob believed me. Anyway, I did so much explaining—I can still vitally remember—that I completely forgot to make a stab for that check I'd gone in to get.

That was five or six years ago, as I've remarked, and for even longer than that I'd been trying to persuade our Great American Playwright to attempt a still more important and intricate art. He had the stuff, I was sure. The man who had the power to pound out *Desire Under the Elms* likewise had the steel in his wrist that a decent rod demands; the man who had the poetry to give us *The Fountain* also had the sensitiveness in his fingers to properly thumb a delicate silk line; the man who possessed the sense of humor and tolerance to turn out *Diff'rent* must pack the courage and patience that all true bass devotees need. I'd always had a strong hunch that Eugene O'Neill would make a fisherman.

Putting the numerous disappointments of many years aside, I had the merry news last summer [1926]: "Come on along, kid, and show me something about bass," wrote Gene. He was up at the Belgrade string of lakes in Maine, at the time, and as my own camp was merely some seventy miles away I cranked up the flivver and stuck the hood O'Neillwards.

It was early in September, and the Maine nights are apt to be brisk at that time of year—too brisk, really, for the best sort of casting. Fingers stiffen from the chill of the metal reel, and a man is fairly well hampered. For, along with Bob Davis, I insist that the night hours are the only ones for shooting a plug after bass. The business of thumbing your cast and respooling your line is made trebly difficult, and you therefore give your opponent the edge instead of having it on him as in the daytime. There simply isn't any argument as far as the sporting side of it is concerned, and you likewise garner about ten times the thrill from a battle in the dark. On top of that, the big boys seem to be rummaging around from about eleven o'clock on, say, to a wee, sma' hour. I handed Gene a hickory rod, adorned with a level-winding reel holding seventy-five yards of line. I warned my pupil that the novice always balled himself up and ran into snarls and backlashes by trying for too much distance at the start. Thirty feet or so every try, I lectured, was better than an occasional sixty or seventy after many precious minutes have been lost in disentangling knots. And—believe it or not, you old-timers—here was one beginner who annexed the lesson of moderation right from the drop of the hat.

Agnes—Mrs. O'Neill—and Gene and I stepped into the Rangeley skiff that first night at precisely eleven, my favorite hour. The water looked like a gigantic chunk of clouded black onyx, with the mist that was hanging over it, and I took the oars and pushed the boat over toward an island perhaps two hundred yards away.

That island looked like nice bass ground, I still insist. It wasn't—I mean that it wasn't on that trip. I didn't care then and I don't care now, for I was looking at something far more vital than a scrap between a red-eye and a worthy human foe—I was looking at the birth of a fisherman. The lad I've always thought was the greatest playwright in the world, even before his stuff had been put on, was standing up there and showing me that he was a genius with a rod and reel. He was game, too. He cast for an hour—for two hours—and he didn't get a strike. To prove what I mean by genius, let me state that in all that while he got precisely one backlash. I don't think it takes an expert to realize that this is pretty nice business for a man who's playing with a plug for the first time in his life.

I started to row back to the camp, finally, stopping about half way across the cove where a batch of pond lilies were and telling Gene to send a few casts around the edges. The Northern lights began to do their radiating, then, and although Agnes and I called his attention to them Gene kept on working his rod:

"Purty?" I said, quoting Simeon in *Desire Under the Elms.*

"Ay-eh," agreed Gene, as Peter does in the play.

Chung!

It's the only way I know how to express it, that inimitable sound made by a striking bass connecting with a top-water plug. As I saw the rod hold its curve, I knew that Gene had his first bronze-back hooked. I'm afraid I yapped out advice—and so did Agnes, as I look back on it—but I saw instantly that it wasn't necessary. He weighed exactly a pound, did that small-mouth, but remember that he belonged to the tribe that carries more gameness ounce for ounce than any other living breed. He came in on his tail, spinning over that clouded-onyx surface; he dug down for the weeds at the bottom, looking for a spot where he could stick in his nose; he leaped out of the water in beautiful curves, doing his darndest to shake the barb free or snap that terrifying line with his tail. But it couldn't be done. Gene manipulated him as—well, tossing all modesty aside, as Bob or I might have, and in three or four minutes I'd stuck the net under him and had him in the boat.

Agnes and I did some congratulating, and I guess I kept on slapping Gene on the back while I eagerly waited for the words that would proclaim him a hopeless addict. They didn't come, and I should have known better, for where verbal enthusiasm is concerned Gene has always slightly reminded me of the Punch cartoon:

A brace of British youths have taken a stance in the Swiss Alps, gazing at

Mont Blanc: "Not bad," drawls one, as the sun begins to sink. "Don't be so demmed enthusiastic," retorts the other, lazily covering a yawn as he turns his head.

"How about it, old kid, ain't it the grandest sport in the world?" I wanted to know. "Ain't it got all the thrills—"

"Yeah," said Gene, going right on casting.

I tried darned hard, for the next ten days, to extract the glad word from Gene that would conclusively proclaim him a hopeless and dyed-in-the-wool fisherman. Luck was against me, though, mainly in the form of the weather. I don't mean maybe either when I say it was cold, for after sundown the thermometer hovered consistently close around the freezing mark. Not that this is so bad on the body when you're properly rigged out, but don't forget that metal reel that cramps up your fingers and sends the chill right along into your spine. Also, I've never found that bass did any prolific striking on cold nights, although brisk afternoons in September and October are apt to bring decent results if you troll slow and deep with live bait.

I've said that the big boys are usually out sporting during the nocturnal hours, and I'll leave it to old Bob Davis or any other tried and true veteran if that doesn't hold good in nine cases out of ten. This was the tenth, all right, all right. I never saw the bronze-backs average smaller, and I've somehow managed to get in five or six hours a night at the art of plug casting, all through the season, for fairly close to the past twenty-five years. To prove that this Belgrade adventure was about the worst stretch I've known when it came to size, let me state that during one session I hooked and landed eleven small-mouths—not bad for any man's lake, eh?—but that I tossed every one of 'em back because not a single specimen came up to a pound. "We must have struck the children's department," as Gene put it.

Don't get the idea, you fishermen, that I'm kicking. With Grover Cleveland[74] I indubitably and unalterably agree that the next best thing to going fishing and catching fish is—going fishing. I am complaining at not having stuck the barb into any big ones, purely, for the reason that I know it generally takes a somewhat hefty prize to make a man a rabid and enthusiastic angler. Not that I mean, in any way, that Gene wasn't game. He was there every way from the ace, never yelping at the bum luck and getting better all the time in his casting, his action smoother and his distance gradually increasing. Still, I didn't get the word that would happily assure me that he was a hopeless and helpless addict. And I guess any bug who's ever wet a line will know the type of stuff I was hankering to hear.

I thought I was going to get the desired earful, my last night at Belgrade. The weather got warmer and I could sort of smell bass in the air. Gene hooked and landed a small one and on his next cast I saw his rod stiffen almost as soon as his plug spanked the water:

"You got him," I said.

"Feels like a good one," admitted Gene.

He looked it, too, when he came out of the water on his first and only leap, shaking his jaws as he tried to get rid of the hook, showing the sheen of his scales against the background of the pines on the shore. He dug down, after that, apparently electing to make it an under-surface tussle. He pulled some good stuff, during the next hectic five minutes, but Gene met his tactics in a way that made me proud. When he was safely in the boat, unhooked and held up for inspection, I certainly had my ears ready for the long-expected enthusiastic remarks.

"What'll he weigh?" demanded Gene, looking at the beauty just—well, just a trifle gloatingly.

"Around three," I opined, still hopefully waiting as I watched Gene studying that bronze-back.

"Pretty good fight," he admitted with a pleased smile—but that was all.

It was about two in the morning when we got back to camp and the kitchen scales weren't to be found. Agnes was sweet enough to rout herself out of bed and lug in the ones used for balancing Oona, the youngest O'Neill.

Two pounds and eleven ounces!

That was how that small-mouth tipped those tested scales, and I hurriedly and eagerly went right on to explain that any fish of that weight unquestionably loses a couple of ounces in the natural shrinkage and blood-letting due to death. I fervently went on to hand out the further information, too, that it was a pip of a bass. Hadn't the guides said, I reminded, that the last three weeks had been the poorest of the year? Hadn't all the boys up at the store, where angling was discussed, told us that a two-pound specimen hadn't been taken in the last ten days? Hadn't he beaten an old-timer like myself at—

"How much did that one weigh that you've got mounted?" interrupted Gene. "Six, wasn't—"

"Six pounds and three ounces, since you gotta know," I answered, for once speaking bitterly when it came to mentioning one of my most highly prized trophies,

"A baby like that ought to put up a scrap," said Gene, looking a trifle wistful-eyed.

"He did—and you're gonna listen to the story once more," was my comeback.

I had one more chance left in that fastly waning season—and the best chance yet, I figured—for Agnes and Gene agreed to come along for a few days and sample my own lake. It has the best bass waters in the State o' Maine, I remark and strongly reiterate, although due to what most people term an overabundance of pond lilies and pickerel grass it's probably one of the most difficult to cast. But that, of course, is what makes it so luscious. It takes a good man, if I say it as shouldn't, to handle a plug there on a black night—or on any kind of a night or even in the daytime. Still, I had a lot of faith in my promising pupil.

The first night at my bass bailiwick snuggled at the foothills of the White Mountains, it was cold, but we bundled up in a manner that suggested an Arctic voyage and sallied forth. I had decided to use my ace-in-the-hole first, for I knew it wouldn't be possible to do much casting. The old red bridge had never failed me, and I have always held it in reserve for the pinch. Big boys lurk under that planking, and hold guard along the stone foundations on either side. A noble spot; a treasure-house fit for a master.

But what's the use? I don't know whether to blame it on the cold alone or not—they just weren't hitting. Every bass man knows what that means. You can give 'em everything you've got in the tackle box, served up faultlessly, and they won't look at it. For a solid hour, anyway, Gene covered that ground while I handled the boat—covered it without a backlash, without a poor cast, his work with the rod being fully as artistic and perfect as any line he has ever written. It was with a sad heart that I aimed the craft for home. The following day was to be Gene's last at camp, and there didn't seem to be any prospect of the weather changing.

It didn't change, either. There was so much kick in the air the next day that I gave up hoping for a favorable night. We agreed to try some afternoon work, drifting around to a cove close to camp that was fairly well protected from the wind that was tearing down from the North. It was nice territory, at that, even if it was better pickerel than bass cover. Gene still kept up his great form, putting the plug along the fringe of the lilies and grasses so neatly that it partially lightened my heavy heart. He did it for an hour—for two hours—and then he turned to me with a yawn and a stretch:

"I guess we'd better call it a day, hadn't we?"

"Put one over there," I pleaded. "In that pocket in the lilies at your left—just one more, Gene!"

With indulgent courtesy my pal did as I requested.

Wham!

It was a big fish, although in what we fiction mechanics term our heart of hearts I knew it wasn't a bronze-back. A pickerel, all the bets said, and I was sure of it as I caught a glimpse of his glinting yellow-and-black side when he dug for the weeds. A pickerel, yes—but a grand old warrior:

"You got him, kid—and *hold* him," I yelled.

I'm supposed to be a cool customer myself, so they tell me, when I'm tussling with a tough one, yet the way this absolutely rank novice manipulated that hellion at the other end of the line darned near got my goat. There's such a thing as *too* much *aplomb* and *savoir-faire* under certain circumstances, as I've got a hunch every fisherman will chime in with me.

One ounce under five pounds, that jet-and-gold baby weighed, and the man who calls me a liar is a liar himself. He was the biggest pickerel taken out of my lake that year, the nearest thing to him having run an even four pounds. I stated this to Gene—and I stated it right vociferously—while I also handed out the congrats that were certainly due. Did I get the desired cry of joy? Did I hear the hilarious news that the piscatorial microbe had penetrated to the very veins of our Great American Dramatist?

"Pretty nice fish," says Gene.

"Don't be so demmed enthusiastic," I couldn't help retorting.

Get me straight on this, before I continue. Don't think that Gene is a frozen-faced guy who never gives three rousing cheers—he ain't. He can put more expression in his eyes when he smiles—more unalloyed friendship or appreciation—than any man, woman or child I've ever known, including the Scandinavian. You've got to remember that we fellers who fish, though, want a little more than that; we want the riotous old hip, hip, hoorah!

And I was going to get it, too, although I didn't know it at the time. As Bob Davis and all other fishermen will agree, it would have been far sweeter if a bass instead of a pickerel had been the medium of making my wish come true. This isn't rapping the babies with the long jaws, either, for fish are fish. Still, bass are bass, too. I don't hear any dissenting voices, do I? . . . I'll tell the world I don't, all right.

But back to the story.

When we returned to camp with the walloping pickerel, Gene decided to wait over another day before beating it back to Belgrade. Candidly, I think my neighbor, John Martin, had something if not a good deal to do with it. A great old State o' Mainer, is John—another lad with as clean an eye and as clean a mind and as clean a heart as O'Neill has. He was born on a sun-kissed, pine-fringed hill that overlooks my glorious lake, over fifty years ago, and what he doesn't know about the pickerel in them there waters wouldn't make a hack writer rich telling about it. Yes, he knows 'em, even though he is a poor, pathetic ignoramus when it comes to bass. Anyway, when he saw that beautiful monster that Gene had captured, he also opined that he wouldn't break camp for another day. If Gene would stay over, he declared, he'd take us out and show us some real pickerel fishing. And so it was arranged.

Clear and cold is right, when it comes to the way the next day broke. More than that. There was a terrific wind up but that did not stop us. Armed with the eighteen foot bamboo poles of the pickerel skitterer, Agnes and Gene and John and I pushed off into the breeze early the following afternoon, after having spent most of the morning in gathering a comfortable supply of frogs. Sucker Brook was the selection of our guide—one of the inlets to the lake that winds sinuously through the marshes for a fair couple of miles, and where I like to paddle in the spring to watch the deer come down and gorge on succulent roots.

That brook didn't measure any two miles this particular September P.M., in my far from humble opinion. It was more like six, or even eight or a dozen. Hard going—mighty hard going. A narrow ribbon of water at best, the late-season shallowness and high wind gave us little room in which to navigate. Even so, we managed to do passably well—but once again it just wasn't the day. The pickerel hit, as I don't deny, as they always do in Sucker Brook, but, like the bass of Belgrade, they had no heft to them. Small, all small, not a one running over a measly fifteen or sixteen inches.

We couldn't blame it on old John Martin, though. He showed Gene his favorite spots, methodically scrutinizing each and every pond lily and patch of grass before giving the edict to send one in. He took the first pickerel we caught and ceremoniously cut off the choicest strip of belly, baiting the hook himself for Gene so that only the big boys would be enticed.

But it was a thin day. We all took a crack at skittering, although I've got to admit Gene nobly did more than his share. An untirable guy, was my verdict, and I guess it was John's, too. He stood up there and whaled away without a whimper, and if you don't think it's apt to be wearing on the wrists and shoulder sockets, just go ahead and try it. That six yard stick gets heavy, after a while, but Gene manipulated it as deftly as he had the bass casting outfit. A born fisherman is correct, and I was praying that the Gods of the Wild would be good to me, in some miraculous way, in the short time that was left of that 1926 season.

The sun had gone down, but the wind was raising more of a hullabaloo than ever, and Agnes had nestled down in the bow of the boat while I stayed with the oars and unashamedly shivered. John, pickerel fiend though he is, had to keep blowing on his hands between every two or three casts, but the author of *Beyond the Horizon* went right on working with a light in his eyes that was getting grimmer and grimmer.

"What have we for dinner, Harold?" Agnes asked me.

"I think we have some veal chops, for one thing," I answered most audibly, knowing we did, and likewise knowing that Gene was somewhat partial to 'em.

Silence from The Great God O'Neill.

"I—I used to like veal chops before I had to go on this diet," said John, sort of suggestively, if you get me.

Nothing stirring. That weather-proof idiot in the stern went right on slapping out his bait.

"You're sure you're not getting cold, Agnes, dear?" I petitioned to know, coughing so rackingly that it would have touched a guy with a heart of ice.

"No—no! . . . Oh, no—not a bit," Agnes assured me, like the game fellow she is.

"It—it is a mite perky," admitted Mr. Martin, lowering his own pole and turning up the collar of his coat.

It didn't do any good, raising that collar. A man needed a fur overcoat out there including ear-muffs. I know that John and I were game, all right, but—well, chivalry isn't altogether dead, I don't think, so we gazed at Agnes with what I suppose is called dumb appeal.

She rose to the occasion gloriously, for I don't believe I have ever heard airy casualness so perfectly intoned:

"Gene, dear. Don't you think we'd better call it a day?"

That Eskimo who should have been up in an igloo turned slowly. His brow was furrowed and his jaws were set. He took a fresh grip on his bamboo—a grip that intimated he was preparing for a long, long siege—and he spoke with contumely:

"Hell," said he, snapping his bait against a bunch of tanlacs, "that's what I said yesterday just before I got that five-pounder!"

Purty?

Well, Bob Davis and I aim to wet a night line together, next summer, and I'll bet my best rod against a fishhook that Gene'll be right there with us!

# 32 / Brooks Atkinson

Justin Brooks Atkinson (1894–1984) was born in Melrose, Massachusetts, and graduated from Harvard in 1917. He was the preeminent American drama critic in the mid-twentieth century, writing for the *New York Times* from 1925 to 1960. He was among the first critics to recognize the exceptional quality of playwrights Eugene O'Neill and Tennessee Williams, and his support for the Off-Broadway movement in the 1940s and 1950s was vital to its survival. O'Neill and Atkinson became friends and corresponded a great deal.

Source: Brooks Atkinson, journal entry, Louis Sheaffer Collection of Eugene O'Neill Materials, Department of Special Collections, Charles E. Shain Library, Connecticut College, New London.

September 22, 1927—At luncheon today with Manuel Komroff[75] and Eugene O'Neill. I had never met O'Neill before except in passing. I have long admired him from afar as one of the heroes, living in the far-off realm of poetry but firmly rooted in human existence.

It was all very pleasant and simple. O'Neill, still in his thirties, is graying around the edges and his face is marked with experience. It is not tired. It is vivid; there is something immediately magnetic about his personality. He has the physical strength of one who understands the strength of nature. Although he is generally unconscionably shy, even awkward, he was at ease today and talked on many themes. About his own work he is neither modest nor presumptuous. He talks of art—of Lazarus Laughed and Strange Interlude, both unproduced—frankly, and smiles agreeably over his practical difficulties. With the arrogance of the true artist he is contemptuous of directors and actors who are not capable of producing him; he is charmingly frank in despising rich men who do not put huge sums of their private fortunes at his disposal for producing his work in proper style. I like him immensely for his ability to see all these minor forces in true perspective. Although he is gentle and sympathetic I am sure he would trample down anything in his path. He is not to be denied. He spoke with contempt of Katharine Cornell's[76] plan of first making her reputation secure by playing tricky modern drama and then devoting herself to great art. O'Neill points out that she will have accumulated so many facile mannerisms by that time that she will be lost to the ways of genius.

We talked of human character, Maugham, Galsworthy,[77] the current stage, the Dempsey–Tunney[78] fight last night, and other natural subjects. O'Neill is naturally a recluse. I was delighted to get on so swiftly with him. But he is the kind of man whose seclusion one instinctively respects, and, on his side, he never takes the initiative. He left me with a glow all afternoon. I felt that I had been in contact with the genuine article.

# 33 / Calvin Hoffman

Calvin Hoffman (Leo Hochman) (1905–1986) was an American theater press agent, drama critic, and writer. His book *The Man Who Was "Shakespeare"* (1955), reissued as *The Murder of the Man Who Was "Shakespeare"* (1960), was highly influential in promoting the argument that the playwright Christopher Marlowe (1564–1593) was actually the author of the plays attributed to William Shakespeare (1564–1616). At his death in 1986, a sizable bequest established the Calvin & Rose G. Hoffman Marlowe Memorial Trust, dedicated to supporting research into the life and work of Christopher Marlowe.

Source: Calvin Hoffman, "Of Eugene O'Neill Remembered," typescript, Louis Sheaffer Collection of Eugene O'Neill Materials, Department of Special Collections, Charles E. Shain Library, Connecticut College, New London.

It was the third week in March, 1928. I was 18[79] and the greatest day of my life had arrived. I was on the threshold of meeting the idol of my thoughts and dreams—dramatist Eugene O'Neill, author of the then-contemporary, ever-haunting and incomparable *Anna Christie*, *The Hairy Ape*, *Desire Under The Elms*, *The Great God Brown* and other plays of sinew and vitality—all of which I scrupulously read, re-read and digested to the last word of dialogue. I committed to memory most of the lines written. The Scriptures, to me, were no more sacred than O'Neill's plays.

How for more than a year previous to 1928 I had tried to meet this (I had read) strange, brooding, elusive man. O'Neill was described as a recluse by nature and there were few people on earth whom he cared to know or meet. Moreover, he was, in 1927, living in Bermuda and seldom visited New York. He had a pathologic abhorrence for city-living.

All this appeared to place the stamp of finality on my quenchless yearn to meet the great American playwright. Nevertheless, a compulsion to at least *talk* to him persisted, mounted, then obsessed me. I craved to pour out my admiration for those matchless dramas and pined to discuss the characters with the author—characters whom I intimately *knew* as I subliminally knew their creator.

To achieve this became the goal of my youthful days. Only those who have felt the gnaw of unrealized desire can conceive of the painful void unfullfilment (born of adoration) leaves. A year passed, 1928 had arrived and my hounding drive to meet the dramatist, who represented the heaven of creation to me—reached the breaking point. The thought of journeying to Bermuda to see my demi-god passionately engaged me. Toward this end I endlessly phoned those in New York who might know just where on that sea-isle O'Neill might be living. To my delight and astonishment I was informed by a Provincetown Theatre director that "Mr. O'Neill sailed yesterday (Wednesday) for New York and would stop at the Wentworth Hotel on West 46th Street for some time." Feverishly ringing the hotel I was told that the playwright was expected Friday—tomorrow—before noon!

If one has not, also, experienced the anticipatory ecstasy of youth's dream come true, one has not, I submit, sounded the well spring of emotion.

This, then, was Thursday the day before O'Neill's arrival on the now long-scrapped Furness Bermuda liner *Victoria*. Though I couldn't sleep that night, tossing restlessly about was the sweetest of agonies—hours of pure happiness.

Early Friday morning I drove to the pier and met the *Victoria* and waited near the gangplank. Hordes of tourists streamed off the boat. Suddenly *the sight* strode into view! Frozen in reverence I observed my writing-god walk to shore looking every inch the mortal I envisioned him to be. (O'Neill was 40 years old at the time.)

But this sovereign sight was merely one "truth . . . told as happy prologue to the swelling act of the imperial theme."

That afternoon (callow lad) I rode the elevator to what I now recall was the 9th floor of the Wentworth Hotel and, unheralded, rang the bell of O'Neill's suite. My heart was thumping, my face flushed and I felt faint. Crucifying thoughts whirled through my head. What if he'd slam the door in my face? Merciful heaven, not that! Or tell me he couldn't be annoyed? I'd melt away in disgrace! Or perhaps peremptorily say he just did not want to see me and shut the door. Die, heart, then and there! A moment or two of waiting encompassed eternity. I suddenly experienced nausea, and my stomach wanted to yield burdens; I broke out in body-sweat. My mouth dried, my throat parched, my legs quivered. Had the door not opened that instant I would have dropped, death-resigned, in a fainting heap.

It opened only as wide (about an inch) as to enable the opener to see who was at the door. Dimly I saw the face that imaged the world. With almost tearing eyes I stammered out: "I'm sorry—terribly sorry! Please forgive the intrusion, but I *had* to—*had* to—*had* to see you!" Large, raven eyes, burning and penetrating, scanned me head to toe—stern eyes, black, mournful and misanthropic glowered at me. I looked at those eyes pleadingly—beggingly. The fierce tiger, lean from hunger and ready for the kill would have relented in pity at such a victim. A tortured moment elapsed before the great god spoke ("'tis true, this god did speak") then the door fully opened. A granite-grim, self-tortured, torturing face miraculously melted as snow in fire. It metamorphosed into an all-warm, boyish, understanding half-smile. O'Neill seemed to stammer himself as he responded, at last, in a low, guarded monotone: "Come in, son."

I had reached the top-most hill of heaven!

During the ensuing weeks I saw a lot of Eugene O'Neill. Our visits ripened into a kind of friendship. I suppose the playwright was flattered by my idolatry and no less pleased that he had met someone who could recall lines without end from *all* his dramas. I assume, also, he felt I possessed some sort of vague critical faculty because many times he asked my opinion of certain characters in his plays. He was particularly interested in what I thought of Caligula in *Lazarus Laughed*; Dion Anthony in *The Great God Brown*; Ephraim Cabot in *Desire Under the Elms*.

Of an afternoon during one of my visits (soon after our first meeting) the dramatist told me he came to New York with the final draft of his latest play, *Strange Interlude*, to deliver to the Theatre Guild for production. Not even that organization, he confessed, had yet read the whole play in its fully revised and corrected form. Lawrence Langner[80] (now dead), co-director of the Guild had read some, but not all, of the acts (there were nine) O'Neill told me. "Would I" he asked, "like to read the manuscript?" My words thunderclapped back: "I'd like nothing better in all the world!"

From the mantle-piece [*sic*] where the script was lying he pitched a thick-laden bundle of typewritten pages to me—*nine acts* of a play which became a monument of modern drama, the finest and most discussed play of the American theatre up to that time.

Putting on his hat and coat O'Neill left the room without further comment. I was alone now in the living-room of an unpretentious bed-room suite with a treasure in my possession—the chaste manuscript of the most recent and unproduced drama of America's most renowned writer—a writer (little did I, or anyone, know) destined to win the Nobel Prize in Literature a few years later.

I began reading *Strange Interlude* (a landmark in itself for length) slowly, methodically, analytically drinking in every word, nuance, stage-direction. After almost six time-benumbing hours I completed the play and my immediate reaction was electric. I was transported to heights previously unknown. No O'Neill tragedy compared to it in drive, sweep, scope, character-analysis and insight. This, surely, I thought, was the journey's end of O'Neill's development.

Their author returned late that night. Neither of us uttered a word, not even of greeting. A chicken dinner was ordered brought to the suite. (O'Neill never dined in a restaurant if he could help it.) We made feeble attempts to eat. It was useless. I was bursting to tell him what I thought of the play. But knowing something of his personality by this time, I properly waited for the cue.

A long silence made this speechless interlude unbearable. Then, without warning, O'Neill walked over to my chair, and, his brow furrowed, aimed one of his side-piercing glances into my baffled eyes knotting his strong jaw and mouth as if ready to devour me. An act of mayhem would have been his next logical move. I shuddered within. Nerve-charged words (the description is not unapt) droned from his mouth. "'Well?" he icily queried. I began to stammer. "I—I—I—." Then like an ogre: "Did you—did you finish it!" I could endure no more. My almost paroxysmal state forced me to ejaculate superlatives in the best Hollywood tradition: "I did!. . . I did . . . .I did! It's mammoth! Wonderful! Colossal! The best—the best of all your plays! Nina Leeds—Charlie Marsden—they're great . . . . It's all wonderful!"

From the menacing expression a few tickless seconds ago O'Neill's face transformed instantaneously to a radiant, disarming, almost blushing smile. He walked away, smoked a cigarette, seated himself and mused darkly. He was evidently pleased.

Certainly I couldn't let my intimacy pass without asking him to inscribe some of his books to me. Needless to say I owned a copy of each edition ever printed, from his first "vanity published" work, *Thirst and Other One Act Plays* (which he paid Richard Badger, of Boston, to print) to his very latest.[81] I selected five books for the precious O'Neill autograph. He wrote flattering inscriptions into each of them. Into one volume I particularly cherished because it contained one of my favorite plays, *The Great God Brown*, he wrote the following words which issue from character Billy Brown, mystically possessed of the soul-destroying, life-denying personality of Dion Anthony (another character in the play):

> "Sssh! This is Daddy's bedtime secret for
> today: Man is born broken. He lives by
> mending. The grace of God is glue!"[82]
>
> To Calvin Hoffman—in the nature of advice—with all
> sincere friendship.
> Eugene O'Neill

A year later, when my wanderings led me to Boston, I was desperately in need of money and I sold the volume for ten dollars (because of the inscription) to the owner of a bookshop just outside Harvard University. (The Grolier

Bookshop, I think—above which lived the poet Conrad Aiken.[83] I *know.* A wild drunken party lasting far more than a day, took place in Mr. Aiken's apartment of which I was a fortuitous guest.) Our understanding was that I would be given the privilege of purchasing back the book for the same ten dollars at a future date. Six months later, more than willing to pay for what I had sold *The Great God Brown* I sent Grolier Bookshop my check. In the best Yankee tradition of horse-trading the price asked was $150.00, a sum I couldn't possibly afford. A few years later the figure doubled. When my subsequent lush days availed me to pay even that huge sum I was told that the book, in the meantime, had been sold to an unknown purchaser and that it was now, in the bookseller's words, "God knows where." It is still "God knows where."

O'Neill's fingers were unusually long, sensitive, prehensile and appeared to be invertedly arched. I couldn't help comparing this quality with the fingers of a monkey or ape, especially when he was writing and held his rust-colored fountain-pen in his hand. Their shape absolutely fascinated me. It was while I observed him penning a letter one morning that I noticed a spasm, a quiver, or a shake in those fingers. (This was probably the seed of an ailment that eventually killed him—Parkinson's disease.)[84] In all youthful candor I drew attention to what caught my eye and mentioned it to O'Neill. He brushed it off as "Nerves. Just nerves." "Nerves" it surely was because on numerous occasions I drove him to, and from, his neurologist on Park Avenue in my Whippet car. (He could barely fit into it.) Neurologists, he told me, were treating him a long time. He never specified the particular condition that afflicted him even when I saw him during the ensuing years.

The best tonic for nerves, the dramatist said, was swimming, which he daily engaged in off the shore-front of his Bermuda home. He loved gliding through the warm aquamarine-colored waters of the sea-gem island and there wasn't a stroke, he said, he couldn't master. His favorite was the Australian crawl. Swimming, and an occasional set of tennis with an invited house-guest, played on the court of his grounds, were his chief physical delights. But swimming was his real love.

Our affinity, I was elated to know, was not, then, of mind and spirit alone since there was nothing *I* enjoyed more in the animal world of exercise than swimming—and tennis! And, like O'Neill also, I preferred swimming. Two summers previously (I was strongly built for my age) I had been a life-guard at a Maine beach resort.

It was May, warm and leafy. The breath of summer was in the air. I dared hint to my man-god the possibility of joining me in a swim at a nearby beach. He reflected a moment then replied, almost somberly, that he would love to but on one condition only—the beach would *have* to be a quiet one, without anyone about, else he could not accept. He repeated this stern proviso making the importance of it deadly clear. I told him we could make an early morning start, swim for a while, then leave, avoiding anything like even a cluster of people. He agreed.

A date was set two days hence, weather permitting. (O'Neill had either a morbid fear, or a rooted hate, of being among people and lived as reclusive and hermit-like an existence as any civilized person could in a bee-hive world.) The appointed day arrived as we set out in my car for the odd-hour drive to a Long Island beach. To the playwright's purring content and my own profound relief the beach was absolutely deserted. Behind untenanted huts we undressed, donned bathing suits and then, running, plunged into the cold sea. Beholding O'Neill naked was a sight I shall never forget. He was by all odds one of the thinnest, board-lean adults I had seen, up to, or since, that time. Litheness and wiriness would be mere euphemisms. He was just plain bone-thin. He paid the penalty bodily, I suppose, for his stupendous nervous gifts.

Nevertheless, in his bathing suit, he cut a handsome figure. Rather tall, his hair silver-grayed at the temples; his features were chiseled and his body erect—a body tanned bronze by the Bermuda sun; his whole mien was like a lean-ribbed, fine-fettled stallion. He was the ideal figure for sculpture. We dove into the giant combers and cavorted like dolphins reveling in the sea-joy of it all. Suddenly, O'Neill saw *someone* swimming a few hundred yards away. This was his cue to swim to shore at once. His allergy to "crowds" was made manifest beyond all dreaming because while home-bound, he spoke little to me and what he did say was in the nature of an upbraiding for having brought him to a beach where crowds congregated!

During our many talks he sometimes shocked me with confessions of his life so intimate that I wondered why he revealed so much to a youth of 18. Recollections of his family-life generated fits of anguish (especially remembrance of his adolescent years which eventually nurtured the seed that produced *Long Day's Journey Into Night*) after which a brooding dolor, a suffering silence would consume him. Reminiscences of his sailor-days and drinking bouts in South America—on tramp ships and at "Jimmy-the-Priests" saloon on the New York waterfront—were nostalgic glorification of a bravado past which never left him. (I think it is true that O'Neill's external *and internal* experiences ceased in his late twenties. Unfortunately, those self-limiting experiences were his entire reservoir of total living both within *and* without. This might be why his later drama became his artistic Achilles heel of creation. He never flowered into the mature, transcendental dramatist.) For me, however, stories of his past were tales that teemed with excitement! I longed to emulate those experiences, some of which I faithfully did.

Details of his sexual life, of which he was as prone to boast I think, left me (a paragon of purity) a-shudder. No doubt about it: O'Neill spoke with authority about tarts, trollopes [*sic*] and tramps and there were confessional aspects of his bouts with that breed which I, for one, will never be cajoled—even on pain of threatened torture—to repeat. But that he was abnormally concupiscent (to put it politely) there can be, I think, no doubt.

One midnight soon after *Strange Interlude* opened on Broadway at the old Golden Theatre on West 58th Street (the play won unprecedented critical acclaim to a degree hitherto unknown in America) O'Neill and I were sitting alone, chatting quietly.[85] With an insouciance which I later observed was a characteristic he let drop a bomb. He was, he told me, sailing shortly for the Orient, thence to Africa and France; that he would be gone seven or eight months and (final blast) he would be travelling—not with his wife but—with the woman he loved! Pointing to a framed photograph of a striking, alluring brunette on his dresser I asked (suspecting as much; I had seen the picture since my first visit) whether she was the woman. He nodded she was. Then he told me he thought I had better be going as she was arriving shortly. I departed into the midnight wonder.

The woman in question was actress Carlotta Monterey whom he had met seven years before while appearing in his play *The Hairy Ape* at the old, stable-renovated Provincetown Playhouse. He married Miss Monterey soon after obtaining a divorce from Agnes Boulton, his second wife (then living at Spithead, Bermuda) who bore him two children—Oona (now the wife of Charles Chaplin) and Shane, the once-afflicted dope-addict now living, I believe, in Ireland. His first marriage at nineteen endured a year and produced a son, Eugene O'Neill Jr., who taught Greek at Yale University before his suicide—he put a bullet through his head—in Greenwich Village many years ago.[86] There were no offspring from this third and last union.

Eugene O'Neill died in 1953 at Marblehead, Mass., (at age 65)[87] where he spent his remaining years, broken in body and perhaps in spirit. A chronicle of those years cries out to be written. It might disclose a story grimmer than any he ever put on paper. And it might properly be called *The Tragedian's Tragedy*. An elegy, published 330 years earlier in memory of an infinitely better and more famous dramatist (i.e. William Shakespeare) could equally apply to the last years of O'Neill's life:

> "If tragedies might any Prologue have,
> All those he made, would scarce make one to this."[88]

And what of my reaction to O'Neill after that memorable excitement-fraught year of 1928 when I first met him? Our meetings during the ensuing five years were as compact of enthusiasm (on my part) and idolization as ever. But I must confess—quite gratefully, I might add—that at age twenty three the hero-worship neurosis disappeared forever. It left me because I began reading, and loving, the time-tested classics, which gave me an esthetic perspective heretofore lacking. I realized there had been dramatists in the world who had reached heights of grandeur to which O'Neill, *at his best*, could never approach. By comparison with the giants of dramatic literature O'Neill was puny and puerile—earth-bound-writing competently enough for, and of, the glorious (and glorified) stereotypes of the times, ordinary humanity made heroic by an unheroic contemporary talent. O'Neill was imprisoned in his own captive outlook.

Aeschylus, Sophocles, Euripides, Marlowe, Shakespeare, Corneille and other dramatic gargantuans[89] (who treated their heroes in an uncommon fashion and *therefore* created uncommon heroes) were the antibodies that saved me from the insidious O'Neill infection.

But, looking back, I cherish the association I had with Eugene O'Neill. He was the first writer to enkindle in me a love of tragedy. He respected those primary, inarticulate passions which link man to his primeval past. If for nothing else Eugene O'Neill will be remembered. He had the ability to impart, better than any other modern playwright, elemental passions in an elementary manner!

# 4
# Europe, Georgia, the Theatre Guild, California (1928–1937)

In 1928 O'Neill left his second wife, Agnes. He sailed to Europe with Carlotta Monterey and, after spending some time in a rented villa in southern France, they traveled to China. They settled into the Château du Plessis (the name of which they frequently abbreviated to "Le Plessis"), near Tours, France, in June 1929, and were married in Paris the following month. In 1929 O'Neill received the Pulitzer Prize for *Strange Interlude*, and *Dynamo* was produced by the Theatre Guild. In 1931 he returned to the United States for the Theatre Guild production of *Mourning Becomes Electra*, a critical and popular success. After living briefly in New York, the couple moved to Sea Island, Georgia, where they built a twenty-room house. After the failure of *Days Without End* in 1934, O'Neill began work on the nine-play cycle, "A Tale of Possessors Self-Dispossessed," which he intended to be his major work, but he was plagued by health problems. Looking for a better climate, the O'Neills moved first to Seattle, then to Danville, California, outside San Francisco, where they built Tao House. O'Neill was awarded the Nobel Prize for Literature in 1936.

In these reminiscences Louis Fladger describes his shipboard friendship with O'Neill. John Lardner speaks of O'Neill's reverence for the newspaperman Sparrow Robertson. Bennett Cerf recounts his trip to Georgia to sign O'Neill as one of the first three writers for his new Random House publishing company. Lawrence Langner, Theresa Helburn, and Rouben Mamoulian describe O'Neill's relationship with his long-term producer, the Theatre Guild. Brooks Atkinson interviews O'Neill about *Ah, Wilderness!* in 1933, and George Jean Nathan describes him in France and in New York. When Eugene and Carlotta O'Neill moved to California in 1937, Maxine Edie Benedict was hired to serve as a private nurse. She describes her developing professional and personal relationship with the O'Neills.

# 34 / Louis Fladger

Louis Fladger (1894–1963) was born in Boston and served in World War I. After the war he lived in San Francisco and served as a purser for several shipping lines. In 1929 he moved to the Hartford area, where he spent most of his time before moving to Miami, his final home.

Source: "Eugene O'Neill Friendship Formed by West Hartford Man while on Shipboard," *Hartford Courant* 14 October 1929: 13.

A glimpse of Eugene O'Neill which ripened into friendship, a dance with royalty, acquaintances with world-known personages and strange foreign ports, all these have been a part of the work-a-day life of Louis Fladger, of 29 Ardmore Road, West Hartford, until recently purser on the Dollar Line steamship *President Monroe*. Possibly no one aboard ship has the opportunity to become acquainted with the passengers as does the purser, and in the nine round-the-world voyages made by Mr. Fladger in the three years he served the Dollar Line he became acquainted with many well-known persons.

Mr. Fladger became acquainted with Eugene O'Neill early this summer, when the famous playwright was aboard his ship on the way to Italy after an attack of tropical fever which had left him wasted and an invalid.[1] The author of several well known plays based on sea life and a former sailor himself, O'Neill was forced to spend much of his time in his cabin. He was traveling incognito and required certain special service which came under the direction of the purser, and in this manner Mr. Fladger met him.

On the voyage he was under the care of the ship's surgeon, and a nurse or his fiancée were constantly with him during his waking hours. He became attracted to the young purser, and the two spent long hours in discussing matters of common interest. When Italy was reached he insisted on having the purser come with him on a long shore trip and with O'Neill's fiancée, the two men made visits to several inland cities by motor.

O'Neill and his fiancée remained in Europe and were married some time later, but Mr. Fladger keeps up a correspondence with the playwright, and was recently informed that O'Neill has recovered much of his strength and the couple are living happily in a villa in Italy.[2]

# 35 / John Lardner

John Abbott Lardner (1912–1960) was a son of the famous writer Ring Lardner (1885–1933). Like his father, he was a humorist who wrote mostly about sports. His sportswriting has been collected in the *John Lardner Reader* (2010), edited by John Schulian.

Source: John Lardner, "O'Neill's Back," *Look* 26 February 1952: 4.

At about the same time *The Shrike* set up shop,[3] two plays were revived from the works of a great writer who has at times been accused of circus effects, of involuntary hokum—of lack of control, as they say in baseball. *Desire Under the Elms* and *"Anna Christie,"* both by Eugene O'Neill, came back to Broadway.[4] It turns out that there is no patch of clumsiness or over-writing in either of these that can make you forget for a minute that they are true, profound, enduring plays. *Desire Under the Elms*, in spite of its old fashioned trimmings of language and manner, seemed especially timeless and real; it is one of the best of O'Neill's non-marathon pieces. Celeste Holm, an extremely chic and well-tailored girl in her previous performances, demonstrates that *"Anna Christie"* is every actress's dream by playing the sad and seedy heroine nearly as well as Garbo did, years ago.[5] In short, Mr. O'Neill keeps his place as the best playwright this country has ever had.

I will carry on no further in these reverent, literary terms about the maestro, because experience has taught me that it can lead to embarrassment. Once, when O'Neill lived in the south of France, a party of worshipful, deeply drama-minded critics made a pilgrimage from Paris to see him. With them, just for the ride, went a part-time sports writer who was a fugitive from Pernod and the pawnshops. For a day or so, the conversation at O'Neill's shrine dealt with dramatic technique and greatness from Sophocles to O'Neill. Then O'Neill interrupted it to say "Does anyone here know Sparrow Robertson?" The late Sparrow Robertson, sports columnist of the *Paris Herald*, was illiteracy's most famous product, the worst writer in Europe, the strongest prop of the brandy trade.[6] The visiting sports writer admitted he knew Sparrow. "He's my hero," said O'Neill eagerly. "Tell me all about him." From then on, the talk was only between O'Neill and the sports writer, and only about Sparrow Robertson.

"I'll get you his autograph," said the sports writer, when the party broke up, and O'Neill beamed.

# 36 / Bennett Cerf

Bennett Alfred Cerf (1898–1971) was born and brought up in New York City, receiving his BA from Columbia University and a Litt B from the Columbia School of Journalism. He worked briefly as a reporter, and was made vice president of Boni & Liveright publishers after investing in the business in the early 1920s. There he became acquainted with Eugene O'Neill. In 1925 he and his friend Donald Klopfer (1902–1986) bought the Modern Library from Liveright and founded Random House, which would eventually grow to become the biggest publishing company in the United States. Cerf became a popular figure as a television show panelist and compiler of joke and riddle books in the 1940s and 1950s. Eugene O'Neill was the first important author he signed for Random House, and they remained friends as well as author and publisher for the rest of O'Neill's life.

Source: Bennett Cerf, *At Random: The Reminiscences of Bennett Cerf* (New York: Random House, 1977), 33, 81–86.

Eugene O'Neill was too much of a brawler for me in those early days, a real wild man, but I loved him. He spoke very slowly and hesitated several times in a sentence. He'd say, "Let's . . . uh . . . take a walk . . . uh . . . down Broadway tonight." But to Gene, I would listen patiently. He'd already published *The Moon of the Caribbees and Six Other Plays of the Sea* and had won Pulitzer Prizes for *Beyond the Horizon* and *Anna Christie*. [. . . ]

A few months before Horace's[7] death his old firm had gone into bankruptcy and its assets had been sold for a fraction of their real value. It is ironic to consider that if Pell's advice had been heeded back in 1925[8] and Horace had not sold The Modern Library to Donald and me, both he and his company might have weathered the Depression. We prospered because of that purchase and built a base for major expansion in the thirties, during which we added some illustrious names to the Random House list. The first two of these became available, also ironically, because of the Liveright difficulties.

After the firm's collapse, it was obvious there was going to be a raid on what few important authors it had left. Everybody was making offers for Eugene O'Neill, and also for one of the leading American poets who was on the Liveright list, Robinson Jeffers. Those were the two I wanted most, and I also wanted Sam Adams—Samuel Hopkins Adams.[9] But O'Neill was the prize. His agent was Richard Madden, and every publisher in New York made a beeline for him when it became known that Liveright was in difficulties. I had a much better idea; I flew down to Sea Island [Georgia], where Gene and his wife, Carlotta, lived. Gene met me, and I spent two days with the O'Neills. Carl Van Vechten and Fania Marinoff,[10] his wife, were also there at that time.

Eugene O'Neill was the most beautiful man I ever met, and when I say beautiful, I mean in the sense that to look at him was soul-satisfying. He looked just the way a great playwright ought to but practically never does—brooding, piercing eyes, a wonderful smile and a superb figure. He was a great swimmer; he could swim five or six miles at a stretch. As I have said, he talked very slowly, and he would often hesitate in the middle of a sentence. I'm a very impatient man and I keep interrupting everybody all the time. I'm not even aware of it; I even did it with President Roosevelt.

But Eugene O'Neill was the only man I ever knew who without trying could shut me up. I would sit quietly and wait for him to finish his long sentences with the long pauses in the middle. He was one of my heroes, and when anybody asks me to name five or six great men I have met in my life, Eugene O'Neill is always one of them.

At Sea Island, I found him much changed from the wild man I had known at Liveright. He had lived down along the waterfront in those days, among all those men in flophouses, a bunch of drunks who were always in trouble. He was so often at Bellevue to dry out that they knew him there by his first name. He had stopped drinking now, partly for health reasons and partly because he had matured; instead of being a young carouser, he had become a dignified gentleman having honors thrust upon him, which at first he avoided. Gene never went to one of his first nights; instead, he'd wander around the city. The night *Strange Interlude* opened he met an old sailor friend, who said, "Gene O'Neill! What the hell are you doing these days?" At that very minute his greatest hit was being played on Broadway!

It was down on Sea Island that I really became Gene's friend. Up until then I was just one of the adoring public that he knew from Liveright, where I was a kid who would hang around him like a faithful little dog. But this time I was becoming somebody, and Gene was the great American playwright. We took long walks on the beach and talked and came to know each other.

Of course, from sixty to eighty percent of the time spent with any playwright or novelist is usually devoted to talking about that author's work. Obviously, a writer loves to talk about himself, and it's a publisher's business to let him. Also, O'Neill fascinated me. This was the life I had chosen for myself, and when he was talking about himself and his plays, I was in heaven; so we got along very well. One thing he talked about at length was a project already in his mind: the Cycle of Seven Plays, which was going to be the story of an American family through many generations, starting back in the Pilgrim days in New England and coming down to the present. The history of this family would be the history of America. The Cycle never came to pass. O'Neill became sicker and sicker, and finally died—leaving only a few of those plays finished, including *A Moon for the Misbegotten*; but none of them was yet ready for production.[11]

When I saw him in Sea Island he had not been married to Carlotta too long, and he was still quite a vigorous man. Carlotta is a story in herself—one of the most beautiful girls in America, brought up in a strict Catholic way out in California, I believe, and then off to New York. When I first met her she was living with Ralph Barton, the famous *New Yorker* illustrator, the one I got to do a catalogue cover for Boni and Liveright.[12] When I went to make that deal [see figure 10] with him, the hostess at his place was Carlotta Monterey. But when I got to Sea Island, she pretended she had never seen me before. She knew damn well she had, and I knew damn well she knew she had, too, but the circumstances under which we had met were not permissible for discussion.[13]

When Ralph Barton died years later, he had never forgotten Carlotta, who was not an easy woman to forget. Barton left a suicide note, saying that the only woman he had ever really loved was Carlotta. Someone called her at the Madison Hotel and said, "Mrs. O'Neill, we want you to know that Ralph Barton has died and left a note about you." She snapped, "Why are you disturbing me while I'm having my lunch? I haven't the faintest interest in Mr. Barton," and slammed down the phone. That's the kind of woman she was.[14]

Gene had met her in 1922, when she was acting in *The Hairy Ape* [see figure 16], his play about a brute stoker down in the hold of a boat and a society girl up on deck who is mesmerized by him. Louis Wolheim, a very wonderful actor who later became famous in *What Price Glory?*, played the hairy ape, and Carlotta Monterey was the society girl.[15] Gene saw her and fell for her. By the time I got down to Sea Island, Carlotta had become a saintlike creature who raised an angry eyebrow when you used the word "damn" in front of her—she was now the great lady. Gene absolutely adored her, but as life went on, theirs came to be more and more of a love-hate relationship.

So while all the other publishers were besieging Richard Madden with offers, I signed up Gene O'Neill personally. We shook hands and the whole deal was made. Madden got his commission, but he was very surprised when O'Neill told him that he was going to come with Random House, since all the big publishers wanted him and we were still beginners.

One of the conditions made by Eugene O'Neill was that I give a job to his old friend Saxe Commins,[16] who had come to Liveright as his editor just about the time I was leaving. We gave Saxe a job, and he turned out to be one of the great men of Random House, a wonderful man, and was our senior editor for many years, until he died.

I came back to New York elated. We had O'Neill, and this gave me a leg up on getting Robinson Jeffers, whom I had never met because he had never visited the Liveright office, but luckily I was the one who had written to him when we were getting his poetry together, so he knew about me. I hustled out to California and signed him up. So we got Liveright's two prizes. [. . . ] Eugene O'Neill was quite different from other playwrights; his books were great best sellers.

Around the middle of 1933 we proudly sent out our notice: "Random House is pleased to announce that it has become the exclusive publisher in America of the books of Eugene O'Neill and Robinson Jeffers." We listed as "available for immediate delivery" eleven volumes of O'Neill plays and five books of poetry by Jeffers—at prices that would not be believed today! Also: we would publish that fall *Give Your Heart to the Hawks* by Jeffers and two new plays by O'Neill.

The first play we did of O'Neill's was absolutely out of his general line. Instead of writing one of those brooding, morbid tragedies he was so famous for, he wrote the comedy *Ah, Wilderness!* It starred George M. Cohan.[17] It was the first time Cohan had ever appeared in a play other than his own. The book was a huge success, and it was a happy start. Our second O'Neill play was *Days Without End*, one that he loved, but it was a complete failure.

# 37 / Lawrence Langner

Lawrence Langner (1890–1962) was born in Great Britain but lived most of his life in the United States He was a patent attorney who had a great interest in the theater and in 1914 was one of the founders of the Washington Square Players. In 1918 the Players disbanded, but Langner, along with Philip Moeller (1880–1958), Helen Westley (1875–1942), and Theresa Helburn (1887–1959), reconstituted it as the Theatre Guild, which was to become the preeminent Broadway producing organization for drama that made a claim to literary quality, particularly the plays of George Bernard Shaw and Eugene O'Neill. The Guild produced seven of O'Neill's plays, starting with *Marco Millions* in 1928 and ending with *The Iceman Cometh* in 1946.

Source: Lawrence Langner, *The Magic Curtain: The Story of a Life in Two Fields, Theatre and Invention, by the Founder of the Theatre Guild* (New York: E. P. Dutton, 1951), 228–37, 281–82, 283–87.

I first met Eugene O'Neill at Provincetown in the summer of 1917. He lived on the edge of the ocean in an abandoned Coast Guard Station, which was formerly the home of the famous Mabel Dodge,[18] and to reach his home it was necessary to trudge for about three miles across the sand dunes. Rumor had it that Robert Edmond Jones had decorated the house in the gay blue-and-white color scheme which it then wore, and the large room which formerly contained the coast guard lifeboat was now the living room.

On the beach just below the house was the wreck of a large schooner, and O'Neill, costumed in a bathing suit, took me onto the beach where, somewhat superfluously, I emptied the sand out of my shoes. The resounding surf, the background of the wrecked sailing ship, and the lithe, muscular body of O'Neill, his dark Irish eyes set deep in his sun-tanned face, made an appropriate O'Neill setting for my first meeting with our foremost playwright, with whose destiny my own was later linked for so many years. We talked over the production of *In the Zone* by the Washington Square Players,[19] after which he invited me to join him in a swim. This I refused, being no swimmer in a high surf (or even in a low one), whereupon O'Neill plunged in and displayed his prowess with a swift overarm stroke of which he was very proud. Like Bernard Shaw, O'Neill's favorite sport is swimming; indeed it is the only form of athletics in which he has indulged during the time I have known him. My last view of him, as I bade him farewell at this first meeting, was his silhouette at the side of the house, the ocean behind him and the wind blowing his hair awry. It was also my last view of the old Coast Guard Station, for the restless Atlantic swallowed it up a few years later and not a trace now remains but the endless ocean and the lonely dunes.

Ever since I read O'Neill's first volume of one-act plays, I regarded him as our outstanding American dramatist. In the days of the Washington Square Players I helped bring about the rapprochement between that organization and O'Neill, which resulted in our producing his *In the Zone* which was later booked in vaudeville by Al Lewis and Max Gordon.[20] O'Neill once expressed the opinion that the Provincetown Players were artists while the Washington Square Players were an "uptown" commercial theatre and not worthy to be regarded as competition. We in turn regarded the Provincetown Players as "amateurs" in everything except their playwrights, O'Neill and Susan Glaspell.

I was determined to bring the Theatre Guild and Eugene O'Neill together, but all my early attempts ended in failure. 'Gene, on his side, wanted to work with the Guild.

[. . .]

Later on, hearing that 'Gene was writing a new play, I got in touch with him and learned that he was working on *The Fountain* and *Welded*. We were much interested in the actor Jacob Ben Ami[21] at the time and were looking for a play for him. I visited 'Gene at his home in Ridgefield, Connecticut. It was called Brook Farm, and was a low-lying colonial farmhouse with Revolutionary associations. 'Gene met me and was very cordial. We talked about the Provincetown Players and the necessity for better acting of their plays. Later on, he permitted the Guild to read *Welded* which did not meet with the Board's approval. Finally, we bought *The Fountain* but decided later not to produce it. Thus, all my efforts to bring the Guild and O'Neill together had failed. Five plays were offered by 'Gene and five refusals were made by the Guild.

[. . .]

In the spring of 1927 I suffered from a severe cold and was advised by my doctor to take a couple of weeks off to recuperate. By this time the producing firm with which O'Neill had associated himself had dissolved,[22] and O'Neill spent most of his time in Bermuda. I had a hunch that a visit to Bermuda might not only restore me to health but also enable me to restore the personal relation which had formerly existed between O'Neill and myself, and which had very naturally become cloudy for the reasons I have explained above. My hunch turned out to be correct.

O'Neill welcomed me warmly and we had some talks about the possibility of the Guild producing *Marco Millions.* From that he went on to discuss the future of the American theatre, and what he hoped to contribute toward it. Walking up and down the sandy beach near his white-roofed coral house which had been built by a Seventeenth-Century privateer, and stood at the edge of the sea, 'Gene explained that he was experimenting with ways and means to break down "realism" in the theatre, and had just finished a play in which the characters not only talked to one another but also spoke their thoughts in a form of aside which he thought the audience would accept. The idea fascinated me and I asked him if I might read the play, which he informed me was called *Strange Interlude.* He also told me that it would take six hours to play it. In view of our experience with *Back to Methuselah,* this did not daunt me.[23]

A few days later I was invited to O'Neill's home for a swim and dinner afterward, and I spent the evening with him discussing the theme of the play. He told me that he had already promised it to a well-known American actress who was his first choice, but that if I liked the play and she did not, I might have it for the Guild.[24] Meanwhile, I could read it and let him know what I thought of it. He then handed me the first six acts of the manuscript, which I still possess. It was half again as thick as an ordinary play, for not only was it a double-length play, but so long that nearly forty pages were subsequently cut out of it. Clutching the precious manuscript to my bosom I returned in the horse cab which had been ordered for me (there were no automobiles in Bermuda at the time) and drove along the shore road in a gale which at times seemed so strong that I feared horse cab, *Strange Interlude* and myself would all be blown together into the sea.

I went to bed intending to read at least part of the play before I fell asleep; the storm outside grew more and more violent as the play grew more and more exciting. The tropical thunder and lightning, and the fierce howling of the gale which began to assume hurricane proportions, failed to interrupt me. All night long I read and read, and at four o'clock in the morning, my eyes strained and throbbing, I finished the sixth act. Before I went to sleep I examined my feelings about the play as far as I had read. I judged it one of the greatest plays of all time.

The storm died down during the night, and the next morning was bright and clear; as soon as I was awake I telephoned 'Gene and told him how enthusiastic I was about the play. He invited me over to his home again. This time he definitely promised me that if the actress to whom he had offered the play did not care to do it (and he thought there were certain reasons why she might not), the Theatre Guild could have it. Then he gave me a breath-taking exhibition of his overarm stroke which I photographed with my cine-kodak. 'Gene at this time was about thirty-eight years old,[25] and at the height of his mental and physical powers. He was built like an athlete, his deep black eyes set in a sunburnt Irish face, as handsome as one could hope to see anywhere, and the skin of his lean body was the color and texture of mahogany with underlying muscles of whipcord. At no time before or since have I seen him in such good health. I luckily recorded his appearance at the time with my movie camera.

O'Neill, after condensing both *Marco Millions* and *Strange Interlude*, came to New York, and he stayed at our home on Eleventh Street. He was with us for about two weeks, and we went into all phases of the two plays. He saw very few friends while with us but he finally consented to our giving a small party for him. "The reason I avoid parties is because I'm extremely bashful," he told me. "In my younger days I used to drink in order to get up the nerve to meet people. Since I've quit drinking, it's become worse. When I once started, I was like a sailor on shore leave—a holdover from my sea-faring days." He told me in Bermuda that he had entirely sworn off drinking, and gave as one reason the effect of alcohol on the brain as explained to him by a doctor friend. "It's just like turning the albumen in your brain into the white of a poached egg!" This vivid and horrible picture made me a hesitant drinker for the many years which have intervened.

During all the time I knew O'Neill, and this goes back to when we were both in our twenties, I never saw him drink any kind of liquor. However, he assured me that he was, in his youth, a notoriously stalwart drinker, and he, in my opinion, built this up into the proportions of a legend. He told the story that at one time he was seated in the Provincetown Playhouse watching one of his plays when a young woman in the seat in front of him remarked to her escort, "Do you know that Eugene O'Neill, the author of this play, is a terrible drunkard?" "No," replied the young man. "Yes, and not only does he drink to excess, but he takes drugs, too." This was too much for 'Gene. "Excuse me, Miss," he said to the young lady, "you are wrong there. I do not take drugs!"

During the many visits I had with 'Gene I learned to know him not merely as a writer but as a person. I always felt in his presence that I was in the presence of greatness and nobility of thought. The kindness of his smile, the gentleness of his spirit, the philosophical detachment of his mind, his Olympian view of human destiny, were not only inspiring but so endeared him to you that you wanted to lay down your life in his service. This ability to inspire hero-worship in me, which both he and G.B.S. [George Bernard Shaw] had in common, was not always conducive to my doing my best work in their interests, for I was often too willing to give in to their foibles when my own better judgment told me to put up a tougher fight against them for their own good.

[. . .]

With an excellent cast which included Earl Larimore, Glenn Anders and Tom Powers, the play [*Strange Interlude*] went into rehearsal and opened at the John Golden Theatre on January 23, 1928. The rehearsals were marked by considerable argument, for time after time 'Gene insisted on cutting out comedy lines or "laughs" when, in his opinion, they interfered with the emotional build of a scene. Philip Moeller,[26] who directed the play so brilliantly, adored the comedy and every time 'Gene solemnly cut out an amusing line, Phil would plead vociferously for its return. "I hope he doesn't realize that line is funny," Phil once remarked to me, "for if he does, out it'll go." Every now and again 'Gene would retire to the lounge with me, and give vent to his feeling about some of the acting in language he certainly did not learn in school at Stamford.[27] He was never too pleased with his actors in rehearsal, and once told me that he adopted the technique of asides which showed what the characters were thinking in *Strange Interlude* because the majority of actors were incompetent to do so. This, however, can be taken with a grain of salt, like some of Shaw's remarks on the same subject. No author ever succeeds in getting a complete realization of the part he has created, and he blames the actor because the actor is unable to achieve the impossible. On the other hand, I have seen many creative actors add dimensions to a part of which the author never dreamed.

[. . .]

In the spring of 1933, 'Gene and Carlotta invited us to spend a week with them along with Fania Marinoff, who was one of Carlotta's good friends. In due course we arrived at Casa Genotta, a beautiful home in Spanish style which the O'Neills had built a few yards from the broad sandy beach [in Sea Island, Georgia]. The house was arranged around a courtyard, and Carlotta had the architect design one wing so that the end which looked out over the ocean was in the form of the stern of a medieval sailing vessel, and in this end was located 'Gene's study in which he wrote his plays.

Carlotta, one of those rare women who was born beautiful and will remain so all her life, had spent a considerable part of her early life in England and the Continent, and was at home anywhere.[28] All her talents and efforts at the time went into making an attractive home and surroundings in which 'Gene could have privacy for his work, and to this she dedicated herself with almost fanatic fervor. Her home at Sea Island was decorated with unerring taste, and her mixture of Danish and Dutch blood made her a meticulous chatelaine. Armina,[29] who prides herself on her housekeeping, always returned from the O'Neills' with a feeling of inferiority. "I'll never be able to run a household as smoothly and successfully as Carlotta," she would say in despair.

In Casa Genotta the household revolved around 'Gene's writing. In the morning he worked in his study until noon. Then, attired in his dressing gown, he came down to the beach where Carlotta, Armina, Fania and I were sunning. After a while we went swimming in the sandy colored water which is, to me, one of the most unattractive features of Sea Island. 'Gene was the best swimmer and swam far out to sea, followed by Armina; the rest of us hugged the beach.

The island was at its best at the time of year we were there, but it was humid and hot in summer and by no means the paradise the O'Neills expected it would be. Indeed, so damp was the atmosphere that special bronze had to be used for all the window hardware, for ordinary metal would rust away. Another unpleasant feature of the island came to light when I asked Carlotta why all the bushes in the charming patio were clipped up from the ground for a foot or so. "That's so we can see if there are any snakes under them." Then she explained that the island abounded in rattlesnakes, and 'Gene added smilingly that these were relatively harmless compared to the pretty little pink coral snakes which also disported themselves in this paradise. Fania, who hated snakes even more than I did, trod very gingerly around the countryside after this, and I was never quite at ease either. But our visit was happy and restful, and we talked over plans for the future.

'Gene, it appeared, was writing a new play, *Days Without End*, which would show that love could last beyond life. In writing it, it seemed as though he had gone back to his early religious feelings and was affirming his belief in the afterlife. I have always believed that this play was inspired by Carlotta and that in it 'Gene sought to express his hope for a love which transcended mortal life and could last forever. This romantic desire for the permanence of love on the part of both of them could be explained by their earlier unhappy experiences, as well as by the romantic streak which made 'Gene sail before the mast and roam around the world. The regularity of home life at Casa Genotta made for ideal working conditions, and just as Le Plessis had produced a background for the enormous task of *Mourning Becomes Electra* so, here on Sea Island looking out over the ocean, 'Gene brooded over other plays to be written in the future.[30]

[. . .]

On August 14th [1933] I wrote him that, for a variety of reasons, we preferred to produce the comedy first. During the rehearsals of *Ah, Wilderness!* 'Gene attended the theatre regularly and made considerable cuts. Indeed he was usually extremely co-operative in regard to cutting, and once he was in a cutting mood, he cut faster than the director asked in rehearsals. He was not at all happy, however, when the play took to the road, and he had to spend a week in Pittsburgh. I had the greatest difficulty in getting him to come to the theatre at all after the dress rehearsal, and even then he would come in only for certain scenes. I asked him why he had this phobia against attending performances of his own plays, and he told me that it did not relate to his own plays, but to being present in a crowded theatre, which made it very difficult for him to sit still and watch the play. On other occasions, I have been with him in crowded arenas such as Madison Square Garden where he would spend hours watching the six-day bicycle race, and more recently at prize fights in Madison Square Garden, where he did not appear to have the slightest discomfort in mixing with crowds of thousands in a large arena.

[. . .]

In March [1934] Armina and I spent some days at Nassau, and on our way back we paid a second visit to the O'Neills. I found 'Gene deeply engrossed in his new cycle (I called it his six-day bicycle race) for which he was stripped for action like a pugilist. His habits were most regular, and everything ran like clockwork in Carlotta's comfortable and tastefully decorated home.

The first morning I was there, after doing his morning's work, 'Gene came out and sat on the beach where I was taking a sun bath and as we both looked out over the ocean, the waves breaking at our feet a few yards away, he told me about his plan for his new plays.[31] They would take literally years to write. We were not to expect to receive the first of them until the last was completed because he would be making changes in them until the very last one was done. Each play would be complete in itself, yet each of the plays would be part of a whole, which he called *A Touch of the Poet*. The plays would deal with several generations of a family, an admixture of old Puritan New England stock and Irish-American blood, and it was the Irish in the admixture which gave the cycle its title, for the touch of Irish blood gave the touch of the poet. Characters were to be in their youth in one play while they would be parents or grandparents in later plays in which the main stories were based on the lives of their children and children's children. Galsworthy's *The Forsyte Saga*[32] seemed like child's play in comparison, as 'Gene traced the effect of the grandparents on the children and their grandchildren, reminding me of the Biblical prophesies [*sic*] as to the sins of the parents being visited upon their children unto the third and fourth generations. I marveled at the scope of the work he was attempting, and wondered whether, in the hot damp climate of Sea Island, he would have the strength to last out the ordeal he had set for himself. Later on, Carlotta and Armina joined us. We went in swimming and 'Gene swam out far into the sea, his head and powerful arms pushing through the green-brown water like a lonely amphibian, belonging neither to the sea nor to the land. But I was troubled about the climate of Sea Island and its effect on 'Gene. No matter how hard Carlotta tried, she fought a losing battle against the dampness coming from the warm sea air laden with salt moisture, and the continuous heat of summer. 'Gene continued with his work and reported the progress he was making in a letter to me of August 12, 1936.

> I hope you yourself don't believe the Cycle is "an American life" in any usual sense of the word, or you're going to be disappointed. I mean, I'm not giving a damn whether the dramatic event of each play has any significance in the growth of the country or not, as long as it is significant in the spiritual and psychological history of the American family in the plays. The Cycle is primarily just that, the history of a family. What larger significance I can give my people as extraordinary examples and symbols in the drama of American possessiveness and materialism is something else again. But I don't want anyone to get the idea that this Cycle is much concerned with what is usually understood by American history, for it isn't. As for economic history—which so many seem to mistake for the *only* history just now—I am not much interested in economic determinism, but only in the self-determinism of which the economic is one phase, and by no means the most revealing—at least, not to me.

He added:

> Try a Cycle sometime, I advise you—that is, I would advise you to, if I hated you! A lady bearing quintuplets is having a debonair, carefree time of it by comparison.
>
> A hell of a hot oppressive summer here. Carlotta and I are neck and neck toward the Olympic and World's sweating record! We just continually drop and drip.

The dropping and dripping ultimately became too much for 'Gene, and with considerable reluctance, they left Sea Island in the hopes of finding a better climate in the Pacific Northwest. It was during this period that 'Gene won the Nobel Prize for literature, which of course pleased all of us greatly. Later, at my request, he showed me, with almost childlike pleasure, the black box which he opened to display the large gold medallion symbolizing the greatest honor awarded to an American playwright. There was not the slightest suggestion either of undue pride or modesty on his part. He took it in his stride.

# 38 / Brooks Atkinson

For information about Justin Brooks Atkinson, see the headnote to chapter 32.

Source: Brooks Atkinson, "O'Neill Off Duty; He Tells in an Interview What Is and What Is Not Autobiographical in *Ah, Wilderness!*" *New York Times* 8 October 1933: X1.

With *Ah, Wilderness!* off his chest and the notices enthusiastic and the prospects cheerful, Mr. O'Neill felt like talking about anything. He was even willing to listen; and from the point of view of the interviewer that was bad. Mrs. O'Neill efficiently intercepted the telephone calls, the messengers and the waiters, thus isolating a corner of New York where an amiable dramatist could call his soul his own. And at high noon on the day after the premiere his soul was in excellent condition. Until December when his next play, *Days Without End*, goes into rehearsal he was to be scot free. His enthusiasms spread the conversation alarmingly. Sea Island Beach, the Adirondacks, Medan in Sumatra, swimming—climates, Cecil Rhodes,[33] George M. Cohan—it hardly mattered what or which he talked about. After all, he did not have to write the interview. And so he could genially waste time by observing that the whippoorwill family (suborder Caprimulgi) has four branches in North America—chuck-will's-widow, Eastern whip-poor-will, Eastern nighthawk and Florida nighthawk—as though it mattered on Broadway. By careful checking in the manuals that statement of scientific classifications turns out to be true, but nothing journalistically constructive is ever accomplished by such discussions.

As for *Ah, Wilderness!* the new play at the Guild Theatre, it is "a comedy of recollection," as the title-page of the printed text explains, and it is full of things for which Mr. O'Neill has great affection. The romantic biographers have given him a picturesque background of pot-houses, ships, sailors and farmers. But he is eager to point out that that is not the complete story. Most of his summers and at least one full year he spent in New London, Conn., where his father had a house and owned a good deal of property, including the Monte Cristo garage, which was the local agency for the Buick car.[34] There are fragments of autobiography in *Ah, Wilderness!* In 1906 Mr. O'Neill was 17 years of age, like Richard Miller in the play. At that time Mr. O'Neill also was reading *The Quintessence of Ibsenism*,[35] Swinburne [36]and Omar Khayyam,[37] and he, too, was convinced by what bowdlerized information he could get that Oscar Wilde's crime was bigamy.[38] There are other family items strewn through the play. Like Nat Miller, the newspaper proprietor of the play, Mr. O'Neill's father always believed that "there's a peculiar oil in bluefish" that invariably poisoned him, although he ate bluefish under the name of weakfish all his life; and he also repeatedly told, each time as though it were new, the story of how he saved a boyhood chum from drowning. On these occasions it was the custom of the two O'Neill brats to lower their heads politely and snicker to themselves.

But the historical background of *Ah, Wilderness!* hardly goes deeper than that. Crack-brained and turbulent as Mr. O'Neill may have been in his high school days, his experiences were not those of Richard Miller, and James O'Neill, the romantic actor, was not the prototype of Nat Miller, the newspaper publisher. Nor were there a younger brother and sister in the O'Neill family. A brother ten years older than Eugene was the only other offspring.[39] So the members of the spirited Miller family group are to be taken as representative folk of that time in any one of those "large small towns" in Connecticut, and the episodes are drawn from things that he saw and heard quite apart from personal history. He has great affection for the sort of solid family life *Ah, Wilderness!* discloses. If he had to choose among people, he would select the same kind today; and he believes that fundamentally they remain very much what they were in those nostalgic days—loyal, kindly and high-minded. His boyhood, particularly in Stamford, where he went to school; and in New London, where he spent his Summers, was a good period of his life; he enjoys recalling it. Perhaps that is why *Ah, Wilderness!* was the easiest of all his plays to write. A year ago last August the central idea came to him just after he had drearily finished the second draft of *Days Without End*, and he plunged straight into *Ah, Wilderness!* completing the first draft in six weeks. Now that it is on the stage, and acted very much to his taste, with George M. Cohan playing Nat Miller to the hilt, Mr. O'Neill is his own best audience. He is ashamed to admit how much the comedy amuses him. Some things have to be confidential.

At this point, as well as at nearly every other point, the interviewer put in his two cents' worth. Is it not a fact that *Ah, Wilderness!* might as well be tragedy as comedy? Are not the episodes of Lily's blighted love and Richard's wild rebellion against life tragic impulses? In fact, if Mr. O'Neill had written about the Millers in 1924 would *Ah, Wilderness!* have been after the malefic style of *Desire Under the Elms*? In other words, can a writer of tragedy become a writer of comedy by virtue of increasing maturity? But it seems not. For tragic characters are driven by the mad strength that is in them to violent conclusions. Ephraim Cabot of *Desire Under the Elms* goes passionately on to a merciless decision as the result of the flaming will of his own character. And in *Mourning Becomes Electra* Lavinia Mannon seals herself up in a house of doom because she is too overwhelmingly powerful to submit to compromises. Although the characters of *Ah, Wilderness!* face many problems, they are not children of fate. They are not foredoomed by the smashing force of destiny; and *Ah, Wilderness!* is no token of Mr. O'Neill's conversion to the comic mood.

One thing it has done. It has helped Mr. O'Neill to free himself from a formula of tragedy that had begun to imprison him. When he began writing plays some fifteen years ago he was determined to break the formula that had engulfed the American stage. *The Hairy Ape*, *Desire Under the Elms*, *Strange Interlude* and *Mourning Becomes Electra* made it possible for him to speak in any style he chose, and *Strange Interlude* in particular brought into the theatre some phases of character delineation that had previously been the property of the novel. But now Mr. O'Neill suspects that his own formula had begun to enslave him and to control somewhat the fate of his characters. *Ah, Wilderness!* is a holiday in another genre. But in *Days Without End* Mr. O'Neill has broken with the formula. Apparently that period in his career is finished.

To judge by his plans and projects there is a great deal more to come. At the age of 45 Mr. O'Neill is a little grayer around the temples and the lines are a little more firmly drawn on his face, but his eyes have the luster of a man who is in good health and spirits and who is eager to go on vigorously with the job. It is this interviewer's private opinion that the tension has relaxed a good deal. Mr. O'Neill seems to be having a pretty good time; like a good many of the rest of us, he can laugh without brilliant provocation. Unless he disciplines himself to be less genial on the occasion of a formal interview it will soon be impossible to remember exactly what he said. What the interviewer said is always easier to recall.

# 39 / Rouben Mamoulian

Rouben Mamoulian (1897–1987) was born in Tbilisi, Georgia, at that time under Russian rule. He immigrated to England in 1922, where he began directing plays, and moved to the United States the following year to direct plays and opera for the Eastman School of Music in Rochester, New York. His Broadway career began in 1927 with the direction of the Theatre Guild's production of *Porgy*. He directed O'Neill's *Marco Millions* the following year. Mamoulian achieved fame as a director of musicals, including *Oklahoma!* (1943), *Carousel* (1945), *Porgy and Bess* (1935), and *Lost in the Stars* (1949), and he had a twenty-year career as a film director, including the 1931 classic *Dr. Jekyll and Mr. Hyde* and *Blood and Sand (*1941).
For information on Louis Sheaffer, see chapter 3.

Source: Louis Sheaffer, "Interview with Rouben Mamoulian, March 26/59," Louis Sheaffer Collection of Eugene O'Neill Materials, Department of Special Collections, Charles E. Shain Library, Connecticut College, New London.

When *Porgy* opened *Marco Millions* was already being prepared.[40] Lee Simonson[41] had already designed the sets and costumes, with Helburn and Langner supervising, and Phil Moeller was going to direct it. Mr. O'Neill dropped in and saw *Porgy* and made a beeline for their office, told them, "This is the man (Mamoulian) to direct my play." When they told me about this I was very flattered, and they gave me the published play to read. I didn't think it was a very good play . . . I thought the production should be a combination of spectacle and play, a rhythmic production. *Porgy* was highly stylized, rhythmic, and Gene saw that and that's why he wanted me for *Marco*. The critics thought it (*Porgy*) very realistic, but actually it was rhythmic. Reinhardt wrote a letter to Woollcott and put his finger on it.[42]

Well, I read *Marco* and felt that it needed cuts, to give more dramatic flow and tempo. When I told this to the six directors [of the Theatre Guild], about the cuts, they all laughed, and said I couldn't have been around much or I would know that O'Neill doesn't cut. When I said I felt very strongly about them, they said, "You haven't met him yet, why don't you talk with him." An appointment was made, at the Hotel Wentworth, and I took my copy with the cuts marked and question marks (so I wouldn't look too rigid about them). When the door opened and I saw him for the first time the impact was of meeting someone very beautiful, like meeting a Michelangelo or seeing Gary Cooper for the first time in cowboy clothes, to give you a gamut . . . He had burning eyes—they overwhelmed me—very handsome and at the same time inarticulate. Talking was difficult for him . . . It was a small room, about half the size of this one [. . .] with a bed, a bed stand, a little table, one chair, and one window. He sat on his bed and I sat on the one chair and told him, "I want to thank you for the compliment, I'm terribly excited and honored at your wanting me" . . . Suddenly I got cold feet, how could I tell him I felt it needed cutting, but it was a point of no return and I told him. He's one of those men who blush very easily, he flushed, his face got red and he turned and looked at me, "I don't cut my plays afterward. If I'd thought it needed cuts, I'd have made them before it was published."

Mamoulian, "You're a great dramatist and this is a good play—but as long as I'm here why don't you let me show you what I mean." . . . Long pause, and O'Neill, "Show me." I held it out and he told me to sit next to him on the bed . . . I did and put the book on his knees. There was a cut on the first page and I explained why I thought so . . . He didn't say a word but reached out, suddenly for a thick dark-blue pencil on his bedside table and made a large X on the page, and I told him it was too much, just down to here, and he made the change (with his pencil like Zeus with his fork) . . . Every cut I suggested was made. He never once said, "Well, I don't know . . ." but took the pencil and made the cut. Each time it was immediate, he thought about it quickly, agreed, and made the cut.

When this was over, I told him, "Mr. O'Neill, I don't have to tell you my being in the theatre is for poetry and stylization and rhythm." . . . O'Neill, "Well, that's why I want you for this." And I told him I'd like to take up a few things with him about the production. "I've seen the production designs, and they're all too small. This not a small play, physically. I told him of the changes I had in mind regarding sets, costumes and the number of people" . . . He was in complete agreement . . .

When I told the Theatre Guild about this, they said, Do you realize it will raise the cost five to $10,000. The production cost around 32 to $35,000 . . . When Gene attended rehearsals he always sat in back of the theatre. He didn't come every day. He never liked the actor playing Kublai Khan (neither did I, he was under contract), and used to refer to the Khan who is not a Khan.[43] He never talked to the actors. We'd go out to lunch and would talk about the play . . . He wore a long coat with a fur collar, and seemed very proud of it. Said he'd always wanted a coat with a fur collar, and now he could afford one.

He once asked me if I were interested in Americana, something typically American, and said if I were, the best place to see what the American character was like was at the six-day bike races. Would you like to go with me? . . . We sat there for hours, about four hours, on the wooden seats and ate sandwiches and had coffee from paper cups. Nobody recognized him, and that suited him fine.

I didn't see him again until MGM asked me to do a musical version of *Ah, Wilderness* [. . .] The film was eventually called *Summer Holiday*.[44] I had certain ideas about this musical I wanted to talk over with O'Neill. He was staying then at the Barclay, he didn't know I was coming east to see him. When I told the Langners about it, wanting to see O'Neill, they said it was impossible, Carlotta wouldn't let anybody see him. The next day I phoned the hotel and I guess it was Carlotta I spoke to first, told her who I was, and Gene got on, asked me to visit them the next day.

This was the first time I saw Carlotta. She was heavy but I could see that she had been a strikingly handsome woman. She was still attractive, even then . . . We talked about his illness. What hurt him bitterly was that if this were a payment for what he had done in the past, payment for any sin, it wouldn't be so bad. The thing that drove him to distraction was that it wasn't from drinking too much or carousing too much. And he kept saying "But why me, why did it have to happen to me."

She called him "Baby," kept referring to him as "Baby," and seemed terribly concerned about his comfort.

He told me "I know they're going to make this musical but I'll be damned if I know why." . . . I told him, "You wrote a perfect play and I don't have to tell you how I feel about you perfectly [*sic*]. I feel the play says what it set out to say and does it brilliantly. That's why I want to change it. No point in using the play as you wrote it and just adding songs." . . . He said, "Will you repeat that. Because you love me and like my play, you're going to change it." . . . I explained on the stage it was exactly right as it was, but the screen has greater scenic possibilities, and the advantages of color. As an example I told him of the scene where the boy meets the prostitute in the pub. I wanted to start it in a very dull, shabby saloon. As the boy started drinking and with each drink became more drunk, the scene got lighter and lighter, the room changed and the girl changed, became more glamorous and romantic, all this seen through the boy's eyes . . . His eyes sparkled and he said, "Now I'm excited about it. I didn't like the idea at first, making a musical, but now I want to see it."

We had talked for an awful long time and I said you probably ought to rest now, and put on my heavy coat. It was winter, in late 1945 or early '46 . . . He said he'd like me to read a new play but he had only the one script, and Carlotta said, I have my copy—it was very nice of her—and brought it out . . . On the hall desk, there was a drawing of him by the Chinese artist (Mai-Mai Sze)[45] and Gene asked me if I liked it, and when I said yes, he said, "I do, too, this is my favorite, I like it better than any of the photographs. Would you like a copy? Of course I said yes, and he brought out a photostatic copy from the bedroom, asked if I'd like something written on it, and when I said yes, he said, "You'd better take your coat off and talk to Carlotta." . . . From the corner of my eye I saw him pull up a chair and just sit there, an interminably long time, finally took a pen, rested a long time, and all this took half an hour to write one line, "To Rouben Mamoulian, With love and great admiration."

The third and final time I saw him was in Doctors Hospital, in 1947 or '48, and again I was told it was futile to attempt to see him. I called Doctors Hospital, talked with him and said I would like him to meet my wife, Azalea. He invited me for the next day. He had a nice corner room, a shawl, a plaid, over him. I never found him so expansive and so articulate as on this occasion. He was awfully glad to see me, and I told him I was sure he knew what had been happening in the musical theatre, *Oklahoma* and *Carousel*, something new, an integration of all the elements that had gotten away from the conventional musical. Mamoulian, "I wish you would write something special for the musical stage, a musical tragedy." . . . O'Neill, "You know I can't, I can't be funny." . . . Mamoulian, "No, nothing like that—but a musical tragedy. It could be very exciting." . . . He became very interested at the idea, then thought of his hands, "But I can't write, I have to do it in long-hand." . . . I suggested he try a tape-recorder or a sympathetic secretary who could take short-hand, but he said he had to write it out himself.

My wife and I had just come back from a trip to South America, all over South America, and I told him about it . . . He started talking about the time he spent down there, on ships, sleeping on benches, and he was fascinating. For the first time he talked the way he wrote. He'd never been so eloquent and graphic and articulate. It was just fascinating. I felt a great nostalgia in him for those days. He talked of sleeping on benches like Zeus would talk of sleeping on a cloud. He talked for several hours, his talk was really flowery, he looked healthy and young, you know the way a person will when he's enthusiastic and excited.

# 40 / Theresa Helburn

Theresa Helburn (1887–1959) grew up in New York City and graduated from Bryn Mawr College, where she directed and acted in plays, afterward attending George Pierce Baker's Drama 47 Workshop at Harvard. She was a founder of the Theatre Guild, the preeminent Broadway producer of literary plays, along with Lawrence Langner, Philip Moeller, and Helen Westley, and served as its executive director. Under her direction the number of subscriptions went from 135 to 6,000 in five years. She was known for discovering new talent, such as casting Alfred Lunt (1892–1977) and Lynn Fontanne (1887–1983) together for the first time, and putting together the collaborators who created *Oklahoma!* and *Carousel.*

Source: Theresa Helburn, *A Wayward Quest: The Autobiography of Theresa Helburn* (Boston: Little, Brown, 1960), 256–79.

Eugene O'Neill made his first appearance at the Theatre Guild in 1929, thanks to the continuous efforts of Lawrence Langner, who made a special trip to Bermuda in 1927 and coaxed Gene into the Guild fold. That season we produced both *Marco Millions* and *Strange Interlude.*

Without question, Gene was the giant among American playwrights. Never was there any question of casual or unfinished craftsmanship on his part. Never any doubt as to what he wanted. Like Shaw, he knew his craft from the ground up, he knew the effects he wanted to achieve, and he knew the techniques by which to attain them.

I can see him now, sitting quiet and impassive in the front row, watching rehearsals hour after hour. He had spent so much time on the preparation of his script that he was ready to answer promptly and without any hesitation every question thrown at him by director and actor.

By the time it went into rehearsal, indeed, O'Neill had devoted more work to it than many playwrights do to half a dozen plays. He wrote longhand, such tiny writing that I can decipher it only with the help of a magnifying glass. He worked slowly, laboriously, painfully. He spent more time in preparation than in the actual writing of the dialogue. His original notes for a play would have filled a book; they served only as a background for his characters, giving them depth, so that Gene knew them thoroughly.

After writing a first draft he would put it away for three months so that he could regain his perspective, and then rewrite it from the beginning. This draft was put away for a year. Then he wrote his third draft. If necessary, he would do even a fourth.

We found Gene almost as difficult as Shaw on the subject of cutting. He believed in saying he was going to say something, then saying it, then saying he had said it. He seemed to fear that without this painstaking reiteration of ideas he could not make his meaning clear to his audience. I have always believed that he could have saved a couple of plays that proved to be failures in his later days if he had been willing to cut. As the years went on and the scope of his plan for plays became bigger and bigger, more and more complex, he became more prolix.

Later on I learned that I could not argue with Gene. He was very self-confident. I would suggest cuts here and here and here. He would shake his head. He needed it all. He had to be complete.

"Well, Gene, go home and think it over," I would say.

Occasionally he would come back and make a few insignificant cuts. Then he would smile, that sweet, gentle, lovely smile of his, and I would know I was beaten. None the less, for us the play was the thing and we gave him, as far as we could conceivably do it, what he wanted. This was particularly true of *The Iceman Cometh*, at which time he was feeling ill and insecure about cutting a play written while in better health several years before its production. That this way may not always have been the most successful is indicated by Eric Bentley's comment: "I had seen what came of author-worshiping directing in the Theatre Guild production [*The Iceman Cometh*] where all O'Neill's faults were presented to the public with careful reverence."[46] Well, Gene respected his craft; I saw no reason why we should not respect his point of view.

*Strange Interlude* was a daring experiment for us. In some ways, I think it was one of the most daring experiments in the theater. There were, as everyone knows now, nine acts; the play ran from five in the afternoon until eleven at night with an hour for dinner. It played through one of the hottest seasons on record and in an uncooled theater. But for a year and a half every seat was filled.

I had to go to Europe that summer and left just after rehearsals started. The afternoon I returned to New York, I went from the boat straight to the theater and sat through the performance enthralled, before I went home to unpack.

I remember writing, more than a year after *Strange Interlude* opened, to tell

Gene that the play was still attracting standees. He replied: "This treads on fanaticism, it seems to me. Myself I wouldn't stand up 4 ½ hours to see the original production of the Crucifixion!"

I feel strongly that the two greatest plays the Guild ever produced were Shaw's *Saint Joan* and O'Neill's *Strange Interlude.* Certainly the latter was the finest serious production that Philip Moeller ever staged. He was at the peak of his brilliance as a director at that time, with *Volpone*[47] probably his greatest work in comedy.

When we followed *Strange Interlude* with *Dynamo*, Eugene O'Neill was traveling from China to the Basque country and did not supervise the rehearsals. At that time, his marital difficulties had become almost too much for him. He loathed the newspaper stories, which he regarded as an outrageous invasion of his privacy; he hated the emotional turmoil and uncertainty, which made it difficult for him to do creative work; and each letter or cable warned us solemnly not to divulge his whereabouts to anyone.[48] None the less, he was happier than he had ever been in his life. His great love for Carlotta Monterey, who later became his wife, was to dominate all the rest of his days.

[. . .]

When we opened *Dynamo* he cabled: "Wish I could be with you but domestic deadlock unchanged and will never return States until Carlotta and I are married."

Some eight months later, Carlotta, then Mrs. Eugene O'Neill, wrote fervently, "We feel we have earned our happiness!"

But if Gene was not on hand to supervise the production of *Dynamo* in person, he, like Shaw, bombarded us with suggestions by mail. I have before me eight sheets marked "Suggestions, instructions, advice, along with sundry snooty remarks and animadversions as to the modern theater for *Dynamo*." Some of the "suggestions, instructions," etc., are particularly interesting for the light they cast on O'Neill's theories and what he was trying to achieve in the theater. Especially on *how*.

> I may seem to be a bug on the subject of sound in the theatre [he wrote], but I have reason. Bobby Jones once said that the difference between my plays and other contemporary work was that I always write primarily by ear for the ear, that most of my plays, even down to the rhythm of the dialogue, have the definite structural quality of a musical composition . . . although it is the principal reason why I have been blamed for useless repetitions, which to me were significant recurrences of theme . . . This is a machine age which one would like to express as a background for lives in plays in overtones of characteristic . . . sound and rhythm—but

> how can one unless a corresponding mechanical perfection in the theatre is a reliable string of the instrument. . . . The only answer is, it cannot be done. Looking back on my plays in which significant mechanical sound and not music is called for (nearly all of the best ones) I can say that none of them has ever really been thoroughly done in the modern theatre although they were written for it.

In regard to casting he said of one feminine character: "I have no suggestions—only a warning that if whoever plays it is ever conscious of being funny for even a moment or rides her lines for laughs, I will swim back all the way from China with a kriss [*sic*] between my murderously gritted teeth and slay that actorine."

*Dynamo* was a good play but not, I think, one of Gene's great ones. Gene wrote me from China that the play was about a mother complex, but that was never clear to me, and I'm sure it wasn't to the audience. I remember it chiefly for the wonderful stage set, and for Claudette Colbert[49] in a tight-fitting red dress running up and down stairs.

Gene began writing to us about *Mourning Becomes Electra* nearly a year before we saw the script. I wish all young playwrights would read and reread his letter about it. It might send them back to their scripts for more work. If the masters find rewrite so rewarding, certainly the apprentices should, too.

> I got to Paris today [Gene wrote in 1930] after finishing getting over my second draft. I did so much on this job it practically amounts to a third draft. We are off for a month's motoring in Spain now. When I come back I will type a fourth and (I hope) final draft . . .
>
> This fourth draft will probably take two or three months. Then I will send you a copy and you can all see what you think. After that, I will have six to seven months leeway before next fall to lay it aside for a lengthy period and then go over it a fifth time if I feel that is necessary. This looks like a good scheme to me and I ought to get a first draft of a new one done in that interval, too, if the gods are good.
>
> [. . .]

In April 1931 Gene wrote from Paris:

> I am sending you the script of *Mourning Becomes Electra* by this same mail—two scripts—so that the Committee can get quick action on it.
>
> As you will see, no departures in technique are involved. *Interlude* soliloquies and asides only got in my way in these plays of intense passions and little cerebration. The masque idea has also gone by the board. It simply refused to justify itself in the final accounting. It confused and ob-

scured instead of intensifying. All that is left of it is the masklike quality of the Mannon faces in repose, an effect that can be gained by acting and makeup. The dialogue is colloquial of today. The house, the period costumes, the Civil War surface stuff, these are the masks for what is really a modern psychological drama with no true connection with that period at all. I think I have caught enough Greek sense of fate—a modern approximation of it, I mean—out of the Mannons themselves to do without any Greek theatrical effects.

*Mourning Becomes Electra*, O'Neill's trilogy, was produced during the depression. One night after the performance, I was standing in the lobby as the audience streamed past me. I heard one man say to another, "Gosh, isn't it good to get back out into the depression again!"

Two years after we did *Mourning Becomes Electra* we produced *Ah, Wilderness!*—O'Neill's delightful comedy. Gene, unlike many playwrights, who expect to do half the work on the play after it opens out of town, usually saw absolutely no point in tryouts. He wanted no part of them. *Ah, Wilderness!* was the only time when he agreed to an out-of-town tryout.

Unlike his other plays, *Ah, Wilderness!* was full of comedy. We knew that it was only fair to try it on the road so that the laughs could be timed and the actors could get a sense of the pace of the play. At length, Gene agreed, though reluctantly. We opened in Philadelphia, and it was some time before he would even come down for a performance. He saw it through and returned to New York. "You see," his attitude suggested; "I knew all the time it was unnecessary."

After *Ah, Wilderness!* there was silence. Gene had embarked on the great project of his life, a *comédie humaine*, a cycle of eight—later nine—plays into which he planned to put everything he knew. And then time passed. Gene, at his Sea Island beach home in Georgia, which he called Casa Genotta, had withdrawn into the private world in which he immured himself for the great project.

I knew of it first in a letter from Carlotta, who wrote: "Gene has started on plays that give him some scope for his ideas—his next will be a history of the human race."

Of course, both Lawrence and I were tremendously excited and we began to question him about the project. "It is only fair [Gene wrote me in March of 1936] to warn you on this point, too. As I am writing [Lawrence] I'm not going to discuss this series of plays with anyone, nor release any of them for production until I have at least three of them completed—and up to date only three-fourths of one of them is done."

A few weeks later I went to Georgia to visit the O'Neills. At Casa Genotta, a lovely house which Carlotta described as "bastard Spanish peasant style,"

Carlotta and I talked and drank coffee all morning. After lunch I talked with Gene in his study, which was built like the master cabin of an old sailing vessel. There he spoke to me about his prodigious plan for the great cycle, discussing particularly *A Touch of the Poet*, showing me the endless notes and the detailed scenarios.

Later we walked along the endless beach outside his house. At least, it seemed endless to me, for I have never been a good walker. Like most shy people, Gene was at his best when with only one other person, and that day, though the walk was rugged and the wind blew sand in my eyes, I made my first discovery of the real man himself. After my return to New York I wrote:

> [. . .] I realize what a privilege it will be to work for and toward the achievement of your *comédie humaine*. But I realize, too, that the special problems and size of the task before us probably precludes any thought of a company not definitely focused on these productions, because working on your cycle will absorb all our surplus energy and more for the next two or three years. But we must continue this summer and next fall to organize our acting material so that we will have sifted through and tested out both its caliber and its spirit before our O'Neill season begins. You are quite right in feeling that work, conceived and carried out as yours is, demands from all concerned an approach rare in the theater today.
>
> Of course, the sooner we can read a draft of any of the scripts, the sooner we will be able to judge whether the people we have in mind for association with us will fit practically into the scheme of things.

The idea of any pressure being applied, even such mild pressure as I had used, appalled Gene; although, considering the immense scope of his project and the vast amount of work and financing it would require, I had felt, in the interests of the Guild, that the point should be made.

> This is a word of warning [he wrote] in regard to planning ahead that I feel bound to repeat now, in justice both to the Guild and me. Don't begin to plan for the production of the cycle, except in a very general way, until you receive finished plays from me to plan on. Don't expect first drafts. I hate letting anyone see first drafts. Mine are intolerably long and wordy—intentionally so, because I put everything in them, so as not to lose anything, and rely on a subsequent revision and rewriting, after a lapse of time with better perspective on them, to concentrate on the essentials and eliminate the overweight. But to a person reading a first draft, that draft is the first impact of the play on them, and it is apt to

be a very misleading impact indeed. My first drafts always bore me for long stretches, so I can hardly expect them to do less for other people. And being bored by a first draft would be a disheartening approach to this Cycle for the prospective producer.

And don't rely on receiving the first plays at any definite future date, for though I may do some speculating about the matter, I cannot honestly even tell myself just when it will be. It depends on so many things which cannot be foretold. For example, the old subconscious might get on the job in great shape, and I might find myself in a surge of creative energy when I could keep going on, in first draft, from one to another until five or six or even all eight were written. In which case, as you will appreciate, I would be insane to pause for any interruption—especially such an exhausting interruption as production is for me, followed always by a long period of blank uncreativeness. It would be better in the long run, from both our standpoints, for me to go on without a break, even if it meant a delay of one or two years. It would be much better, from your angle, if, from the start, you had all eight to base a company on.

[. . .]

Later, after the O'Neills gave up their Georgia house and moved to California, I did a piece on Gene for the *Saturday Review of Literature*. To my chagrin, the magazine, in the same issue, published a sharp attack on him written by Bernard De Voto.[50] I wrote to tell Gene how sorry I was and in reply he wrote cheerfully that he never subscribed to a clipping bureau, he hadn't read the article and he had never heard of De Voto. Anyhow, "a too unanimous chorus of approval would make me feel a tombstone was planted over my head! The only writers that all writers agree are good writers are dead!"

That year Gene won the Nobel Prize but he was too ill to go to Stockholm. He was in a hospital. "I am beginning to feel as old as the Nile myself," he wrote in reference to a book I had sent him, "waiting for Carlotta to return, so very long does this first real separation of ours seem, each day the reign of an Egyptian dynasty, so to speak. Such are the pangs of love and how lucky I feel to be panged! . . .

"Lucky I didn't go to Sweden! My appendix would probably have burst as I was making my speech at the Nobel banquet, and ruined the occasion."[51]

I continued to sound out O'Neill on the great Cycle. He had been working on it for some six years or more. What was happening? Where were the plays? When was the Guild going to launch the great project? I didn't ask how we were going to do it. We'd find a way, all right. But unhappily, it wasn't necessary to look around for ways and means. The plays were still a great secret.

> No [Gene wrote me firmly] absolutely no hope for any play next season. I don't even want to think of production until I have four or five of the nine finished, and (if I can do it without winding up in the Poorhouse or the Home for the Aged and Infirm), I'd like to wait until all nine are completed. This last is the ideal, of course. Then we really could engage a repertory company for the whole Cycle—show the actors and actresses we have parts that would make it worthwhile, out of pure self-interest, to tie up for several seasons under our conditions. No stars, of course, but show the young and ambitious their chance to become stars through this Cycle . . . I'm very obdurate on this point. In fact, to be blunt, I won't allow it to be done any other way.
>
> But when will I be ready with even the minimum of four or five plays—let alone the full nine? . . . I did manage to finish the first draft of another play—the new No. One of the nine—last summer and fall and early winter. This makes three I now have in first draft. But two of them are still far from what I want them to be and have to be rewritten. The other—No. Three—is in pretty good shape for a first draft and won't need much work . . .
>
> Another thing, writing one of the units in this Cycle is a much more complicated business than doing a single play, or half of *Strange Interlude* or one of the *Electra* trilogy. Often I start a work day writing dialogue for the play I'm on and wind up writing suggested notes on a scene in the eighth or ninth play! Of course, this will all be very valuable in the later stages but it does eat up time and energy and slow up progress on the immediate job.

Another year passed and Gene was still laboring at his great project, none of which we at the Guild had as yet seen.

[. . .]

Gene wired that there was to be no finished play for us that season. I wrote back promptly, still ridden by that dream of mine for some new kind of musical play.

> I am sorry we cannot look forward to doing some new O'Neill this season or next season but there is another idea that has been on my mind for a long time—and that is, to make a musical version of *Marco Millions*.
>
> Today, I had lunch with Kurt Weill,[52] who is extremely intrigued with the idea and who, I think, might do a very good job. Do you know Weill's work and does the idea appeal to you? We also thought of Dick Rodgers and Larry Hart[53] but they are involved in a musical with George Abbott[54] for next season.

[. . .]

I learned, to my chagrin, that Oscar Hammerstein[55] was at work with Jerome Kern[56] on the Byron *Marco*, so that project was brought to an end. Gene, however, was genuinely interested in the whole idea of making musicals of his plays. He wrote: "Another play to think of in musical connection is *The Hairy Ape*. Coates,[57] the conductor, was once going to make an opera of it. He didn't. I mention this to show you that the idea had occurred to a famous musician. But I'm not thinking of grand opera now but of something more like *Porgy and Bess*.[58] Give this idea a little pondering, will you? With the right composer, it could work out into a most striking and out of the ordinary rut affair. And very timely. Because I think we are all a bit sick of answers that don't answer. *The Hairy Ape*, at least, faces the simple truth that, being what we are, and with any significant spiritual change for the better in us probably ten thousand years away, there just is no answer."

That season Lawrence and Armina's Westport Country Playhouse[59] presented a revival of *Anna Christie*. Bennett Cerf, who was staying with the Langners, sat beside me during the performance and told me he thought Gene was working on a new play which was not to be part of the Cycle. I wrote Gene about the success of the *Anna Christie* revival and hinted that we'd like to hear about the new play Bennett had mentioned.

There wasn't, Gene replied, going to be a new play. "It's good to learn the production of *Anna Christie* at Lawrence's theatre was so well done. As for it being a grand play, it isn't for me. It's dead as hell. But there does seem to be a lot of theatrical life left in the old trollop . . . I had thought it had been movied and radioed until nothing remained to interest anyone."

Periodically reports appeared, from one source or another, that Eugene O'Neill had broken with the Theatre Guild. One report, published by *Variety*, declared that he had joined the Playwrights Company. "I'm about as fed up with these rumors [Gene wrote me] as I imagine you all are. They're as unfair to the Guild as they are to me. I bitterly resent that as soon as the Guild has a run of bad breaks these rumors started. Seemingly it is assumed that I am the kind of heel who would naturally try to get away from you the moment you had tough luck! I don't like it. And it's all so damned idiotic, too, when you consider that I am not in a position yet to talk production of plays with anyone!"

Another report was that Gene was leasing the Broadhurst Theatre to put on the Cycle himself. "Of all the bloody nonsense I ever heard that is the worst," Gene wrote furiously to Lawrence. "Can you picture me leasing the Broadhurst to embark on a producing career? Two preliminary steps would be necessary before that could happen. No. 1, I would have to be adjudged insane and committed to an asylum. No. 2, I would have to escape."

[. . .]

Later that year, Gene sent *The Iceman Cometh* to Lawrence, who read it at once and wrote to express his enthusiasm. "I'm damned pleased you liked it so well [Gene wrote him on August 11, 1940]. Personally, I love it! And I'm sure my affection is not wholly inspired by nostalgia for the dear dead days 'on the bottom of the sea' either. I have a confident hunch that this play, as drama, is one of the best things I've ever done. In some ways, perhaps the best. What I mean is, there are moments in it that suddenly strip the secret soul of a man stark naked, not in cruelty or mock superiority, but with an understanding compassion which sees him as a victim of the ironies of life and of himself. Those moments are for me the depth of tragedy, with nothing more that can possibly be said."

But O'Neill did not want any part of his Cycle to be produced during the war:

> Later on, after the victory in the war which must be won is won, and the reaction to the realities behind the surface of the peace sinks in, there will again be an audience able to feel the inner meaning of plays dealing with the everlasting mystery and irony and tragedy of men's lives and dreams; plays which are propaganda only for life as the artist attempts to illuminate it and transmute it into Art. People are too damned preoccupied with the tragedy of war now—as they should be—to want to face such plays. And I don't blame them. I'd rather spend an escapist evening with legs and music myself—or with pipe dreams that were treated as truth . . .
>
> My health has been bad—Parkinson's disease much worse, for one thing. Some days I can't write—I mean physically can't write longhand—and couldn't type even if the old dog could change tricks and compose on a typewriter. However, I've done some work in '42, despite these annoyances and a generally futile feeling of "What's the use?" But I've had to give up the physical work around the grounds—I used to take care of quite a lot—because it brings on spells of complete exhaustion when I feel like a wet anaemic fly crawling up a cold windowpane.

[. . .]

I wrote Gene about the possibility of selling *Mourning Becomes Electra* to the movies: "As you know, ever since I was in Hollywood in 1935, I have been trying to interest various picture companies in *Mourning Becomes Electra*. Even at that time I had the idea of Garbo and Hepburn[60] in it. The answer was always frustration, frustration, frustration. Then, as you know, we got Hepburn excited and she did her best to sell it to Metro-Goldwyn-Mayer. She says the scene was fantastic and finally Louis B.[61] said only over his dead body.[62] Surprisingly, Kate didn't shoot him on the spot."

Gene sent me a long typed reply, with insertions in his microscopic handwriting. It reveals much of his attitude toward his work, his fine sense of responsibility for the way his ideas were to be presented to the public, and a touch of exacerbation [*sic*] that was rare in him but which his worsening physical condition explains.

I've never liked having distorted pictures made of my plays, and the picture medium has never interested me. I thought long ago when I saw *Caligari*[63] that there could be a genuine, original art form developed along that line. Talking pictures seem to me a bastard which has inherited the lowest traits of both parents. It was the talkless part of *The Long Voyage Home*—the best picture ever made from my stuff[64]—that impressed me the most . . .

So you may understand what my feeling is about a film sale of a favorite play I know Hollywood will distort. Let's consider *The Hairy Ape*. It remains one of my favorites. I have an enduring affection for it as drama, the more so because so few people have ever seen what it was all about. But let that go. I sold it because, with Tao House and ranch overhead on my neck, I had to sell it or sell some of my securities whose income pays the alimony! . . . I didn't really want to sell because I knew no one in Hollywood had the guts to film *my play*, do it as symbolic expressionism as it should be done, and not censor it into imbecility, or make it a common realistic stoker story. I remember that its first stage production was one of my most satisfying times in the theater. I remember Wolheim was practically perfect as "Yank" and was also a pal of mine. I don't want to have that memory spoiled. So when I tell you I am not going to see the film—nor read one word written about it—nor even admit that it exists, I sure mean it! But all the same, I will always feel guilty. The memory of what *The Hairy Ape* is, was, and should be, will, in a sense, be spoiled for me. The picture, even if financially a hit, will be soon forgotten, and the play will remain as if no picture had every touched it. But still, I will always regret.[65]

About *Mourning Becomes Electra*, I am sure Hepburn would be splendid as Lavinia. The rest I'm afraid would be a dreadful hash of attempted condensation and idiotic censorship, as the *Strange Interlude* film was.[66]

How about General Mannon's speeches about war, death, etc., and what Orin has to say of war when he returns? Would these be ruled out as morbid pacifism or something? Yet to me these contain an implication, at least, of deep spiritual truth. Do you remember when Orin says to Lavinia in Act III of *The Hunted*: "I had to kill another in the same way. It was like murdering the same man twice. I had a queer feeling that war meant murdering the same man over and over, and that in the end I would discover the man was myself!"

But I'm getting away from the point—and also, getting to the point where I wonder if we ought to sell *Mourning Becomes Electra*, at any price. After all, it was a splendid Guild production—your high spot, as a theatre, I think—a great Guild achievement against great odds—an event that was a high example of the combined acting, producing, and writing art of the American theatre—so compelling that in the depth of the depression this tragic trilogy brought packed houses to the theater in late afternoon for weeks at a six-dollar top! [*Strange Interlude* was produced in boom days.] And to me, it is also a high spot. It did more than any other single play to win the Nobel Prize. In every capital of Europe where it was done before the war it was an event. And it still goes on, despite the war, thirteen years after your production, and will go on. Only a year ago, it was produced in Lisbon and later revived there—a great success. People came to the theater in the early evening, something they'd never done before except for Wagnerian opera. It has been done in Switzerland since then. Now they want to do it in Madrid. It is no boasting but plain fact that, no matter what exceptions are taken here and there by this or that, for this or that reason, it is generally regarded in Europe as the high point of American dramatic writing. Well, all that belongs to the Guild, too. And whether people of this country give a damn about it or not—and they don't—it belongs to them. Furthermore, you of the Guild and I are—well, being you're a lady, I won't say growing old but at least entering the period when one begins to select, if one can, some memories of one's work in life worth cherishing and keeping untarnished.

Do we want to let Hollywood debase it (as it must, being at heart, even with the best intentions, merely a commercial mob-amusement racket), the *Mourning Becomes Electra* of our memories, the achievement that had great significance, whereas the picture will have none?

Am I being sentimental? The Guild will probably think so, since I notice that *Mourning Becomes Electra* is not even included in the list at the bottom of your letter paper—presumably a list of your greatest achievements, box office or no box office. You omit *Mourning Becomes Electra*, although any international jury composed of critics of dramatic art would tell you it is the most significant modern play you have ever produced since the Guild began. Why, Christ, compared to it, a lot of the plays on your list are, as far as fine drama is concerned, merely things to hang on a hook in a backwoods privy! The jury I speak of would, I know, agree to that judgment with enthusiasm.

Well, the above has rankled for a long time. Now you have it. It doesn't matter a damn, I admit, except that I can hardly be expected to see it as an expression of loyalty to my finest work—or, what is worse, loyalty to yourselves for the important work you have done for American drama and an American theater (as distinct from the Showshop Business).

In 1946, the Guild brought out two O'Neill plays: *The Iceman Cometh* and *A Moon for the Misbegotten*, neither of which fared well commercially.[67]

The last time I saw him, Gene said, "These audiences don't want my plays."

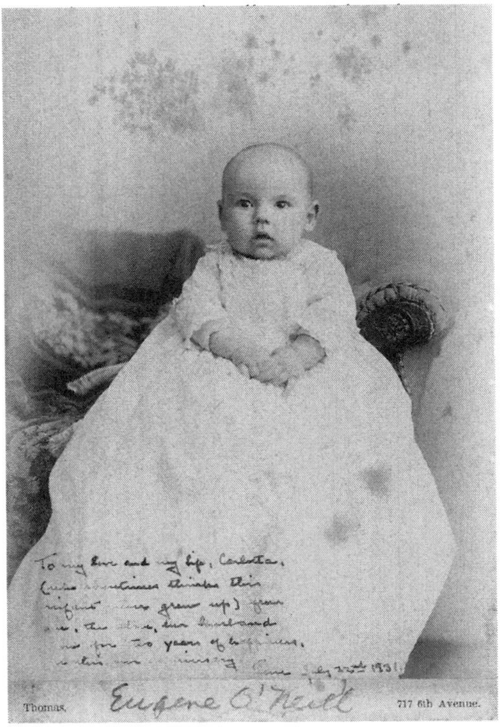


Figure 1. Portrait of Eugene O'Neill as a baby, ca. 1889. Source: Yale Collection of American Literature, Beinecke Rare Book and Manuscript Library

Figure 2. Monte Cristo Cottage. Source: Photograph taken by Brenda Murphy

Figure 3. The living room of Monte Cristo Cottage. Source: Photograph taken by Brenda Murphy

Figure 4. Studio portrait of Mary Ellen Quinlan O'Neill, ca. 1870s. Source: Yale Collection of American Literature, Beinecke Rare Book and Manuscript Library

Figure 5. Eugene O'Neill (reading) with his brother Jamie and his father, James, on the porch of the Monte Cristo Cottage, ca. 1900. Source: Yale Collection of American Literature, Beinecke Rare Book and Manuscript Library

Figure 6. Eugene O'Neill as a child. Source: Yale Collection of American Literature, Beinecke Rare Book and Manuscript Library

Figure 7. Postcard of the Peaked Hill Bar life-saving station that became the O'Neills' home, c. 1908, H. I. Robbins, Boston. Source: Collection of Brenda Murphy

Figure 8. Eugene O'Neill in his Provincetown Players days. Source: Library of Congress, Reproduction Number: LC-B7901-36.

Figure 9. Eugene, Shane, and Agnes Boulton O'Neill at Peaked Hill Bar, Cape Cod. Source: *Outdoor America*, May 1928, copyright Izaak Walton League of America, Reprinted with Permission.

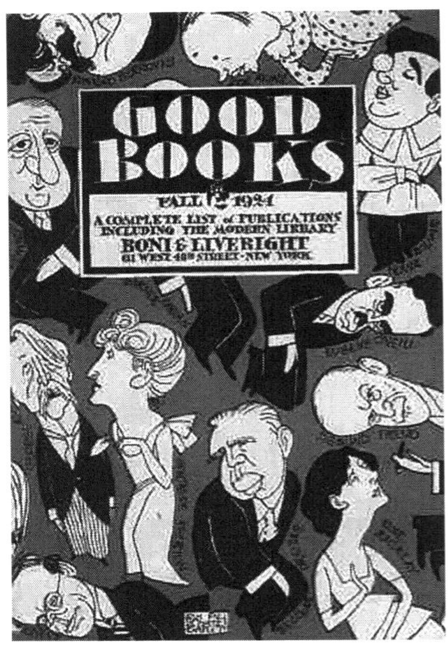


Figure 10. Ralph Barton's cover of the Boni & Liveright catalog, including a caricature of O'Neill. Source: *Good Books*, Boni & Liveright, 1924.

Figure 11. Eugene O'Neill at Sea Island, Georgia. Source: Library of Congress, Prints and Photographs Division, Carl Van Vechten Collection

Figure 12. Carl Van Vechten photograph of Eugene and Carlotta O'Neill. Source: Library of Congress, Prints and Photographs Division, Carl Van Vechten Collection

Figure 13: Eugene O'Neill in his Bugatti in front of the Château du Plessis, ca. 1930. Source: Yale Collection of American Literature, Beinecke Rare Book and Manuscript Library

Figure 14. Carl Van Vechten photograph of O'Neill. Source: Library of Congress, Prints and Photographs Division, Carl Van Vechten Collection

Figure 15. S. J. Woolf drawing of O'Neill. Source: Reproduced with permission of Deborah W. Hobson

Figure 16. Carlotta Monterey in *The Hairy Ape.* Source: Yale Collection of American Literature, Beinecke Rare Book and Manuscript Library

Figure 17. The gravestone of Eugene and Carlotta Monterey O'Neill. Source: Photograph taken by Brenda Murphy

# 41 / George Jean Nathan

George Jean Nathan (1882–1958) was born in Fort Wayne, Indiana, and grew up in Cleveland. His mother attended the same convent school as O'Neill's mother, Ella Quinlan, and the two women remained friends. After graduating from Cornell University in 1904, Nathan moved to New York and did newspaper work before joining the *Smart Set* as drama reviewer in 1908. In 1914 Nathan and H. L. Mencken became joint editors of the magazine and exerted great influence over the cultural values and opinions of the 1920s generation. As a reviewer, Nathan practiced what he called "destructive" criticism and liked very little, but he set a high value on O'Neill's work and became one of his closest lifelong friends. Nathan published more than forty books, mostly collections of his drama criticism.

Source: George Jean Nathan, *The Intimate Notebooks of George Jean Nathan* (New York: Alfred A. Knopf, 1932), 21–38.

In all the many years of our friendship, I have heard Eugene O'Neill laugh aloud once and only once. We were walking, after dinner one evening in July [1930], up the long, lonely road just beyond the chateau he was then living and working in at Saint Antoine du Rocher in Touraine. In the country, men who live in cities generally find themselves talking out of character. If they are sober, sedate fellows in the city, they become orally frisky in the country; if they are flippant in the city, they become more or less solemn and even wistful at the smell of flowers and manure. Their discourse alters with the scene. O'Neill, who in the city—for he is essentially a man of cities despite his inability to write save a cow is mooing or a sea is swishing beneath his window—has the mien and the conversational *élan* of an embalmer, presently proceeded thus: "When Princeton, after kicking my tail out of place as an undergraduate because I was too accurate a shot with an Anheuser-Busch beer-bottle and hit a window in Woodrow Wilson's house right where it lived,[68] some years later suddenly got proud of its old beer-bottle heaver but magnanimously allowed Yale to claim the hoodlum for its own with an honorary degree, I found myself in New Haven late one night viewing a number of old boys of the class of 1880 or thereabouts having a hot reunion with themselves. Three of them in particular, that I ran across on one of the street-corners, were so grandly stewed that I had to stand still and watch them. One of them, it appeared, was president of a big bank in New York; another was vice-president of one of the big railroads; and the third was a United States Senator. After playing leap-frog for about ten minutes, during which one of them fell down and rolled half-way into a sewer, the three, singing barber-shop songs at the top of their lungs, wobbled across the street to the opposite corner where there was a mail-box. With a lot of grunts and after much steaming and puffing, the bank president and the vice-president of the big railroad got down on their knees and hoisted their old classmate, the Senator, up on their shoulders in a line with the slit in the mail-box. Whereupon the Senator proceeded to use the mail-box for a purpose generally reserved for telegraph poles and the sides of barns."

The boisterous roar that followed his recollection of the scene marked, as I have said, the only time within my knowledge of O'Neill that he has laughed outright at anything. In all the years I have known him, the most that has ever issued from him has been a quiet little chuckle and I have only, in all that time, heard him chuckle twice, once in New York when he indulged in a reminiscence of the wonderful free-lunch that he and his brother Jim used to get with a five-cent glass of beer (and live on) in a saloon opposite the old Madison Square Garden, and once at Le Plessis, in France, when he handed me a newspaper article in Spanish, treating of the time he once spent in Buenos Aires during his sailor days, asked me to translate it for him, and I inserted several imaginary paragraphs describing in rich detail his great proficiency as a tango dancer. He is constitutionally the antithesis of *l'homme qui rit*.[69] Nothing even faintly amuses him, unless it be the remembrance of his dead brother's gift for Rabelaisian monkeyshines, the singing (in a voice capable of just three notes, all sour) of old barroom ballads, or remembered tales of his father, the late James O'Neill who, during the years when he was a matinee idol, used to parade Fourteenth Street at high noon daily—after at least three hours spent in dolling himself up—by way of giving the girls a treat, and who always made it a practise on Sundays to get to church half an hour late by way of staging an effective entrance for himself.

Contrary to finding amusement in the world, O'Neill finds endlessly the materials for indignation. The body of his dramatic writing reflects him more closely, I venture to say, than that of any other playwright in the present-day American theatre. Let the dramatic critic of some yokel newspaper in some yokel town that he has never even heard of write that he isn't all he should be as a dramatist, and he lets out a vituperative blast of such volume that, once done, he finds himself completely exhausted. Several times I myself have been denounced, if somewhat more politely, for expressed opinions on his work. Once, he let me read the manuscript of his play, *Welded*, in which he had great faith. When I reported to him that all I could discern in it was some very third-rate Strindberg, he sharply observed that I couldn't conceivably understand any such play as I had never been married, put on his hat, walked out and didn't let me hear from him for two months afterward. When, several years later, he sent me the manuscript of *Lazarus Laughed* and I wrote to him that I didn't care for it, he replied in the next mail that my judgment of it couldn't be taken seriously by him because I was lacking in all religious feeling and was therefore prejudiced against any such play, and that it was really a masterpiece whatever I thought about it. On this occasion, he was so disgusted with my critical gifts that he didn't write to me again for three months. The same thing happened in the case of *Dynamo*, which in a preliminary manuscript reading struck me as being close to caricature. Even after the play was produced and almost unanimously condemned, he stuck to his loyalty toward it and to his conviction that all the critics were dolts. "It maybe wasn't all it should have been," he subsequently admitted to me, "because I was going through a lot of trouble in family matters when I was writing it, but just the same you're dead wrong about it." And—I happened to be visiting him at the time—he sulked for the rest of the day and condescended only to exchange a curt good-night with me at bed-time. If a newspaper or any other kind of photographer snaps him without his formal permission, he seethes. If he gets a letter with something in it that displeases him, he mutters sourly over it for twenty-four hours. The petty nuisances and annoyances that every man suffers and quickly dismisses from mind and attention cause him something bordering on acute agony.

After many years of being very hard up, his plays gradually began to make him money. But real money came only with the tremendous success, both as a performed play and published book, of *Strange Interlude*, which netted him close to a half-million dollars. Since boyhood, he had had just two wishes: one, to have some shirts tailored by a first-class London shirt-maker and, two, to own a carriage dog such as he had seen loping after the rigs of the rich in his youngster days. His greatest satisfaction in *Strange Interlude* was that it had made the gratification of the two wishes possible.

He has a dislike of meeting people that amounts almost to a terror. Even with his few close friends he is generally so taciturn that it is sometimes necessary to go over and poke him to make certain that he is neither asleep nor dead. He sits glumly for hours at a time without opening his mouth, brooding deeply over some undecipherable concern which, upon ultimate revelation, turns out to be a worried speculation as to whether his wife has ordered spaghetti, his favorite dish, for dinner for him that night. Having sat at different tables with him countless times, I have, with rare exception, heard him during the course of a meal say more than two words and they have invariably been—in reply to an inquiry as to whether he would care for any more of this or that—"Why sure." The way to lose O'Neill's friendship is to ask him for oral expressions of opinion on anything (if he feels like expressing an opinion, he will write a letter, and a satisfactorily long one), or to introduce him to any man other than one who knows a great deal about professional sports and who will confine his conversation to that subject. The one great admiration that he has temporarily achieved for any man in the last four years was for Sparrow Robertson, the chief sporting writer of the *Paris Herald*, whom he met just once and found to be "a grand bird." He has a great respect for Sean O'Casey,[70] but beyond that an aversion to most men of his own profession, asserting that the majority of them are not worth the powder to blow them up, and of all those whom he has met in later years only W. S. Maugham and H. R. Lenormand have any interest for him.[71] He goes to a theatre about once in every five years and then only in Europe because he has heard that some play of his is being done there in a language that he cannot understand. I have known him on only one occasion really to admit that he had been in a theatre. That was when the Russian Tairoff did *All God's Chillun* in Russian in Paris several years ago. He professed to have found it the best production of any of his plays that he had ever seen. "But," I protested, "you don't know a word of Russian. How could you tell?" He looked at me pityingly. "You should have seen the way Tairoff's wife, in the role of the girl, brushed those books off the table in that scene in the last act!" he replied with grave seriousness.

Displaying outwardly all the glow and effervescence of a magnum of ice water, he is internally given to huge enthusiasms of all sorts and varieties. Whatever piece of work he happens currently to be working on arouses him to such a pitch of incalescence over its virtues that he will go around all day wreathed in broad, mysterious smiles. And when O'Neill thus smiles, it is as if any other man stood gleefully on his head, waved his arms and legs and let out a bellow that shook the heavens. Familiar with all his longer, as well as with a number of his shorter plays, since their manuscript infancy, I recall only one time when doubt over a script that he was writing assailed him. In all the other cases he was as excited over their merits as a child of the wealthy anticipating on Christmas Eve the gifts he was certain to get. The one exception was a trilogy which he had undertaken. "Would to God," he wrote me, "that this damned trilogy of mine were off of my neck! I'm beginning to hate it and curse the day I ever conceived such an idea. The notion haunts me that I've bitten off a good deal more than I can chew. On my return, the first two acts of the first play struck me as not right, so I've started to rewrite them. And so it goes on! It looks as if the rest of my life was doomed to be spent rewriting the damned thing. I honestly feel very low about it and am anxious to get done with it and free my mind from the obsession of it and get on to something else. When these two acts are done, for better or worse, I'm going to call quits. I don't think I can go through the ordeal of typing it myself now. I'm too fed up. Think it wiser to get it typed. It would bore me so that before the end I would probably burn it."[72]

But not so usually. Confidence generally permeates his being, warming him to the very toes. He says nothing, or at best very little, but the mysterious smiles embroider his features. Of *The Straw*, he informed me, "I have complete confidence in my own valuation of it." *Where the Cross Is Made*, was "great fun to write, theatrically very thrilling, an amusing experiment in treating the audience as insane." "I would like to stand or fall"—in each instance—"by *Bound East for Cardiff*, *The Long Voyage Home*, *The Moon of the Caribbees*, *Beyond the Horizon*, *The Straw* and *Gold*," he wrote me. Each of these plays, he duly announced, was "my sincerest effort and was written purely for its own sake." Of *All God's Chillun Got Wings*—"Well, I've got it done and I'm immensely pleased with it!" Of *Desire Under the Elms*—"Its poetical vision illuminating even the most sordid and mean blind alleys of life—that is my justification as a dramatist!" Of *Marco Millions*—"there's a whole lot of poetical beauty in it and fine writing." *The Great God Brown* was "a devastating, crucifying new one." *Lazarus Laughed* was "*far* the best play I've ever written." Of *Dynamo*—"I thoroughly disagree with you about the play. It is not *far*, far below me. I'm sure of that! Wait and see! It will come into its own some day when it isn't judged as a symbolical trilogy with a message to good Americans about what's wrong with them and what to do about it. I think you're wrong this time—as wrong as about *Lazarus Laughed.* Not that you're not right about the excessiveness of the stage directions, but then I thought you knew that my scripts get drastically weeded out in that respect when I read proof and that I always let them slide as they first occur to me until then. A slovenly method, perhaps, but the way I've always worked. Then again, I don't think it's fair to take the speeches of a lot of admittedly inarticulate characters in a particular play as expressions of the general underlying theme of a trilogy—which I obviously never intended them to be." Indeed, even in the case of the later trilogy, *Mourning Becomes Electra*, about which there were the preliminary doubts already recorded, I received, when the play at length was finished, this comment: "It has been one hell of a job! Let's hope the result in some measure justifies the labor I've put in. To get enough of Clytemnestra in Christine, of Electra in Lavinia, of Orestes in Orin, etc., and yet keep them American primarily; to conjure a Greek fate out of the Mannons themselves (without calling in the aid of even a Puritan Old Testament God) that would convince a modern audience without religion or moral ethics; to prevent the surface melodrama of the plot from overwhelming the real drama; to contrive murders that escape cops and courtroom scenes; and finally to keep myself out of it and shun the many opportunities for effusions of personal writing anent life and fate—all this has made the going tough and the way long! And even now it's done I don't know quite what I've got. All I *do* know is that after reading it all through, in spite of my familiarity with every page, it leaves me moved and disturbed spiritually, and I have a feeling of there being real size in it, quite apart from its length; a sense of having had a valid dramatic experience with intense tortured passions beyond the ambition or scope of other modern plays. As for the separate parts, each play, each act, seem better than I hoped. And that's that."

Wherever he happens to be at the moment happens enthusiastically also to be the place of all places for him to be and forever live in. Provincetown was "ideal, quiet and the only place where I could ever work." When in Bermuda, he wrote me, "I didn't start this letter with any view of boring you by an expounding of inner principles. It was rather to recommend Bermuda to you as a place to 'take the waters' in case you're planning a Spring vacation. The climate is grand. The German bottled beer and English bottled ale are both excellent. And the swimming is wonderful, if you like such, which I do above everything. It has proved a profitable Winter resort for me. I've gotten more work done than in the corresponding season up North in many years." When at Belgrade Lakes, in Maine, he sent me a postcard: "There's tranquillity here. A place to think and work if ever there was one! Ideal for me." "Well, after a week in London," he wrote, "I am strong for it! It seems to me that if it were possible for me to live contented in any city this would be the one. There is something so self-assuredly nerveless about it. Of course, the weather has been unexpectedly fine—warm and sunny every day—and that helps. In short, I've been happier here since I left New York than ever in my life before." While he was living in Guéthary in the Basque country, I received the following: "The Basque country and the Basques hit me right where I belong! According to present plans and inclinations it is here that I shall settle down to make a home for the rest of my days. Europe has meant a tremendous lot to me, more than I ever hoped it could. I've felt a deep sense of peace here, a real enjoyment in just living from day to day, that I've never known before. For more than the obvious financial reasons, I've come to the conclusion that anyone doing creative work is a frightful sap to waste the amount of energy required to beat life in the U.S.A. when over here one can have just that more strength to put into one's job." When he was in Indo-China, this arrived: "This is the place! There is nothing more beautiful and interesting in the world. It is grand!" Settled for several years in Touraine, he wrote: "This is the place for me! The most beautiful part of France. Here is the ideal place to live and work!" During a motor trip through Spain, I received three postcards from him at different times. One, from Madrid, conveyed this message: "I've never seen a more beautiful spot. It would be a great place to work in." One, from Granada, this: "Spain is most interesting and I'm darn glad we picked it out for a vacation. Granada is quiet, peaceful and immensely attractive. What a place to live and work in!" One, from Malaga, this: "This is the best place I have ever struck in Europe—really good stuff! It'd be a swell place to live and work in." Returned to New York again, he said to me, "Why I ever left here, damned if I know. There's life and vitality here. It's the place for ideas! This is the spot for me and my work!" His present passion is for a small island off the Georgia coast. "The best place to live and work I've ever found!"

O'Neill and Sinclair Lewis[73] are alike in one respect. Both have naturally a boyish quality, an innocent artlessness in a number of directions, that will doubtless remain with them to their last years. In it lies much of their charm. Lewis is as excited over a party as any debutante, and a trip to Hoboken on the ferry works him up to a degree of delight comparable only to Robert Fulton's first sensation when he saw his steamboat actually working. O'Neill, for all his solemn exterior, gets an unparalleled pleasure from splashing around in a swimming pool and making funny gurgling noises, from putting on the fancily colored dressing gowns he bought several years ago in China, from singing raucous duets with a crony—"Rosie, You Are My Posy" and "'Twas Christmas in the Harem" are two of his favorites,—from lying on the ground and letting Blemie, his pet dog, crawl over him, the meanwhile tickling him on the bottom, from watches with bells in them, from the idea that one day he may master the accordion and be as proficient a performer as the vaudeville headliner, Phil Baker,[74] and from drinking enormous glasses of Coca-Cola and making everyone believe it is straight whiskey. When his very lovely wife, Carlotta, comes down to dinner in some particularly striking gown, his face lights up like a county fair. She knows well the effect it has on him and quietly lays in a constantly replenished wardrobe for his relish. "Do you like it?" she will delicately ask on each occasion. And, though his infinite satisfaction is clearly to be perceived, like a little boy who doesn't want to give in and admit anything too quickly, he will invariably mumble, "Well, it's pretty, but I like blue better."

Years ago, he was a drinker of parts. In fact, there were times when he went on benders that lasted a whole month and times when he slept next to the bung-hole of a whiskey barrel at Jimmy the Priest's and when Jimmy, the proprietor, coming to work the next morning, found the barrel one-eighth gone. About four or five years ago, however, he hoisted himself onto the water-wagon and has since sat thereon with an almost Puritanical splendor and tenacity. Like many another reformed bibber, he now views the wine-cup with a superior dudgeon and is on occasion not averse to delivering himself of eloquent harangues against it and its evils. It is not easy to forget his pious indignation when Barrett Clark once ventured to mention his old drinking bouts to him. "Altogether too much damned nonsense has been written since the beginning of time about the dissipation of artists!" he exploded. "Why, there are fifty times more real drunkards among the Bohemians who play at art, and probably more than that among the people who never think about art at all. The artist drinks, when he drinks at all [note the whimsy of that *at all*], for relaxation, forgetfulness, excitement, for any purpose except his art!" So today, it is Coca-Cola, followed by Kalak,[75] with a vengeance.

O'Neill is very slow in making friends. He tests a potential friendship much after the technique of a fisherman, trying out various personal and metaphysical lines, flies and worms to determine what kind of fish the stranger is and to what degree, personally or philosophically, he resembles a sucker. Once he has made a friend for himself, that man remains a friend, in his eyes, until Hell freezes. In all the world I suppose that there are not more than five men at the very most whom O'Neill really regards as friends, and at least three of these are relics of his early more or less disreputable days in Greenwich Village and the adjacent gin-mills. I had known him for exactly ten years until we got to the point where we called each other by our first names.

He has done much of his more recent writing in an enormous chair that he had manufactured for himself in England. It is a cross between a dentist's and a barber's chair, with all sorts of pull-in and pull-out contrivances attached to it and with a couple of small shelves for reference books. A board is so arranged that it can be manœuvred in front of him and on it he rests his pad. Stripped to the waist—he never works, if he can help it, with anything on above his navel—and with his legs stretched out to their full length, he writes everything in long hand and his chirography is so minute that it takes a magnifying glass for average eyes comfortably to read it.

I have never known him to tell a smoking-car story and, if someone happens to venture one while he is around, he sits silent and wide-eyed at its conclusion, as if he couldn't possibly understand it and wonders just what the point is. As for himself, he has just one story and will repeat it, to his apparent own infinite amusement, on the slightest provocation. It is the venerable one known as "The Old Bean," and concerns the braggadocio of an old souse who, despite all the dire catastrophes that befall him, imagines that the tremendous shrewdness of his intellect allows him on all occasions to get the best of everyone else. It is a long story, lasting at least an hour if related at top speed, and I have heard it from him regularly twice a year. Once, telling it to me again and embroidering its details, it occupied the entire time it took us to walk the seven miles from Le Plessis to Tours. The sole other occasion for unwonted loquacity on his part is the reminiscence of his vagrant New York days at the dive known as the Hell Hole and at Jimmy the Priest's where, with a pot-companion named Joe Smith, he shared a room—which they always referred to as "the garbage flat"—for the fine sum of three dollars a month. His particular comrades at Jimmy's, in addition to Joe, included a number of odoriferous colored gentlemen, a press-agent for Paine's Fireworks named Jimmy Beith, and one Major Adams, a red-nosed inebriate of sixty-odd who had been cashiered years before from the British army. This fraternity, hardly ever with more than fifty cents at a time in its combined treasury, subsisted on raw whiskey for breakfast and on what free lunch it could cabbage off the end of the bar during the rest of the day. From time to time, other habitués of the place were accepted into the fold, including an old sea captain named Chris Christopherson, whom O'Neill in later years incorporated name and all into his play, *"Anna Christie,"* a sailor named Driscoll, whose name suggested to him the Driscoll of *Bound East for Cardiff*, *The Moon of the Caribbees* and *In the Zone*, and a septuagenarian miser who had lived in a small, bare room above the saloon for twenty-two years, who never could persuade himself to throw away a newspaper and who could hardly find room enough to sleep on the floor for the enormous stacks of accumulated copies of the *New York Times*. The favorite tipple of the brotherhood, when one or another of the members—usually O'Neill, who at intervals would contrive to cozen a dollar out of his father—managed in some way to get hold of the price, was, aside from the breakfast rye, Benedictine drunk by the tumblerful. But such treats were rare and makeshifts were necessary. Alcohol mixed with camphor was found—after one got used to the taste—to have a pretty effect. Varnish diluted with water was also discovered to have its points. And there were days when even wood alcohol mixed in small doses with sarsaparilla, with just a soupçon of benzine to give it a certain bouquet, was good enough, in the brothers' view, for any man who wasn't a sissy.

For weeks on end, the brotherhood would sit, or lie, in Jimmy's without stirring out for even a moment's breath of air. That is, all save the Major, who had a hobby for collecting old and wholly useless books of all descriptions, which he never read, and for attending funerals. If he came home any evening without at least three frowzy books garnered from God knows where or without having attended at least two funerals of persons entirely unknown to him, he would mope for the rest of the night and would regain his cheer only after he had drunk a half dozen or so toasts to His Majesty, the King, in beakers of varnish. It was apparently not the royal toasts, however, that caused the Major's demise, but something ponderously diagnosed by a hastily summoned neighborhood medico as "malicious liver complaint." The Major's funeral was a gala affair, with the remaining brotherhood so melancholiously but none the less richly in its cups that no fewer than three of the mourners lost their balance and tumbled into the grave on top of their late brother's coffin.

Nor was it the nature of the brotherhood's refreshments that unwound the mortal coil of Brother Beith. Learning one night, while full of Pond's Extract mixed with one-eighth whiskey and three-eighths gasoline, that his dear wife, whom he had forgotten all about in the fifteen years he hadn't laid eyes on her, had run off with a fellow in South Africa, he committed suicide by jumping out of one of Jimmy's upper windows.[76] Beith's suicide, together with certain personal emotional misfortunes in an encounter with Cupid, weighed upon O'Neill's mind and—now it may be told—a month or so after Beith took his life the man who was to become the first of American dramatists attempted, with an overdose of veronal, to follow suit.[77] When, one afternoon at two o'clock—the conventional hour for rising and having whiskey breakfast—O'Neill failed to stir, failed even to respond to the brothers' nudges, pokes and peremptory kicks, an ambulance was quickly summoned and our friend was carted off at a gallop to Bellevue. With the brothers grouped solicitously about his cot, two internes worked over him for an hour before he again gave signs of life. Three hours later, the dose of veronal not having been so large as he believed, O'Neill was back in the world once more and, with a whoop of joy, the brothers put on their hats and moved mysteriously toward the door. "We'll be back soon," they observed significantly—and were gone. Four hours later, they reappeared, all beautifully and magnificently drunk. It developed that they had rushed to O'Neill's father and had got fifty dollars from him to pay the hospital fee for his son's resuscitation. "You dirty bums!" groaned O'Neill, with what vocal strength he could muster. "How much you got left?" Thirty-two dollars, they reluctantly informed him. "All right, divide!" he insisted. And with his sixteen dollars safe in hand, he rolled over, grinned satisfiedly, and went happily and peacefully to sleep.

We were sitting one late Summer afternoon about two years ago in my rooms in the Avenue Maréchal Foch, in Paris, looking out at the merry-go-round of motor cars in the Etoile and at the Arc de Triomphe in the sinking sun. I asked him—his reflective mood seemed to inspire the question—what he would like more than anything else out of life.

"The Nobel Prize?" I hinted out of the side of my apéritif glass.

"On careful consideration—and no sour grapes about it because I have had no hopes—I think the Nobel Prize, until you become very old and childlike, costs more than it's worth. It's an anchor around one's neck that one would never be able to shake off," he answered, gulping his tea.

"A more intelligent critical appraisal of your work?" I smiled.

His ears, as is their wont when critics and criticism are mentioned, stood setter-like and challenging on end. "I expect denunciation! It's generally sure to come. But I'm getting awfully callous to the braying, for or against. When they knock me, what the devil!, they're really boosting me, with their wholesale condemnations, for the reaction against such nonsense will come soon enough. These tea-pot turmoils at least keep me shaken up and convinced I'm on my way to something. I know enough history to realize that no one worth a damn ever escaped them—so it gives me hope. When I'm generally approved of, I begin to look in the mirror very skeptically and contemplate taking up some other career I might succeed at. So it's all tonic."

He finished his tea.

"I'll tell you what I want and it's the God's truth. I want just what I've now at last and for the first time in my life got! Life has certainly changed for me in the last year or so and for the first time in God knows how long I feel as if it had something to give me as a living being quite outside of the life in my work. The last time I saw you I told you I was happy. A rash statement, but I now make it again with a tenfold emphasis. And, believe me, it has stood tests that would have wrecked it if it wasn't the genuine article. I feel younger and more pepped up with the old zest for living and working than I've ever felt since I started working. I may seem to slop over a bit, but you don't know into what a bog of tedium and life-sickness I was sinking. I was living on my work as a fellow does on his nerves sometimes, and sooner or later my work would certainly have been sapped of its life because you can't keep on that way forever, even if you put up the strongest of bluffs to yourself and the world in general. Now I feel as if I'd tapped a new life and could rush up all the reserves of energy in the world to back up my work. Honestly, it's a sort of miracle to me, I'd become so resigned to the worst. So be a little indulgent and don't mind my unloading a little of the pop-eyed wonder of it at you!"

At this point Carlotta, his wife, came in, put her arm around him and kissed him.

"Where've you been?" he asked, his face suddenly lapsing again into that perverse little-boy expression. Carlotta gave him another little kiss. "I've been shopping for dresses, Genie dear," she said. "Blue ones."

# 42 / Maxine Edie Benedict

Maxine Edie Benedict (?–2007) was O'Neill's private duty nurse in San Francisco in 1936 when he had his appendix removed. She was a 1936 graduate of the Samuel Merritt School of Nursing in Oakland, California, and nursed both Eugene and Carlotta at various points throughout their lifetimes.

Thalia Bradford Brewer (1907–2002) was born in Frankston, Texas, and attended the University of Mary Hardin-Baylor and the University of Texas. She was a journalist who wrote for the *Austin Statesman*, the *San Antonio Express*, the *New York Herald Tribune*, and the *New York Times*. In 1951 she moved with her family to Danville, California, where Eugene and Carlotta O'Neill had recently left Tao House. As cofounder of the Eugene O'Neill National Monument Association (1968) and the Eugene O'Neill Foundation (1974), her work was instrumental in the designation of Tao House as a National Historic Site in 1975.

Source: Thalia Brewer, interview notes with Maxine Edie Benedict, 18 October 1977, Louis Sheaffer Collection of Eugene O'Neill Materials, Department of Special Collections, Charles E. Shain Library, Connecticut College.

Last Sunday evening I had a long and interesting conversation with Maxine Edie Benedict, who lives in Falls Church, Virginia. Her first comment was, "I've been thinking about the O'Neills off and on all day." The sixteenth, of course, was Eugene O'Neill's birthday.

Barely twenty at the time, Maxine Edie was a private duty nurse assigned to O'Neill at Merritt Hospital[78] when he was hospitalized there in the winter of 1936–1937. She said she was on call by Carlotta and Eugene for the rest of their lives. She found both of them "warm and friendly." A lasting impression of O'Neill was of "an humble and sweet man." She said she once told him, "I like you much better than your plays."

After O'Neill left Merritt Hospital, "If someone sneezed, I would be called," Maxine said. "It was really a privilege" to attend them in the Bay Area, first—after the hospital stay—at the residence they rented on Avalon Street, Berkeley; the estate in Lafayette which they rented while Tao House was being built; and then at Tao House itself.

She remembered, particularly, caring for Carlotta following Carlotta's eye surgery which was performed by Dr. Hans Barkan, an ophthalmologist, in San Francisco. Maxine mentioned that Carlotta's seemingly haughty demeanor was caused by the eye problem which necessitated, for the sake of comfort, holding the head aloft and slightly backward.

At Tao House, Maxine remembers the extensive watch and small clock collection that O'Neill kept in his bedroom—a bedroom much smaller than Carlotta's. She recalls Esteban, the stuffed toy monkey (about three feet in height) which Carlotta kept on her bed. Esteban had been a gift from Eugene. Maxine remembered seeing it again years later in the O'Neills' New York apartment.

Maxine recalled that "Papa Gene," often called by this name with affection by his wife, loved to dance to the slow, rhythmic blues emitted by Rosie [O'Neill's player piano] or to music from his records of which he had a large collection. Maxine's mother was invited from time to time to have dinner with the O'Neills, along with Maxine. "After dinner he enjoyed dancing with my mother, who was a marvelous dancer."

Maxine did not get the impression that Eugene was ever anything more than kind and charming and fatherly to Jane Caldwell, the daughter of Carlotta's old friend, Myrtle, who was married to Dr. Charles Caldwell.[79] "Carlotta and Eugene were wrapped up in each other. He was as possessive as she." But, Maxine went on to say, there seemed no love left at the time of O'Neill's death. Carlotta told Maxine some time after his death that both she and Eugene had been overly medicated while they lived at Marblehead.

Shane O'Neill and Maxine were about the same age, and "Eugene and Carlotta tried to stir up a romance between Shane and me when he visited at Tao House. They were just teasing us, of course."

The O'Neills always remembered Maxine on her birthdays and at Christmas. They gave her a number of lovely gifts which included a star sapphire ring, a gold watch, a clock, a desk, and a riding vest and shirt. (Maxine did some horseback riding.)

[. . .]

In 1947, when Maxine and her husband were stationed at Stewart Air Force Base at Newburgh, N.Y., Carlotta wrote that Eugene wanted to spend his 59th birthday with them. Bennie and I cooked a birthday cake and put one candle on it. It was a luncheon, so they could get back to New York without its being too late. Some of the people at the base who saw them arrive at our quarters in their black limousine—driven by a chauffeur—were impressed. We loved having them, and they were happy to be with us. We had dinner with them on several occasions in their New York apartment.

# 5
# California and New York (1938–1948)

After the move to Tao House in 1937, despite his deteriorating health, O'Neill worked on the cycle plays and wrote *The Iceman Cometh, Long Day's Journey Into Night, A Moon for the Misbegotten*, and *Hughie.* Unable to complete the cycle plays, O'Neill burned his notes and several of the manuscripts for unfinished plays. Claudia Andreasen Fetzer, who lived near Tao House, recalled the O'Neills' isolated life in California: "The community was not impressed with celebrity and his taciturn demeanor did not endear him to those whom he encountered. Apparently he had no interest in his neighbors and the feeling was mutual."[1] In 1944 the O'Neills sold Tao House and moved into San Francisco, and in 1946, they left California to come to New York for the rehearsals of *The Iceman Cometh.* As the only Nobel Prize–winning American dramatist, O'Neill had achieved an unparalleled position in the American theater and was received by the New York press with as much reverence as it is capable of. He was also failing in health and watched over relentlessly by his wife, Carlotta, which made interviews difficult.

Karl Schriftgiesser, S. J. Woolf, and Herbert J. Stoeckel describe their various experiences with O'Neill at this point. In a 1956 interview with Seymour Peck, Carlotta talks about these years. Paul Crabtree, Marcella Markham, and Mary Welch describe O'Neill's interaction with them as young actors when Crabtree and Markham were appearing in *The Iceman Cometh* in 1946 and Welch in *A Moon for the Misbegotten*, which was produced by the Theatre Guild in 1947 but closed in St. Louis before it reached New York for its intended Broadway production. Ingrid Bergman speaks of her meeting with O'Neill and their discussion of the cycle plays that he ultimately destroyed. Sean O'Casey writes of his friendship with O'Neill. Saxe Commins and Bennett Cerf give their accounts of O'Neill's years with Carlotta at Tao House in California.

# 43 / Carlotta Monterey O'Neill

Carlotta Monterey O'Neill (1888–1970) was born and educated in California, and first became publicly known as the winner of a beauty contest representing that state. She became an actor, making her Broadway debut in the play *Taking Chances* (1915). She met O'Neill in 1922, when she played the role of Mildred Douglas in his play *The Hairy Ape* (see figure 16). In 1929 they were married, shortly after O'Neill divorced his second wife, Agnes Boulton. They lived for short periods in France, in Georgia, in California, and in Massachusetts, Carlotta supervising either extensive renovations or the building of new houses in each new place, and controlling the couple's life with increasing restrictions on O'Neill's communication with old friends and associates. They fought with mounting intensity, finally separating when O'Neill, impaired by the degenerative disease of the brain that plagued his later years, apparently stormed out of the house in Marblehead, Massachusetts, fell in the snow, broke his leg, and was left there by Carlotta until the family doctor came. They eventually reconciled, moving to a residential hotel in Boston, where O'Neill died in 1953. Carlotta moved to New York and lived in a hotel until she entered a nursing home in Westwood, New Jersey, where she died.

Seymour Peck (1917–1985) grew up in New York City and graduated from City College of New York. He wrote for the newspaper *PM* and its successors from 1942 until he went to work for the *New York Times* in 1952, where he eventually became Sunday drama editor, editor of the Sunday Arts and Leisure section, and the *Times*'s cultural news editor. When he was killed in an auto accident at the age of 67, he was still serving as an editor on the Sunday *Book Review*. He served on the nominating committee of the Tony Awards and was known for his encyclopedic knowledge of the theater.

Source: Seymour Peck, excerpts from an interview with Carlotta Monterey O'Neill, 2 October 1956, transcript in Louis Sheaffer Collection of Eugene O'Neill Materials, Department of Special Collections, Charles E. Shain Library, Connecticut College, New London.

O'NEILL [. . .] *Strange Interlude*—he really made some money. So I encouraged him to have everything on earth he could have that he had never had. I thought it was good for him. I thought it would give him a sense of—well, I don't know—feeling just as well dressed as the next man. And it did help him. Of course, there was many a quarrel about he should not have shoes made to order. Was awful about that because I was making him a gigolo, or something, but finally I got him there, and he ended up by having seventy-five pairs of shoes before we got back to America. Then I introduced him to tailors. He had all clothes. In short, when he returned to America he never bought a suit, a pair of shoes or anything. Maybe a pair of sports things or something, but he had a complete wardrobe, and he was ever so pleased that he had it because in the midst of all this—when it was finished, I should say,—the depression came. So, it was very good, he had a wonderful wardrobe and everything.

[. . .]

We could never go to the theater here. If we did, somebody in the audience when they were walking back and forth, you know, somebody would spy him and they would say—OH, MR. O'NEILL, OH, IT'S SO WONDERFUL, you see, and people would gather around. And I could just see him sort of disintegrate. It was terrible, so we just stopped at home. Now there were very few people he really liked—you know that, don't you? Very few, because he did not feel at home with them. [. . .] He hated to come to New York for a production because as he sat and watched—I used to sit by him and take notes and things—as I would sit there and watch his play—like in *Mourning Becomes Electra* we sat seven weeks. I never was bored a minute, it was wonderful. And he was so fascinated by the characterization of Nazimova and Alice Brady and also of Earl [*sic*] Larimore but particularly the two women.[2] But as the play went on he became more fascinated by them but they were less what he wrote, you see. These were totally different characters but they made them so wonderful from their point of view of characterization that they did no harm to the play. But it wasn't what O'Neill had fancied. For instance, this New England father and Alice as a New Englander—her Irish and French which was so wonderful. And the things like that would disturb him so. And then in different plays, when they would be put on, they would come to him and feeling badly—he spoke very, very quietly and rather indistinctly—and they would come to him and say—Mr. O'Neill this play is running fifteen minutes too long. And he would look at them, say nothing, and then they would look at him and become a little embarrassed. Well, the people who come from Westport or Long Island have to catch the last train. He would say—They don't have to come to the play if they have to catch the last train. I don't give a damn if they come to the play or not, and I don't care if they miss their train. This is my play. And then, of course, the fight would begin, you see. All that kind of thing which worried him and disturbed him and everything.

[. . .]

When we lived in France Gene had a (check spelling) Begotti Racer,[3] and he had a marvelous time with that [see figure 13]. And, when he was very nervous and tired, he would go out in this racer and drive 95, 98 miles an hour and looking— not a wrinkle, you know, 19 years old and perfectly relaxed. He took me out one day and they almost had to get me out of the car. I was gone, I was so terrified. But when he came back to this country he never drove a car because it meant driving in traffic, and he said I'm no chauffeur for anybody and there was no place and so we always had a chauffeur.

[. . .]

When this war thing began, you see, here [he] was with this big house [Tao House], 158 acres and Gene would have pets. He had to have chickens of all things . . . . . The things he liked as a little boy, you know, and could never have enough of because his parents were on the road and he had no home. He was put in school at six. So, he got quite bronze—I'll never forget—and I spent my life typing with two fingers.—I didn't know how to type.—writing, you know, getting data for all these chickens and things, and he kept ordering chickens. [. . .] Well, it was all right as long as we had servants there but when the war came and everybody left, here was Carlotta feeding the [chickens], looking after the swimming pool, making the beds, scrubbing the floors, cooking and everything, it was no fun.

[. . .]

He never had any vacations—as they went on, or went home to their parents or [were] taken off to the mountains or anywhere. He had an old English nurse,[4] and he said that she was marvelous . . . this darling old woman sometime in the summers would take him to her house or where her cousins lived or something, and she would take him to the aquarium that used to be downtown. Or, she would take him to the zoo or she would take him to all sorts of places. And treat him as a little boy should be treated. And he had wonderful times. She took him to the circus once, he told me. As I told you, those three afternoons [in fall 1926], I sat and listened to this man and at first I was a little worried and then I was deeply unhappy. I thought of all people to be so stricken, a man who has talent, and he has worked hard and all and his face would become sadder and sadder and he would talk and talk and then finally he would say—do you know what time it is, do you have a watch? And I would say there is a clock there. And he would look at it and say—I have to go, I have to go and he would rush out and come back the next day and go on. Well that's what got me in all my trouble with O'Neill, my maternal instinct came out—this man must be looked after, you see. But he told me different things in his life. He was very sensitive in a way and yet could be very cruel. That's like all real sensitive people, don't you think?—They turn diametrically opposite.

[. . .]

And he would tell me how he had been offended by not being able to keep up. For instance, at Princeton even his father gave him so little. Now when he went to Baker's class at Harvard—Monte Cristo we always called him to differentiate—Monte Cristo gave him the magnificent sum of $10 a week. He was to pay his board, his room, his streetcar fare, his laundry, anything. . . . it wasn't drinking, of course, he was studying very hard and he told me this—that every now and then he would want an ice cream soda. And if he did he would have to walk all the way to where he went and back. He boarded with a Mennonite family.[5] He said they were very good to him, and the woman was a very good cook, and he had plenty to eat. That was one Godsend, and he had a clean decent little bed. But he was fortunate in that because God knows what he would have gotten if he had gone to other places. And then he would explain how, you know, other boys—because he was a man and he had been to sea and he had been all this—he didn't have anything for anything. And that was another thing that broke my heart. I couldn't bear this child I had adopted had suffered these things. And then he was very bitter, more bitter—he was never against his mother because you see she didn't know what she was doing. It was all a vicious circle. The father came over in the steerage when he was about twelve years old, Monte Cristo. I forget how many brothers and sisters he had, and his father and mother, and they went to Cleveland because they had some distant relatives there. And they had a terrible time. They didn't find any gold in the streets, they found that they had to work and there wasn't much pay. And they were terribly poor, terribly poor. And the Mother had to go out and work, Monte Cristo's mother. But the father, he never worked, he just loitered around and somehow managed to drink and everything else.[6]

Etc. Etc. Etc. [in transcript]

[. . .]

O'NEILL: When [James O'Neill] got back, he bought this very shabby looking little house.

PECK: The house in New London? Have you seen it Mrs. O'Neill?

O'NEILL: Yes. Unfortunately, my husband took me when we got back from Europe, and after we had lived in the Chateau he wanted to go back to see the house in New London. And I said don't do it darling, don't do it.—don't ever try to go back. Keep your ideas but don't go back. No, he must go. So we took the car and we went up. We went down Pequot Avenue, and he said I can't find it, I can't even see it. It can't be Pequot Avenue. Well, to be brief, this house had grounds that went directly to the water. But in the time that Gene had been away, the town or the city had cut a street through and built little houses along here to the water and he couldn't find it. Well, I was thunderstruck when I saw this quaint little birdcage of a house sitting there. And he said, I shouldn't have come. And I said, well never mind, you have come, now let's get out of here. And he said, yes, let's get away. I don't want to look at it. Well, that was that. He bought the cheapest furniture. It was terribly shabby—it was horrible or so Gene told me. I do not know, I never was inside it. But somebody had bought it.

PECK: You never had been inside it at all.

O'NEILL: Oh, no. You couldn't have dragged me in. And somebody was living there anyway. He just wanted to see it. This nostalgic thing that is always around to give way to.

[. . .]

PECK: How long would you say it took him to write [*Long Day's Journey Into Night*]?

O'NEILL: I don't know because I don't know how long—You see he would always make notes. He was always working on three or four plays at a time. And you must remember he was doing a cycle, and he kept adding the plays to the cycle. First it was to be seven, then nine and then I don't know how many it was. And he always meticulously wrote scenarios and then [would] go over them and then cut and change. And then after a year or so read them all and tear them all up and start all over again. But this he worked on when he once got down after the notes and after the scenario. When he once got to the dialogue it didn't take him long because he knew exactly what he wanted to say.

[. . .]

PECK: Did he work very long hours? Did he start very early in the morning?

O'NEILL: He worked just the same as a person would work in a shop, or anyplace. When he was working he got up at a certain hour, had his breakfast at a certain hour brought up to him.

PECK: For instance, what time would you say?

O'NEILL: Well, he would rise about half past seven and he would dress and his breakfast would be brought up to him on a tray, and then he would go into his study. And my job was to keep the house quiet and nobody to go near him. Orders were, not even if the house is on fire . . . . He is to be disturbed and at one o'clock, he tried for a bit to come downstairs to luncheon [but] it was very bad because he would sit there, I would sit here and actually his whole mind was on his play, acts, lines, ideas and he could not talk, and I would have to sit there perfectly dumb and I didn't want to even make a sound with a chair or anything. I didn't want to disturb him. It made me very nervous and it made him nervous seeing me sitting there you see. So we decided the best thing [was that] he have his lunch on the tray also, which worked out very well. Then he would sometimes, if he had been working very hard, he would lie down for a bit or if he were just at a place he wanted to go on he would go back and work a bit. He generally took a rest sometime in the afternoon. If the weather was nice, he would swim later or after that he and I took a walk, and again, if he were at a part of the play he wanted to look over or change or add something then he would go back again. He very rarely worked after dinner, very rarely, except again if he were at a place he wanted to get it absolutely so he would not lose the trend by going to sleep or something.

PECK: He would talk over the play with you in the evening?

O'NEILL: Always, always talk over.

Do I look too athletic in my sweater?

PECK: You look like Marilyn Monroe.[7]

O'NEILL: Not me dear, you didn't look well.

[. . .]

PECK: Would you say that it was more difficult living with him during these periods when he was so hard at work?

O'NEILL: Oh, heavens no. It was a privilege to live with him because it was mentally stimulating. My God, how many women have husbands who are very stimulating? I had to work like a dog. I was his secretary, I was his nurse, I built his house. I did everything, he wrote the plays. I did everything else. I looked after everything, tended to the business, did everything. Heavens no, I loved it. We used to argue because when we first began this, of course he didn't know anything about people anybody like me and I had never met anybody like him so we had to sort of get acquainted and once in a while we would have to stop and look [at] what we had got into. We had both read, my father was Danish, my mother French and Dutch, I was educated in England and France and my reading had been very seriously pointed out to me, my father tended to all this,[8] I must read, and read and read and when we married and his library and my library finally got into our home, he thought I had played a trick on him, I don't see how he could figure anything out because we had ninety percent the same books. He thought it was the funniest thing he had ever seen and I said "How would I know what you had, why would I waste, money. . . so then we simply took the best editions and kept them but we had had the same thing and I think that was the first thing, that we could talk, we were interested in the same things.

[. . .]

PECK: Was the sense of release in finishing [*Long Day's Journey Into Night*] greater, would you say, than with some of his other plays in so far as it was such a deeply personal expression?

O'NEILL: I imagine it was but he never said it but I could tell by his actions. He would simply come out and say "Well, thank God, now that is finished." Gene was not, he was not a chatty person, and even when the very few people did come to our place, because you see we worked all the time, except Christmas Eve—we didn't work Christmas Eve—but while he was working he never saw people unless he had to, sometimes what he would call his business associates. They would turn up from odd points of the globe and they would talk and then he would go back again. He was wonderful because you see in the evening we always had enormous fire places unless it was a hot summer or something, but we always had a fire and we had a Dalmatian dog we adored. I must send you Blemie's will.[9] It was one of the most charming things Gene ever wrote. I would love to do that. And he would sit there and read and I would sit here and read and Blemie would sit first by me and then by him not to hurt anybody's feelings you see. All he would say to me [was], listen to this, and he would read me something. He was very fond of poetry and so was I and some nights he would read Yeats[10] particularly those charming Gaelic things you know. And if he had a sense of humor and felt very gay he would act them out. He was wonderful. He could be the worst ham you ever met. He was very charming. But if he was sick, he would be silent and just sit and think.

PECK: There is no particular hoopla or gaiety attached to the writing of a play?

O'NEILL: Oh mercy, no. There was no hoopla in our house. Even his humor when he was most funny, he did it very quietly, didn't he, sort of you had to be on edge to hear.

[. . .]

I will tell you the strange thing about him and it was real. Honors never meant anything nor did adverse criticism, because he one day said to me: "I know when a play is lousy, and I know when it is good. I know much more about a play than they do. So what is the difference. If they praise me, well that is nice, it is charming of them. I am glad they appreciate it. But, if they don't, no, no. . . And you know after a play [was written] we never saw a play played. We were there every day at rehearsal, then we saw the dress rehearsal and when the dress rehearsal was over the car would be outside with the chauffeur and bags. We would hop in and go. Nobody knew where we were. Half the time we didn't even know where we were going. That saved a lot of trouble. Of course, we didn't tell the chauffeur anything because we made up our minds after we got started, and a great many times he never read criticisms of an opening because he was already at work on a new play. You see he had been thinking about it while the rehearsals were going on.

PECK: Then in the last years you wouldn't say there was an increase in depression over the lack of popular interest.

O'NEILL: He never paid any attention to popular interest, but he was too much worried about not being able to work. He always used to say to me, again and again and again: "If I could only just write and never have to bother to go to New York and produce," but we had to eat and we had other many responsibilities. And there you are. All he thought of doing was writing.

# 44 / Marcella Markham

Marcella Markham (1922–1991) was a stage and screen actor. Her first Broadway role was in the farce *Vicki* in 1942, and her biggest role was as Betty in *The Threepenny Opera* at the Theatre de Lys in 1954. She did a good deal of television work between 1963 and 1984, playing Nancy Astor in the miniseries *Winston Churchill* in 1981.

Paul Ryder Ryan (1932–2006) was a journalist, poet, novelist, editor, and teacher, with a long and varied career. He grew up in Rye, New York, and graduated from Harvard University. Although he wrote five works of fiction on Asian topics, in the 1970s, he edited the *Drama Review*, contributing articles on such topics as the Living Theatre in Brazil and theater as prison therapy, as well as writing on theater for other periodicals.

Source: Paul Ryan, "Eugene O'Neill: A Hundred Years On," *Drama: The Quarterly Theatre Review* 4 (December 1988): 27–30

Just as the *Iceman* rehearsals were about to start, the young Marcella Markham virtually gate-crashed the Theatre Guild's offices and persuaded the producers to allow her to read for a role in the play. "They started to throw me out," recalls Markham today, "and I thought O'Neill would never be able to get the words out to say 'no'—I knew he wanted me to stay. Anyway, he finally said it, and I read with him for the role of Cora, one of the tarts in Harry Hope's bar. Curiously enough, when he read the Parkinson's didn't bother him. He read very well." Marcella Markham read well, too, and was given the job. She remembers the 58-year-old O'Neill attending every single rehearsal. He was gaunt and suffering from a permanent tremor as a result of the disease, but he was tanned from the years he had spent in California where he and his third wife, Carlotta Monterey had built a house. "He was a very beautiful man," says Markham, "terribly handsome and very gentle. And he loved actors, just adored actors. I find that everybody makes him out these days to have been a serious, ponderous man—he wasn't. *The Iceman Cometh* was a series of comic turns . . . I mean every turn was amusing and sad, but they were vaudeville turns. That's why he got Eddie Dowling, an old vaudevillian, to direct.[11] I think he meant *Iceman* to be an entertaining piece."

# 45 / Ingrid Bergman

Ingrid Bergman (1915–1982) is best known for her role as Ilsa in the film *Casablanca* (1942). During her long acting career, she won three Oscars, two Emmys, and a Tony Award for Best Actress. She appeared in *"Anna Christie"* in Santa Barbara, San Francisco, and Maplewood, New Jersey, in 1941. Carlotta O'Neill went to see her performance in San Francisco.

Source: Virginia Floyd, "A Meeting with O'Neill," *Eugene O'Neill: A World View* (New York: Fredrick Ungar, 1979), 293–96.

I just heard about this meeting two days ago.[12] I only came to New York to celebrate Christmas and New Year with my children and grandchildren, but I was pleased to be invited. It may be that you are right. Perhaps it is again Mr. O'Neill coming to tell me that I should be present. It started with *Anna Christie* in San Francisco in 1941. After a performance his wife, Carlotta, came backstage. She said that he was too ill to come but that he would like to meet me. I said that I would like to meet him very much. I was very flattered that he wanted to see me at all, and she said she would come and pick me up two days later for lunch. She pointed out that I must not bring a photographer. I said, "No. I did not bring photographers; they were usually there already." I added: "Be very careful that they do not come without your knowing it. I will not mention to anyone that I am visiting you."

On the way to their beautiful Tao House, Mrs. O'Neill told me that she would give me a sign when I should leave. She stated that he was tired and would not want to stay very long with me. She would nod, and then I should say that I had to go. I promised her that I would do that. So I arrived, and, of course, I was very young and terribly impressed because I knew what a great playwright Mr. O'Neill was. I was also deeply concerned about my part as Anna Christie. The house was very white, and the architectural style was Chinese. There was very little furniture, and the house was airy.

Mr. O'Neill was very tall, but standing there before three staircases—platforms

—he looked even taller. He was a very handsome man but quite thin. He came toward me, and there was a silence about him that was so effective. It was the stillness that impressed me. One hardly dared to speak to him. Then, as he came closer, I saw those eyes. They were the most beautiful eyes I have seen in my whole life. They were like wells; you fell into them. You had the feeling that he looked straight through you. Then he sat down, and we talked. He told me that his wife appreciated what I had done with *Anna Christie*. Then we had lunch. I was so awed by the whole thing I cannot remember what we spoke about.

After lunch, Mr. O'Neill made a sign to me that I should come up to his working room. Mrs. O'Neill immediately made a sign that I should not, that I should go home now. I looked from one to the other, and I decided that I would follow him. We went up to his study, which was a remarkable room. He had the nine plays of the Cycle all laid out. He was working on all nine at the same time. He said: "I am writing one hundred and fifty years of American history. It is the same family, and they go from young to middle-age, to old and dying, and then on to the next generation. It is going to be about American history and a family that we follow through the ups and downs of this country." I looked at these plays. They were not finished. He worked on them all at the same time. When an idea came to him, he wrote it into the period where he thought it would be most effective.

Then he said: "I want a company that stays with me. After all, it is the same family that goes through many generations, and I want the same faces. In one play you will have a big part, and in another one you will have a small part. You will play a sister, an aunt, a young daughter." I stood there. I had just started my career in Hollywood, and I had an idea of all the wonderful movies I was going to make. I said to Mr. O'Neill: "But nine plays! You want me to be in nine plays?" He said: "Yes. I want this company to stay together for four years. In four years we will have produced them all." Of course, being young and very anxious to have a career in the movies (it was 1941), I said, "No, I am not going to do them." I regretted having to refuse. I remember he looked at me and said: "You're abandoning me." I said, "Not really. Perhaps some other time. Maybe later." I felt terrible about turning down nine plays!

As we know, Mr. O'Neill became very ill, and he never finished the nine plays. He completed *A Touch of the Poet* and the play that follows it, *More Stately Mansions*, but all the others were destroyed. He wanted to destroy *More Stately Mansions* also. I do not know if Carlotta, whom I got to know later when I was doing *More Stately Mansions* here, hid the play in a drawer or it was left in a drawer by mistake. She told me how she cried, how very difficult it was to sit there and tear up all these plays. But one copy of *More Stately Mansions* survived and was found. The play was not finished. It was about six hours long if you read it. Mr. O'Neill had just put everything into it; he had not ended it. He had put all of his ideas into this play.

Jose Quintero came to me—I was then in France—and asked me if I would read it and consider playing it. That's when I remembered Eugene O'Neill standing there saying: "Are you abandoning me?" Then I said: "This time I shall play it—never mind what the play is like." We started out on a version that was different from the Swedish version.[13] There was so much material that we had to select what we wanted. And, of course, the play was not really praised by the critics; they did not like it. However, I thought it was important that the play had been found and that we were producing it. After all, O'Neill is one of America's greatest playwrights. Even if *More Stately Mansions* is not his best play, it was written by a playwright who will go down in history as the greatest of America.[14]

# 46 / Sean O'Casey

Sean O'Casey (1880–1964) was born in Dublin, Ireland, to a poor Protestant family, and began working at manual labor at the age of fourteen. He joined the Gaelic League in 1906 and learned the Irish language, becoming a passionate Irish nationalist, labor union activist, and member of the paramilitary Irish Citizen Army. In the 1920s, his radical experience served as the basis for his early plays *The Shadow of a Gunman* (1923), *Juno and the Paycock* (1925), and *The Plough and the Stars* (1926), which were first produced by Dublin's Abbey Theatre. O'Casey moved to London in 1928, and his antiwar play *The Silver Tassie* (1928) was rejected by the Abbey the same year. O'Casey got to know O'Neill through the critic George Jean Nathan when he came to New York in 1934 for the production of his allegorical play *Within the Gates*. *Rose and Crown* is one of six volumes of autobiography that O'Casey wrote between 1939 and 1956, collected under the title *Mirror in My House* in 1956. In it O'Casey writes of himself in the third person.

Source: Sean O'Casey, *Rose and Crown* (New York: Macmillan, 1952), 321.

The five minutes had passed, and the liner swung out into the harbour, with Sean leaning over the side watching New York drawing away from him. It was a calm day, crispily cold; the evening was falling over the city, and Sean saw it fading in the half-light of the dusk, its towering buildings darkened, and a myriad lights from hill and valley of windows gleamed like friendly eyes watching him go: a city that is the outcome of many civilisations—of Stonehenge, of Peru, of Mexico, medieval Europe; melted down, remoulded, and cast out into the modern America; before all men, with all its faults, tremendous, terrible, inspiring. Many thoughts about many he had met were embedded in his memory for ever: the long, lean figure of Eugene O'Neill in the latest of Daks,[15] with a warm, welcoming smile softening his sombre face, the deep-set eyes of the great dramatist burning with a light like what would glow in the eyes of a battle-scarred crusader staring from a rocky, sun-browned hill at the distant city of Jerusalem; his wife, Carlotta, caring for him, a dark flame of loveliness; the clever, voluble Sinclair Lewis praising the goodness of the corn-cob; the sturdy Elmer Rice quivering with rage at the thought of what Nazism would do to the world.[16]

O'Casey, Sean. Letter to Otto Brandstädter, 18 July 1955; letter to Louis Sheaffer, 28 January 1957; letter to Brooks Atkinson, 25 May 1957; letter to Lester Osterman, 19 November 1959; *The Letters of Sean O'Casey*, ed. David Krause, vol. III, 1955–58 (Washington, DC: The Catholic U of America P, 1989), 165, 310–11, 435; vol. IV, 1959–64 (Washington, DC: The Catholic U of America P, 1992), 83.

To Otto Brandstädter[17]
TC. O'Casey 18 July 1955
[. . .]

Orwell,[18] to my thinking, was just a bitter raging disappointed man; riddled with disease, and one who, instead of fighting his ailment, wasted his life railing at those healthier than himself; and most of those who laud and adore him are ones who fear to do else, because their pay-packets are dependent on what they say and how they behave. O'Neill was in a very different class. He was a dear friend of mine, a very charming man, hating humbug, cruelty, and hypocrisy, who did not fully understand life—which of us can?—one who was always seeking the truth, and never even thinking of yielding his integrity for anyone or any reward. Look a little deeper into THE ICEMAN COMETH, and see what he says, implicitly, about the informer, who, alone of all the characters, if I remember right, commits suicide. And all written before the McCarthy[19] came to glorify shame and the meanest of crimes—betrayal of a comrade.

To Louis Sheaffer
MS. Sheaffer
28 January 1957
Dear friend, (all lovers of O'Neill are friends)

No one's a stranger to me, tho' all strangers aren't friends. I haven't answered your first letter because a bruising blow just borne by the death of a young beloved son kept me careless about other things.[20] As you say, I, too, have to try to deal with a few requests out of hundreds. I'm afraid this letter may be disappointing to you, for I have little to say; but what I have, here I say it: I first heard his name from the great Irish Labor Leader, Jim Larkin[21]—not unlike O'Neill in stature, & one, too, who once went down to the sea in ships. Larkin was a beloved friend of mine, knew I was interested in the theater, saw "The Hairy Ape" in New York; told me about it, & said, "You should get this play, Sean; O'Neill has a great gift, and will be heard of in days to come." A good prophecy, by God! Long afterwards, I got the play, with others, & immediately entered into understanding of the greatness of the man who wrote them. Like the towers of Ilium, he was topless. Dramatic glory shows round about him. Of course, he wore a mask at times; he didn't appear naked before every Tom, Dick & Harry; but in his plays, he revealed himself, body, soul, and spirit; and in his last play, *Long Journey* [*sic*], he holds up a flaming torch showing the nooks & crannies of a younger life, and transcends it with a poetic vision. Oh, Eugene, Eugene, your going is a great loss to the Theater. There was a giant in the American Theater in his day.

O'Neill wasn't a ready correspondent. He concentrated on his plays in a wise way. He wasted little time. So I got few letters from him—three or four; but where they are now, God only knows so I can't send them to you, for it might mean a hunt of weeks among the MS. letters, etc., I have in a big chest; and I haven't the heart or energy for a search. The friend of his youth & riper years—a very dear friend—is G. Jean Nathan, and he must have many, if he has kept them. He mentions Eugene many times in his books. GJ. is now very ill, & shouldn't be disturbed; but Mrs. Julie Nathan[22] might help you. If I remember right, Eugene wrote to me from California & from Georgia. His publishers got out a Brochure about him years ago and I wrote a few comments for this booklet. I met Eugene in New York, and was with him several times. I can honestly say I was a friend of his. The first visit was with Mr. Nathan, when Eug. feeling lonely in Calif, came to N. York, and was staying in a hotel in Madison Avenue—the Madison Hotel? On the way, Mr. Nathan—a soul-friend (anam-cara, we call this in Irish) of Eugene's, bought a few little toys for his friend—it was Eug.'s birthday, I think—, & this, meant as a joke, was none, for Eug. was a child as well as a great man to the end. Eugene wore a new pair of Daks—present from Carlotta, and was very proud of them in a child-like way. The moment we met, we got close together, & were at once Eugene, Sean, and George. Carlotta was there, of course, and presented herself as a very beautiful woman, devoted to Eug. She, too, became a friend, & I was Sean to her & she was Carlotta to me. We spoke of many things from Daks to the Drama. When I told Eug. what I thought of him, he was pleased, but took the praise like a shy child. He wasn't really conscious of his greatness: he took this in his stride, &

was concerned only in the work he had done & that which he thought of doing. The last time, when I was going, we embraced, & realised that our feelings for one another came close to love. Of course, Eug. was of Irish extraction, but he was thorough American; tho', on the strength of this extraction he accepted association with the Irish Academy of Letters founded by W. B. Yeats, the Irish Poet.[23]

O'Neill is one of the most famous Gaelic names Ireland has; a great Ulster name given to Ireland's greatest Clan Chiefs, and many Septs branch from this prime O'Neill clan name; so certainly Eugene was of Irish extraction, & a famous one, too.

I can't see a reason why Carlotta should put any obstacle in the way of a Life of O'Neill. His life, in my opinion, should be recorded, however hard the work may be. It was a full life, an adventurous life in many more ways than one; and a great man should have mention made of him, however inadequate the mention may be. We can never get to know the whole man, for that wasn't known even to himself; but we should set out to get to know as much as we can of one who took such a great and influential part, not only in the American theater, but in American life.

I do hope Carlotta may see this to be so. If you ever see her, give her the love of O'Casey.

I'm sorry I can't do more than this; but, unfortunately fate put many thousands of miles of space between him & me. "An' seas between us braid ha' roared."[24]

All good wishes to the big work you set yourself to do.

*Yours sincerely,*
*Sean O'Casey*

To Brooks Atkinson
TS. Atkinson 25 May 1957
My very dear Brooks and Oriana,

It was very pleasant to hear from you, though I often do, indirectly—I have just been reading your Review of A MOON FOR THE MISBEGOTTEN. A sad history of a self-lost brother. Eugene was inclined to be too compassionate, too inclined to torture himself by the sin of omission in others who were near and dear to him. Frailty thy name is man as well as woman, and all that Eugene could do about it was nothing; and so it was futile to grieve. I've seen over years great talents in my own brothers, not one, but three, wasted either through drink or vanity; but it availeth me nothing to go into perpetual mourning about it.

To Lester Osterman[25]
PC. *New York Times*
19 November 1959
Dear Mr. Osterman,

You do well to honor a theatre-building with the great name of Eugene O'Neill; for what finer memorial could a great Dramatist have than that of a temple dedicated to the Art he loved, and to which he added many a wide and deep honor, and, more than once, a glory.

The soul of O'Neill was a restless one, always seeking out the storm, crying out from the midst of tumbling waves, loudly enough to be above the tumult of the strongest winds, till the dark lull of death brought silence and a well-earned peace.

Yet this man could be gay. Yes, indeed, for I saw him so; I was with him a number of times in the company of his dear friend, George Jean Nathan, and then we talked and talked merrily in the surge of a gay time together; and then often I saw the somber face of the Dramatist break into the sunniness of deep and generous laughter. It was good to have met this remarkable man; to have looked into his deep wine-dark eyes; to have pressed his hand as the hand of a friend in joyful and lasting affection; and to have heard his laughter.

I am glad that in his American soul there was, not only the touch of a poet, but also the touch of an Irishman, for the O'Neills had their origin in Ireland. This great Dramatist of America and the world tells me again that our Shamrock twines a leaf or two around every flower symbolizing each State of O'Neill's great and urgent Country. The Shamrock is an unassuming and humble plant, but it is always there.

May this Theatre in New York, dedicated to Eugene O'Neill, be ever worthy of the Name's greatness and the Name's pride.

Sean O'Casey

# 47 / Karl Schriftgiesser

Karl Schriftgiesser (1904–1988) was born in Boston and educated at the Goddard Seminary in Barre, Vermont. As a journalist he worked for the *Boston Transcript*, the *Washington Post*, and the *New York Times*, where he served as acting drama editor during World War II. He also wrote a dozen books, including *Families: From the Adamses to the Roosevelts* (1940), a biography of Henry Cabot Lodge, and several works about American politics, including *This Was Normalcy* (1948) and *The Lobbyists* (1951).

Source: Karl Schriftgiesser, "*The Iceman Cometh*," *New York Times* 6 October 1946: X1, 3.

Eugene O'Neill, comfortable in old corduroy slacks, blue sport jacket and dark red carpet slippers, relaxed in his penthouse living room the other afternoon and talked about his new play. *The Iceman Cometh*, whose long four acts will be seen for the first time Wednesday afternoon, is his first drama to be produced in a dozen years.

Relaxed is not exactly correct. Even after all these years, during which Mr. O'Neill has won three Pulitzer awards and the Nobel Prize for Literature, he is still a shy man, diffident toward publicity, not anxious to talk about himself or his work. Although he has been in New York for several months he has shut himself away from interviewers naturally curious about what promises to be one of the most exciting events in recent theatre history. Besides, he was just recovering from a brief but angry attack of the flu.

At first he talked slowly, choosing his words with care. But as the afternoon wore on the thin, nervous, intense man warmed to his subject. The conversation ranged over many years and many things, especially the time when he lived downtown on the West Side along the waterfront—the scene of *The Iceman Cometh*.

This play which he has written is one in which Mr. O'Neill has great faith. He is not worried about its holding the interest of audiences for the four hours, plus dinner intermission, which it takes. As he talks about it his deep, brooding eyes now and again seem to lighten his thin, almost haggard face. An excitement lifts his voice, at most times so low and hesitating that even when sitting near him it is difficult to hear.

As the blue smoke of his Egyptian cigarettes hazed the bright sunlight breaking in bars through Venetian blinds, he went back to that time in his life, the early years of the century, which is the period he writes about in his play. The year is 1912. The place a squalid, smoky, whisky-reeking saloon, a drab oasis transformed by the long-forgotten Raines Law into an equally squalid "hotel."[26] There, in a forgetful darkness, are gathered the down-and-outers—the bums and prostitutes—that O'Neill knew when he was a sailor and was young.

"I knew 'em all," he said. "I've known 'em all for years." His voice dropped gropingly into his remembrance of things past. "All these people I have written about, I once knew." Another long pause. "I do not think that you can write anything of value or understanding about the present. You can only write about life if it is far enough in the past. The present is too much mixed up with superficial values; you can't know which thing is important and which is not.

"The past which I have chosen is one I knew. The man who owns this saloon, Harry Hope, and all the others—the Anarchists and Wobblies and French Syndicalists,[27] the broken men, the tarts, the bartenders and even the saloon itself—are real. It's not just one place, perhaps, but it is several places that I lived in at one time or another"—he let his brooding eyes wander over the present living room, with its books and comfortable furniture, and his beloved collection of records neatly stacked on shelves—"places I once knew put together in one.

"What have I done with this setting? Well, I've tried to show the inmates of Harry Hope's saloon there with their dreams. Some, you see, have just enough money from home to keep them going; but most of 'em keep from starving with the aid of the free lunch. This old Tammany politician who runs the place lives with his dreams, too, and he loves these people for he is one of them in his way.

"You ask, what is the significance, what do these people mean to us today? Well, all I can say is that it is a play about pipe dreams. And the philosophy is that there is always one dream left, one final dream, no matter how low you have fallen, down there at the bottom of the bottle. I know, because I saw it."

The time of which he writes, he recalls, marked the end of one of the great labor movements in America: the days of the old Knights of Labor, the Syndicalists, the Wobblies. Although much of this comes into the play, and more than one of his characters was in the thick of the violence, *The Iceman Cometh* is not a play about Labor as such. Its philosophy is eternal and universal, O'Neill thinks: "It will take man," he says, "a million years to grow up and obtain a soul."

O'Neill talked, too, about the title. To him titles are a matter of great importance, "I always try to get into the title the surface meaning and at the same time the deeper significance."

The surface meaning of *The Iceman Cometh* stems from a sardonic wisecrack, often repeated by one of the characters, who tells people he has left his wife safe at home with the iceman. The play revolves around this. But as it proceeds the "iceman," who started as a ribald joke, takes on a different, deeper and even terrifying meaning and before the end becomes Death itself.

The idea for *Iceman* came to him suddenly. Because he knew all the characters so well there "was not so much hard work as if I had had to dig them out." Once started, the work "flowed right along, page after page," he recalled, his deep eyes happy with the memory. Later he revised it once.

*The Iceman Cometh* apparently was created more easily than others of his plays. "I don't just write plays," he explained, "I make many notes over a long period. Then I write a scenario of 20,000 or so words. I draw out all the scenes from my own strange conception of perspective, which I understand, even if directors don't always."

Mr. O'Neill seemed happier with the conversation away from his writing and his plays. But somehow the conversation did not stay long away from the new play. Mrs. O'Neill arrived to serve coffee and bring the bad news of a change in the time for an important rehearsal. Mr. O'Neill attends rehearsals faithfully and was especially anxious for this one. It appears they had been having a little difficulty with the last act. He thought he could do a little judicious pruning and straighten things out. And that led to the inevitable question about why he wrote such long plays.

"They're much easier to cut," he said, a ghost of a grin spreading over his sad, intense face.

Source: Louis Sheaffer, Karl Schriftgiesser interview notes, Louis Sheaffer Collection of Eugene O'Neill Materials, Department of Special Collections, Charles E. Shain Library, Connecticut College, New London.

E[ugene] O['Neill] asked Times to submit a list of prospective interviewers—given about a half dozen. Chose Schriftgiesser, knew him slightly. [. . .]

About the most uncomfortable interview K[arl] S[chriftgiesser] ever had, partly because of EO's tremor, partly because of C[arlotta] M[onterey] hovering around, constantly interjecting comments (she was so protective, bossily protective); partly because of Heidt's nervousness,[28] he was so eager for the interview to go well; partly because Heidt had exacted a promise from KS that he would say nothing about EO's physical condition, his tremor, his illness (Also KS pity for EO)

EO evasive on questions re the Cycle.

Talked a good deal about N[ew] L[ondon], about having been a reporter . . . Seemed at times to be a bit mentally confused, apparently mixed-up about where KS had worked, seemed to assume that KS had worked in New London on a paper [. . .]

KS felt EO was in a reminiscent mood and that interview would have gone well if CM hadn't been there—she constantly hovered around, interrupting.

KS thot [*sic*] EO's mind had been affected to some extent by his illness.

At end moved to table and CM served coffee—fine strong black coffee. EO couldn't hold cup even with both hands, CM had to help him get it to his mouth.

# 48 / S. J. Woolf

Samuel Johnson Woolf (1880–1948) was born in New York and educated at the City College of New York and the Academy of Design. He built a unique career as an artist-journalist by drawing and interviewing famous people, including Mark Twain, George Bernard Shaw, Oliver Wendell Holmes, Winston Churchill, and every American president from Theodore Roosevelt to Harry Truman. An exhibition of his portrait drawings was held at the Museum of the City of New York in 1946. Even after he was stricken with ALS, Woolf continued to work, conducting an interview with Henry Fonda just before his death.

Source: S. J. Woolf, "Eugene O'Neill Returns after Twelve Years," *New York Times Sunday Magazine* 15 September 1946: 6, 61, 62.

Posing for me [see figure 15] in his Manhattan apartment, O'Neill made it clear that length is one theatrical problem that does not interest him. When I asked him how long a play should be he said: "As long as necessary to tell the story. No play is too long that holds the interest of its audience. If a short play is tiresome it is too long and if a long play is absorbing until the fall of the last curtain no one will pull out his watch to look at the time."

*The Iceman Cometh*, along with two other unproduced plays, *A Moon for the Misbegotten* and *A Touch of the Poet*, was written on the West Coast, where the author and his wife lived from 1931 until this year. O'Neill remarked that while he settled in turn in Seattle, Oakland and San Francisco, he never at any time lived near Hollywood. Before moving to New York the O'Neills disposed of much of the furniture in their California home, but they brought with them their vast collection of books and phonograph records, some favorite Chinese antiques and a large drum (made from a tree trunk) such as plagued the Emperor Jones as he slunk through that tropical forest.

Even among his prized possessions O'Neill seems a curiously detached person. He is tall and thin, with a repressed manner that is almost shy. Greenwich Village, where his plays first attracted attention, has left no apparent impress on him. He dresses immaculately, his hair is neatly brushed and when he smokes, as he does almost continuously, he is careful to have an ash tray by his side.

His voice is low, and as he speaks he knits his eyebrows and his large, dark eyes become more than ordinarily intense. From time to time a quiet, repressed note of humor comes into his talk and an alarmingly sudden smile breaks over his face. In repose his face is sad. In retrospect one forgets his haggard cheeks, his thin gray mustache above a soft mouth and his slightly bulbous nose. What one remembers best is his mournful eyes that look oddly like those in portraits of Poe. Like Poe, too, he looks as if he were surrounded by an aura of mysterious sorrow.

Most of O'Neill's talk, while I was sketching, was of the theatre, and much of it was reminiscent. Several times he mentioned his father, the celebrated James O'Neill. As a child, the playwright traveled widely with the elder O'Neill's troupe. "Almost the first words of my father I remember," he said, "are, 'The theatre is dying.' And those words seem to me as true today as when he said them. But the theatre must be a hardy wench, for although she is still ailing, she will never die as long as she offers an escape.

"It was when he was starring in The Count of Monte Cristo that my father decided the theatre was dying. I can still see him in that play with outstretched arms, rising from a canvas sea shouting, 'The world is mine.' It was a time when artificiality was as prevalent on the stage as it was in everyday life. The simplest lines had to be declaimed. Virtue always triumphed and vice always got its just deserts. A man was either a hero or a villain and a woman was either virtuous or vile.

"It was a prudish age which has left its impress in the form of present-day censorship. This to me is one of the biggest obstacles to the artistic development of the theatre. Now, before a play can be safely produced, somebody has to say that it will not corrupt the morals of 6-year- olds. But, to tell you the truth, I think some of the 6-year-olds could give pointers to many of us oldsters.

"I remember when the censors got after one of my plays. The result was a sudden increased demand for tickets, but the tickets were bought by the wrong kind of people who laughed at the wrong places and went away disappointed because they had not seen a smutty show."

O'Neill regards the refusal of many producers to experiment as another theatrical curse. "Many theatrical managers," he said, "fear to keep abreast of the times. They know that a certain type of play made money ten years ago and they keep to the same formula. It was the little experimental theatre which opened the eyes of the commercial producers to the fact that the taste of the public was better than they thought."

It was no surprise that a dramatist who has consistently written "experimental" plays should talk at length about theatre technique. New techniques, O'Neill pointed out, often amount to no more than fads. He mentioned expressionism as one fad that had waxed and waned in the modern theatre, and while he poked fun at that movement's excesses, he was quick to add that it had had "some good influence in playwriting. The trouble with a fad—and this holds true for any form of art—is that it affords an opportunity for people who do not know the technique to pose as artists. There are as well-established rules for the theatre as there are for painting and music. The only ones who can successfully break the rules are the people who know them. A knowledge of rules is necessary, even if adhering to tradition is not."

It is in comments like these that one catches a glimpse of O'Neill's profound interest in craftsmanship. He gets around to craftsmanship even when speaking of what he considers the bad influence of motion pictures on the stage.

"The motion picture," he asserted, "has hurt the stage. In the first place, as soon as young actors and actresses make good, Hollywood grabs them. In the old days there were many more good actors and actresses available for stage productions than there are now. In addition, many plays today are written with Hollywood acceptance in mind. Artistic concessions are made in them with the hope that they will be bought by some movie company.

"This does not mean that I am opposed to moving pictures. I enjoy many of them. I recently saw a new picture based on the life of Nurse Kenny that I liked tremendously.[29] It was written for the screen and it shows the opposition against which she has had to contend—the fate, after all, of all innovators. Some adaptations from stage plays are good. Several of mine have been extremely well done. But the entire technique of moving pictures is different. The only way a good stage play can be written is for the author to forget all about the screen. If eventually it is to be turned into a movie, it should be done by somebody who knows how to write for the screen."

Radio, too, O'Neill insists, has its own technique. He put himself on record as being opposed to the condensing of full-length plays into broadcasts that run an hour or even less.

"It is possible to write well for the radio," he added. "Norman Corwin[30] has shown that to be true. But I feel that radio should stick to its own medium and not try to act as a substitute for the theatre. It has a field all its own. When television becomes more prevalent, still another method will be used. But no matter what happens, neither films nor ether waves will ever take the place of reality."

He sat still for some minutes, saying nothing and staring out into space. In one of his thin hands was the ever-present cigarette—a mild brand with a cork tip and cotton filter. His thoughts seemed far away and I hesitated to break the silence. Suddenly he looked up and a smile spread over his face. He said that he had been thinking of the past.

Eugene O'Neill was born 58 years ago on the third floor of a hotel that stood on the corner of Broadway and Forty-third Street. After he had grown up and made a name for himself, he often stood across the street and looked up at the room. "But New York had changed," he said. "The old hotel had had several stories added to it. The green horse cars we used to take when we went to see friends who lived at Seventy-seventh Street had vanished, and above Fifty-ninth Street the Boulevard had become Broadway."

[. . .]

When I asked O'Neill which was his favorite among his plays he said he thought it was *The Great God Brown*, in which the actors wore masks. He also revealed that he had intended to use masks in *Mourning Becomes Electra* but gave up the idea when he couldn't obtain the kind he wanted.

"I hesitate to re-read my own plays," he said. "Few people realize the shock a playwright gets when he sees his work acted. Alice Brady and Alla Nazimova gave wonderful performances in *Mourning Becomes Electra* but they did not carry out my conception at all. I saw a different play from the one I thought I had written. As I look back now on all my work, I can honestly say there was only one actor who carried out every notion of a character I had in mind. That actor was Charles Gilpin[31] as the Pullman porter in *The Emperor Jones*."

He added: "I am not saying that some of the actors and actresses who interpreted my plays did not add something to them. But, after all, even an owl thinks her owlets are the most beautiful babies in the world and that's the way an author feels about his stage children. It is for this reason that I always attend the rehearsals of my plays. While I do not want to change the personalities of the artists acting in them, I want to make it clear to them what was in my mind when I wrote the play.

"I confess, though, that I have never been completely satisfied with anything that I have done and I constantly rewrite my plays until they are produced and even then I always see things which I could improve and I regret that it is too late to make more changes.

"For, after all, anyone who creates anything must feel deeply. Like Shaw, he may cover up his sincerity with humor, he may make light of his efforts, but those efforts are nevertheless heart-breaking."

The production of *The Iceman Cometh* ends a long silence, but in that silence O'Neill has not been idle. The war, he says, made it difficult for him to concentrate on work that seemed "trivial" compared to what was going on in the world. Yet there were times when he managed to forget the outer turmoil and to draft a new drama cycle about which he is loath to speak. At all times, he indicates, he works slowly. He is not adept at typewriting and he finds dictating to a secretary difficult. Accordingly, all his plays have been written in longhand.

Whatever reception *The Iceman Cometh* may receive, it is undoubtedly the work of a man who takes both the theatre and life seriously. The setting may be a bar, but it will not be the most unlikely place in which O'Neill has staged a tragic drama. In the past he has found drama of stature in the jungle, the New England village, the Midwestern farm and the forecastle. And the emotions of his characters invariably transcended the specific time and place.

# 49 / Max Gordon

Max Gordon (1892–1978) was a well-known theatrical producer. He began his producing career in the 1920s, forming the firm of Lewis and Gordon with his partner, Albert Lewis (1885–1978). He went out on his own with *Three's a Crowd* in 1930, however, and produced many plays, from musicals, revues, and operettas to such literary works as *Dodsworth* (1934) by Sinclair Lewis, an adaptation of *Ethan Frome* (1936) by Owen Davis (1874–1956), *The Women* (1936) by Clare Boothe (1903–1987), and Shakespeare's *Othello*. His final production was *The Solid Gold Cadillac* by Howard Teichman (1916–1987) and George S. Kaufman (1889–1961), which ran for 526 performances from 1953 to 1955.

Source: Max Gordon with Lewis Funke, *Max Gordon Presents* (New York: Bernard Geis, 1963), 90–91.

The firm of Lewis and Gordon represented class, style and quality. How many one-act plays we actually produced over the years, I do not know. Nor can I now describe more than a dozen in detail. But there is one for which I do have a special fondness: *In the Zone*, by Eugene O'Neill. It is a moving play, a poignant one, about a seaman whose mail is rifled by his shipmates. We picked it up among a batch of one-act plays that we had purchased from the old Washington Square Players, a Greenwich Village group that meant much to the development of the young O'Neill and to the American theatre itself. From its ranks the Theatre Guild was born.

Shortly before we were going to produce *In the Zone*, O'Neill sought us out. He wanted an advance of fifty dollars against his royalties. When I asked him why, he said that he wished to marry. *In the Zone* proved to be an artistic success on the Orpheum Circuit, but I did not hear from or see O'Neill again until many years later.

The meeting was arranged by Richard Madden, one of the country's leading play agents at the time and O'Neill's personal representative. O'Neill, Madden said, had been talking about the old days of vaudeville, about the glorious days of George M. Cohan, and had expressed a wish to hear some of the old Cohan songs. Madden said he could think of no one other than me who would remember some of those songs. When I started to say something about not being much of a singer, Madden stopped me. "Look," he said, "that's not really important. You may not have heard it, but Gene's a very sick man. He's got Parkinson's disease. Now, if you could see your way clear to visit him and sing some of those songs, you would be performing a great act of kindness."

O'Neill was gay enough as we talked and grew sentimental and nostalgic. Among the songs he wanted to hear was the one about a young Negro who says:

> I'm gonna get right up
> And put on all my clothes,
> I'm gonna go round
> And take in all the shows.
> I'm gonna ride around in an open carriage,
> And if ah meets mah girl, there's gonna be a marriage.

Another song I sang to him that night had never been published. In it Cohan described his ambitions to be a playwright and confided these to a friend, asking his advice. His friend answered:

> Go get a flag,
> Because you need it, you need it, you know you do.
> Go get a flag
> And always save it and wave it, and they'll stand for you.
> Hire a lot of chorus girls
> And fire these bum legits,
> Get yourself a Yankee Doodle gag,
> Put some real songs in your shows
> And sing the damn things through your nose;
> For Godsake, go and get a flag.

It was one of those odd evenings that occur once in a lifetime. I remember it with a strange mixture of amusement and sadness.

# 50 / Herbert J. Stoeckel

Herbert J. Stoeckel (1896–1967) was born in Hartford, Connecticut, and had a career as a journalist and popular historian, writing books like *The Strange Story of John Hanson, First President of the United States* (1956). A collection of his notebooks is housed in the Hartford History Center of the Hartford Public Library.

Source: Herbert J. Stoeckel, "Memories of Eugene O'Neill," *Hartford Courant* 6 December 1953: 3, 16.

"He doesn't like to be interviewed, and as a rule he says very little when he is. The mass interview he gave to the press just before the opening of *The Iceman Cometh* in 1946, is an exception and a notable one."

So writes Barrett H. Clark in his oft-reprinted *Eugene O'Neill: The Man and His Plays* (1946 edition). The O'Neill biographer and bibliographer is here referring to the interview the late playwright granted in early September, 1946, at the offices of the Theater [*sic*] Guild in New York City.

Clark also says that for some reason never made clear to him, the interviewers were reporters, with only a few critics present. There was no stenographer to take down what O'Neill might deign to say in answer to the myriad questions fired at him. Which was a pity, since O'Neill showed every disposition on that red-letter occasion to talk frankly about his life and work and to reveal publicly the core of his philosophy.

I happened to be present at the interview. Considering its now historic significance in the O'Neill saga, I have refreshed my memory of the event. This memoir is based on the story I wrote at the time, plus other relevant material from notes which were pigeon-holed.

My version of what took place differs from the others since it touches primarily on the Connecticut and Long Island background of O'Neill's colorful career. Why this is so had best be told chronologically.

In 1946 I was writing features for the *Nassau Daily Review-Star*, a Long Island newspaper. John M. Greene, for many years sports editor of *The Courant*, was the paper's managing editor. Greene had conceived the idea of a series of personality profiles on stage, radio and screen celebrities whose permanent homes were in Nassau County.

In obtaining these informal profiles, Times Square and Radio City became my beat.

After 12 long years of silence on the Pacific Coast, O'Neill and his wife, Carlotta Monterey, had come East with three new plays, *The Iceman Cometh*, *A Moon for the Misbegotten* and *A Touch of the Poet*, all future Theater Guild shows.

Joe Heidt, the Guild's publicity chief, had received so many inquiries about O'Neill's re-emergence, his future plans and the three plays that he persuaded the reluctant O'Neill to be interviewed en bloc and have done with the matter. Lawrence Langner's oak-paneled sanctum with its huge Tudor fireplace, was packed.

Frankly, I wasn't as keenly interested in O'Neill's current dramaturgic output as I was in the possibility that since the O'Neills intended to remain in the East, he might locate again on Long Island where he had been a former resident. That was the rumor, and such a move on his part seemed logical. In other words, I regarded Eugene O'Neill as perfect copy for another Nassau profile.

Again I was interested in him as a fellow-Nutmegger, for he was so indexed in my portfolio of Connecticut greats and superfolk. Hence the more intimate nature of my own questions. However, I instinctively jotted down some of the high spots of the interview even though it wasn't the material I really wanted.

Right on the dot, O'Neill walked in briskly and took the chair, in the center of the room, reserved for him. I saw at once that he was unwell. Always uneasy and inarticulate in public, his dramatic appearance was made more difficult by the palsy-like ailment already manifesting itself in the tall, wiry frame. At times speech was an effort for him. But he did his duty.

Yes, O'Neill admitted to the blue-stocking from a highbrow stage magazine, he had been influenced by foreign playwrights. Ibsen and Strindberg, for instance, but a more profound influence had been New England. For he considered himself a New Englander, although he had been born in New York City.

As an artist, he replied, he felt closest to the battle of moral forces in New England and as a person he loved "that region best," considering it "his home."

Here was my cue. I cut in: "Mr. O'Neill, weren't you almost born in Connecticut? Wasn't it just happenstance you were born in New York?"

That was true, he answered, turning towards me. Many of the Gotham scribes fumed a bit and glanced at me scornfully. They thought the matter quite irrelevant.

However, I had hit a nugget of O'Neillian reminiscence; thanks to it, he seemed disposed to talk about his advent in the world. He let drop a biographical fact never known before.

He told how his boyhood and youthful years had been spent in and around New London where his actor father, James O'Neill of *Monte Cristo* fame, and his mother were prominent residents.

It was only by the narrowest margin of circumstance, he continued, that he wasn't born in Connecticut. At the time his father was starring with the Union Square Stock Company. His mother, who was expecting the stork any day, had just joined her husband in New York. The big event occurred in the Barrett House, then an uptown family hotel, later the Hotel Cadillac at Broadway and 43rd Street, in the heart of Times Square, the city's future theatrical center. He humorously observed: "The Cadillac was demolished some years ago, which was a dirty trick."

I shall never forget that O'Neill smile when he said it was "a dirty trick" to raze his birthplace. Throughout the interview it seemed as if he were wearing a tragic mask of concentrated sorrow.

Then, without warning, he flashed an ear-to-ear smile, as if another mask had been suddenly superimposed. Then, instantaneously, this fleeting mask of comedy disappeared, and the mask of tragedy was donned again. One was shocked by the swift transition.

"The human race has been so damn stupid," he said, pulling no verbal punches, "that in 2,000 years it hasn't had brains enough to learn the secret of happiness, contained in one simple sentence—the Golden Rule. When you think any grammar school kid could understand and apply it, then it's time we dumped the human race down the nearest drain and let the ants take over."

Someone asked: But hasn't the Golden Rule made some progress?

O'Neill: "Oh great! When I read the papers after the World War, I thought: What's the use? It's a little different now. A little."

When someone told him he was paradoxical, he countered:

"What did Walt Whitman say?: 'Do I contradict myself? Very well then, I contradict myself.'"

Abruptly he said that the United States is "the greatest failure in the world," explaining he meant spiritual failure as he meant spiritual death in *The Iceman Cometh*.

Everything had been given the early nation, he went on, but about the time of the Mexican War, Uncle Sam started "the old game of trying to possess his own soul by possessing something outside of it, and thereby lost it."[32]

He finished this cryptic statement by quoting: "What shall it profit a man . . . ?" Sean O'Casey, he declared, is the greatest living playwright and the most beautiful things ever made in the United States were the clipper ships of New England. Of all his plays, he liked best *The Hairy Ape*, although the world seemed to prefer *Mourning Becomes Electra*.

Another revelation was his casual disclosure that among his scripts is *A Long Day's Journey Into Night* [*sic*], not to be published until 25 years after his death. When asked to give the reason for this singular provision, he remained silent. It is said that this play, which he considered his best, is autobiographical. Will the O'Neill family and New London perhaps figure in it?

After 90 minutes the interview was over. Joe Heidt had provided refreshments. However, most everybody made for the door. Only a few remained to buttonhole O'Neill and ask some more questions. O'Neill jocosely told the small group around him that in his old drinking days he would never have passed up the "refrescos." That sudden smile again.

Finally there was hardly anyone left. O'Neill stood there alone. I approached him.

"I want to talk about Long Island and Connecticut," I began. "And 'High Dive.'"

George Nathan had written in his *New York Journal American* column about "High Dive." In his talks with Nathan, O'Neill had confessed to a pent-up desire to own and run some day, as a sideline, an old-style water-front saloon, like he frequented on South and West streets in New York—and very likely in New London—in his sea-faring and Bohemian days.

I asked Nathan about it. "It's been a whim of his for years," Nathan said.

With a smile O'Neill verified this. "I haven't forgotten it. Nathan and Henry Mencken can handle the bar but I want to be at the cash register."

This inspired the question where O'Neill might settle down since he had evidently decided to stay in the East. He said that in San Francisco Carlotta and he had occupied an apartment.

"We're still living in an apartment in New York but that's not my idea of living," he told me. "Our next and permanent home will likely be on Long Island. Somehow I incline to the North Shore. Of course, the new house will overlook the Sound or the ocean."

"How about Connecticut?" I asked.

"We'll be able to see Connecticut. Besides, there isn't much difference, is there? Connecticut and Long Island were once one. When I was in New London, the North Shore coastline of Long Island was a familiar sight."

I mentioned how Walt Whitman, whom he had quoted, came from an old Connecticut family that had moved across the Sound to Long Island. O'Neill nodded and said it was just like commuting. Briefly touched upon were his New London newspaper days, school days at Betts Academy in Stamford and his T.B. experience at Gaylord Farm in Wallingford.

He confirmed what he had once said that at Gaylord he really thought about his life for the first time, that there his mind got the chance to establish itself, thus starting him on his career. It was in Wallingford that he felt he wanted to write more than anything else.

After leaving the "san"—his term for it—he lived in New London with his family for a while. When his father took to the "road," O'Neill stayed with an English family whose place overlooked the Sound.[33]

Here, on the porch, he wrote steadily, chiefly plays, completing his first important play, *Bound East for Cardiff*, in the spring of 1914.

The accompanying illustration is an enlargement of a rare snapshot of O'Neill as he looked at this time while taking a polar bear dip in Long Island Sound in 1914.

I am indebted to Dr. David Russell Lyman, former superintendent of The Gaylord Farm Sanitorium, Wallingford, for this interesting Connecticut O'Neill item.

O'Neill was a reporter on the old *New London Telegraph* when his right lung went back on him in 1912. He entered Gaylord on Christmas Eve, 1912, and after five months there was discharged as an arrested case.

He sent the snapshot to Dr. Lyman with the following New Year message written in ink thereon: "Taken—cross my heart!—Jan. 1, 1914. New London, Conn. Water—39 degrees."

Underneath, quoting Kipling, O'Neill wrote:

"The uniform 'e wore
"Was nothin' much before
"An' rather less than 'arf o' that be'ind."[34]

To prove that it was winter and that he wasn't kidding, O'Neill, it will be noted, drew an arrow at his feet, pointing to the snow on the beach.

Then O'Neill and I discussed something that struck a mutual chord: the Collings case.[35] In 1931 he was living in Northport on Long Island's North Shore. Naturally the house had a commanding view of his beloved Long Island Sound.

He fixed the time when he reflected a moment and said: "Let's see, it was just before *Mourning Becomes Electra*." In this famous play, then due to have its initial production, he again adapted, in terms of American life, Aeschylus' theme of fate overhanging a household.

"I was living in Northport when the Collings case broke," O'Neill stated.

Many *Courant* readers will recall this famous Long Island Sound mystery. The Collings family was from the Connecticut shore and the family boat was registered there. The case has never been solved.

Since this bizarre mystery of the sea had its setting off Northport near O'Neill's very house, the playwright followed with absorbed interest the unfolding of events in the sensational case. Here too an inscrutable fate had hung over a household, resulting in violent murder and family tragedy—a case which itself possessed all the elements of startling melodrama.

O'Neill's mention of the Collings murder—and it came from him—suddenly brought back memories. I swiftly saw again the Penguin leaving its safe mooring in Connecticut . . . the "pirates" boarding the Collings craft anchored that night off Northport . . . the callous flinging overboard of its owner, his hands and feet cruelly trussed . . . the cutting of the boat adrift with the five-year-old daughter, its lone occupant, aboard . . . the attack on the young wife-mother who was left unconscious on a motorboat anchored miles away in Oyster Bay.

"Were there ever any new developments in the case?" O'Neill asked. "I've been away, you know."

I shook my head.

So ended my personal interview with Eugene O'Neill. I said goodby to him and Joe Heidt. I was the last of the "guests" to leave.

O'Neill finally settled neither on Long Island nor in Connecticut. He decided on Marblehead, Massachusetts. Carlotta and he moved into a veranda-flanked wooden house at the tip of exclusive Marblehead Neck, with a broad view of the sea that has figured so prominently in many of his plays.

Here he lived in virtual seclusion until recent years when he moved to Boston to receive closer medical care. And there—in a Back Bay hotel—the final curtain fell the other day.

# 51 / Saxe Commins

Saxe Commins (1892?–1958) was born in Rochester, New York, and graduated from the University of Pennsylvania with a dental degree, although he had literary aspirations and had a play, *The Obituary*, produced by the Provincetown Players in 1918. He gave up a thriving practice in Rochester to come to New York and begin working as an editor for Horace Liveright. O'Neill, having come to like and trust Commins, made it a condition of his signing with Random House that Commins would be hired as his editor. Commins rose to become the senior editor at Random House and the director of the Modern Library Series, and to become famous as the editor not only of O'Neill but of William Faulkner, Sinclair Lewis, Gertrude Stein, and many other important writers. His friendship with O'Neill far exceeded his role as editor.

Source: Saxe Commins, "*Love and Admiration and Respect": The O'Neill-Commins Correspondence*," ed. Dorothy Commins (Durham, NC: Duke UP, 1986), 218–25, 229.

Upon the O'Neills' return to New York in fall, 1945, Saxe began to see them regularly in their suite at the Hotel Barclay. His account of that period follows:

> At dinner there one evening I was witness to a painfully embarrassing display of cruelty and vindictiveness. It was not the first time that I had been made privy to domestic scenes of spite and violence on one side and a tormented meekness on the other. The origins of the sparks that detonated this explosion of malevolence could only be sought by an examination into the nature of evil.
>
> Gene had brought with him from California a varied collection of manuscripts, the harvest of many years of intensive work. Principally they were finished plays, notes in long hand running to 125,000 words, tentative drafts, character sketches, scene divisions, snatches of dialogue, stage directions and the like for the nine plays of the cycle in progress on the

general theme of the tyranny of possessions and the consequence to those possessed by them. Among the completed plays was *A Touch of the Poet* which dealt with the founder of the family that was to proliferate from his seed through many generations to become the symbols of O'Neill's pervasive theme of the havoc wrought by the passion for possession. Of incidental interest was the choice of the name of the leading character in *A Touch of the Poet*. He was called Melody, a man who had fought under Wellington in the Peninsular Wars and had migrated to Boston, there to establish himself as a tavern keeper. The name was given him after a talk we had long before the writing of the play about prizefighters remembered from our youth. One of them, a Negro lightweight out of Boston, bore the mellifluous professional name of Honey Melody. After repeating it many times and delighting in its euphony, O'Neill said it would be a fine name for a character he had in mind.[36]

Our dinner was a dismal affair; eaten in silence and gloom. It was all too apparent from Gene's nervous anxiety and Carlotta's angry gibes that something serious had occurred. When the table was cleared I learned the cause of the tension; the manuscripts were lost. They had disappeared mysteriously during the day and there was no clue to their whereabouts.

We tried to recapitulate every event and every contingency from the time the manuscripts were last handled to the moment when it was discovered that they were missing. Gene was certain that he had not taken them out of the hotel suite when he went that morning to the offices of the Theatre Guild. He was sure that he had locked the door and delivered the key at the desk the few times he was obliged to leave the hotel. He recalled how he had packed the manuscripts in the trunk in California and how he reassured himself about their safety when his baggage was brought to their hotel rooms in New York. For a few days after that he simply assumed that they were where last he had seen them.

Carlotta disclaimed having seen the manuscripts at any time since they had left California and made matters worse by insinuations that Gene's memory was failing him, that he was growing senile and was less than aware of what he was doing most of the time. I ventured the suggestion that we make another thorough search of the suite and perhaps, like Poe's purloined letter, we would find what we were seeking in the most obvious of places. Whereupon we went through every trunk, closet, cupboard and bureau drawer in the apartment, all to no avail. Carlotta taunted us while we explored likely and unlikely places of concealment, omitting only an examination of the drawers in which she kept her lingerie and other items of a personal nature. When we stopped there, she insisted with growing resentment that we should not let delicacy deter us and she flung open the bureau in which she kept her underwear. Gingerly and embarrassedly we removed every garment, but still no manuscript came into view.

As the search continued, Gene's nervousness manifested itself in an uncontrollable tremor of his hands and a quivering of his lips. He was trying desperately to prod his memory and thus solve the mystery of the missing manuscripts, but he was completely blocked. Our systematic examination of the apartment convinced us that they had disappeared without a trace. We gave up the search and I went home.

Two days later when Gene and I were alone for a moment, he whispered to me that the manuscripts had been found and begged me to forget the entire unhappy episode. He explained, as if he were trying to condone a sick child's perverse behavior, that Carlotta had taken them out of the apartment and hidden them to punish him for reasons totally obscure to him. She knew where the manuscripts were during all the time of his torment and of the vain search. Only Strindberg, he observed grimly, would understand his predicament and know the motivations for such wantonly calculated cruelty.

When Edward Sheldon died in 1946,[37] the O'Neills gave up their suite at the Hotel Barclay and rented and refurbished his penthouse apartment. The elevator door opened directly upon a large hallway, to the right of which was Carlotta's room, furnished with a canopied bed, a blue-black paneled mirror, an elaborate dressing table and deep closets for clothes. A glazed porcelain Chinese hip-high idol stood a grotesque guard at the foot of her bed.

Gene's room, farther down the hall, was austerely furnished. In the drawers of his natural-wood desk were kept his manuscripts. At this desk we worked on the texts and proofs of his plays. A Victrola and a cabinet containing many jazz records stood against the wall beside his dresser. In the hallway near at hand were ceiling-high shelves stacked with phonograph discs.

The large living room, where Sheldon held court from his raised bier for so many years, served as a library and dining room. Its walls were lined with books and its tables covered in neat array with current magazines. A French door led to a spacious roof garden, canopied for about a quarter of its length with a large roll awning. From this roof could be seen the Metropolitan Museum of Art, Central Park and the towering apartment buildings that framed it to the west.

It was to this apartment, always associated with the living corpse of

Edward Sheldon, that I came two or three times each week, either to work or to talk haphazardly about events and ideas and books and, for the most part, a past summoned to remembrance by a phrase or a name or any one of the accidental keys that open the locks of speech and thought and communion. Our own home at the time was on East Ninety-fifth Street, only eleven short blocks away, and with or without invitation we visited each other in neighborly fashion. Neither of us had many other visitors.

Where Ned Sheldon had lain in state as a procession of callers came and went, we, the seeing and living, sat in isolation with an invisible wall around us, believing hopefully that we could exclude the world. Gene, always seclusive, now built even higher barriers against intrusion. His physical affliction, Parkinson's disease, had advanced considerably and the tremor of his hands and his slowness of speech were so manifest that he became more and more conscious of the impression they made on others. To avoid explanations and apologies he withdrew farther and farther into silence and self-effacement. Occasionally I would bring my children to visit him and now and then he and Carlotta would come to our home for dinner. . . .

Those were the quiet times. Friends and neighbors were at peace. It was the calm before a great storm. When it blew, the hurricane left a wake of destruction.

We were at dinner in the room in which Ned Sheldon's ghostly presence still lingered. Carlotta, Gene and I had moved to more comfortable chairs away from the table to drink coffee. The telephone bell rang and Carlotta answered it. The tone of her voice underwent an abrupt change when she heard the name of the caller; it was all too apparent that her annoyance was mounting. Holding her hand over the mouth-piece, she turned to Gene and said icily: "It's one of your friends, I won't talk to her." Thereupon she began to pace the floor nervously while muttering to herself.

Timidly Gene went to the telephone. All I could hear was his share of the conversation. It went somewhat like this: He said "Hello" and waited a little while. Then he said: "Of course, Fitzi, I'll do anything I can . . . Will one hundred be enough? I'll be glad to make it more . . . are you sure? . . . I'll mail you the check right away . . . Let's hope it's not as serious as you fear . . . . Count on me." Then he hung up.

While he was talking, Carlotta continued her restless pacing of the floor, wringing her hands and working up a seething rage. She was close to hysteria, her eyes blazing and her voice hoarsely incoherent with words of imprecation. When Gene came away from the telephone, her rage had mounted to fury. All of Gene's former friends were roundly cursed, blamed for his illness and branded as parasites and hangers-on. Fitzi, particularly, was singled out as the worst miscreant, as a bum and scrounger who was interested only in preying on Gene. This was M. Eleanor Fitzgerald, the friend and consoler and steadfast encourager during the days of poverty and anonymity. Mildly and placatingly Gene tried to say that Fitzi had helped him when he was in need and now he could do little less than try to repay her for her many kindnesses. She was sick and in desperate need of help and even if she was all and more than Carlotta charged, he still was bound to lend a hand. Patiently he tried to explain that the call came from Mount Sinai Hospital, where Fitzi had been taken after suffering severe abdominal pains. At first glance the doctors suspected a malignant growth and there would have to be X-ray examination and perhaps even an exploratory operation. Meanwhile Fitzi had to find enough money to pay the deposit demanded by the hospital before admission to cover the initial costs of room, nurses, laboratory fees and the like. But Fitzi was without funds and in desperation she had called Gene and she was right in doing so, Gene tried patiently to explain. She had helped him when he had known trouble and the least he could do was to respond to the appeal of someone who had befriended him.

So reasonable a statement, instead of abating the storm, lashed it into an even greater fury. Carlotta cursed Fitzi in language that was far less than ladylike and gave special emphasis to a word that for her had the worst possible connotation—bohemian! That epithet coming from Carlotta had an obscene inflection; it represented all that was evil and reprehensible to a person who made great pretensions to an aristocratic lineage. She, the lady, abandoning refinement, heaped abuse upon contempt for the people Gene knew during his days of struggle; they were criminals, bloodsuckers, thieves, bastards, scum—and bohemians. As the tirade gained momentum, Gene tried vainly to defend them and himself, to explain old loyalties and to justify his past. This brought on another eruption.

I cowered in my chair, not saying a word and hoping against hope that a favorable opportunity for a quiet exit would present itself. It came when a servant entered the room to clear the coffee cups. I pleaded that I was tired, that I had to go to work early next morning, that my family were waiting up for me and stuttered in that vein as I meekly backed out of the room to the elevator. I walked a short distance to my home, embarrassed for having been a silent witness to a family upheaval and quite ashamed of myself for having made no effort to mediate the quarrel or, worst of all, for failing to speak up in behalf of Fitzi who had always been kind to me.

The following morning I was wakened early by a telephone call. It was Gene asking me to come over without delay to his apartment. On my arrival I saw no sign of Carlotta. I soon learned from Gene what had happened after I had left the night before. Immediately after the elevator door had been closed behind me, Carlotta renewed her attack on Gene's friends with increased virulence, heaping the major portion of her hatred on Fitzi. The outburst continued for a long time, a one-sided harangue in which the central theme was Gene's weakness and cowardice in tolerating his bohemian friends. He remained silent, but that silence lent fuel to the fire and at its height it culminated in an explosion of violence.

Carlotta rushed into Gene's room and lifted the glass that covered his dressing table over her head and crashed it to the floor where it broke into hundred of splinters. Underneath this glass Gene had kept the only picture he had of his mother and himself as a baby. Carlotta, now at the summit of her frenzy, snatched the picture and tore it into bits, crying, "Your mother was a whore!"

This was the last straw. Gene slapped her face. Whereupon she screamed maniacally and ran to her own room. There she hastily packed a bag, dressed for the street and made a melodramatic exit, swearing she would never return.

Gene waited for dawn to call me. Soon after my arrival and after having learned from him the sequence of events that led to the wild parting, we took counsel. First of all, someone would have to stay with Gene and we immediately thought of Walter Casey, a boyhood friend from New London and a man of unswerving devotion.[38] Within an hour after we called him, Casey arrived with a handbag containing his clothes and toilet articles. He understood the situation without detailed explanations and began to take charge by preparing breakfast. I was then able go to work and left for my office with a somewhat easier mind.

Within twenty-four hours we were aware of the presence of detectives assigned to watch the apartment and whoever came or left. Always in pairs, the sleuths stood guard on the street corner. They employed a mysterious system of waving white handkerchiefs, to what end none of us could guess.

Gene's remorse over the night's quarrel was pitiful and in a sense degrading. He reproached himself for having lost his temper and, because of that, his wife. There were, he pleaded, extenuating circumstances which we could not possibly understand. There was guilt on both sides and the marriage of two quiveringly sensitive people required an expansion of forbearance. It was he who should have exercised greater control and no matter what the provocation should have shown more tolerance.

The Parkinson tremor became more and more acute. Alarmed, we called Dr. Shirley Fisk,[39] whose offices were nearby on Fifth Avenue. When he arrived we explained the entire situation to him. He prescribed sedatives and urged that someone remain at Gene's side twenty-four hours a day. He also recommended frequent cups of black coffee as a means for controlling the agitation of his arms and legs. But more important, Gene was to be watched constantly lest he come by an injury accidentally or self-inflicted.

For ten days Casey and I alternated on sentry duty. We sat in the kitchen percolating coffee and trying to formulate plans for the future. Most of all, Gene insisted on discussing measures whereby he could learn where Carlotta was hidden. He wanted to hire a detective and actually did so, only to learn that his lady was, for the time, incommunicado at a mid-town hotel.

On the night of January 28, 1948, I became sleepy as the hour dragged by. At midnight I asked Casey whether he could remain in charge while I went home for some rest. He assured me that there was no need for me to wait, that he was certain that Gene would sleep well into the morning and that even he could retire for a few hours. So I went home, thinking of little else but the comfort of my bed.

I was awakened at six in the morning. Dr. Fisk was on the phone. He urged me to dress quickly and come over at once, for Gene had fallen a few hours before and broken his arm. The doctor had been summoned by Casey after the accident and he had found Gene on the floor of his bedroom with Casey leaning over him, afraid to move him lest he do him further injury.

While I was on my way to the apartment Dr. Fisk ordered a Keefe and Keefe ambulance. It arrived soon after I did and after the doctor had briefly outlined what had happened and what had to be done. Apparently Gene had tried to walk in the dark to the bathroom and had slipped on the highly glossed floor and fallen over a low stool, fracturing his right arm as he wildly tried to break his fall. Now all that could be done would require hospital facilities. At the moment he was in a semi-comatose condition because of the injection given him by Dr. Fisk but still suffering severe pain.

The ambulance arrived and Gene was bundled onto a stretcher and carried down the elevator. Its siren screaming, the ambulance, with Dr. Fisk and me seated beside Gene, drove heedless of red-light traffic signals to Doctors Hospital on East Eighty-seventh Street. While Gene was being trundled into the X-ray room, I registered for him, paid the ambulance fee and declared myself next of kin on the hospital admission form. The X-ray plates revealed a compound fracture of the humerus. An orthopedic specialist was summoned and he and Dr. Fisk reduced the fracture and applied a plaster of Paris splint from the shoulder to the wrist. In spite of the acute pain in setting and splinting the broken arm, there was no word of complaint from Gene. Only the haunted, melancholy eyes showed his suffering. Once in bed and made relatively comfortable by his French-Canadian nurse, he fell asleep under heavy sedation.

For a few days his only visitors were Casey and I, and we always came separately. Casey was reluctant to leave the apartment unoccupied because he was concerned most of all about the manuscripts in the desk drawers. Gene was especially worried about them because the elevator door opened directly upon the apartment and he feared that such easy access would tempt a thief—or somebody. He then asked me to have Casey take all the manuscripts out of his desk and bring them to Random House, where they could be placed safely in the company vault.[40]

I did as I was asked and telephoned Casey. At about 11 in the morning he drove up in a taxicab to the Fifty-first Street entrance to Random House and with the aid of the driver carried in two cartons containing all of Gene's manuscripts. They were deposited in the vault and labels were attached to them on which were written notices that these boxes were not to be moved or opened by anyone but Eugene O'Neill or me. That done and the vault locked, Casey went back to the apartment.

I tried to do something about earning my pay. While thus engaged in the mid-afternoon my telephone bell rang. A blast assaulted my ear. It was Carlotta's voice. "What do you mean, you thief, by stealing my manuscripts! I caught you this time.

I'll send you to jail. My detectives saw it all. They followed Casey. They know you engineered it. I know how to handle the likes of you!"

"Just a minute, Carlotta," I managed to interrupt. "I didn't steal Gene's manuscripts. Don't you know that he has been in Doctors' Hospital for several days with a broken arm? He asked me to put them in a safe place. That is all."

"You are a liar, and so is Gene. He couldn't tell the truth. I don't give a damn what happened to him."

There followed a cascade of curses. The veneer of the lady had been rubbed off and the mind and the language of the show girl were exposed. The tirade became an outpouring of obscenities.

I tried to stop it by interjecting that she could say anything she pleased about me, but she had no right to revile Gene in this way. He was sick and helpless and unable to defend himself. These last days had been ghastly for him and now, alone in the hospital with a broken arm, he deserved the utmost consideration. Whereupon she reacted against me with all the hatred and evil she could compress into three words.

"You— —bastard!" she screamed into the phone and banged her receiver into its cradle.

Stunned, I sat looking at the telephone in bewilderment and chagrin. Then I wrote out from memory as accurately as possible a transcript of what had been said over the telephone, omitting the grosser obscenities.

*To Eugene O'Neill from Saxe Commins.* tl(cc) 1 p.
COPY

February 26, 1948
Dear Gene,

At 2:30 this afternoon—five minutes ago—Carlotta called me at the office. I want to set down, while it is still fresh in my mind the exact conversation so that there will be no distortion later.

After identifying herself, she asked:

"Have you given those scripts to Dodds of Princeton[41] or whatever his name is?"

"What scripts?" I asked.

"The ones Gene has been lying about. You know what a God-damned liar he is."

"I won't listen to that, Carlotta. Gene is not a liar; he has never lied, and you know it."

"He has always been a liar. Did you take those scripts out of the desk?"

"You can't talk that way to me. I did not take any scripts out of the desk."

"I've got enough on you to send you to jail after all you've said about me."

"Carlotta, I've never mentioned your name to anyone. You ought to know that. I've always treated you with respect and I deserve a little from you."

"Respect, hell. God-damn you, I'll show you. I'll have you in jail where you've belonged for years."

"Please, Carlotta, what is it that you want?"

"Don't lie to me. You know you took those scripts out of the desk."

"I did not."

"Well, they're either in Random House or Princeton and you know it."

"Don't ask me about them. They are not mine."

There followed a string of abusively vulgar epithets and the phone was violently slammed down.

The fact that Carlotta called me about the scripts indicates that she knows about their removal from the desk and that she is in a state of sick bitterness about it. Her virulent language can only be explained by her state of agitation and a deep-seated illness. Her hatred is now turned toward me and with great violence.

What else could I have done, Gene, but tell her that I did not take the scripts? Without authorization from you, I cannot even mention them. Under the circumstances, I want you to know and approve of whatever I say or do whenever it touches you.

Always

Saxe's memoir continues:

That night at the hospital I showed Gene what I had written and asked him whether, under the circumstances, I was to come to see him again or stay away altogether. He read the sheet of paper slowly and then paused for a long time.

"Try to understand," he said, "She's sick, terribly sick. Don't you leave me too."

I promised I would not.

*To Eugene O'Neill from Saxe Commins.* als 1i p.

On stationery headed: Random House, Inc. The Modern Library / 457 Madison Avenue / New York 22, N.Y. / Saxe Commins, Editor

March 2, 1948

Dear Gene,

I have been giving much tormented thought to the possibility that my frequent visits to the hospital and my daily phone calls of inquiry might have been causing you embarrassment. Nothing, as you must know, could be farther from my mind or heart. Yet if it will save you the slightest need of explanation, I shall stay away until you summon me. All I want you to know is that as long as I live I'll be available, when the chips are down or at any other time, on the moment of your call.

With all devotion<br>
Saxe

Shortly after this episode, the O'Neills were reconciled and planned to resume life together someplace on the New England coast. They arrived in Boston late in the spring of 1948 and soon purchased a small cottage at the tip of Marblehead Neck, twenty miles north of Boston. While they were having their new home remodeled, they spent several months in a suite of rooms at the Ritz-Carlton Hotel. From there, Gene wrote to Saxe.

*To Saxe Commins from Eugene O'Neill*, als 2 pp.
On stationery headed: The Ritz-Carlton / Boston 17, Massachusetts

July 26 '48
Dear Saxe:

Much gratitude for the inscribed book.[42] I feel as if I'd read it already, you've told me so much about it, but I know I will have a new pleasure reading it.

The big news with us, which I meant to write you long ago, is that we had the good luck to get in first on the sale of a house right on the ocean near Marblehead—first sale of waterfront property in its vicinity for many years. Carlotta bought this out of her reserve fund. It is a tiny house with little rooms, the upstairs ones with sloping eaves—built in 1880. Reminds me of the first home my father bought in New London, also on the waterfront when I was a kid. We both love this new place. Of course, a lot has had be done to modernize it—as to kitchen, etc. and to thoroughly insulate it into an all year round home—our last. Everything to cut down overhead and make it a cinch to run with just a cook. No car. We won't need one. The aim is to simplify living and gain as much security for our old age as is possible. I feel I shall be able to write again, and again have some roots—of seaweed—with my feet in a New England sea. It is like coming home, in a way, and I feel happier than in many years, although we are still stuck here in a hotel impatiently awaiting the completion of the work on the place.

As to health, we are both much better and will be better still when we are in our home. My arm isn't right yet and won't be for six months, they say, but it steadily improves. No swimming this summer, of course. But next year—! The tremor is better, too, but I'm just cursed with it for life, I guess, and the best to hope for is to circumvent it. This letter, for example, is written during a good spell, and it's not so bad, eh? And why complain when the world itself is one vast tremor.

All best to you, Dorothy & the kids!
As ever, Gene

P.S. Remember me to Bennett, Haas,[43] Klopfer

*To Dorothy Commins from Carlotta Monterey O'Neill*, tls 1 p.
On stationery headed: Point O'Rocks Lane Marblehead Neck, Massachusetts

October the 21st 1948
Dear Dorothy:

Gene has asked me to tell you how pleased he was to receive your birthday wire.[44] You were sweet to remember him.

When it was time for Gene to leave the hospital it was necessary to make a home for him—and away from New York which he grew to loathe, as I did! So, we came to New England (that I have always loved) and I have been doing my best to make a home. Am afraid I have lost my resiliency to this and that, but the home will be finished in another week or so. It is the smallest house I have ever seen! (Which we both wanted) And cost the most! I had the beautiful idea that if I sold all the securities I had left I would have enough to re-do some little house and, when finished, go to Master O'Neill and say, "Here, young man is a home for you all ready made!" But, like everything I have attempted with the Master it did not work out that way. I bought a very small house for $25,000.00 being told $25,000.00 more would put it in condition. To make a long story short I put all my money in it, then was forced to go to Gene for $15,000.00 and now I have to mortgage the place for $20,000.00 to pay the last payment.[45] I am stoney—Gene hard-up—but, we have a home! Life goes on, and what more can one say! I hope things go well with you and yours. And, again, let me thank you for your remembrance of Gene.

As always,
Carlotta

# 52 / Bennett Cerf

For information on Bennett Cerf, see the headnote to chapter 36.

Source: Bennett Cerf, *At Random: The Reminiscences of Bennett Cerf* (New York: Random House, 1977), 86–88.

I continued to be O'Neill's admirer, publisher and friend for the rest of his life, which became increasingly unhappy and difficult. Toward the end Gene developed Parkinson's disease and his hands started shaking. He became more and more of a recluse because he was ashamed of the fact that when he'd eat, his food would fly all over the place. It is a dreadful disease.

During this time Carlotta had become more of a jailer than a wife; she alienated his lawyer and a lot of his best friends, including the Langners of the Theatre Guild. She just threw them out of Gene's life and took possession of him herself. They sold the house on Sea Island. He got tired of it, she said. I don't know what the facts are, but I thought he loved it down there. But he was a restless soul. They bought a house out in California about twenty-five miles from San Francisco, across the bay, in Mill Valley. For some reason or other I was still in Carlotta's favor, and I went out to spend ten days with him in Mill Valley. It was very sad. Here was this great playwright living close to San Francisco but rarely getting into the city, seldom seeing anyone. Carlotta had electric gates installed, and to get onto their property, you had to go through not just one gate, but two; and unless a button was pushed at the top of the hill, those gates didn't open. She could watch over the terrain like an old feudal lord guarding against invading armies.

Gene by this time was quite sickly and very thin. He was still working, but it was getting harder and harder for him. He always wrote standing up. He had a tall desk and he would stand at it and write in longhand in tiny script. In some New Orleans whorehouse he had bought—I don't know how he found it—a player piano which he named "Rosie": it was white, with naked ladies painted all over it. And Carlotta, the great religious girl, thought it was terrible, so Gene had it down in the cellar. He'd sneak down once in a while and drop nickels in the slot, and while it played old ragtime tunes he'd sit there with an ecstatic look on his face. He loved "Rosie."

When I got out there, the first thing Carlotta told me was that Eugene, Jr., and his bride were due shortly after I left. (He was the son who later committed suicide.) Carlotta hated him, as she hated anybody who had anything to do with Gene. She said, "He married a girl who looks like a Minnesota fullback. They think they're going to stay two weeks. Ha, ha, ha! I'll have them out of this house in four days." Those were her words. And she did, too. She also pushed his other children, Oona and Shane, completely out of his life.[46]

But Gene, the afternoon I arrived, beckoned me with his finger, like a mischievous little boy, and we went down to the cellar and I sat there while he played me a couple of rolls on the player piano. He was having a ball. In the middle of it, Carlotta found us and screamed, "You ought to be ashamed of yourself, bringing Bennett down here. You're in pain, remember?" He had forgotten all about his pain, but she reminded him of it and ordered us upstairs. If I'd had a baseball bat, I think I'd have clobbered her over the head. But Gene meekly went upstairs.

At the end of 1945 Gene and Carlotta came to New York, where he worked on the Theatre Guild production of *The Iceman Cometh*. They decided to remain in the East, and in the spring of 1946, took an apartment in the Eighties and began to see old friends. I remember one night Gene and Carlotta were at the Russel Crouses' for dinner.[47] The Irving Berlins[48] were there, too. After dinner Berlin began playing the piano. I can still see Eugene O'Neill standing over him, singing "Alexander's Ragtime Band" in a very bad voice but having the time of his life. And he remembered a song of Irving Berlin's that Berlin himself had forgotten. Gene sang him the song and Irving then recalled it, and the two of them sang it together. It was a great sight.

Another evening Carlotta and Gene came to our house for a dinner party. My wife, Phyllis, and I had invited Burl Ives,[49] who brought along his guitar, and after dinner he sang a few songs. Gene always had to be warmed up, and I knew how to do it. After Burl had entertained us for a while, I said, "Gene, Burl can accompany you on anything. Do you remember some of your old sea chanteys?"

Gene smiled and said, "I guess I could think of a couple of them." Then he sang a few chanteys, one or two of which Burl knew and the others he picked out. As Gene warmed up, Carlotta got angrier and angrier because Gene was remembering dirtier and dirtier songs. After a little while she said, "I will not be a party to these goings-on. We're going right home, Gene," and Gene stood up, for once in his life, and told her, "I wouldn't dream of it. You go home without me."

I said to Carlotta, "Don't worry, we'll get him home." So she swept out in a rage, and when she was gone, it was as though Gene had been released from prison. He went on singing those obscene sea chanteys, with Burl playing the accompaniment. It was an enchanting evening. Carlotta didn't want him to have a good time; she wanted to own him. They loved each other—but what a way they had of showing it! When Gene would go into one of his Irish furies, he would hurl things at Carlotta. He once threw a wall mirror at her, and if it had hit her, it might have killed her. There were two sides to the story—there always are.

# 53 / Paul Crabtree

Paul Crabtree (1918–1979), a writer, director, producer, and actor, began his career in 1943 as a replacement performer in *Oklahoma!* He played Don Parritt in the Theatre Guild's production of *The Iceman Cometh* (1946) and directed *The Silver Whistle* (1948) and the musical *Texas, Li'l Darlin'* (1949) on Broadway before he moved to Hollywood and became a writer for television, where his credits included series like *The Loretta Young Show* and *Death Valley Days*.

Source: Louis Sheaffer, Paul Crabtree interview notes, Louis Sheaffer Collection of Eugene O'Neill Materials, Department of Special Collections, Charles E. Shain Library, Connecticut College, New London.

So much written about [O'Neill] makes him out to be a bitter dark character, like someone from his own plays. I found him to be a very humorous man, he had a good sense of humor. I didn't even know he was Eugene O'Neill first time I met him . . . It happened while I was directing a group of performers from various shows, *Oklahoma*, *Carousel*, *Annie Get Your Gun*,[50] just for practice, in the large room at Theatre Guild. We were going to put on a bill of short pieces, including a musical thing, *Elmer and Lily*, Saroyan had written for the American Negro Theatre.[51] One afternoon I found a dignified old gentleman sitting near me, and he sat there for almost an hour, from 4:30 till end of rehearsal. Something about it being an imaginative piece of work. One song had a line about baseball and he said he was interested in baseball. We got talking about the Yankees, Giants, Dodgers, and he told me stories of the old days, before baseball got so organized. One story was a player who had a special hip pocket added to his uniform, because when he went to bat he always stuck his glove in the pocket, and if he had to get hit, would twist his hip quickly and get hit on the glove . . . He told the stories with humor . . . Several times I noticed Lawrence Langner, Theresa Helburn and Mrs. Langner looking over the half-door, but we talked on, got around briefly to talking about the theatre, and we were there till nearly 7 o'clock. This was probably in April or May, 1946. He spoke hesitantly but seemed very relaxed. . . . There was great humor in his eyes, but if you didn't catch the humor in what he was saying, he'd let it go . . . On the landing, the whole place quiet, we found the whole Theatre Guild sitting there (two Langners and Helburn) with their overcoats on, and Mrs. Langner said in a very sharp voice, "Well, Paul, I see you've met Mr. O'Neill."

I hadn't realized he was O'Neill because in the pictures I knew he had a square mustache, smaller, and he looked so dark, but then his hair was gray and his mustache had spread . . . Maybe if I'd known he was in New York, I'd have guessed . . .

Langner asked [Crabtree] to read for part of Don Parritt in *Iceman*, and when they met again O'Neill recalled that their first meeting had kept the Guild heads waiting an hour and half . . . [Crabtree] had an office at the Guild, and O'Neill always dropped by for a talk . . . One day he came by, held out a hand, and it was steady as a pole. "The gotdamdest [*sic*] thing happened to me. I went to the dentist and he had some rather painful work to do, and wanted to give me some novocaine, but I told him no, didn't want any local anesthesia. I wanted to see how my power of concentration was, thought I'd concentrate on something so hard that maybe I wouldn't feel any pain . . . I started thinking of *The Iceman Cometh*, about the characters as I'd drawn them and the real people I had known [that] the characters were based on, and the next thing I knew the dentist was all through, I hadn't felt any pain, and my hands didn't shake . . . There's something medical in this. They ought to look into it . . ."

O'Neill came to rehearsals practically every day, right after the lunch break, at 1 . . . Mrs. O'Neill[52] was the most beautiful woman I'd ever known, I fell in love with her, she was delicious! She always came with him (: this is contradicted later, by humorous incident at Gilhooley's) . . . Once I was sitting near her and she [said] to me, "Look at him sitting there reading that script – and he doesn't have his glasses on!" He seemed to be following every word, and turned the page at the right time. She laughed and said, "Now watch what will happen," and gave me her glasses in a case, and asked me to put them on the table by him. I waited for a break and went over between him and Dowling, said something to Dowling, and quietly left the glasses by O'Neill. He put them on and said, "Alright, let's get started again," picked up the script and then elaborately turned it upside down, looked at his wife, and winked. We all burst out laughing . . . I still don't know whether he'd actually had the wrong side up or was going along with the joke.

We didn't go out of town with *Iceman* . . . We were in the set for two weeks . . . Some tables would be out of sight of the audience, and O'Neill often took a seat at one of these tables. Tom Pedi,[53] a soft-hearted Italian, used to serve him a glass of beer when the action called for him to pass around the beer, and you could tell O'Neill felt he was right back there at one of his bars. He had to look sideways to watch the action, and there was one scene—he loved the girls—with Pearl that always had the tears rolling down his face . . . He talked to us one afternoon about our characters and said all of them were people he'd known. Some characters were composites of people he'd known. He loved Harry Hope, talked a good deal about him, and he loved Larry, but he didn't talk much about Hickey, as I recall . . . maybe he didn't talk about Hickey at all. He talked quite a bit of the lawyer, Willie Oban, and said he was based on someone with one of the most vivid vocabularies he'd ever known. "The vocabulary was at ease with him."[54]

Crabtree read two or three times for Dowling, who didn't okay him. They auditioned hundreds and finally Langner had Crabtree read for O'Neill. Out of room about half-minute when [they] called him back, and said he had the part . . . When [he] first read for it, [he] slicked down and wore a double-breasted green suit with a white stripe, [which] had belonged to a brother-in-law who went into the service. Wardrobe fixed Crabtree with three or four outfits, because O'Neill didn't like them, finally O'Neill recalled the suit Crabtree had worn at the first audition, thought that would be right. Crabtree says he would gladly have contributed the suit but union regulations [were] against it. The $34.50 suit was sold to Brooks Bros., which gave Crabtree $75, then changed it to single-breasted, pegged the trousers, both O'Neill's suggestions, and charged the Guild $300 for it.

Bobby Jones[55] a true genius. He had all his colors, pieces of chalk, in a cigar box. He'd go to the back of the theatre, study the set, then go up on the stage and rub a bit of chalk on the set. It seemed pointless to me, but then I learned what he was doing. He was highlighting and low-lighting the set with chalk.

O'Neill's theatrical sense of technique was fantastic. The lighting man told me he didn't know another play that followed lighting so logically. The time of day, as specified in the script, starts off with early morning. The morning light starts working on the tables, first one, then another, and it wakes up the people as it spreads . . . Contrary to most plays, in which the published script has stage directions added after it was written, directions the director had put into the production, this one was already printed when we went into rehearsals and it already contained the directions.[56]

Re O'Neill being dissatisfied with Dowling's direction: There was some talk around about that, and we knew it was true. What Dowling put in in the morning O'Neill would take out in the afternoon . . . Frankly, Dowling was right most of the time, he was trying to put some action and life into a very talky play, but O'Neill didn't want any unnecessary action, he was almost obsessed about it. He didn't want anything that might take attention away from the words. Any action was held to a minimum.

Barton[57] was perfect for Hickey in most ways but it was too much for his age. He had trouble remembering all those lines. O'Neill was very annoyed and unhappy with Barton.

Digges had a heavy makeup job and didn't care to go out to eat at the one-hour dinner break. Neither did I, so I had a hot plate and used to make soup, other things to eat, and I used to take him a bowl. Once I asked him—I'd noticed he always did this—why he always patted his feet while talking, like a man pedaling at a piano. Digges, "The old memory, it isn't what it used to be—I don't want to lose the O'Neill rhythm . . ." Not that he ever had any real trouble, maybe a line or so occasionally.

Final dress rehearsal held for O'Neill alone. Yes, I'm sure Mrs. O'Neill was there, too . . . She told me it took him half a day to write each inscription, for members of the cast . . . Inscription to Crabtree: "To Paul Crabtree—A million thanks for all your sensitive interpretation of 'Don Parritt' does to make *The Iceman Cometh* live. I can never be grateful enough to you! / You have a grand future before you, and every upward step in it will have my cheers and friendship! / Eugene O'Neill / October 1946."

When time came to take it on road, Langner told me because of size of cast and the expense it could be toured only if it gave eight performances a week, which meant matinees, and that it would have to be cut. He knew how stubborn O'Neill was set against cuts but felt *Iceman* had so much repetition that maybe O'Neill would agree if he prepared his case properly. Langner told me to check the number of times it repeated the line "The lie of a pipe dream is what gives etc . . ." I went through the play and found it said 32 times, and told him so. Three or four days later Langner called me and said he wanted me to be with him when he met with O'Neill—he had an appointment with him—to discuss the possibility of cuts. I asked him not to put me on the spot with O'Neill, because I liked and admired him so much. When we got together, Langner talked about taking it on the road, that we'd have to play eight times a week, that the play had repetitious things and said, "For instance, the line 'The lie of a pipe dream . . ." O'Neill interrupted him, "I know, it's said 32 times. I want it said 32 times." And that ended it. It went on the road with no cuts.

Mrs. O'Neill's manner toward [Eugene] was like any ordinary human being. When the time came to leave, she'd say, "All right, old man, here's your coat." Or, referring to his actions at rehearsal, "He'll take the fun out of it." (Crabtree agreed with my comment that her attitude was one of affectionate disparagement.)

Once we went to Gilhooley's on 8th Ave. for lunch, O'Neill, Digges, Carl Benton Reid and I, and they wouldn't serve us. We were in costume and looked like bums. O'Neill was dressed neatly, of course, but he didn't tell the waiter he was treating us. He kept saying, "Go ahead, Harry (he called us by the names of our characters) dig into your sock and show him you've got money, go ahead, Harry." None of us, except O'Neill, had any money because we were in costume. Finally, after O'Neill'd gotten all the humor he could from the situation, he told the waiter it was all right, he had money for all of us . . . Yes, he ate with us. He seemed very relaxed with us . . . I think he smoked with his left hand.

Bobby Jones once at Westport told us that a group of six or eight friends—O'Neill among them—had concocted an imaginary family that did things, travelled. All the members were clear in their minds and they'd write letters to each other, kept this up for years, about meeting so-and-so or one's high blood pressure bothering him again . . . It was a game with them.

Re Joe Marr's[58] comment that some *Iceman* play[er]s compared notes and found they were having nightmares, often of a suicidal nature: . . . Crabtree said he had bad dreams but particularly recalls that when *Iceman* was in Philadelphia, possibly [from the] strain of eight performances a week, a feeling hit him as he approached the theatre, found his fingernails digging into his hands and face getting tighter. Had the Guild release him from the play but they made him return in a week or ten days.

While *Iceman* was in rehearsal, Earle Larimore was released from the Sanitarium, actually to die, but he didn't know it.[59] The Guild made a to-do over Larimore, introduced him to the company as the famous O'Neill leading man, said he'd recovered his health, and was going to understudy Hickey, Larry and Willie Oban. He was around rehearsals all the time, and when time came to rehearse him, [they] found he wasn't up to the toughest parts. Not told Hickey and Larry taken away from him but other understandies [*sic*] lined up for them, and at the end was just understudying Willie. He was given Willie's part when we went on the road, but couldn't really handle it. Wasn't that he was drinking really but his health wasn't good. . . . Willie, you know, just has one real speech. I was seated at the next table, and used to feed him a line . . . It was the most gripping thing I've ever known in the theatre. He was tremendous. There wasn't a dry eye on the stage. It's the only time I've ever seen an audience stand up, not all but a good many, and applaud . . . One of those wonderful, impossible things that can happen in the theatre. He achieved that again. He died not long afterward.

Saw O'Neill around Guild year so later, *Moon*[60] time. Moved slower, seemed failing.

# 54 / Mary Welch

Mary Welch (1922?–1958) was born in Charleston, South Carolina, and grew up in San Diego. She was an award-winning drama student at UCLA before moving to New York in 1944, where she made her Broadway debut in the role of Jo in *Little Women*. She had had some success in the theater before she was chosen to play Josie Hogan in the Theatre Guild's 1947 production of *A Moon for the Misbegotten*. She replaced Kim Hunter (1922–2002) as Stella in the original production of *A Streetcar Named Desire* (1947) and garnered attention as Amelia Shotgraven in the long-running *The Solid Gold Cadillac* (1953). She was playing Marguerite "Missy" LeHand in *Sunrise at Campobello* (1957) at the time of her death.

Source: Mary Welch, "Softer Tones for Mr. O'Neill's Portrait," *Theatre Arts* May 1957: 67–68.

Since Eugene O'Neill's death on November 27, 1953, there have been many tributes which mourned "our greatest American playwright." Most of these spoke of the tremendous talent and challenge he brought to the theatre, and then went on to discuss his many plays. Few words were written about O'Neill's daily life or his contact with people, however. If anything was said about his private life, for the most part we received the legendary picture we had while he was alive—that of a lonely, passionate, tormented genius, living in isolated spots as far from Broadway as possible, and remaining completely aloof from any contact with the needs and problems of other people. Having had direct, personal contact with him, I would like to add some warmer, softer tones to what I feel is an overly stark and limited portrait of O'Neill. I want to recall his sensitivity and generosity toward me during the preparations for the tryout of the last of his plays to be staged in his lifetime.

It was in May, 1946, that I first read an item in a New York newspaper which began: "The Theatre Guild is desperately searching in America and Ireland for a tall, Irish girl to play Josie, the lead in Eugene O'Neill's new play, *A Moon for the Misbegotten*." The next morning I walked into the imposing building which housed the Guild. I had just returned from a tour of Philip Barry's *The Joyous Season*, starring Ethel Barrymore, and was full of youthful arrogance. I announced that I was ready to play the part for them.

The several casting officials looked me over and concluded. "You are of the right age, temperament and origin, but you have little or no chance. You are too normal! We are looking for a huge girl with some of your qualifications—but in addition, at least another fifty pounds and preferably many more years' acting experience. Josie is the lead and only woman in Mr. O'Neill's play. She is a great mother-earth symbol, and the actress who plays her should have a range from farce to Greek tragedy."

This protest only made me more interested. I answered them with a long list of plays I had done in college and stock, which more than covered this small range. I don't remember when I have been so tenacious. Back of my boldness was this line of thought: "What do you have to lose? At least you might get a peek at your hero, Eugene O'Neill. How many other actresses can say the same?"

Completely snowed under by my self-praise, the weary Guild officials said, "It seems ridiculous but we'll give you a quick interview with Mr. O'Neill next week when he will be screening many actors."

Despite the Guild's doubts, my daydreams during the following week had their own range, from how I would impress the great O'Neill to how I would take my curtain calls. I arrived for my appointment at least eight pounds heavier (also padded) and dressed in green. I waited more than a full hour, sitting among girls whose proportions made me feel tiny. Finally Armina Marshall, one of the Guild producers, said, "You're next for Mr. O'Neill!"

I was shown into a small den furnished with only a big desk and two chairs. Behind the desk, four feet from me, sat Eugene O'Neill.

No wonder the many legends exist. He did look exactly as I had always seen him in all the photographs and drawings. He was "gaunt," "intense," "tragic." I didn't have to take time to adjust the reality of his appearance to my expectation, as one frequently does on meeting a distinguished person for the first time. While Miss Marshall talked to him about me, I had a chance to study him more. He was impeccably dressed in an expensive dark suit but he seemed more bone than flesh. I liked him immediately; I like the look of men who carry no excess baggage.

O'Neill nodded pleasantly but remained silent as he was told my qualifications. He seemed embarrassed by this kind of talk. It wasn't until we were left alone that he seemed to relax and then try to put me at ease. His searching eyes focused constantly right on my face, but instead of arousing a self-conscious behavior in me, they seemed to put me on my absolute honor to express myself as clearly and as simply as I could. In those days, like many young actors,

I smiled too much in my desperate anxiety to please. He must have sensed this when I first entered the room, but instead of being irritated, he just kept staring, as though he were burning me down to a purer core. I always felt the same way with him—as though I were purified. I had to be completely myself because I knew he would detect the slightest tendency to impress or charm him.

His first questions were, "Are you Irish with that pug nose? What per cent? From what part of Ireland are your people? I want as many people as possible connected with my play to be Irish. Although the setting is New England, the dry wit, the mercurial changes of mood, and the mystic quality of the three main characters are so definitely Irish."

I answered, "Of course, Irish, 100 per cent, County Cork."

His first smile appeared on "County Cork." It made me bold enough to slip into a brogue and tell him about my grandmother who used to say, "I'll never eat a plate of stew—those dishes of mystery!" This and a joke about a friend of hers getting caught in the wrong field of "taters" made him laugh. We were both off on Ireland and didn't mention the play. Relaxed, I could have gone on talking with him for hours, forgetting my first mission, but the next actress was growing insistent and I realized I should leave.

As I got up to go, O'Neill said, "Here now, take the play with you and come back and read for me in two weeks." As he handed the script to me I noticed for the first time the severe tremble in his hands, caused by Parkinson's disease, which made him suffer so greatly during his last years.

I started reading the play on the subway on my way home, but it took me many hours to finish it. I had to keep stopping constantly to recover from the emotional impact of each act; I had never felt so identified with a part. In those days I kept a diary and I wrote, "Every bluff and hurt and discovery of Josie's seems to have occurred to me. This is what every actor looks his whole lifetime for—*his* role. This is my role. For once I feel moved by fate. I know I have to play this part and will."

The next time I saw O'Neill was two weeks later, at the first official reading in a luxurious room on the third floor of the Theatre Guild building. He was there with his wife and the Guild producers to weed out the final candidates for the role of Josie. O'Neill's previous warmth and my own overwhelming love and desire for the part had given me courage to memorize large sections of the play, and boldly to use Josie's main prop, an old broom—thereby giving myself over to the part instead of delivering the customary stumbling first reading. The Guild seemed impressed by the long preparations I had made, but there was still an element of worry.

"The reading was good."

"The accent is perfect."

"But she still seems too normal for Josie's problem of feeling misbegotten."

Mr. O'Neill, who had written the dimensions for his leading lady, then proceeded to overlook his own measurements. "That doesn't matter to me," he retorted. "She can gain some more weight, but the important thing is that Miss Welch understands how Josie feels. These other girls, who are closer physically to Josie, somehow don't know how tortured she is, or can't project it. The inner state of Josie is what I want. We'll work the other problem out in clothes and sets. I think the emotional quality is just right."

The Theatre Guild and the director, however, still had to be convinced, so in the next few months I gave at least three more auditions in costume and in make-up, and with each new appearance I had added five more pounds on a diet of potatoes, bananas and pies. Finally came the day of decision when I would meet and read with James Dunn,[61] the leading man.

The day before this final audition I received a phone call from a Guild secretary, who said that O'Neill wanted me to meet him and his wife in their apartment an hour before my appointment at the theatre. I had no idea what to expect and was afraid that this meeting might mean an easy letdown. When I arrived at the door of the O'Neill penthouse apartment in the East Seventies, the very patrician and beautiful Mrs. O'Neill greeted me warmly and took me across a large living room into her husband's den.

"Hello, Miss Welch—Mary. I thought we'd just have a chat and a cup of tea before the final inquisition."

He had simply wanted to put me at ease and build my confidence. His eyes twinkled as if he were ready for a minor skirmish and was sure he would win.

"Now don't worry, I don't care what anyone says. You are my choice and you are going to play Josie."

It seemed unbelievable to me that I was sitting in the O'Neills' lovely living room, filled with books and plants and one of the first television sets ("given to me by a friend so I can watch the fights"), and that I was listening to Eugene O'Neill bolstering my shaky actor's ego. We spoke of other things, too. O'Neill brought up his earlier plays, particularly the ones he had written about the Negro people. He had felt deeply about them, and his face grew bitter and forceful as he recalled how some of the New York professional theatre crowd had accepted these works. His words were, "They didn't really understand what I was writing. They merely said to themselves, 'Oh look, the ape can talk!'" These words shocked me; but besides ringing with true bitterness, I am sure they were spoken to furnish the pride and arrogance I lacked.

I remember Mrs. O'Neill getting all of his winter wraps ready for him, and insisting that he put on his overshoes. In the taxi on our way to the theatre he was still telling me not to be afraid of any doubts I might have about myself.

That day I signed a contract to play Josie, and it had this very unusual clause: "The artist agrees to gain the necessary weight required for the role."

I next saw O'Neill at our first rehearsal, when the whole cast was gathered to read *A Moon for the Misbegotten* for the first time. James Dunn and I both had to stop several times because we were weeping. And when we raised our eyes from our scripts and looked at the playwright and all three Guild producers, we realized that we were not alone in this. O'Neill came over to us at the end of rehearsal and said humorously, "Oh, here we go again. I wept a great deal over Josie Hogan and Jim Tyrone as I wrote the play. I loved them." The day ended with Mrs. O'Neill adding a homey touch, passing around a box of chocolates.

Mr. O'Neill was ill during most of the three weeks of rehearsals, but he was able to come three times to give us notes which proved a definite help. His first major note was that we were playing the tragedy of the work too early. *A Moon for the Misbegotten* is almost farcical in places in the first act, though it becomes almost Greek in its tragic stature in the fourth and final one. The playwright often told us jokes about his early days. He seemed to look for humor everywhere. And always I felt he understood my terrible worry over the responsibilities of such a large part. He made me feel he really believed in me. On the three occasions when he was at rehearsals, I dared to be as free as I always should have been.

Illness prevented O'Neill from attending the premiere in Columbus, Ohio, but he came to bid us good-by in New York. Once more he said, "I know you will play Josie the way I want it." We embraced and I told him some of the personal reasons why the part meant so much to me— things that I have told no other person. I recall that when he left a rehearsal one afternoon in New York, I said to myself, "This man compels me to behave at my best level, to express the absolute core of whatever is my soul. I can only be me—honest, sincere, no matter how revealing." I felt an unaccustomed relief on shedding all the layers of convention I had felt it necessary to assume for contact with other people.

I want to mention another incident at that rehearsal, and this will surprise many people. O'Neill cut several sentences from his finished script, upsetting the legend that he steadfastly refused to cut a single line, once a script was handed over to the producer. He performed this operation at the bidding of James Dunn and myself, and it came about when he realized that we were obviously upset at having just too much to say. After this I always felt that he might have made some appropriate cuts in his other plays, if people had had the courage to approach him—provided, of course, that they had had his respect.

Several weeks later when the play was on the verge of being closed by the police in Detroit on the false claim that it is "a slander on American motherhood," other cuts had to be made to satisfy the local politicians. I shall never forget a meeting with the local police officials, who actually set themselves up as editors of O'Neill. And we were forced to listen to them in order that we might open again that evening, the second night of the engagement; we couldn't even wait for the cuts the playwright had agreed to make so that the tryout tour might continue. One of their more brilliant contributions was: "Well, you can't say tart, but you can say tramp."

The tour began February 20, 1947, and closed the following March 29. We played Columbus, Cleveland, Detroit, Pittsburgh and St. Louis. Some of the critics were profoundly moved by the work; others missed it entirely, calling it another *Tobacco Road*.[62] We closed after the St. Louis engagement due to a combination of circumstances, foremost among which were O'Neill's illness (which prevented him from working on the play) and casting problems relating to certain of the male roles.

My last communication with Eugene O'Neill (other than the note he wrote after we had closed, thanking me for my work) was in the form of a gift of a dozen red roses on opening night in Columbus, together with card which read, "Again my absolute confidence, Eugene O'Neill." I can think of nothing finer to say to an actress on opening night.

# 6
# Marblehead and Boston (1948–1953)

In 1948 the O'Neills moved into an extensively renovated house in Marblehead, Massachusetts, leaving this in 1951 to move into the Shelton Hotel on the Charles River in Boston. The last five years of O'Neill's life were physically and mentally torturous for him. Because of his degenerative brain disease, he was no longer able to write or to perform many physical tasks. At the end he could not walk or eat unaided. In addition to this, both he and Carlotta suffered from bromide poisoning from medicine they were prescribed, which led to delusions and paranoid behavior as well as violent fights between them. In 1948 O'Neill broke his arm after Carlotta left during one of these, and in 1951 he broke his leg and was left lying in the snow for some time by Carlotta. After both of these incidents, they were reconciled, against the better judgment of O'Neill's friends, Lawrence Langner, Saxe Commins, and Bennett Cerf, all of whom Carlotta cut out of his life after the first or the second reconciliation.

In this section, Commins and Cerf recount their devastating memories of these days. Russel Crouse, on whom the O'Neills called as a kind of mediator during both crises, describes their relations in his diary entries and in an interview with Louis Sheaffer. O'Neill's doctor, Frederic Mayo, describes his relationship with the O'Neills and the incident when Eugene broke his leg in 1951. His nurse, Sallie Coughlin, describes her experience with him afterward. Finally confined to his bed by the state of his health, O'Neill died of pneumonia at the Hotel Shelton on November 27, 1953. In posthumous memories, Carlotta O'Neill tells her side of the story to Seymour Peck; the O'Neills' interior decorator and friend, Earle Johnson, recalls their time at Marblehead; and their friend Carl Van Vechten gives his opinion on the possibility of an impartial biography of O'Neill.

# 55 / Saxe Commins

For information on Saxe Commins, see chapter 51.

Source: Saxe Commins, "*Love and Admiration and Respect": The O'Neill-Commins Correspondence*," ed. Dorothy Commins (Durham, NC: Duke UP, 1986), 229–42.

Saxe's memoir contains the rest of the sad ending to the O'Neills' story:

[In 1948] All communication was cut off and even matters pertaining to Gene's work had to be transmitted through Miss Jane Rubin of the office of his literary agent, Richard Madden. I had been purged, as had all of his old friends and, most unfortunately as it turned out, his children, Shane, Oona, and Eugene, Jr. The son who bore his name was, more than anyone else, in desperate need of communication with his father.

Young Gene was then undergoing a time of adversity. His three marriages had failed miserably. His academic career, in the beginning rich in promise, was in decline. He had given up his post at Yale University as an Assistant Professor of Greek and the Classics, a position he had attained after a notable scholastic record as an undergraduate. The promise, unfortunately, was greater than the performance, and both he and the university were disappointed. . . .

Through the good offices of Professor [Whitney J.] Oates, young O'Neill was tendered a place in the Classics Department at Princeton in 1947, but the experiment, after a year's trial, did not succeed. He then drifted from one institution of learning to another, including Fairleigh-Dickinson College in Rutherford, New Jersey, and the New School for Social Research in New York, and dropped gradually in status until he reached the bottom of the academic ladder.

A bearded giant of a man, perhaps six foot three in height and massively built, he had a basso-profundo voice of which he was inordinately proud. He made himself believe that with a little training he could become Chaliapin's[1] successor. With his resonant voice to recommend him he sought engagements with radio networks and actually found some radio assignments as a reader of books for the benefit of the housebound. He also appeared occasionally on the program known as *Invitation to Learning*, a weekly half hour informal discussion of the world's great books. Always in need of money, the earnings he came by so infrequently and precariously were never enough for his needs. Let it be said for him that in the face of heartbreaking discouragements he tried his skills at whatever presented itself and never betrayed his love of scholarship.

He had bought a small piece of land near Woodstock, New York, on the Ohmayo Mountain where he hoped to build a home. It carried a mortgage of $4,000, sponsored by the endorsement of his father. The time came when the mortgage was due for renewal and all that was required was a re-endorsement. That formality, he was confident, would be observed without difficulty. As the due date approached he made every possible effort to communicate with his father, but to no avail. Letters remained unanswered, telegrams were ignored, telephone calls never went beyond the vigilant monitor and guard at Marblehead. In a panic he appealed to whoever might have access, but every avenue of approach was blocked. He persuaded W. E. Aronberg, O'Neill's attorney in New York, to intercede but his messages were intercepted and never relayed to the father. Desperate, the junior O'Neill tried to raise the money by appeals to his friends, but they were as impecunious as he.

He came to my office on Thursday, September 21, 1950, to seek my counsel, even though he knew that I had been forbidden communication of any kind with his father. He told me of all the stratagems he had used to break through the barrier and how he was always repulsed and turned back. His hatred of Carlotta was almost maniacal; it was she, he insisted, who was the cause of his desperation. If only he could have the mortgage renewed and find some work, his problems would be on the way to solution. He was a scholar of considerable reputation among his peers; he had a voice of deep sonority and great appeal; he was a strong man and could do manual labor. He asked me to try to induce five or six book publishers to underwrite a radio program in which he could offer thumbnail comment and criticism of current books in a weekly broadcast. This was indeed clutching at a straw, for even if he was qualified by scholarship, voice and judgement, the problem still remained to bring five or six publishers into accord, a thirteenth Herculean labor. Nonetheless I promised to do what I could and actually explained the proposal to a few publishers, all of whom merely wondered whether I had taken leave of my wits.

When he left me on that Thursday, there was no way of foretelling from his despair that it would carry him as far as it did. On the following Monday afternoon at about three o'clock, a telephone call from Woodstock brought the hysterical voice of Frank Meyer, a neighbor of young Gene and the man from whom he had bought his land, crying out: "Gene has just killed himself. He slashed his wrists and ankles. My wife found him dead at the bottom of the stairs in his house."

Would I notify his father?

In my own panic dread of such an assignment, trying either to evade the delicate task or to act as rationally as possible, it seemed to me then that a doctor or a lawyer should be asked to perform it. I forthwith telephoned Bill Aronberg to convey the shocking news and to seek his advice more than to shift the burden onto him. He said without hesitation that it was his duty as O'Neill's lawyer to notify him of the disaster. After all, he was, he said, on a retainer and this was his responsibility, not mine. He promised that he would telephone Marblehead and then call me back to report how the father withstood the shock.

A half hour later his call came and I realized at once from the tone of his voice that he was disturbed and blazing with anger. He said he wanted to give me a verbatim report of his long-distance conversation.

When Carlotta answered the telephone, Bill Aronberg said: "Hello, Carlotta. This is Bill Aronberg. I have terrible news for you. Try to be brave and break this gently to Gene. Young Gene has just committed suicide."

Whereupon Carlotta answered: "How dare you invade our privacy?" and slammed the receiver down. That was the entire conversation.

Young O'Neill was beyond insult and injury. No inquest could reveal that he died as much from a thwarted effort at communication as by his own hand. A note found near his body tried to convey a sardonic if somewhat theatrical last message of bluster and defiance. It read: "Never let it be said of an O'Neill that he failed to empty the bottle. Ave atque vale!"[2]

Less than five months after young Gene had written his final hail and farewell, Bill Aronberg, still Eugene O'Neill's lawyer, Lawrence Langner, director of the Theatre Guild, and I were involved in what Carlotta chose to call a conspiracy to kidnap and transport her husband from Salem, Massachusetts, to New York City. Also implicated in the "criminal conspiracy" was the late Dr. Merrill Moore, physician and psychiatrist and the only begetter of thousands of sonnets.[3]

The sad episode had its beginning in Marblehead in the first week of February, 1951. What I know of that act in the tragic drama that was his life came to me from Eugene O'Neill's own lips as he lay immobilized in a bed in the Salem Hospital. This is what I learned from him when I was summoned to his bedside:

On the cold February night of the 5th he and Carlotta had had a quarrel, the nature of which he would not divulge. At any rate, to escape her wrath, he explained, he walked out of the house, coatless, and wandered in the darkness about the grounds of their Marblehead home, following the path that led from the door to the road. The night was colder than he at first thought and he decided to return for an overcoat. As he approached the door he mistook one of the stones, sharply angled at the top, which lined the driveway for a shadow. Unheedingly he stepped on it and fell, stunned by a sharp pain in his knee as he lay sprawled on the ground. On trying to rise, he discovered that his leg would not support him and fell again. He realized at once, from the pain and his inability to flex his leg, that serious damage had been done to his knee.

He began to call for help. There was no answer. For an hour he lay on the roadway, helpless and unable to move, crying all the while for aid. With no coat on his back, he suffered from the severe cold and felt, besides the pain, fear of the consequences of long exposure. He continued to cry for help and finally the door of their house was opened. Carlotta stood framed in its small rectangular proscenium, her figure lighted by the vestibule lamp. She made no move. After a long silence, she delivered in histrionic tones these lines:

"How the mighty have fallen! The master is lying low. Now where is all your greatness?"

Wherewith she closed the door.

Fortunately, the doctor who had been due an hour earlier to administer medicine to allay Gene's Parkinson's tremor was late. When he arrived, he heard Gene's cries from the path and hastened to his side. At a glance he could tell that the knee had been broken and nothing less than hospitalization could be of any help. He threw his own overcoat over Gene and went into the house to summon an ambulance from Salem. While telephoning it was apparent to him that he had two patients, not one, for Carlotta was in a state of hysteria.

When the ambulance arrived he had Gene placed on the stretcher and lifted into the vehicle. He tried to persuade Carlotta to accompany them to the hospital, but she refused. In the very early morning she was seen wandering on the road by a policeman making his habitual rounds. Carlotta demanded that he take her to her husband in the hospital. [The two preceding sentences are from Saxe's notes and were not part of his memoir.]

While in the lobby, she created a scene, screaming maledictions on Gene's head, insulting the doctors and nurses, and threatening them with arrests and lawsuits and whatever else came into her disturbed mind. So great was the disturbance caused by her wild behavior that the police were called. They merely escorted her outside the building and appealed to her to calm down. Outdoors she continued her incoherent tirade and it reached such a peak of violence that the police decided to call a psychiatrist. He, at first ignorant of Carlotta's identity, saw the urgency of the situation and at once had her committed to a hospital for mental patients. The psychiatrist was the poet Merrill Moore.

That is how matters stood when I arrived by train from New York. Gene, in severe pain and trembling with nervous shock, his leg encased in a plaster cast that stretched from mid-thigh to ankle, lay on his hospital bed and pieced out the story for me haltingly and with desperate sadness. Little could be done for him now beyond attending to his needs, making him comfortable and trying to assure him that the doctors and the nurses of the hospital staff were eager to serve him with all the facilities at their command. Before I left he made me promise that I would come to him as often as possible.

Once a week thereafter I went to Salem from New York, by air rather than by train, because it was quicker and more convenient to travel by taxi from the Boston airport to Salem than to go by train to Boston, drive across the city, take another train to Salem and then be transported by taxi to the hospital.

Each visit brought more and more confirmation that, although Gene's knee was healing under the cast, his nervous condition was steadily becoming more aggravated. Consultation with Dr. Frederick B. Mayo and other physicians in Salem ended with their recommendation that the wisest course would be to take Gene to New York, where he would have his own physician and the best possible orthopedic and neurologic care. When first told of the doctors' counsel, he vetoed the plan because he was gravely concerned about Carlotta. He had learned that she had taken steps to gain release from the institution to which she had been committed. Since she was not a voluntary patient and because she had been admitted in an emergency by a psychiatrist, she was within her rights to demand immediate dismissal. This was accomplished without any intervention on Gene's part and Carlotta left her hospital for parts unknown.

The doctors in Salem again urged upon Gene the wisdom and necessity of going to New York and he was finally persuaded to undertake the trip. Bill Aronberg, Lawrence Langner and I arranged ways and means of bringing about the transfer. We decided, with the doctor's consent, to engage a trained nurse as a traveling companion, take a room on the train to which he would be brought in a wheelchair with his physician in attendance and run the risk of his withstanding the journey to New York. Aronberg, Langner and I met him at the Grand Central Station and with the aid of the nurse carried him to a waiting wheelchair. A limousine was in readiness to drive us to a Madison Avenue hotel where we were joined by Russel Crouse, a staunch old friend whose good sense and reliability in any crisis were always unfailing.

Within a few hours it became evident to the nurse and to us that a hotel room would not be adequate for his needs. The nurse had to return to Salem and we would have to engage three shifts of nurses to take her place. Then, too, sleeping quarters and food would have to be provided for them. Under these circumstances we agreed to telephone Doctors Hospital to arrange for a room and to call Dr. Fisk who was again to be in charge and would select an orthopedic specialist.

The nurse from Salem and our entire group attending, we accompanied Gene to Doctors Hospital where he was assigned a comfortable room overlooking the East River. He remained there for a month. X-rays showed that his knee was healing satisfactorily, but his general physical and nervous condition had undergone obvious deterioration. He was down to ninety-seven pounds.

Every day for four weeks we visited together for at least one hour, usually in the evening after work. His nights, he told me, were hideous, haunted by spectres and delusional terrors, asleep or awake. He was taking frequent doses of chloral hydrate at the time, both to reduce the Parkinson tremor and to induce sleep. Once, while I was with him, he sprang from the bed before I could grasp him and cowered in a far corner of the room nearest the door, crying out: "She's on the window sill. She's coming toward me. Please keep her away!" Whereupon he scraped the wall with his fingernails, trying vainly to get a finger hold so that he could climb the wall, cast and all, and escape whatever was pursuing him in his overwrought, phantom-ridden mind.

It was not entirely a sick fantasy that she was near. Upon her insistence and certainly within her legal rights, Carlotta was released from the sanitarium to which she had been committed by Dr. Moore and, after a brief delay, came to New York. There she engaged a room in Doctors Hospital underneath Gene's. Several times during my visits she telephoned him. Whenever she did so I waited in the hall until the conversation came to an end. It was all too manifest that she was regaining control.

Even in the face of Gene's imminent return to captivity, our group tried to make plans for an uncertain future. Bennett and Phyllis Cerf found and were about to sign a lease for a New York apartment for Gene to which he could move upon his dismissal from the hospital. This plan was vetoed and the option on the apartment was dropped. My wife and I had gained his half-consent to setting up an establishment in Princeton, New Jersey, where we would try to minister to his needs. Carlotta's appearance summarily disposed of this notion. Other friends generously suggested alternatives, to all of which he listened patiently but would not respond affirmatively or negatively. All of us soon began to realize that our good intentions only paved the way to nowhere.

As Gene grew a little stronger, he began to analyze or, more properly, to explain and rationalize his predicament. He realized, as we were beginning to do, that the tie that bound him to Carlotta was too firm to undo. Yet he was acutely aware that submission meant the final severance from all his old friends and repudiation of his own past. He realized that he would need constant care, would have to be fed and nursed and guarded. On that score alone he was unwilling to impose upon his friends. There was, on the other hand, the risk of other quarrels with Carlotta and perhaps other broken limbs. Consideration, too, had to be given to his Parkinson affliction; it had advanced to the point where he could not possibly live without close moment-to-moment help.

Essential as this was, it cut a deep wound into his pride. After all, Carlotta had lived with him and it for almost a quarter of a century, and when she was not in a state of acute disturbance, she could be competent and devoted and even sacrificial in her imperious and managerial way. Hers was not a radiant future, he argued as much to convince himself as me, and she had relinquished a life of ease as a woman of conspicuous beauty in order to be at his side through all those years, for better or for worse. As the wife of a famous man (he smiled wanly at the use of the adjective), she had expected to be surrounded by all that wealth and recognition could bring. But, instead, the latter years had been bitter for both of them, and not only was he sick and unproductive, but so was she and hers was a peculiar sickness only he could understand and had to forgive. Together, they might help each other; apart there could only be even greater torture and then dissolution. And, finally, his chief article of faith was that doom had to be his companion to his last hour.

To Bennett Cerf and Saxe Commins from Eugene O'Neill, tl 1 p. On stationery headed: Random House, Inc. The Modern Library / 457 Madison Avenue New York 22, N.Y. / Bennett A. Cerf, President

March 17, 1951

Dear Bennett and Saxe:

Please let this note serve as my official permission to Random House to publish, prior to production, individually or together, my two plays, *A Moon for the Misbegotten* and *A Touch of the Poet*. I rely on your judgment as to the appropriate publication date and the general format of the book.[4]

Sincerely,

Eugene O'Neill

Saxe and I visited O'Neill on May 16, 1951, the day before he left New York to return to Boston and to Carlotta. Saxe had brought with him a letter which Oona, long estranged from her father, had asked him to relay to him. Saxe gave it to O'Neill, who put it under his pillow; whether he ever read it is uncertain. Oona never received a reply. As we were leaving, O'Neill put his arms around Saxe and said, "Oh, Saxe! Goodbye, my brother!" It was so utterly sad I could not suppress my tears.

We never saw or heard from the O'Neills again. Accompanied by a nurse, O'Neill arrived in Boston on May 17, 1951, and went straight to the Hotel

Shelton, where Carlotta awaited him in a two-room suite that became his final home. There, in isolation and loneliness, death came to O'Neill on November 27, 1953. Carlotta outlived him by seventeen years and survived to orchestrate the O'Neill "revival" of the 1950s by releasing the rights to *Long Day's Journey into Night* (which won for O'Neill his fourth Pulitzer Prize), *A Touch of the Poet*, *More Stately Mansions*, and *Hughie*. She died on November 18, 1970.

After we saw O'Neill for the last time, Saxe wrote to Oona about our visit. He wrote her again after O'Neill's death.

[. . .]

The conclusion of Saxe's memoir provides a fitting epilogue to the O'Neill story:

When after his death in November of 1953, Eugene O'Neill's will was probated in Boston on December 24th of that year, it was revealed that he had disowned his two surviving children, Shane and Oona, and had named his widow as his sole beneficiary and executrix. The sentence cutting off his two children read:

"I purposely exclude from any interest in my estate under this will my son Shane O'Neill and my daughter Oona O'Neill Chaplin and exclude their issue, now or hereafter born."

The reason for this exclusion was incomprehensible at the time and gave rise to surprise and wonder. But it was not long before the mystery was solved.

In mid-1954, Bennett Cerf, President of Random House, was called on the telephone by Carlotta O'Neill and asked whether he had read the copy of *Long Day's Journey into Night* which had been hidden for many years in the company safe. To this he answered that indeed he had not because he was not allowed legally to do so and therefore he had never so much as seen nor opened the package; the seals were still intact and he had no intention of breaking them. In reply to this, Mrs. O'Neill said she wished he would read it at once because she wanted it published as soon as it was possible to do so. Before Cerf consented to read it, he wanted, he told her, to think about the matter and would then call her back.

He immediately consulted with me and asked my views. I suggested that he learn from our lawyer, Horace Manges, whether this violation of a dead man's wishes would be legally, if not morally, condonable, and second, that he insist upon a public statement, to be printed on the jacket and within the book itself, signed by the widow, to the effect that publication rights were granted with her full authorization. The last suggestion was offered with the view of averting the possibility that Random House or Bennett Cerf might be accused of vandalism. We were clearly faced with the alternative of undertaking publication with clean hands or relinquishing our right to do so altogether.

When Cerf communicated this decision to Mrs. O'Neill, she exploded with fury and vented most of her wrath on me, accusing me of having instigated a plot against her, of having ruined all the O'Neill plays on which I had worked with him and charging me with about as many crimes as are included in the penal code. To which, with characteristic loyalty, Cerf replied in a letter that was as gratifying as it was bolstering to my vanity. This letter alone, if I could live up to it, was a solace for the hurt inflicted by the unforeseen termination of a nearly forty-year friendship. For Cerf's act of devotion I hold him in high esteem, but even in greater respect for his determination not to compromise his principles as a publisher by violating a dead man's wishes.

We were shocked when we learned from our attorney that a strict interpretation of the law provided that the instructions of the deceased may be superseded by those of the sole beneficiary and executrix of a will. Therefore, Mrs. O'Neill was within her legal rights if she caused to be produced and published a play for which there had been a legal, if no longer binding, stipulation against such publication or production. There was no mention of the restricting document or the wish itself in the will.

At last the mystery was solved. Now it became clear why Eugene O'Neill had been induced to disown his two surviving children. Had they been legitimate heirs in the eyes of the law, the widow would not then have been sole beneficiary and the claim, within a strict interpretation of the law, to the right to produce and publish *Long Day's Journey into Night* before the stipulated time, which would have been in 1978, would have elapsed.

Astounded and bewildered by this development we could not at first let ourselves believe that, legally or morally, such a flouting of a dead man's wishes, explicitly stated in a signed document, would be permissible or justifiable. Unfortunately, we were laboring under moral illusions only, but our legal misapprehensions were more decisively against us.

Lawyers for Mrs. O'Neill overruled our naive contentions and confirmed the opinion of the attorney retained by Random House. That made it unanimous. Two distinguished members of the Boston Bar, successors to many colleagues who had been hired and fired by the relict of the playwright, called on Bennett Cerf to reach a determination about the publication of the posthumous play. Their errand was quickly accomplished; Cerf relinquished all rights to publication.

These counsellors were the successors to Mr. Melville Cane,[5] poet and essayist and an able and trustworthy lawyer, one of the many who had served their terms and been rejected. Long ago Cane and I had had a brief encounter in which at first I was the victim of his client's wrath. He was to feel its lash much later.

For more than ten years Mrs. O'Neill and I had maintained in our joint names a large safe-deposit box in the Manufacturers Trust Company which had its banking offices at 57th Street and Fifth Avenue. In it were stored many manuscripts, certificates of stock, mementoes and some rather expensive jewelry. During the time the O'Neills lived in France and California, letters, cables and telegrams came to New York asking me to remove certain items from the box and ship them wherever they were at the time. Sometimes I was asked to add things to the contents of the box. But no article of mine was ever placed in this receptacle, nor did I ever have occasion to use it for my own purposes. The reason for the joint rental of the safety-deposit box was so that I could always have access to it and deposit or withdraw anything the O'Neills might request.

Once an anxious series of telegrams and letters came from Mrs. O'Neill. She was nervously concerned about the loss of some valuable jewelry. Reference to the inventory of jewels locked in the box revealed that they were quite safe and intact. Her telegram on receiving the good news expressed happiness, relief and gratitude at my having found them where they were all the time. There also came the request to ship all the jewels in the safety box in the bank to California by registered mail. This was done and the acknowledgment of their receipt was in the language of rejoicing.

During the first of two separations between the O'Neills—once when his arm was broken and then his leg—I received a peremptory letter from Melville Cane. He demanded that I relinquish my key to his client's safety-deposit box and made the statement that my access to it was not only questionable but also suspicious. The implication was that I planned to make off with its contents. To this letter I replied with bitter reproach to him for impugning my honesty and also with a full explanation of the circumstances under which the box had been rented and used for more than a decade. The key was enclosed with the letter.

Gene was in Doctors Hospital at the time convalescing from a fractured arm. I brought him Cane's letter and the carbon copy of my reply. He was furious. His anger expressed itself in a rather irrelevant but humorous manner. First of all, he disparaged Cane's literary work and then rebuked me for not writing a more scathing response. Then, with a broad grin on his face, he asked me whether we had in our office printed rejection slips for manuscripts that were not worthy of a personal letter. When I told him that we had such standard forms and used them only for the utterly hopeless manuscripts submitted to us, he said that what I should have done was to let one of those printed rejection slips serve as my answer to his letter.

Fortunately my little contretemps with Melville Cane was resolved many years later when he was no longer Mrs. O'Neill's attorney. He remembered our exchange of letters and at last could explain why he had to act as a lawyer under the orders of his client. He knew all along, he said, that I had never used the safety box for my own purposes and was certain that I had discharged my part of the bargain scrupulously. We later came to respect each other with genuine understanding.

Now Melville Cane belongs to that growing company of lawyers who were given rejection slips by Mrs. O'Neill. The two gentlemen from Boston who called on Bennett Cerf about the publication by Random House of *Long Day's Journey into Night* were also honored in this manner and can now consider themselves alumni. They were succeeded by a constellation of attorneys whose names on their letterheads are an awesome directory. It was they who arranged for the posthumous publication of the play by Yale University Press, after Random House had relinquished all rights to it, twenty-two years before Eugene O'Neill had intended to issue it.

For several years prior to his death in 1953, Eugene O'Neill had contributed manuscripts, notes and correspondence to the archives of the Yale University Library. After his death all his papers were given to Yale for safekeeping and for the ultimate use of scholars. Under these circumstances and even if a quid pro quo was not involved, it was logical and certainly legal, regardless of the moral distinctions entailed, to over-ride the author's living wish and have Yale University Press publish *Long Day's Journey into Night* with deserved success.

When the play was produced in 1956, first in Stockholm and then in New York, the question of the propriety of bringing it to the stage was overshadowed by the unanimous acclaim of the critics and the whole-hearted support of the public. O'Neill's own misgivings about the effect his work would have on the reputations of the dead and the susceptibilities of the living proved in the end to be baseless. The play was accepted, as it so richly merited, not as a rattling of skeletons in a family closet, but as a work of art dealing with a universal rather than a personal experience. It has been, from all accounts, magnificently acted and produced. I have never seen the play in whose history I was, in a strange sense, an unlisted member of the cast acting an anonymous role.

# 56 / Carlotta Monterey O'Neill

For information on Carlotta Monterey and Seymour Peck, see chapter 43. For information on Louis Sheaffer, see chapter 3.

Source: Seymour Peck, excerpts from an interview with Carlotta Monterey O'Neill, 2 October 1956, transcript in Louis Sheaffer Collection of Eugene O'Neill Materials, Department of Special Collections, Charles E. Shain Library, Connecticut College, New London.

O'NEILL: No, it wasn't Parkinson's—he never had Parkinson's. Never. It was printed in all the papers he didn't have Parkinson's disease at all. He had a nervous . . . . . . . When he died I had an autopsy performed because I wanted to know what in the name of God was the matter with this man I had nursed so long. And even then they called it a hereditary nervous disease [. . .] the last two or three years he suffered a great deal. He would fall. Handing his stick to me, he would go to step forward and instead of that he would fall backward and, of course, this was terrible. And it angered him, it embarrassed him.

**PECK: He broke his leg once during this time, didn't he?**

O'NEILL: No, no, this was after that he broke his leg. He broke his leg because he was very naughty, and he wouldn't pay attention and he insisted upon going out at night. He was supposed to take his stick, and this was at Marblehead—he wanted to live on the water our last home we got together—and it was so much on the water that we were tied to rocks by steel cables and when the storms came up, of course they came right over the head. I expected to go out to sea any moment. And he was all dressed up one night in the weirdest garments, and I said, "Where are you going, darling?" and he said, "That was his affair." And he went out. And you know how the rocks stick up and you try to plant a little grass between them and a few little daisies or something to make it look not quite so dreary—and he tripped on one of those little rocks and that is how he broke his leg. And when he died I had an autopsy taken at Massachusetts General. I asked the doctor if it couldn't be done because I wanted to know what was wrong. And there were many things wrong. He was much older than his years. That may be on his doctors that I trusted, and I don't say mean [*sic*] trusted—the doctors whose opinion I valued who knew him better.

[. . .]

**PECK: What are these stories that Mr. O'Neill wanted twenty-five years to elapse before [*Long Day's Journey Into Night*] was produced?**

O'NEILL: Well, I might as well get this over.

**PECK: Please.**

O'NEILL: When we came to New York, from California at the end the very end of '45 and the *Ice Man* was put on by the Guild, very badly. Oh I forgot, my husband showed his eldest son this play and he read it and he said it is a very wonderful play, but he said, "will you promise me something" and my husband said, well what is it, and he said "promise me you will not let them produce this play for 25 years," and he said "why" and he (the son) said, "I don't think it would be good for my social position at Yale." So, when Gene gave it to Random House to put in the safe, he took a little card and stuck it in the middle where the thing was and said not to be produced for 25 years. That was all there was to the contract. When we were in about 1952 and 53 we were very hard up, terribly hard up, my income was getting very low, Gene's was getting low and I was very worried. I was nursing a very sick man and all the rest of it and I was very unhappy, and I suppose I went around with a long face, which is not very good for a nurse to do, and he said to me what's the matter with you? You look as if you had lost your last friend, and I said well gee what do you suppose is the matter with me? He said, what are you worried about? And I said, money, money, money, and he said, but you don't have to worry. We've got a nest egg. I said, where is it? Why, he said, *Long Day's Journey*. Well then I thought he had [gone] completely out of his mind and I said, well, what about *Long Day's Journey*, and he said, well we'll publish it, and I said I thought it wasn't to be published for 25 years, and he said: "Oh, well, that's all over now, we don't have to do that." I said, why not? He said, "Because Eugene is dead." I said, what's Eugene got to do with being dead and you publishing that play? And he said, "Because it was he who asked me." You see he didn't tell me when he had done that at first. I didn't know that till then. Now, he said, if things get worse, we will publish it and then he made a literary trust and paid me the greatest compliment he could have done, and the will in which I have complete and absolute control of everything, and he said to me, (as I told you a little while ago) I could publish it if and when I pleased but the only thing he insisted upon was that inscription[6] and that nobody write it for him, so that was that.[7]

**PECK: In reading the play, it struck me that his relationship with his family was in many ways the same unhappy one that he had with his children. Is that so? Did it bother him that he should have lost a son the tragic way he lost Eugene and his other children should have gone so far away from him?[8]**

O'NEILL: Now listen, Mr. Peck, that is a terrible question to ask me. Of course, it bothered him but he was the type of man who never said anything. I don't like to discuss his children. I think it is very poor taste and I don't think I should but the thing is this, when anything happened to those closest to him, he saw very little of them, they used to come to visit us during the summer or holidays, when they would do anything that he didn't think that was quite good for them, not because he wished it, he would sink into a silence, but then he wouldn't even talk about them, he wouldn't even mention their names, and it became very difficult because he disagreed with what they thought and so it became so that their names were never mentioned. Now when the lawyer phoned, Gene never answered the phone, never talked to anyone unless it was absolutely necessary, but he never answered the phone and I went, it was a New York lawyer at that time,[9] and he said to me, "Eugene has killed himself." I said, "What," and the phone was here and my husband was sitting right over there. So you couldn't expect me to say "Oh, how funny," or something and I said "Are you sure?" and he said "yes" and I said "I don't believe it." "Well, I tell you, I'M sure." And this and that. Well I hung up the phone and you can imagine what I felt like and I sat down and Gene watched me with those black eyes of his and he said, "Well, come out with it, what is it?" And I said, "Eugene is ill, very ill" and he said, "When did he die?" I said, I don't know, and he hadn't told me the exact time, and he said, come on let's talk sense. Is he dead? He said he was. He surely wouldn't ring you up if he wasn't. He lapsed into silence and he never mentioned his name again, except when he said, Eugene is dead, so we can publish the thing. Now, his other children upset him, but always inside, as time went on and this hurt would arrive and that hurt would arrive, there was no criticism, there was no anything, he just became more ill, more unhappy but never said anything. So naturally I never did. That is why I didn't want to go into this.

[. . .]

**PECK: I was very touched by a story that I read about your helping him destroy some six plays of the cycle . . .**

O'NEILL: Oh don't talk about that

**PECK: That began with *The* [*sic*] *Touch of the Poet.***

O'NEILL: We did that in, at the Shelton Hotel because he didn't want to leave any unfinished plays and he said "it isn't that I don't trust you Carlotta," but you might drop dead or get run over or something and I don't want anybody else finishng a play of mine, and it was like tearing up children. It was awful. I had typed these, most of them you see.

**PECK: Six plays?**

O'NEILL: I forget, five or six and it was horrible.

**PECK: They were all uncompleted then?**

O'NEILL: No they were completed, but they needed cutting and revision and he never allowed anyone to touch any of the plays.

**PECK: Was this very close to his death?**

O'NEILL: Well it was in the last. It was between '51, and he died in '53, those two years. But I think it was in the end of '52 and the first part of '53. It was in there about.

**PECK: And he felt he could not get back to the work himself?**

O'NEILL: But he hadn't worked for ten years.

**PECK: How did you actually destroy the plays?**

O'NEILL: Tear them up, bit by bit.

**PECK: Together, or you did it?**

O'NEILL: No we did it together, I helped him because you see his hands, he had this terrific tremor and to do anything, so he had to tear just a few pages at a time because you know if you tear thick pages you know how it would look. [. . .]

**PECK: Did you try to dissuade him?**

O'NEILL: Why certainly not, I'd not be so presumptuous. No one would get very far trying to persuade him to do anything. He was the writer, he was the man. He wasn't that kind of a man.

[. . .]

O'NEILL: I'll tell you speaking seriously about O'Neill, when I say O'Neill I mean the writer, when I say Gene I mean my husband. Gene had a, he was very much of a sadist at times, terribly so, but if he did anything when the moon changed and he realized it, he suffered terribly from guilt if he had hurt anyone that he liked at all. And his guilt, to watch his guilt hurt me much more than when he was a sadist. I couldn't stand to see my child so miserable, you know. But I think his writing showed that, don't you.

**PECK: Where is Mr. O'Neill buried?**

O'NEILL: In Boston, just outside Boston, Forest Hill Cemetery.

**PECK: Very small stone.**

O'NEILL: I carried out every wish of his to the letter and it was very difficult. He wished to keep from the papers, apologies, any letter where he was, in what funeral parlor, anything. He wished no publicity. He wished nobody to be at his funeral. He wished no religious representative of creed or kind. He wished nobody to be there but me and my nurse, his nurse who helped me the last two years.[10] Well, what we went through. We must say. But the people in the hotel and [in] particular two men who were strong of arm and determined, good Bostonians, they were throwing people downstairs and I don't know what. And my nurse who is a Canadian, a very charming person, we used to have to go around blocks and change taxis and everything to finally get to the undertakers which was only two blocks from where we lived.[11] We'd ride miles to keep it a secret. And then my lawyer and I went out and bought the lot. He wished a simple lot, enough for two people. He wished me to be buried beside him and he wished a stone and he drew a little stone and he lettered beautifully you know and he lettered on this pattern Eugene O'Neill whatever the date was, born and died, and Carlotta, my wife, born San Francisco, etc. and rest in peace and a line left open for when I die [see figure 17]. And do you know that I used to go out there when I got very nervous and very unhappy and look at that and feel a sort of content. I had a place to go to. It's wonderful when you are left alone. And there you are. It's very lovely, this cemetery particularly. It isn't like the old-fashioned cemeteries, it's got beautiful trees, enormous rhododendrons, and in the spring and the summer with the dogwoods you know, it's quite, quite lovely. It's awfully hard to keep things private in this world. Mercy.

**PECK: That's part of what Mr. Atkinson would have called his infatuation with oblivion.**

O'NEILL: Yes, it saves a lot of trouble.

# 57 / Bennett Cerf

For information on Bennett Cerf, see chapter 36.

Source: Bennett Cerf, *At Random: The Reminiscences of Bennett Cerf* (New York: Random House, 1977), 88–89.

As time went on, Carlotta became more and more irrational. There was no question about the fact that her mind was now affected. She had become obsessive about Gene. He couldn't do anything without her, in her opinion. They finally left New York and moved to Boston. Then Carlotta bought a house in Marblehead, and it was there that things began to be even worse.

By this time Gene really saw nobody. One night he sneaked out for some reason or other. On his way home it started to snow terribly, and just in front of the house Gene, who was now very frail, slipped and fell down and broke his leg. Carlotta came out and stood over him, laughing at him while he lay in the snow with a broken leg. That's when they put her away. Gene stayed in the hospital until his leg mended. Then Russel Crouse brought him down to New York and put him in a hospital. Gene was terrified that Carlotta would find him. "Keep that woman away from me. She almost killed me." He was in the hospital for weeks. Then we all decided together that he was going to stay in New York and never go back to Carlotta.

At the time there was no space to be had in New York; everything was overcrowded. But Phyllis and I found a place for Gene at the Carlyle Hotel on Madison Avenue. Of course, for Eugene O'Neill they moved heaven and earth. And since he was so weak and would continue to need care, we arranged for a male nurse to call for Gene at ten o'clock on the morning he was to leave the hospital and go with him to the Carlyle. But when the man arrived to get him, Gene was gone! Carlotta (they couldn't keep her confined; nobody would certify that she was insane, and at times she could be absolutely normal, very convincing and charming, and meek and beautiful) had found out where he was and had come down to Doctors Hospital and talked him into going to Boston with her. This was the woman of whom he had said, "Keep her away from me," but he couldn't resist her. He never told Saxe Commins; never told Russel Crouse; never told Phyllis and me. He was ashamed to, and off he went—not a word from him.

Well, of course, we were terribly sorry for him, and furious with him too. He lived for another two years, but we never saw him again. And to finish the saga, when the great Eugene O'Neill died in 1953, this woman allowed not a single friend to come to the funeral. The hearse was driven out to the cemetery, and behind it was one automobile with Carlotta O'Neill and a nurse and a doctor sitting in it—not another soul.

Before Gene died he had delivered to us the manuscript of his long autobiographical play, *Long Day's Journey into Night*, with instructions in writing that it not be published until twenty-five years after his death.[12] We put the manuscript in our safe, fully intending to abide by his wishes; but soon after he died we learned that Carlotta had a different view: she demanded that we ignore Gene's directive and proceed with publishing the play at once. We refused, of course, but then were horrified to learn that legally all the cards were in her hand; what the author wanted, and what he had asked us to do, had no validity if she wanted something else—which she did. When we insisted that Random House could not in conscience publish it, she demanded that we give her the manuscript—it was now her legal property—and Yale University Press, apparently caring as little as she did about what O'Neill had wanted, published it promptly. They therefore had a best seller on their hands and a Book-of-the-Month Club selection, but I do not regret that we took the stand we did, because I still think we were right.

Eugene O'Neill was a great man, the great American playwright. He had a streak in him, too, of boyish enthusiasm that didn't seem to fit. He loved talking about the old days and the sea chanteys he had sung. Then that somber, beautiful face of his would light up and you really loved him very, very much indeed.

A man like this comes along maybe once in a generation.

# 58 / Earle F. Johnson

Earle F. Johnson (1907–?) was a popular interior designer in the Boston area. Carlotta and Eugene O'Neill met him when he worked at Carbone, Inc. in Boston and hired him to decorate their house in Marblehead. The relationship deepened into friendship, with Carlotta calling Johnson on the telephone and asking him to come for social visits. He later established his own business in Wellesley, Massachusetts. Johnson occasionally lectured on "New England Interiors" for local women's groups and other organizations.

Michael Burlingame (b. 1941) was born in Washington, DC, and educated at Phillips Academy, Andover, and Princeton before earning his PhD at Johns Hopkins University. He has taught at Connecticut College and the University of Illinois in Springfield. A prominent Lincoln scholar, he is the author of *Abraham Lincoln: A Life* (2008), *Lincoln and the Civil War* (2011), *The Inner World of Abraham Lincoln* (1994), and many other books. In the 1980s he wrote several articles for the New London newspaper the *Day.*

Source: Michael Burlingame, "O'Neill Recalled Warmly," *Day* [New London] 21 July 1988: E1, 3.

One of the few people Eugene O'Neill saw regularly in the last five years of his life was Earle F. Johnson, an interior decorator who had helped the playwright and his third wife, Carlotta, furnish the last home they would share (a cottage by the sea in Marblehead, on Boston's North Shore). Last weekend, Johnson, a genial dapper gentleman who looks much younger than his age (82), publicly shared for the first time his memories of the O'Neills in an interview with *The Day.*

Sitting in the Monte Cristo Cottage (the playwright's boyhood home) in New London Saturday, Johnson reminisced with animation. Among other things, he recalled that Carlotta so disliked O'Neill's elder son, Eugene, Jr., that she would immediately burn the sheets that he and his lady friend had slept on when visiting the Marblehead home. She also had the playwright's personal library burned when she could not persuade Yale or the Salvation Army to take it after his death.[13]

Many years ago Arthur Gelb, a high-ranking *New York Times* executive who, with his wife Barbara, co-authored a biography of O'Neill (published in 1962), asked Johnson to tell him about the playwright, but was rebuffed.[14] Speaking with obvious affection and warmth about his friends the O'Neills, Johnson explained why, even though Gelb intimated that "it would be worth my while" if he cooperated, he could not do so: "Shortly after I met the O'Neills (in 1948), they said to me, 'Please, Earle, don't commercialize our friendship.' I agreed, and I keep my promises. But now Carlotta's gone (she died in 1970) and I'm sure she would approve my talking with you."

Johnson was at the Monte Cristo Cottage to donate O'Neill's cane and deck chairs, which Carlotta had given him after her husband's death in 1953. The hand-made cane, which the playwright used regularly in his last years, resembles a cross between an Irish walking stick and a shillelagh. The deck chairs, purchased from Abercrombie and Fitch, were a birthday present from Carlotta to her husband, given at a party where Johnson was the only guest. He and O'Neill sat in them during some of Johnson's many visits to the Marblehead home between 1948 and 1953.

"O'Neill had the cane with him the first time I met him and his wife," Johnson recalled. "One slow Wednesday they came to the store where I worked (Carbone's in Boston) to ask advice about decorating the house they had bought in Marblehead. I didn't recognize them, though they were an unusual looking couple. After they left, a colleague of mine said, 'Don't you know that was Eugene O'Neill?' That afternoon Carlotta called and said, 'The master is as interested in you as I am.'"

Johnson recalls her adding that "she was surprised that her husband took an interest in decorating the house. I think she thought, 'This is good. Maybe we'll be doing something together.'

"The next day they invited me over to their suite at the Ritz Carlton Hotel, and the following week we went to the house. They gave me the job then."

Johnson said he almost lost it, however, through a misunderstanding. In September 1948, the playwright gave him a copy of *The Iceman Cometh*, which Johnson asked him to inscribe. With Johnson holding his hand to help steady it (O'Neill suffered from a congenital tremor of the hands that tragically forced him to abandon writing plays during his last decade) O'Neill wrote "To Earle F. Johnson, with deep gratitude for his many kindnesses to us O'Neills."

(Johnson started to read the play, but could not bring himself to finish it. He told O'Neill, "You look like an angel. How could you write such stuff.")

After Johnson showed the volume to colleagues, a customer who had overheard the story called Carlotta to request that her husband autograph a play of his to be auctioned for charity. Carlotta, who resented intrusions on their privacy, was furious, but when Johnson explained that he hadn't encouraged the request, she forgave him.

After finishing his formal task for the O'Neills, Johnson was often invited to visit as a friend. "I went there quite a bit. The visits would last from 15 minutes to two or three hours. I never went on my own or with my wife. Carlotta would call me saying she wanted to see me or Gene wanted to see me, that he was lonesome. It was always during business hours in the week. She told me to tell my boss that I had to go out there for business reasons. O'Neill always sat at the dining room table. He was always dressed up. I never saw him in casual clothes."

Although this period was a stormy one in the O'Neills' marriage, Johnson says he noticed no antagonism between them. "They were two different types of people, but I never saw anything like tension between them. He never took a negative attitude toward her. He loved her and she idolized him."

O'Neill, Johnson recalled, was hardly a chatterbox. "When I would arrive, he would sometimes just nod. Other times he'd say, 'Good morning, Earle.' She would always bring some coffee or something like that and we'd just sit there. Sometimes I could get him in conversation, especially about the sea, which he called his solace. It gave him peace of mind. In good weather we sat outdoors on the deck chairs. When he had very little to say, he just seemed to enjoy the fact that I was sitting beside him. If he wanted to say something to someone, I was there. How much could he talk to Carlotta about?"

O'Neill seldom mentioned his family, Johnson said. "I sensed that whenever I thought about asking him about his family, he was thinking, 'Don't ask me.'" Nevertheless, Johnson remembers that "he was disappointed with his father because the old man criticized him a lot. He felt he never really had a father. He did not mention his mother. He was also disappointed in his boys (Eugene, Jr., and Shane) but he was pleased with Oona (his daughter). He said she was the only sensible one of the three because she had married somebody with money (Charlie Chaplin). He did not get excited when talking about his children. The only time there was any bitterness you could sense was when he talked about his oldest son (Eugene, Jr.)."

Carlotta especially disliked Eugene, Jr. She told Johnson, "he'd bring a slut on visits (to Marblehead)." She said, "I didn't like it, but I had to respect the Master." She always called him that—never 'my husband' or 'Gene.' Eugene, Jr., she said, 'was full of disease.' That's why she'd burn the bedsheets after they'd left. 'I can't get the linen off the bed fast enough after they'd left,' she said."

Carlotta was far more voluble than her husband. "She talked all the time. I think she was desperate for company. We'd talk about our Scandinavian backgrounds—my family comes from Sweden, and hers from Denmark. It was very down-to-earth, simple conversation."

Johnson recollects that the O'Neills cared little about social status. "With Carlotta, she didn't care what your station in life was. She befriended the garbage man and the mailman." When they left Marblehead to move into a Boston hotel in 1951, Carlotta wanted to give Johnson some of the things he had helped select for the house, but she could not reach him, for he had left Carbone's to establish his own business in Wellesley. So she gave many household items to the postman and the garbage man.

Johnson sadly recalled that "I lost touch with them. I'd call the Marblehead number but no one would answer. Then one day on Newberry Street in Boston I saw her. She embraced me and cried as she apologized for being unable to give me some of her husband's possessions as he had intended. 'You know me, Mr. Johnson. I like to give things to people who were nice to me.' She added that 'the only people who were nice to me were the garbage man and the postman.' She offered me some things that had been put in storage, but I refused, though I did offer to help sell them and take a commission. I did so, and got good prices for them."

In November 1953 Johnson received a call from Carlotta: "She told me, 'The Master is gone. It would have been my wish that you could be present at the burial, but I must do what the Master requested. I am a Christian, but he called himself an atheist and wanted to be buried as an atheist. He said that all the bad things happened to his family while they were Catholics. He wanted a simple white shroud and black coffin with only me and the nurse in attendance at the interment.' After the burial she called to say that she had by the grave site fallen to her knees and recited the Lord's Prayer.

# 59 / Frederic B. Mayo, MD

Dr. Frederic Breed Mayo (1916–2000) was a young internist practicing in nearby Swampscott when he treated Eugene and Carlotta O'Neill in Marblehead. It was he who found Eugene when he fell and was left freezing in the snow. For information on Louis Sheaffer, see chapter 3.

Source: Louis Sheaffer, interview notes with Dr. Frederic B. Mayo, Louis Sheaffer Collection of Eugene O'Neill Materials, Department of Special Collections, Charles E. Shain Library, Connecticut College, New London.

[Carlotta] called me one evening to come over—there was a lot of snow around —and when I approached the front door I heard this moan. I investigated and found [O'Neill] in the snow, alongside of the house, very thinly dressed, shirt, sweater, no rubbers, not dressed for outdoors in that weather. I lifted him up and helped him into the house . . . He didn't say anything that I could remember, he must've been in too much pain to talk. He had injured his right knee . . . linea [*sic*] fracture down the shaft, fractured tibia but not compound . . . I guess he stumbled on a rock buried under the snow. (He had come out the door and come right to the side of house, about where swimming pool is now.) Planning to kill himself? It's possible, it looks as tho he was headed for the water, but that's only a guess. He never said anything, never said how long he was out there. This happened on Feb. 5/51 . . . I had him taken to the hospital in a private ambulance, tried to keep it out of the papers, but as you know it got in.

That same night, I believe it was, the police called me to see Carlotta. She'd been found wandering around on Marblehead Neck, not acting rational. She was confused and was seen by a psychiatrist. Since Salem Hospital is not equipped to handle mental cases, she was taken to another hospital, not a mental but a private one, McClean [*sic*] Hosp., in Waverly, part of Boston.

He was in mortal fear of her at the time. McClean called to ask if she could come with an attendant and see him. They thought it would be alright . . . When I told him she wanted to come, he broke out in a sweat, "Oh, don't let her come near me, oh, don't let her come here" . . . He seemed afraid she would hurt him. He told me that when he broke his arm in New York and had it in a cast, she took hold of it and moved his arm, causing him great pain.

I first made a house call in October, 1948. [. . .] He definitely had Parkinson's Disease—I don't know why she denies it now.[15] I called in Dr. Jacob Schwab, expert on Parkinson's at Mass. General Hospital to look at him . . . It's difficult to say how bad her arthritis of hip was. Took X-ray of feet, nothing wrong there . . . I visited them on average of once a month, the usual things, colds, not feeling well. She'd call me on sundry aches and pains . . . I think sometimes the calls were just because they were lonely and wanted to see someone else, I felt that with him especially. He was all cooped up there . . . I liked him very much. I'm not particularly interested in the theatre so we talked about the water and boats. I was disappointed to find he liked jazz (implication Mayo a classical music lover). Since he was interested in boats, I once asked if he would like to go for a sail some Sunday afternoon—I have access to a good-sized schooner, told him there'd be nobody but family. He was very enthusiastic, his face lit up, but she put the kibosh on it. When I contacted them, the answer was no. She always answered the telephone.

I'd spend 10 or 15 minutes there, 30 at the most, once, I think. They never mentioned the children at any time, and I made a faux pas once. I asked if any of the family were coming for Christmas, think I mentioned Oona, and she told me, "Don't you ever mention that name in this house again. We've disinherited her" . . . She once complained to me that she'd been a fine actress and could have become one of the best in the theatre but marrying him deprived her of a career and the theatre of a great actress. . . . He was not loquacious but he was a delightful man, very charming and gracious.

His wasn't one of the worst Parkinson's cases. His body didn't tremble violently or all the time, his hands didn't shake violently against his body, as I've seen in some cases. He had a tremor but his trouble was more a rigidity of the muscle. Some days he'd hardly have a tremor, and other times, when upset, would be bad.

I don't think she was violent or abusive that night but we had a hard time getting her into the police car, to go to Salem. I had to give her a sedative. (When I asked Dr. Mayo his analysis of her character, expecting a psychoanalytic reply, he said, "She's a horse's ass.")

[. . .]

I didn't prescribe any sedatives for the O'Neills. I believe he got it—she did too—from their N.Y. doctor. Think it was chloral hydrate.

[. . .]

He (O'Neill) was not in a position to make decisions when he was in Salem Hospital. I don't know whether Langner and Aronberg persuaded him to transfer to New York but he didn't protest, so far as I know . . . Yes, I believe he was reluctant to start working—he'd given up. It was hard to get any enthusiasm or spark for anything from him. [. . .] He told me he first discovered he had Parkinson's when he tried to sign a hotel register and his hands would tremble, became all the more nervous to have people watching him and thinking "That's Eugene O'Neill."

# 60 / Sallie Coughlin

Sallie Coughlin (1895?–?) was a nurse who worked in various hospitals in the Boston area. In 1951 she was assigned to O'Neill at Salem Hospital after he fell in the snow in Marblehead and broke his leg.
For information on Louis Sheaffer, see chapter 3.

Source: Louis Sheaffer, Sallie Coughlin interview notes, Louis Sheaffer Collection of Eugene O'Neill Materials, Department of Special Collections, Charles E. Shain Library, Connecticut College, New London.

Miss Coughlin [. . .] was assigned to O'Neill's case in 1951. He was "just skin and bones" when she met him.

O'Neill told her at the time he broke his leg, there had been an argument and he was desperate to escape Carlotta's voice hammering at him, went outside to get a breath of air, a moment's peace, and fell on a *sheet* (Sallie's term as one used in New England) concealed by the snow. Carlotta had not followed him outside but remained standing in the doorway. When he called for help, on falling, she remained in the doorway, saying over and over, "I hear a little man calling in the wind, I hear a little man calling in the wind, I hear . . ." And he blacked out for a while, for how long he never knew.

First several weeks he was in traction . . . Sallie doubts that he was suicidal for a while, that windows were kept locked to prevent an attempt. Points out that he was in traction and couldn't have gotten out of bed on his own.

Had difficult time at first in getting him to take a daily walk in the corridor, when his leg was healing. Was reluctant because he felt everyone would be looking at him. Sallie took this as a sign of his conceit, that everyone would be staring at the famous playwright, told him that the other patients weren't aware of his being there, that the other nurses and doctors were too preoccupied with their own work to be interested in him. "When you take the walk, all they'll see is not Eugene O'Neill the playwright but a tired old man."

(Sallie, who apparently has a strong family feeling, disliked O'Neill because she had heard he was alienated from his children, didn't have anything to do with them.)

She once said to him: "Why is everything so sordid in your plays? So depressing?" And he told her: "Because that's the way I see life. To me it's sordid, unhappy, brutal—I can only write about it the way I see it."

He slept late, generally didn't have breakfast till about 10:30 . . . "I had a hard time getting him to eat, he had no appetite. He was not a sloppy eater."

For several weeks, shortly after he entered Doctors Hospital, Carlotta, who had learned the nurse's name, used to write her every day from Boston and generally enclosed photos of Gene, and of Gene and herself, which she inscribed on the back, "From happier days" . . . But Sallie never replied, and after a while the letters stopped coming.

Dr. [Robert Lee] Patterson,[16] whom Sallie felt was fond of both Gene and Carlotta, told her of earlier bust-up in 1948 when he had both of them in Doctors Hospital. Dr. Patterson laughed, as though over the antics of two willful, difficult children, when he told of O'Neill wondering to Patterson about her whereabouts, and she was on another floor in the same place.

"He (O'Neill) was only interested in the minds of people, wasn't he? . . . He told me something about a play that was not to be made public for twenty-five years."

There was a man came to see him who wanted to tell him that Oona was getting along fine, that she was well regarded in Switzerland. He didn't want to see him (*???*) but I thought he should . . . The man was in there just a short time[17] . . . I once asked him if he didn't feel guilty about Oona, the way he'd treated her, and he said that everyone has to make their own life, do what they think is best for them.

He felt that life had dealt him a dirty deal through the Parkinson's. I told him, "Parkinson's doesn't kill, it only impairs." But he said it had taken away the thing that meant most to him, his writing. I asked him why didn't he dictate, that I'd be glad to take down what he wanted to say, but he told me he had tried it, and the ideas wouldn't come, that it came when his hand was moving over the paper . . . His tremor wasn't so bad, I felt that he could educate himself to doing it if he really tried. I got him to the desk once and gave him a pencil and some paper. But he pushed it away.

After he'd begun the daily short walk on the corridor, turned balky once or twice about it. One foot was in a brace, and had to put shoe on other foot for the walk. After much persuasion, he agreed to the walk and in the most personal remark he ever made to her, "Please don't get tired of me." Once told me that he gave in sometimes, did what I wanted him to, because he disliked going against me all the time.

Other people put him on a pedestal, but I didn't. I talked to him the way I would anyone else. He was a difficult patient but not a bad one. He never got pettish and pouted or raised Cain about anything, the way some patients are. He was difficult because it was hard to get him to do things that were good for him . . . *You could never get him to do anything he didn't really want to.* . . . He was never disagreeable, never cranky.

She didn't have any trouble understanding him. Not that he talked much. Sometimes I'd say something to him and he wouldn't answer, would pretend he hadn't heard me. And I'd repeat it, ask him if he'd heard me. "If you don't feel like talking, that's up to you, but wiggle your ears or do something so I'll know you heard me," and he would smile. There were days that he wouldn't say anything.

He seemed to feel that everyone who came to see him wanted something from him.

Discounting Shirlee's making considerable point that he did not care to see his mail: "A lot of people in those circumstances don't care to read their mail, just can't be bothered. At a time like this they're all wrapped up in themselves, they're like children."

I felt after I'd been with him two or three weeks that he was looking forward to being with Carlotta again.

Sallie: "I happen to like my job very much." Said that the first day of a new assignment, she can always tell whether a patient is going to be difficult or not, whether she'll be able to get along with him. Sometimes after the first day she removes herself from a case. Her first few days with O'Neill, she regretted being called to take care of him, but after she got used to him, it was all right.

Carlotta phoned Sallie after Dr. Kozol[18] made trip to see O'Neill, on C[arlotta] M[onterey]'s behalf, and she called again shortly before the departure for Boston.

O'Neill was concerned about strain of the RR trip to Boston, and was assured by Sallie that Dr. Patterson had taken care of that. She'd have sedation to give him. O'Neill asked her (?) to accompany him to Boston, wanted someone familiar to him along, to bridge the transition . . . Sallie was supposed to wait as long as possible before giving O'Neill the hyp, at least till half the trip was over but found it necessary to do so before half-way point . . . Asked O'Neill whether he had any discomfort, and he said, "There's no use my saying I'm comfortable when I'm not." Asked if he wanted the hypodermic needle sedation then, and he said yes. He slept most of the trip and was sleeping when the train paused a few minutes at the station in New London, last time he was ever there . . . As promised, Dr. Kozol was waiting at the station in Boston when they arrived, had a wheelchair, and they got O'Neill into Kozol's car.

"I must say, Carlotta handled the situation beautifully. As soon as we walked in, she threw her arms around him, hugged him and kissed him. I saw his face—

he looked so relieved. I was there for a few hours and he smiled more than I'd seen in all the weeks I'd been looking after him. He was happy to be home . . . They wanted me to stay the night, Carlotta in particular, but I knew what they wanted. They wanted me to stay on for a while, indefinitely, but I wanted no part of it. I told them, and it was true I'd made arrangements to go on up to Maine, they were expecting me that same day."

(At Doctors) He didn't appear to want to see anybody. People called, asking for a time to see him, but he'd put them off. There was no telephone in the room, I'd answer the calls at the desk on the floor. Bennett Cerf phoned a good many times wanting to know when he could visit and after a while began to sound very annoyed, as tho, Maybe you don't know who I am, when O'Neill kept putting him off. . . . Langner came very often, sometimes with his wife, and he used to tell me, "If there is anything I can do, just call me." And gave me a number where I could reach him at any time.

(Miss Coughlin, slightly above average height, dark-haired, around fifty-six when she nursed O'Neill, bluntly honest and not unkind, speaks her mind frankly. Did not really like O'Neill. Probably at first O'Neill resented and taken aback by her honesty, compared her unfavorably with Mrs. Bird[19] but after a while came to appreciate her integrity and character, her attempts to persuade him to do things designed to help him get better, to get him to writing again, to eating more . . . She felt she had to nag him to do this.)

When O'Neill told Sallie of CM leaving him out in the snow, his voice was terribly hurt, he felt that he might have died if the doctor hadn't come along . . . He had no idea of how long out in snow.

George Jean Nathan phoned a great deal.

Unlike most patients, who don't resist taking a walk but like feeling of escaping from their room even briefly, O'Neill wanted to stay in his room. As though he was in a little circle. Others felt they were no longer caged but free, while he seemed to like being caged, it was padded, it was comfortable, it had everything he needed.

[. . . .]

When they were preparing to take the train to Boston, O'Neill told Sallie to leave behind everything they couldn't get into the luggage, as he didn't want them carrying any paper parcels. "He wanted to travel like a gentleman. I think he wanted to put up his best front for his girl."

On train ride, O'Neill wasn't in so much physical discomfort, as nervous about what lay ahead, his reunion with Carlotta, after what had gone on between them.

Very few visitors on Sallie's time—the Langners came often—as he didn't have his breakfast until around 10:30.

Miss Beatty, his night nurse, got him listening to WQXR.[20]

Re EO after several weeks looking forward to reunion with CM, Sallie thinks that CM was "someone for him to cling to."

Re EO's feeling that everyone who came to see him wanted something from him, Sallie had this impression particularly from Bennett Cerf's frequent phone calls asking for time to visit and EO continually putting him off. Cerf never saw EO on Sallie's shift. Cerf got somewhat nasty on phone about being put off.

# 61 / Russel Crouse

Russel Crouse (1893–1966) was born in Findlay, Ohio, and grew up in Oklahoma. After graduating from high school, he worked as a newspaper reporter before enlisting in the navy during World War I. After the war he worked at several newspapers in New York until he became a press agent for the Theatre Guild in 1931, when he got to know Eugene O'Neill. He acted briefly and worked on two musicals in the early 1930s, but his career as a playwright really began when he was recruited to work on the musical *Anything Goes* (1934) with Howard Lindsay (1880–1969), a collaboration that became one of the most successful in the twentieth-century American theater, including the book for *The Sound of Music* (1965) and the plays *State of the Union* (1948) and *Life with Father*. The latter ran for an astounding 3,224 performances on Broadway from 1939 to 1947—as of 2016, still the longest run of any nonmusical Broadway production.

Source: Russel Crouse, "Extracts from the Diaries of Russel Crouse: Eugene O'Neill," typescript, Eugene O'Neill Collection, Beinecke Rare Book and Manuscript Library, Yale University, New Haven, Connecticut.

## 1944

August 17 (from Hollywood)—Telephone to Eugene and Carlotta O'Neill and they plan New York in November and maybe Saratoga. Sorry I am not to see them. Gene sounds a little feeble.

## 1945

November 9—Dinner at the Crillon and to see Gene O'Neill and Carlotta. He looks well but so much older. He talks of his plays and we gossip.

## 1946

November 23—E. O'Neill and Carlotta came to dinner and then the long awaited meeting with I. Berlin and Ellin. And it turned into a wonderful party, with Howard and Dorothy and the Cerfs[21] dropping in later, and Irving played his old songs and we all sang them, and Gene sang some we didn't know and Carlotta unburdens herself to me. And we all really had fun.

December 5—To pick up E. O'Neill and Carlotta, and the Lindsays join us at *Annie Get Your Gun*[22] and it's still wonderful. Back to see Ethel.

December 20—At 7:00 to dinner at Bennett Cerfs, and Eugene O'Neill and Carlotta there, and Burl Ives and his wife and the S. Comminses. And after dinner Burl sang.[23]

## 1947

February 20, 1947—Dinner, and Eugene O'Neill and Carlotta came afterward and talk of his play, and Timothy[24] comes down very solemn and they like him.

March 4, 1947— . . . and at 6:15 to Sardi's[25] for dinner with Sullivan and to Eugene O'Neill's *The Iceman Cometh* and it a beautiful play dissipated by over length and diffuse direction.

Monday, April 7, 1947—So to dinner at Lawrence Langner's and Eugene O'Neill and Carlotta there and she beautiful.

April 19, 1947—And to bed to read Eugene O'Neill's play *A Moon for the Misbegotten*.

July 31, 1947—Then home to talk with Hamilton Basso[26] who is writing a profile of Eugene O'Neill and pleased to hear him say Gene counts me among his close friends.

October 14, 1947—Dinner with Eugene O'Neill and Carlotta. Gene slow of speech and the whole picture very depressing, a mind still full of things to say and unable to say through trembling fingers.

January 30, 1948—Up late and I hear the latest chapter in the saga of E. O'Neill from W. Casey—drinking again, Carlotta's exit, the broken arm, the hospital, Carlotta back?

February 17, 1948—I to Doctors Hospital[27] to see E. O'Neill there with a broken arm and other troubles, and we talk of the theatre and atomic terrors.

## 1948

March 3—Carlotta O'Neill calls almost shaking with nerves—her story—it's all a tragedy. Tears.

March 15—To see Eugene O'Neill and hear another story.

March 24—A telephone call from Carlotta O'Neill in hysterics. I go to see her at the Lowell. She in bad shape. I will call her doctor tomorrow.

April 18—Carlotta O'Neill calls to report she and Gene are going to Boston tomorrow—reconciled. I call Gene.

July 16—I call Eugene O'Neill and Carlotta in Boston and they sound fine.

## 1949

June 17—Telephone Gene and Carlotta O'Neill. They low.

August 2—After lunch A.[28] and I drive to Marblehead Neck where we spend an hour with Eugene O'Neill and Carlotta. They are much happier and look better than in many a day. But Gene is no nearer health. They have a magnificent view of ocean in a sea-crag "nest."

## 1950

July 15—Carlotta O'Neill telephones. She and Gene won't be able to come over as he is ill.

## 1951

March 13—On the 11:15 plane to Boston and by taxi to Salem, and to Salem Hospital to see Eugene O'Neill and he frail and halting but we have a good visit. "I have nothing more to say," he says when I ask him about work. And he tells me about Carlotta—and he apprehensive.

March 31—In the afternoon I go to see E. O'Neill at Regent Nursing Home and find him moving to Doctors Hospital so there for a brief visit. His amazing personality is slowly fading.

April 7—I dashed to the hospital to see E. O'Neill and C. Kennedy[29] there. And he tells me a dream and he talks of Carlotta and is "through."

This day at Doctors Hospital Eugene O'Neill tells C. Kennedy and me of a dream: "I dreamt I killed my night nurse last night." Then: "And I dreamt I was in Japan 2,000 years from now and the Japanese were the only surviving race, and they showed me the scientific developments of the day which were wonderful, but they would not tell me how they were done."

April 11—After lunch to see E. O'Neill and he better. And Lawrence Langner there too.

April 15—A call from Carlotta in Marblehead. Tears. And a visit to Gene at the hospital. Depression.

This day Eugene O'Neill in the hospital tells me he is finished and speaks of his confusion of mind. And his nurse tells me has talked of suicide and she has had the windows locked.

April 17—And home to find a call from E. O'Neill's nurse that he wants to see me, so after lunch to Doctors Hospital and his first words to me, "I want to go back to Carlotta." So a session—telephone talks with Dr. Patterson and W. Aronberg and no answer.

April 18—Dinner and, he having called for me this afternoon, I go to see E. O'Neill and he has changed his mind about Carlotta and he is very nervous and shaky.

April 22—And after dinner to see E. O'Neill in the hospital and he better but worried about finances.

April 23—A call to Carlotta in Marblehead. She better.

April 26—A call from E. O'Neill. After dinner I visit E. O'Neill in the hospital. A call from O'Neill's nurse. He wants to see me. A call to W. Aronberg—What to do? A call at dinner from Carlotta, hysterical and bitter. To the hospital at 8:30. W. Aronberg there. Dr. Merrill Moore. He wants me to suggest "the Crouse plan" that they live apart but see each other. I decline. He wants to talk to Carlotta. I agree to call Dr. Kozol. Gene wants to go back to Carlotta, wants none of the Moore separation plan. What am I to do?

April 27—I call Dr. Kozol in Boston and report Dr. Merrill Moore's wishes to talk to him and Carlotta.

April 29—After lunch to see E. O'Neill and he still eager to return to Carlotta but the lawyers are in the way and I don't know what to do about it.

May 1—I talked to E. O'Neill. W. Aronberg tells me today he has given in to Eugene O'Neill's desire to have Carlotta back and has telephoned Merrill Moore in Boston to arrange it with her doctor.

May 2—W. Aronberg gives me carte blanche to act on Gene's orders so I go to see him at 1:00. He wants Carlotta back. I am to tell her. I call Carlotta—a blast! I call Dr. Kozol; an answer so there is hope.

W. Aronberg tells me I can take orders from Eugene O'Neill. I do. But Carlotta is hurt and savage. A severe blast. But I talked to Dr. Kozol and he is [unreadable] and hopeful. I don't tell Gene but will tell him tomorrow when I can be explicit.

May 3—This day began with a telephone call from W. Aronberg, Eugene O'Neill's lawyer, which infuriated me. I talk to Dr. Kozol in Boston and to O'Neill giving him assurances of imminent reconciliation.

May 5—After lunch to see Eugene O'Neill and he calmer than any time in this particular crise.

May 9—So to the Waldorf and meet Dr. H. Kozol of Boston and his wife and he tells me of his conference with E. O'Neill and of Carlotta. Later—but Gene and Carlotta thank me for my part in the near-reconciliation.

May 13—To Doctors Hospital and Gene O'Neill very gay and reports he and Carlotta will live in a hotel opposite Dr. Kozol's office, which is good.

May 16—At 1:00 I go to say good-by to E. O'Neill who leaves tomorrow to rejoin his Carlotta, and he in fine shape.

May 18—I call E. O'Neill and Carlotta, re-united in Boston, and they seem happy.

June 4—I talk to Carlotta O'Neill. A good report.

July 31—And then we (Russel and Anna) to see E. O'Neill and Carlotta at the Hotel Shelton and found them in good shape. Carlotta tells Anna Gene has been on Nembutal and tries desperately to get it.

September 27—So to the theatre for rehearsal. A call from Dr. Kozol and out to see Eugene O'Neill and Carlotta and found them calmer, but she tells me the whole story.

September 28—Up in time to have lunch with Dr. Harry Kozol at the Harvard Club and he fascinating on the subject of Eugene and Carlotta O'Neill.

October 4—The O'Neills say we can do *Moon For the Misbegotten* with M. Janes ?—(Could this be Margo Jones?)[30]

October 17—This afternoon a conference with P. Buner, (?) M. Cave, (?) about E. O'Neill and the Guild.

Nov. 28—At Robert Whitehead's[31] request I talked to Carlotta O'Neill in Boston. Gene is in a hospital.

## 1953

November 23—Boston. Dr. H. Kozol comes to talk to me about Eugene O'Neill and Carlotta, and I talk to him of Merrill Moore.

November 27—So back from the theatre and learn of the death of Eugene O'Neill my friend. Try to reach Carlotta. Long talks with H. Kozol his doctor.

November 28—Up at 11:00. No call from Dr. K. At 12:00 he comes to see me to report a strange conversation with Carlotta. I try to call her again. "She is under the care of her doctor."

December 3—I talk to Anna in New York and she has been attacked by telephone by Carlotta O'Neill.

December 4—Dr. Kozol on the phone. Carlotta has reported to him her attack on Anna and he is full of explanations.

Source: Louis Sheaffer, Russel Crouse interview notes, September 26, 1957, Louis Sheaffer Collection of Eugene O'Neill Materials, Department of Special Collections, Charles E. Shain Library, Connecticut College.
For information on Louis Sheaffer, see chapter 3.

Shane once at Tao House, he was about 18 or 19, quiet, shy, around 1942 or '43 . . . Handsome black-haired boy, he and his father used to smile at one another, and you felt underneath a wonderful rapport . . . he and father shy with one another, didn't really seem to know each other, but at dinner table or by pool, smile at one another . . . had the feeling they could have been very close, if given a chance . . . Gene had a good deal of sentiment but was afraid of it.

[. . .]

He saw *Annie Get Your Gun* on Dec. 5, 1946 . . . Told him I'd let him know shortly before the curtain, so we could slip out and avoid the crowd but when I whispered to him it was about to end, he waved it aside . . . we waited in our seats for crowd to leave and he raved about show and Merman . . . I said would you like to go back and meet her, and he said yes (I had impression Carlotta didn't like it) . . . Chorus kids crowded in for autographs, he signing with shaky hand, till Ethel said, "all right, get the hell out of here."

[. . .]

Gene seemed to be very much in love [with Carlotta] . . . Read *Days without End*[32] with the idea of a man who hated his wife.

Father White (?) Of Catholic Writers Guild called me [Crouse] to have lunch, toward end [of the run] asked me if O'Neill would put in line that wife had died[33] . . . I told him Gene never changed a line for anybody but I'd ask him . . . Gene replied, when I asked him, "If they want to think that she's dead, that's all right with me. But I'm not going to add or change a line."

[. . .]

When brought down to New York from Salem, Langner, Aronberg, Commins, their idea was to have him live alone with a male nurse, but Crouse felt that Gene and Carlotta would get together again and wanted no part of all this . . . Merrill Moore had plan for O'Neills to live apart (and visit with one another) which he wanted Crouse to sponsor, the Crouse Plan, but he refused . . . Crouse checked with Gene when he returned to room to make sure Moore hadn't saddled plan on him.

Gene told Crouse, "I can't live without her" . . . His nurse afraid of suicide attempts and kept windows locked . . . Carlotta wept on phone to Crouse, ask [*sic*] if he had inquired about her, whether Crouse heard from her . . . Gene asked Crouse to tell Carlotta he wanted her back (check on this) but Crouse said he wouldn't do a thing unless he got an okay from his lawyer, Aronberg, and his doctor . . . finally once Aronberg told Crouse to take orders from O'Neill.

[Crouse] felt the O'Neills were fascinated and repelled by one another . . . that isn't an uncommon relationship.

[. . .]

Carlotta's chill toward Crouse began after they were at Shelton in Boston, he visited [O'Neill] once, and Crouse defended Cummins [*sic*], said "Carlotta, you're wrong about Cummins, he's always been a good friend to Gene and to you" . . . Gene just sat there and grinned.

Then when Crouse and Lindsay in Boston in 1953 with *Prescott Proposals*,[34] phoned O'Neills and was told they weren't well, couldn't see him, and he left a message staying at Savoy Plaza and would come at their convenience if [they] wanted to see him . . . Back to New York for a weekend, or a few days, then returned to Boston, worked like devil, and Leland told Crouse that O'Neill had died . . . Crouse called Carlotta but she [was] not taking any calls . . . Kozel [*sic*] came around to see Crouse and explained she wanted solitude. [. . .] Periodically, she still calls Mrs. Crouse.

Carlotta asked Crouse if he had heard she was a lesbian . . . He said he'd heard of [Elisabeth] Marbury[35] . . . She said when she parted from [Ralph] Barton,[36] she was blue and down, and Marbury phoned her to stay with her, that was all.

Gene was in back yard when he broke his leg, after Carlotta had gone to bed, they had had a quarrel (He told Crouse this in Salem Hospital) . . . she told Crouse she had taken sedatives (felt dopey) and was trying to visit him at hospital, was found wandering there incoherent, and was taken in ambulance to MacClean [*sic*] in Belmont[37] . . . Moore signed in O'Neill's name committing her.

[. . .]

[O'Neill] was like someone who'd been locked in a closet: as he warmed up would wag his tail. [. . .] Reminded [Crouse] of stories of somebody locked up for years, fed in tiny room, chained, then let out. [. . .] RE: recreating friendship each time, EO reminded him of wary dog who would meet someone he knew, some one who had always been friendly, yet the dog would eye him for a while, then start to wag his tail in acknowledgment of friendship. When Crouse first saw EO each time, latter would eye him thoughtfully, appraisingly, then suddenly smile.

[. . .]

Recalls CM's cruelty, in Boston, telling EO, "You're thru, you'll never write another play."

[. . .]

O'Neill was not gregarious but on the other hand he was not a recluse. He liked people. [. . .] She (CM) did keep him away from people that would have given him pleasure, that he would like to have seen. In all fairness, I believe she thought she was protecting him but she went too far . . . If you had seen him at the dinner party, singing at the top of his voice while (Irving) Berlin played for him—he was having the time of his life, he loved it . . . And when he went backstage to see Merman, after seeing *Annie Get Your Gun*. The chorus kids flocked around and he was signing autographs, his face beaming like a happy kid . . . He liked people.

Many of EO's friends, when they learned of his death, phoned Crouse in Boston, there for *Prescott Proposals*, to express sympathy and ask for details. Crouse gave CM a list of all who had phoned him, about twenty, among them the names of Langner and Armina Marshall. This infuriated CM and she phoned Mrs. Crouse to blast Russel for including the Langners' names.

Crouse doesn't recall EO ever saying in 1951 hospital that he was thru with CM.

Crouse doubts that EO ever really suicidal when broke leg in Marblehead or later in hospital. Feels that EO's nature demanded that he see something out to the bitter end.

Crouse generally saw EO at 1951 hospital during the day, never stayed long, at most about half-hour, thinks that is one reason EO welcomed his visits. EO often would urge him to remain longer . . . Crouse never had real difficulty understanding EO, his voice would be too low sometimes, Crouse would ask him to repeat something, but it wasn't a case of inarticulate mumble (as Gelb suggests) . . . (Probably EO would mumble when he really didn't feel up to talking to some one or find the effort worthwhile.)

Crouse never questioned EO's sanity in 1951 hospital.

# 62 / Carl Van Vechten

Carl Van Vechten (1880–1964) grew up in Cedar Rapids, Iowa, and graduated from the University of Chicago, after which he began a newspaper career with the *Chicago American*. He moved to New York in 1906 and went to work for the *New York Times*, where he was soon made assistant music critic. His first book, *Music after the Great War* (1915), established him as a champion of modern music. While he continued to write music and theater criticism, he also became a key supporter of the artists and writers of the Harlem Renaissance, and his 1926 novel, *Nigger Heaven,* was a controversial depiction of 1920s Harlem culture. Van Vechten is best remembered now as a photographer, particularly of artists, musicians, and writers, an art he began to practice seriously in the 1930s. His collection of photographs, which he donated to the Library of Congress, contains his portraits of Eugene and Carlotta O'Neill. Van Vechten and his wife, the Russian-born actor Fania Marinoff (1890–1971), knew Carlotta Monterey as early as 1915, and they visited the O'Neills several times in Georgia, in France, and in California.

For information on Louis Sheaffer, see chapter 3.

Source: Louis Sheaffer, Carl Van Vechten interview notes, typescript, Louis Sheaffer Collection of Eugene O'Neill Materials, Department of Special Collections, Charles E. Shain Library, Connecticut College, New London.

[. . .]

She [Carlotta] liked to build houses but always lost interest after building them, and he got restless, thought he could work better in another place.

Never saw Gene in the morning, then to the beach around noon. [. . .] Lunch at Casa Genotta was always buffet, you helped yourself. Dinner always formal . . . Carlotta had the most beautiful dresses, even when they dined alone, she told me so . . . Many of her dresses nobody saw but Gene . . . ordered from Paris.

At Tours a little more relaxed, not working at the time, took us on a tour of the chateaus . . . If they had guests, they didn't want them when they came . . .

But when people drive to an out of the way place, you can't turn them away. She was jealous of his old friends, because he knew them before he knew her.

[. . .]

He wouldn't let anybody come near him at times, except her, he was completely dependent upon her. She did everything for him, he couldn't even go to the bathroom, she'd see he was fed, at night she'd empty out the slops . . . He said, What could I do without Carlotta? . . . Langner wanted him to live at his place, but he told Langner, "You're away during the day" . . . She told them (old friends) he didn't want to see them again.

Bitter, against his brother among others, said he made him drink, taught him to . . . Shane wrote impertinent even scabrous letters, was 13 or 14 at the time.

Junior like his father, very retiring, charming, quiet, erudite.

O'Neill was interested in them (Negroes) as interesting subjects but not as people. Carlotta was very thoughtful of her colored girls . . . Gene was so kind and gentle, and yet he could be hateful and bitter . . . Gene was always very black or white, no gradation . . . Gene bitter on Chaplin.

Very peculiar in this respect—he was very jealous of the past, anybody who ever knew Carlotta . . . Chaplin was a good friend of Ralph Barton, Charley [*sic*] in New York would stay with Barton, and maybe that's why he hated Chaplin.

Barton was furious she'd married somebody more famous than he was, great blow to his ego, had lunch with him at the Hotel Madison the day he killed himself and he talked of nothing but that . . . He wasn't in love with her . . . From all his running around, he couldn't give her all the sex she wanted.

He was under the impression he knew a great deal about Negroes, and he actually knew very little.

Disliked actors, most of all George M. Cohan, mostly because people said it wouldn't have run without Cohan[38] . . . O'Neill said anybody could play the part . . . Didn't want to think any actor rated over his play . . . took great dislike to Judith Anderson.[39]

*Days Without End* more her [Carlotta's] play than his. She loved the play, great disappointment to her.

Very shy man, at Guild rehearsals took over the roof, even rather dangerous, to avoid reporters . . . Every time they moved got rid of some of their past . . . Rosie the piano with nude women painted all over it . . . Liked six-day bike races . . . She [Carlotta] hired his nurses and saw they weren't pretty

[. . .]

Ralph Barton, whom V[an] V[echten] knew intimately, didn't kill himself over love for Carlotta as his death note alleged . . . Left the note "to annoy" Gene, which it certainly did. VV and Marinoff had lunch with the O'Neills their first day back from Europe in 1931, the news about Barton broke . . .

Barton was heavily in debt, had lived beyond his means for years, felt he'd seen and done everything, couldn't go any further, and saw no point in going on.

Source: Carl Van Vechten, letter to Alfred A. Knopf, 30 October 1956, *Letters of Carl Van Vechten*, ed. Bruce Kellner (New Haven: Yale UP, 1987), 264.

> Dear Alfred,
>
> I think it would be impossible for anyone, save in some secret way, to set down his share of the story, to write a frank O'Neill story. Undoubtedly Carlotta [Monterey O'Neill] will have her version prepared and she has already rewritten her diary.[40] Probably anything unfavorable to Gene in her possession has been destroyed. Princeton, Yale, and the Museum of the City of New York share his manuscripts. They have already been informed that if they give out anything she doesn't desire given out she will withdraw the mss. She will INSIST on reading any biography. [Kellner ellipsis] Moreover, I think she will be able to protect his reputation even after she is dead, for a generation or two. Then, everybody who knew him will be dead. The only way to preserve the unadulterated story is to get affadavits [*sic*] from numberless people, including wives and children of Gene (Lawrence Langner has already written his),[41] organize and publish these in some far distant future, without risk of getting sued.* Please do NOT let any one see this letter and do not quote from it. It is for your private eyes, but better keep it in some safe place because this subject will come up many times. Every publisher in America will be after the story.
>
> With love, Carlo
>
> *Of course, this would be an expensive procedure, because most of the witnesses would require a ghost writer.
>
> P.S. Is he worth all this trouble?

# List of Reminiscences

(Reminiscences are ordered by their appearance in this volume. See Works Cited for complete bibliographic information.)

## Part 1. New London, School, and Wandering (1888–1913)

Tyler, George C. in Collaboration with J. C. Furnas. *Whatever Goes Up.*
Hastings, Warren H., and Richard F. Weeks. "Episodes of Eugene O'Neill's Undergraduate Days at Princeton."
Sheaffer, Louis. Interview with Kathleen Pitt-Smith, July 13, 1962.
"O'Neill Bad Actor, Stage Hand Recalls."
Loving, Pierre. "Eugene O'Neill."
Sheaffer, Louis. Interview with Mrs. Mabel Haynes.
Hamilton, Clayton. *Conversations on Contemporary Drama.*
Cobb, Irvin S. *Exit Laughing.*
Latimer, Frederick P. "Eugene Is beyond Us."
Clark, Barret H. *Eugene O'Neill: The Man and His Plays.*
McGinley, Arthur B. "Columnist Recalls Eugene O'Neill as Dreamy Reporter in New London."
Woodworth, Robert A. "The World's Worst Reporter."

## Part 2. Cambridge, Provincetown and Greenwich Village (1914–1917)

Sheaffer, Louis. Interview with Beatrice Ashe Maher, September 1962.
Weaver, John V. A. "I Knew Him When—."
Glaspell, Susan. *The Road to the Temple.*
Vorse, Mary Heaton. *Time and the Town: A Provincetown Chronicle.*
Hapgood, Hutchins. *A Victorian in the Modern World.*
Kemp, Harry. "O'Neill of Provincetown" and "O'Neill as Actor Is Recalled by One Who Saw Him in '17."
Nathan, Adele. "'Eugene G. O'Neill': 1916."
Day, Dorothy. *The Long Loneliness: The Autobiography of Dorothy Day.*
Gardner, Virginia. *"Friend and Lover": The Life of Louise Bryant.*
Sheaffer, Louis. Interview with Dorothy Day, ca. 1957–1958.
Williams, William Carlos. Letter to Louis Sheaffer.

## Part 3. Provincetown Playhouse, Peaked Hill Bar, Ridgefield, Broadway (1918–1927)

Werner, Hazel Hawthorne. “Recollections.”
Throckmorton, Juliet. “As I Remember Eugene O’Neill.”
Sheaffer, Louis. Manuel Zora interview notes.
Wilson, Edmund. *The Twenties: From Notebooks and Diaries of the Period.*
Kennedy, Charles O’Brien. “Eugene O’Neill.”
Boulton, Agnes. *Part of a Long Story: Eugene O’Neill as a Young Man in Love*; statement to Max Wylie.
Sullivan, Dan. “Friend of Eugene O’Neill Tells of Dramatist’s Tie to Brother.”
Young, Stark. “Eugene O’Neill: Notes from a Critic’s Diary.”
Cowley, Malcolm. “A Weekend with Eugene O’Neill.”
Crane, Hart. Letters to Grace Crane, 1 November 1923; 3 February 1924; 30 July 1926; Letter to Charlotte and Richard Rychtarik, 5 March 1924; Letter to Waldo Frank, 3 July 1926.
De Polo, Harold. “Meet Eugene O’Neill—Fisherman.”
Atkinson, Brooks. Journal entry.
Hoffman, Calvin. “Of Eugene O’Neill Remembered.”

## Part 4. Europe, Georgia, the Theatre Guild, California (1928–1937)

“Eugene O’Neill Friendship Formed by West Hartford Man while on Shipboard.”
Lardner, John. “O’Neill’s Back.”
Cerf, Bennett. *At Random: The Reminiscences of Bennett Cerf.*
Langner, Lawrence. *The Magic Curtain: The Story of a Life in Two Fields, Theatre and Invention, by the Founder of the Theatre Guild.*
Atkinson, Brooks. “O’Neill Off Duty.”
Louis Sheaffer. Interview with Rouben Mamoulian, 26 March 1959.
Helburn, Theresa. *A Wayward Quest: The Autobiography of Theresa Helburn.*
Nathan, George Jean. *The Intimate Notebooks of George Jean Nathan.*
Brewer, Thalia. Interview Notes with Maxine Edie Benedict, 18 October 1977.

## Part 5. California and New York (1938–1947)

Peck, Seymour. Excerpts from transcript of interview with Carlotta Monterey O’Neill, 2 October 1956.
Ryan, Paul. “Eugene O’Neill: A Hundred Years On.”
Floyd, Virginia. “A Meeting with O’Neill.”
O’Casey, Sean. *Rose and Crown*; letter to Otto Brandstädter, 18 July 1955; letter to Louis Sheaffer, 28 January 1957; letter to Brooks Atkinson, 25 May 1957; letter to Lester Osterman, 19 November 1959.

Schriftgiesser, Karl. "'*The Iceman Cometh.*'"
Sheaffer, Louis. Karl Schriftgiesser interview notes.
Woolf, S. J. "Eugene O'Neill Returns after Twelve Years."
Gordon, Max, with Lewis Funke. *Max Gordon Presents.*
Stoeckel, Herbert J. "Memories of Eugene O'Neill."
Commins, Saxe. "*Love and Admiration and Respect*": *The O'Neill–Commins Correspondence.*
Cerf, Bennett. *At Random: The Reminiscences of Bennett Cerf.*
Sheaffer, Louis. Paul Crabtree interview notes.
Welch, Mary. "Softer Tones for Mr. O'Neill's Portrait."

## Part 6. Marblehead and Boston (1948–1953)

Commins, Saxe. Memoir in "*Love and Admiration and Respect*": *The O'Neill–Commins Correspondence.*
Peck, Seymour. Excerpts from transcript of interview with Carlotta Monterey O'Neill, 2 October 1956.
Cerf, Bennett. *At Random: The Reminiscences of Bennett Cerf.*
Burlingame, Michael. "O'Neill Recalled Warmly."
Sheaffer, Louis. Dr. Frederic B. Mayo interview notes.
Sheaffer, Louis. Sallie Coughlin interview notes.
Crouse, Russel. "Extracts from the Diaries of Russel Crouse: Eugene O'Neill"; Sheaffer, Louis. Russel Crouse interview notes, 26 September 1957.
Sheaffer, Louis. Carl Van Vechten interview notes.
Van Vechten, Carl. Letter to Alfred A. Knopf, 30 October 1956, *Letters of Carl Van Vechten.*

# Additional Reminiscences


Bird, Carol. "Eugene O'Neill: The Inner Man." *Theatre Magazine* June 1924: 9, 60.

Braggiotti, Mary. "Little Girl with a Big Ideal." *New York Post* 20 December 1946: 6.

Crichton, Kyle. "Mr. O'Neill and the Iceman." *Collier's* 26 October 1946: 19, 39–40, 42.

Demuth, Charles. *Letters of Charles Demuth: American Artist, 1883–1935*. Ed. Bruce Kellner. Philadelphia: Temple UP, 2000.

"Eugene O'Neill Tells What He Thinks about His Plays." *Brooklyn Daily Eagle* 18 May 1930: E4.

Hamilton, Clayton. "Eugene O'Neill Has 'Arrived.'" *Columbia* [S.C.] *State* 18 April 1920: 43.

Hamilton, Gladys. "Untold Tales of Eugene O'Neill." *Theatre Arts* August 1956: 31–32, 88.

Hubler, Edward. Letter to the Editor, *New York Times* 11 December 1953: 30.

Karsner, David. "Eugene O'Neill." *Sixteen Authors to One: Intimate Sketches of Leading American Story Tellers*. 1928. Freeport, NY: Books for Libraries, 1968. 109–11, 118–19, 120–22.

Lawson, John Howard. "Landscape." Rpt. LeRoy Robinson. "John Howard Lawson on Eugene O'Neill. *Eugene O'Neill Newsletter*. 3 (September 1979) eoneill.com.

Middleton, George. "How the Late Eugene O'Neill Assisted the Dramatists Guild–Comments." *New York Times* 20 December 1953: X4.

Nathan, George Jean. "The Bright Face of Tragedy." *Cosmopolitan* August 1957: 66–69.

O'Neill, J. F. "What a Sanatorium Did for Eugene O'Neill." *Journal of the Outdoor Life* June 1923: 191–92, 221.

Sheaffer, Louis. Interviews with James Light, Paul Green, Eddie Dowling, Robert Rockmore, Kathryne Albertoni, Lillian Gish, Charles Webster, Cecil Boulton, Teddy Ballantine, E. G. Marshall, Florence Eldridge, Harold De Polo, Jasper Deeter, Frank and Cecil Shay, Howard Lindsay, Claire Sherman, Daniel J. O'Neil, Anna Crouse, John Marriott, Mrs. Vera Massey, Edwin Justus Mayer, Philip Moeller, Patricia Neal, Katina Paxinou and Alexis Minotis, Hubertine Zahorska, Phyllis Dugganne, John Huston, Sophus K. Winther, Dr. Paul Hugenberger, and others. Louis Sheaffer Collection of Eugene O'Neill Materials, Department of Special Collections, Charles E. Shain Library, Connecticut College, New London.

Vorse, Mary Heaton. "O'Neill's Pet Saloon Is Gone." *World* [New York] 4 May 1930.

Wilson, Earl. "Eugene O'Neill Lets Us in on Why 'The Ice Man Cometh.'" *New York Post* 2 August 1946: 4, 36.

# Biographical Sketches of Important Names

**George Pierce Baker** (1866–1935) was a professor of English who established the 47 Workshop at Harvard in 1912, one of the first courses in playwriting in the country, in which O'Neill enrolled as a special student in 1914. In 1925 Baker moved to Yale, where he helped to found the Yale School of Drama.

**Terry Carlin** (?–1934), a philosophical anarchist and hobo, was the model for Larry Slade in O'Neill's *The Iceman Cometh*. O'Neill and Carlin were rooming together in Provincetown when O'Neill first became acquainted with the Provincetown Players, in 1916. Once O'Neill became financially stable, he continually contributed to Carlin's support and even provided a home for him in his house in Provincetown.

**Oona O'Neill Chaplin** (1925–1991) was the only daughter of Eugene O'Neill and Agnes Boulton. She was born in Ridgefield, Connecticut, and rarely saw her father after he left Agnes in 1928 to be with Carlotta Monterey. She married Charlie Chaplin when she was eighteen and he was fifty-four, and because O'Neill and Carlotta disapproved of the marriage, they cut off all communication with her. She and Chaplin had eight children. Because of Chaplin's political difficulties, they spent the majority of their thirty-five-year marriage in Vevey, Switzerland. Like her father, mother, and brothers, Oona struggled with alcoholism, particularly after Chaplin's death in 1977.

**George Cram Cook** (1873–1924) was born in Davenport, Iowa, and, after a short academic career, became a writer, eventually moving to New York's Greenwich Village along with his wife, Susan Glaspell. He was one of founders of the Provincetown Players and was elected the group's president in 1916, quickly consolidating his power so that the group was thought of as his theater. He installed the famous dome in the theater, which made the unique scenic effects of O'Neill's *Emperor Jones* possible. Partly because he was upset by O'Neill's replacing him as director of *The Hairy Ape* in 1922, Cook and Glaspell left for Greece, where Cook had always dreamed of living. He died there in 1924.

**Robert Edmond Jones** (1887–1954) was one of the most distinguished American stage designers of his generation. After graduating from Harvard in 1910, he studied the New Stagecraft in Europe with Max Reinhardt and then returned to the United States to begin his career in the American theater. He was one of the original Provincetown Players and designed the set for their first simple production in Provincetown in 1915. His Broadway career had begun with his breakthrough design for *The Man Who Married a Dumb Wife*, directed by Harley Granville-Barker earlier that year. Jones went on to a long and successful career as designer, director, and producer and was a member of the Triumvirate, along with O'Neill and Kenneth Macgowan, who founded the Experimental Theatre, Inc. (ETI), which executed Jones's designs for O'Neill's *The Great God Brown* and *Desire Under the Elms*. He also directed *All God's Chillun Got Wings* and staged *The Fountain* and *The Great God Brown* for the ETI and designed *Mourning Becomes Electra* for the Theatre Guild.

**James Light** (1894–1964) was a stage director, a member of the Provincetown Players, and associate director of the Experimental Theatre, Inc., where he and Eleanor Fitzgerald were in charge of the experimental offerings the organization produced at the Provincetown Playhouse. He also worked with the Federal Theatre Project and was dean of the Dramatic Art faculty at the New School for Social Research.

**Kenneth Macgowan** (1888–1963) began his career as a critic, writing several books, including *Continental Stagecraft* (1922) with Robert Edmond Jones and *Masks and Demons* (1923) with Herbert Rosse, which greatly interested Eugene O'Neill, who was experimenting with masks in the 1920s. With Robert Edmond Jones, O'Neill and Macgowan formed the Triumvirate, which founded the Experimental Theatre, Inc., in 1923. Macgowan and O'Neill became lifelong friends, and O'Neill's letters to him have been edited by Jackson R. Bryer in a volume entitled *The Theatre We Worked For* (1982).

**Carlotta Monterey O'Neill** (1888–1970), born Hazel Tharsing in Oakland, California, met Eugene O'Neill in 1922, when she played Mildred Douglas in *The Hairy Ape*. She had a steady, though not remarkable, theatrical career between 1915 and 1924, except for about a year when she was briefly married to Melvin C. Chapman Jr. in Oakland and gave birth to a daughter, Cynthia. Beginning in the mid-1920s, a liaison with a wealthy Wall Street banker, James Speyer, provided her with a trust fund and income for the rest of her life. She married the well-known *New Yorker* illustrator and caricaturist Ralph Barton in 1925, divorcing him in 1926. In that year, she spent the summer at Belgrade

Lakes in Maine, where O'Neill was vacationing with his family, and began a relationship with him that resulted in their going to Europe together and finally marrying in Paris in 1929. They lived first in the Château du Plessis, outside of Tours, France, then in several houses that were built or renovated under Carlotta's direction: Casa Genotta in Sea Island, Georgia, Tao House in Danville, California, and a smaller house in Marblehead, Massachusetts. After O'Neill's death in 1953, she turned her attention to the production of *Long Day's Journey Into Night,* first in Sweden, and then in New York.

**Ella Quinlan O'Neill** (1857–1922), Eugene O'Neill's mother, grew up in Cleveland, Ohio, and was educated at the Convent of St. Mary of Notre Dame in Indiana before she married the matinee idol James O'Neill in 1877. She was the mother of James O'Neill Jr. and Edmund O'Neill as well as Eugene. Her suffering over the loss of her infant son Edmund and her struggles with morphine addiction following the difficult birth of Eugene inform the character Mary Tyrone in O'Neill's *Long Day's Journey Into Night.*

**Eugene O'Neill Jr.** (1910–1950) was the son of Eugene O'Neill and his first wife, Kathleen Jenkins. His parents separated before his birth, and, after one meeting in his infancy, Eugene Jr. did not see his father until he was eleven years old, after which O'Neill made an effort to keep in touch with his son, funding his education at Yale, where he eventually earned his PhD in classics. He taught at Yale, Princeton, Sarah Lawrence, The New School, and Fairleigh Dickinson while pursuing a career in radio in the 1940s. He married three times. He had increasing problems with alcoholism and committed suicide at his home in Woodstock, New York.

**James O'Neill** (1847–1920), Eugene O'Neill's father, was an Irish immigrant who became a promising Shakespearean actor before he became a successful actor-manager who made a fortune in the theater, mostly from playing the title role in a stage adaptation of Dumas's *The Count of Monte Cristo,* in which he toured the country for many years, playing the role more than six thousand times. He was the model for the character James Tyrone in O'Neill's *Long Day's Journey Into Night.*

**James O'Neill Jr.** (1878–1923) was Eugene O'Neill's older brother, known as "Jamie." A promising student in his youth, James was expelled from the University of Notre Dame and spent the rest of his life half-heartedly pursuing an acting career, mostly in his father's company, and distracting himself with alcohol, women, and gambling, eventually dying from acute alcoholism. Although rebellious, he was deeply attached to his parents, particularly his mother, and served as mentor to Eugene from his adolescence in the ways of what Jamie thought of as a sophisticated Broadway lifestyle. He was the model for O'Neill's character Jamie, or Jim, Tyrone in *Long Day's Journey Into Night* and *A Moon for the Misbegotten*.

**Shane Rudraighe O'Neill** (1919–1977), O'Neill's second child, was the son of Eugene O'Neill and his second wife, Agnes Boulton. He lived with his parents in Provincetown, Massachusetts; Ridgefield, Connecticut; and Bermuda, and, after they separated, with his mother. After a difficult youth during which he attended several schools, he lived a bohemian life in Greenwich Village, eventually becoming addicted to drugs. After sporadic attempts to help him, O'Neill essentially abandoned Shane, eventually disinheriting him along with his sister Oona in favor of his third wife, Carlotta. Like his half-brother Eugene Jr., Shane committed suicide.

**Cleon Throckmorton** (1897–1965) was a stage designer. After working in the Washington, DC, area, he joined the Provincetown Players in 1920 to help with the design and staging of O'Neill's *The Emperor Jones*. He also designed the sets for *All God's Chillun Got Wings* and *S. S. Glencairn*, as well as 150 other plays in the course of his career.

# Permissions

The following persons and entities have granted permission to publish the chapters indicated:

Werner, Hazel Hawthorne. "Recollections." Typescript. Louis Sheaffer Collection of Eugene O'Neill Materials, Connecticut College, New London. Reprinted per permission of Anna Avellar.

Sheaffer, Louis. Notes from interviews with Kathleen Pitt-Smith, Mrs. Mabel Haynes, Manuel Zora, Rouben Mamoulian, Karl Schriftgiesser, Sallie Coughlin, Carl Van Vechten, Beatrice Ashe Maher, Dorothy Day, Dr. Frederic B. Mayo, Paul Crabtree, and Russel Crouse in Louis Sheaffer Collection of Eugene O'Neill Materials, Department of Special Collections, Charles E. Shain Library, Connecticut College, New London. Reprinted by permission of Michele Slung (on behalf of the estate of Louis Sheaffer).

Throckmorton, Juliet. "As I Remember Eugene O'Neill." *Yankee Magazine* August 1968: 85, 93–95. Reprinted by permission of *Yankee Magazine.*

Kennedy, Charles O'Brien. "Eugene O'Neill." *Lambs Script* (March & April 1954): 1–4. Permission granted by The Lambs, Inc.

Sullivan, Dan. "Friend of Eugene O'Neill Tells of Dramatist's Tie to Brother." *New York Times* 31 July 1967: 21. Reprinted with the permission of Daniel J. Sullivan.

Young, Stark. "Eugene O'Neill: Notes from a Critic's Diary." *Harper's Magazine* (June 1957): 66–71, 74. Copyright © 1957 *Harper's Magazine.* All rights reserved. Reproduced from the June issue by special permission.

De Polo, Harold. "Meet Eugene O'Neill—Fisherman." *Outdoor America* May 1928: 5–8. Copyright Izaak Walton League of America. Reprinted with Permission.

Atkinson, Brooks. Journal entry. Typescript. Sheaffer-O'Neill Collection, Department of Special Collections, Charles E. Shain Library, Connecticut College, New London. Reprinted by permission of James T. MacIlveen.

Atkinson, Brooks. "O'Neill Off Duty" *New York Times* 8 October 1933: X1. Reprinted by permission of James T. MacIlveen.

"Eugene O'Neill Friendship Formed by West Hartford Man while on Shipboard." *Hartford Courant* 14 October 1929: 14. Reprinted by permission of the *Los Angeles Times.*

Brewer, Thalia. Notes from interview with Maxine Edie Benedict, 18 October 1977. Reprinted courtesy of the Brewer family.

Schriftgiesser, Karl. "The Iceman Cometh." *New York Times* 6 October 1946: X1, 3. Reprinted by permission of Celia Irvine.

Woolf, S. J. "Eugene O'Neill Returns after Twelve Years." *New York Times* 15 September 1946: Sunday Magazine: 6, with accompanying illustration. Reprinted by permission of Deborah W. Hobson.

Stoeckel, Herbert J. "Memories of Eugene O'Neill." *Hartford Courant* 6 December 1953: Sunday Magazine: 3, 16. Reprinted by permission of the *Los Angeles Times.*

"Declining Years" in *Love and Admiration and Respect*, Dorothy Commins, ed., pp. 218–225, 229–35. Copyright, Duke University Press. All rights Reserved. Republished by permission of the copyright holder. www.dukeupress.edu.

Welch, Mary. "Softer Tones for Mr. O'Neill's Portrait." *Theatre Arts* 41.5 (May 1957): 67–68. Permission granted by Samuel R. Ceccarelli, *Theatre Arts.*

Crouse, Russel. "Extracts from the Diaries of Russel Crouse: Eugene O'Neill." Typescript. Eugene O'Neill Collection, Yale Collection of American Literature, Beinecke Rare Book and Manuscript Library, Yale University, New Haven. Reprinted with the permission of Timothy Crouse.

Peck, Seymour. Excerpts from transcript of interview with Carlotta Monterey O'Neill, 2 October 1956, Sheaffer-O'Neill Collection, Department of Special Collections, Charles E. Shain Library, Connecticut College, New London. Published by permission of the family of Seymour Peck.

"O'Neill Bad Actor, Stage Hand Recalls." *Hartford Courant* 3 April 1929: 18. Reprinted by permission of the *Los Angeles Times.*

McGinley, Arthur B. "Columnist Recalls Eugene O'Neill as Dreamy Reporter in New London." *New Haven Register* 28 November 1953: 48. Reprinted with permission of the *New Haven Register.*

Robert A. Woodworth, "The World's Worst Reporter." *Providence Journal* 6 December 1931. Copyright © 1931 *The Providence Journal.* Reproduced by Permission.

Burlingame, Michael. "O'Neill Recalled Warmly." *Day* 21 July 1988: E1. Reprinted by permission from The Day Publishing Company.

Latimer, Frederick P. "Eugene Is beyond Us." *Day*, 15 February 1928: 2. Reprinted by permission from The Day Publishing Company.

"Letter from William Carlos Williams to Louis Sheaffer," By William Carlos Williams, from New Directions Pub. acting as agent, copyright © 2014 by Paul H. Williams and the Estate of William Eric Williams. Used by permission of New Directions Publishing Corp., agents. Reprinted by permission of New Directions Publishing Corp.

Part of the Introduction appeared in Brenda Murphy, "Getting to Know O'Neill," the *Eugene O'Neill Review* 35:2 (2014), pages 247–57. © copyright The Eugene O'Neill Society. This article is used by permission of the Pennsylvania State University Press.

Claudia Andreasen Fetzer has granted permission to quote from her email message of May 22, 2014.

Our efforts to find heirs of Adele Nathan, Calvin Hoffman, Warren H. Hastings, and Richard F. Weeks have been unsuccessful, but we have used their material with gratitude.

# Notes

## Chronology of Eugene Gladstone O'Neill

1. O'Neill used quotation marks in this play's title because Anna Christie was not the title character's real name. Many published editions and productions of the play do not use the quotation marks, but among O'Neill scholars it is the preferred form of the title.

## Introduction

1. Virginia Floyd, *Eugene O'Neill: A World View* 294.
2. S. J. Woolf, "Eugene O'Neill Returns after Twelve Years" 11.
3. Herbert J. Stoeckel, "Memories of Eugene O'Neill" 3.
4. Stark Young, "Eugene O'Neill: Notes from a Critic's Diary" 66.
5. Juliet Throckmorton, "As I Remember Eugene O'Neill" 93.
6. Edmund Wilson, *The Twenties: From Notebooks and Diaries of the Period* 111.
7. George Jean Nathan, "The Bright Face of Tragedy" 66.

## Part 1

1. J. Duncan Spaeth (1868–1954) was a preceptor (1905–1911) and professor of English (1911–1935) at Princeton. He served as the president of the University of Kansas City from 1935 to 1938.

2. Henry Jackson van Dyke (1852–1933) was a professor of English at Princeton from 1899 to 1923. A much-honored poet and Presbyterian clergyman, he also was appointed minister to the Netherlands and Luxembourg by President Wilson in 1913.

3. The Haymarket was a well-known nightspot at 66 West 30th Street in New York's Tenderloin district. It was a three-story building made to look like a theater but was actually a dance hall where women drank for free, men paid a 25-cent fee for joining them, and prostitution prospered. John Sloan (1871–1951) painted a famous "Ashcan School" painting of the Haymarket in 1907, and O'Neill himself wrote a sonnet about it, "The Haymarket," which was published in the *New London Telegraph* in 1912.

4. *Wormwood, a Drama of Paris* by Marie Corelli (1855–1924), first published in London as a three-decker by Bentley in 1890, is the story of the disintegration

of Gaston Beauvais, son of a wealthy Parisian banker and victim of that "absinthe-mania," which, according to Corelli, pervaded all classes in Paris. The following quotation, framed in a lurid red border, appears as a frontispiece to the novel:

> And the name of the star is called wormwood: and the third part of the waters became wormwood; and many men died of the waters, because they were bitter"
> —Revelation, viii, 11.

Below this is the same passage repeated in a French version, where the word "wormwood" is rendered as "absinthe." Although ostensibly written as an admonitory tract against "the Curse" of absinthism, Miss Corelli's novel includes numerous striking monologues, as for example, in the opening chapter.

> "Do not drink that," he said gravely, touching the glass I held. "It will drive you mad some day!" Drive me mad! Good, very good! That is what a great many people have told me,—croakers all! Who is mad, and who is sane? It is not easy to decide. The world has various ways of defining insanity in different individuals. The genius who has grand ideas and imagines he can carry them out is "mad;" the priest who, like Saint Damien, sacrifices himself for others is "mad," the hero who, like the English Gordon, perishes at his post, instead of running away to save his own skin, is "mad," and only the comfortable tradesman or financier who amasses millions by systematically cheating his fellows is "sane." Excellent! Let me be mad, then, by all means! mad with the madness of *Absinthe*, the wildest, most luxurious madness in the world! *Vive la folie! Vive l'amour! Vive l'animalism! Vive le Diable!* . . . [*Princeton University Library Chronicle* note.]

5. Louis Holladay and his sister Paula ("Polly") were to become close friends of O'Neill during his Greenwich Village days. A series of restaurants that Polly owned were gathering places for the Provincetown Players, including O'Neill. O'Neill was very shaken by Louis's death from a heroin overdose in 1918, which took place in the Golden Swan, or "Hell-Hole," bar in his presence.

6. This is a reference to Arthur and Barbara Gelb's biography *O'Neill* (1962), which had just been published.

7. O'Neill was not actually expelled from Princeton but suspended for poor attendance at the end of his freshman year. He did not take his exams and did not return in the fall. He quit the job at the New York-Chicago Supply Company, which his father had gotten for him.

8. O'Neill played The Second Mate in the Provincetown Players' production of *Bound East for Cardiff* in 1916.

9. O'Neill was awarded the Pulitzer Prize four times, for *Beyond the Horizon* (1920), for *"Anna Christie"* (1922), for *Strange Interlude* (1928), and, posthumously, for *Long Day's Journey Into Night* (1957).

10. The National Prohibition Act, informally known as the Volstead Act, was the enabling legislation of the Eighteenth Amendment to the Constitution, which prohibited the production, sale, and transport of intoxicating liquors.

11. Malvolio is the puritanical character who seeks to curtail festivities but becomes the butt of the revelers' jokes in *Twelfth Night* (ca. 1601) by William Shakespeare (1564–1616).

12. O'Neill was thirty-five in April 1924.

13. O'Neill was hired by the *New London Telegraph* in August 1912.

14. The reference is to the well-known writers Joseph Conrad (1857–1924), who wrote the classic sea novel *Lord Jim* (1900), Rudyard Kipling (1865–1936), who wrote travel sketches and poems about the sea, and John Masefield (1878–1967), many of whose sea poems are included in his collection *Salt-Water Poems and Ballads* (1916).

15. Hamilton is probably referring to the plays that were printed in *Thirst and Other One-Act Plays* (1914), of which, as he notes below, he was perhaps the only reviewer. It includes *Thirst*, *Warnings*, and *Fog*, which are set at sea.

16. In his article "A Shelf of Printed Plays," Hamilton wrote that "this writer's favourite mood is that of horror. He deals with grim and ghastly situations that would become intolerable if they were protracted beyond the limits of a single sudden act. He seems to be familiar with the sea; for three of these five plays deal with terrors that attend the tragedy of ship-wreck. He shows a keen sense of the reactions of character under stress of violent emotion; and his dialogue is almost brutal in its power. More than one of these plays should be available for such an institution as the Princess Theatre in New York."

17. *The Moon of the Caribbees* was written in the spring of 1917 and first produced by the Provincetown Players in December 1918. *Bound East for Cardiff* was first produced by the Players in July 1916. O'Neill's earliest version of *"Anna Christie," Chris Christopherson*, was completed in the spring of 1919. *The Emperor Jones* was completed in 1920. It's very unlikely that the latter two would have been in James O'Neill's possession.

18. Maurice Maeterlinck (1862–1949) was a Belgian playwright and poet known for his fantasy and mysticism. Johann Wolfgang von Goethe (1749–1832) was one of the greatest of German writers, best known for his two-part drama *Faust* (1808, 1832), as well as a scientist and polymath. This is a reference to the "Sturm und Drang" period of Goethe's work, characterized by *Die Leiden des jungen Werthers* (1774).

19. This is probably a reference to *Le Cavalier Polonais* (ca. 1655) by the great Dutch painter Rembrandt Harmenszoon van Rejn (1606–1669).

20. This is probably a reference to Beatrice Ashe. See chapter 12.

21. Latimer refers to the poem "The Rime of the Ancient Mariner" (1798) by Samuel Taylor Coleridge (1772–1834).

22. Will Rogers (1879–1935) was a well-known humorist and actor who starred in more than seventy films and Broadway productions in addition to writing news-

paper columns and books. He was known for his homespun good humor, and the statement "I never yet met a man I didn't like."

23. James O'Neill met Edwin Booth (1833–1893) in 1873, when he was playing in the company of James McVicker (1822–1896), Booth's father-in-law, in Chicago. O'Neill made a sensation playing Macduff to Booth's Macbeth, and over the next two years they played in *Hamlet*, *Julius Caesar*, *Romeo and Juliet*, and *Othello* together.

24. This is a reference to the house at 325 Pequot Avenue that James O'Neill would name Monte Cristo Cottage, and that served as the setting for O'Neill's plays *Ah, Wilderness!* and *Long Day's Journey Into Night*. Most people, including Ella and Eugene O'Neill, did not consider it a "fine house," but a cobbled-together residence that was furnished like a summer cottage.

25. Richard Mansfield (Meridan Phelps) (1857–1907) was a British actor best known for his performances in Shakespeare and in Gilbert and Sullivan, for his tour de force performances in both title roles of *Dr. Jekyll and Mr. Hyde*, and for romantic roles like Beau Brummel and Cyrano de Bergerac. Edmund Breese (1871–1936) was a director, actor, and writer who began his Broadway career playing in James O'Neill's 1900 production of *The Count of Monte Cristo*. He is best known for the role of the District Attorney in Ayn Rand's *The Night of January 16* (1935). Nance O'Neil (1874–1965), known as the "American Bernhardt," had a thirty-year career on the stage and in silent film, including such eponymous roles as Magda and Hedda Gabler. Tyrone Power Sr. (1869–1931), the father of the well-known film actor, had a thirty-year career as an actor on stage and in silent film, most notably in revivals of Shakespeare and other classic plays. He was also in one talking film, *The Big Trail* (1930). Mark Ellsworth played a small role in James O'Neill's production of *The Count of Monte Cristo* in 1900. Frederick Debelleville (Frederic De Belleville) (1855–1923) appeared in three films in 1915 as well as in Somerset Maugham's play *Caesar's Wife* (1919).

26. Corse Payton (1866–1934), known as "America's Best Bad Actor," ran Payton's Lee Avenue Theatre between 1900 and 1915, playing two shows a day in the first cut-rate "10–20–30 cent" theater. James O'Neill was well aware of the joke.

27. With the exception of the novelist Theodore Dreiser (1871–1945), all of the writers listed were members of the Provincetown Players, where O'Neill's career as a dramatist originated. Cook and Glaspell are identified in the headnote to chapter 14. Wilbur Daniel Steele (1886–1970) was a well-known short-story writer. Mary Heaton Vorse (1874–1966) was a labor activist, journalist, and novelist. Mrs. Max Eastman was Ida Rauh (1877–1970), a feminist lawyer who was to become one of the Provincetown's best actors. Harry Kemp (1883–1960), the self-styled "tramp poet," was well known in Greenwich Village and Provincetown, where he lived in a cabin on the dunes and was a fixture for many years.

28. Helen Ware (1877–1939) was a popular stage actor who made the transition into silent and talking films through character roles and had a long career.

29. H. L. Mencken (1880–1956) was a journalist, public intellectual, and cultural critic, known for his championing of scientific progress and his contempt for what he

called the American "booboisie." He edited two influential magazines, the *Smart Set* and the *American Mercury.*

30. George Jean Nathan (1882–1958) was an influential theater critic, known for his acerbic style. He is said to be the model for the role of Addison DeWitt in the movie *All About Eve* (1950). He worked with H. L. Mencken on the *Smart Set* and the *American Mercury.* Nathan was to become one of O'Neill's closest friends.

31. Heywood Campbell Broun Jr. (1888–1939) was a journalist known for his writing on social issues and sports, as well as theater. He founded the Newspaper Guild, which gives an annual award in his name.

32. Viola Allen (1867–1948) was well known for her acting in Shakespeare as well as more modern plays. Her signature roles were in *Little Lord Fauntleroy* (1886) by Frances Hodgson Burnett (1849–1924) and *Shenandoah* (1889) by Bronson Howard (1842–1908). In 1910 O'Neill was briefly employed as assistant stage manager for his father's touring company of *The White Sister* (1909), a popular melodrama written by F. Marion Crawford (1854–1909) and Walter Hackett (1876–1944) and based on Crawford's novel of the same title.

33. This, of course, is not accurate. O'Neill's seafaring days were behind him in 1912.

34. Frederick Latimer actually sold the *New London Telegraph* to the *Day* in 1913.

35. James O'Neill Jr. died in 1923, after Eugene had enjoyed Broadway success with *Beyond the Horizon* and *The Emperor Jones* in 1920, *"Anna Christie"* in 1921, and *The Hairy Ape* in 1922.

## Part 2

1. A red hand, cut off below the wrist, appears on the O'Neill coat of arms. A seventeenth-century legend about its origin describes a man named O'Neill who, in a swimming or sailing race to win land by being the first to touch the shore of Ireland, cut off his left hand and threw it onto the beach, thus beating all contenders and winning Ireland for himself. Eugene O'Neill enjoyed telling this story and ascribed his swimming prowess to his O'Neill genes.

2. Aubrey Beardsley (1872–1898) was a member of the Aesthetic movement of the 1890s, along with playwright Oscar Wilde (1854–1900). His elegantly decadent, erotic illustrations and posters were important to the development of Art Nouveau. The most famous of his erotic illustrations were for two plays, Aristophanes's *Lysistrata* (1896) and Wilde's *Salome* (1894). Wilde's play is based on the biblical story of Salome, who, promised a reward for her dancing by King Herod, asked for the head of the prophet John the Baptist on a platter, and got it.

3. O'Neill did not buy Beatrice the stylish clothing, but he did eventually acquire a player piano, which he nicknamed "Rosie." It is still housed in Tao House, his home in Danville, California, which is now a National Historic Site.

4. J. Hartley Manners (1870–1928) wrote the play *Peg o' My Heart* (1912), in which his wife, Laurette Taylor (1884–1946), starred. It ran for more than six hun-

dred performances on Broadway. Taylor also originated the role of Amanda Wingfield in Tennessee Williams's *The Glass Menagerie* (1945).

5. Beatrice Maher sold her copies of O'Neill's poems, along with his letters and snapshots, to the New York Public Library in 1969. They are available in the Berg Collection, and several have been published in *Selected Letters of Eugene O'Neill* (1988).

6. Enrico Caruso (1873–1921), a very popular Italian tenor, made approximately 290 recordings between 1902 and 1920.

7. "Songs of Araby" was an Irish ballad made popular by the Irish tenor John McCormack. It may have been the inspiration for "Araby" by the Irish writer James Joyce (1882–1941), one of the short stories in his collection *Dubliners* (1914), which was an important book for O'Neill. See chapter 21.

8. George Whitefield Chadwick (1854–1931) was an American composer, considered one of the New England School of composers of the late nineteenth century. The years between 1910 and 1918 are called his "dramatic period," including the tone poems *Aphrodite* and *Tam O' Shanter*.

9. Weaver refers to George Pierce Baker's playwriting workshop, which O'Neill joined in 1914. See the Biographical Sketches of Important Names in this volume.

10. Edward Massey (1898–?) wrote *Plots and Playwrights* for the 47 Workshop and had it produced by the Washington Square Players in New York in 1917. It was published in *Modern American Plays* (1915), edited by Baker.

11. The Widener family was one of the major donors to Harvard's library. After Harry Elkins Widener (1885–1912), a passionate book collector, and his father, George Widener (1861–1912), were killed on the *Titanic* in 1912, his mother, Eleanor Elkins Widener (1861–1937), donated $3.5 million to build the Harry Elkins Widener Memorial Library. Felton Broomall Elkins (1889–1944) attended Baker's workshop with O'Neill. He published three of his short plays in *Three Tremendous Trifles* (1919).

12. Edward Brewster Sheldon (1886–1946) was one of the most respected American playwrights of his generation. His *Salvation Nell* (1908), *The Nigger* (1909), and *The Boss* (1911) had all drawn attention as realistic plays dealing with current social realities in the decade preceding 1914.

13. John Frederick Ballard (1884–1957) came to Harvard from Nebraska by way of Chicago. His play *Believe Me, Xantippe* (1913) won a prize at Harvard and was eventually produced on Broadway starring John Barrymore. After earning his MA from Harvard, he had a successful career as a playwright and screenwriter.

14. Cleves Kinkead (1882–1955), like O'Neill, was a special student at Harvard. His play *Common Clay* ran for 316 performances on Broadway in 1915–1916.

15. Lewis Beach (1891–1947) is best known for the realism of the commonplace in his plays *The Clod* (1915), *A Square Peg* (1923), and *The Goose Hangs High* (1924), all of which had respectable runs on Broadway. He was spending an extra year in the Workshop.

16. Asafetida is an obnoxious-smelling root that was used in medicines as a carminative.

17. *Spoon River Anthology* by Edgar Lee Masters (1869–1950) is a collection of

free-verse portraits of the inhabitants of a small American town. It was considered daring and iconoclastic when it was published in 1915.

18. One of the oft-repeated stories about O'Neill, which he encouraged, was that he was expelled from Princeton for throwing a beer bottle through the window of its president, Woodrow Wilson. This was not true. O'Neill was suspended from Princeton for poor attendance and never returned. See chapter 2.

19. Yank, the protagonist of O'Neill's one-act play *The Hairy Ape* is a stoker, and the opening scene of the play takes place in the forecastle of an ocean liner.

20. The Durgin-Park restaurant, located near Faneuil Hall, has been a Boston fixture since it opened in 1827. It is known for its large portions of plain New England food and its no-nonsense service.

21. The Four Hundred is a term used to refer to New York's social elite in the late nineteenth century. It is supposedly the number that could be accommodated in the ballroom of Mrs. William Backhouse Astor Jr.

22. *Abortion* and *The Movie Man* were published in *The Lost Plays of Eugene O'Neill.* Neither was produced. The plot of the published *Abortion* differs from the plot of Weaver's account. *Beyond the Horizon* was, of course, to win the Pulitzer Prize in 1920, as was *"Anna Christie"* in 1922.

23. Frederic (Frederick, Fred) Burt (1876–1943) was a professional actor and a founding member of the Provincetown Players. He also had a Broadway career that lasted from 1901 until 1928.

24. "Jig" was the nickname of Glaspell's husband, George Cram Cook, who was president of the Provincetown Players.

25. The *Glencairn Cycle*, or the *S. S. Glencairn*, was the title often used for the four one-act plays about the sea, *Bound East for Cardiff, The Moon of the Caribbees, The Long Voyage Home*, and *In the Zone*, when they were produced together.

26. John Reed (1887–1920), the author of *Ten Days That Shook the World* (1919), a classic account of the Russian Revolution, died in Moscow in 1920 and is indeed buried beneath the Kremlin wall. His life was intertwined with O'Neill's because of O'Neill's romantic relationship with Reed's wife, Louise Bryant (1885–1936).

27. O'Neill was accompanied on this trip by Harold De Polo (1888–1960), a popular writer who claimed to have written three thousand western and detective stories, as well as several novelettes. De Polo remained friendly with both Agnes and Eugene during their marriage, and, like them, he later moved to Bermuda. Chapter 31 is his account of a fishing trip with Agnes and Eugene.

28. The "fish-house" refers to the Wharf Theater, a structure on a Provincetown wharf that served as the Provincetown Players' first theater.

29. The reference is to O'Neill's *Thirst*, produced at the Wharf Theater in August 1916. The other sea play that was produced in Provincetown in 1916 before the Players moved to New York was *Bound East for Cardiff.*

30. *The Emperor Jones* was first produced by the Provincetown Players on November 1, 1920. The Provincetown Playhouse at 133 Macdougal Street had been a bottling works at one point as well as a stable and a private residence.

31. Fifine Clark (?–1929), a French woman who had married a sea captain and

moved to Provincetown in her youth, had, as a widow, briefly run a boardinghouse in the village before she was employed by the O'Neills as a housekeeper and nanny for their son Shane in 1919.

32. The Experimental Theatre Inc.'s revival of *Before Breakfast* premiered at the Provincetown Playhouse on March 5, 1929, with Mary Blair as Mrs. Rowland, directed by James Light. The play had originally premiered at the Provincetown Playhouse on December 1, 1916.

33. Harry Kemp is listed as playing Davis, one of the sailors, in the program for the Provincetown Players' production of O'Neill's *Bound East for Cardiff* in November 1916 in Greenwich Village. He also had parts in John Reed's *Freedom* (1916) and Susan Glaspell's *The People* (1917). His own play *The Prodigal Son* was produced by the Provincetown Players in 1917.

34. For S. J. Woolf's article "Eugene O'Neill Returns after Twelve Years," see chapter 48.

35. Nathan refers to the eminent European playwrights Arthur Schnitzler (1862–1931), Ferenc Molnár (1878–1952), August Strindberg (1849–1912), Anton Chekhov (1860–1904), Jean-Baptiste Poquelin—known by his pen name, Molière—(1622–1673), and Oscar Wilde (1854–1900).

36. The plays of Theodore Dreiser (1871–1945) include *Plays of the Natural and the Supernatural* (1916) and *The Hand of the Potter* (1918). Nathan probably refers to *A Book of Burlesques* (1916) by H. L. Mencken (1880–1956), which contains some dramatic pieces, and *Washington Square Plays* (1916), which includes four plays by American playwrights.

37. Nathan probably saw the second bill of the 1916 season, which ran from July 24 to 28 and included *The Game* by Louise Bryant and *"Not Smart"* by Wilbur Daniel Steele (1886–1970), as well as O'Neill's *Bound East for Cardiff.* As noted by Harry Kemp in chapter 17, O'Neill had only one line in *Bound East.* Bryant played the female lead in her play.

38. This is a reference to *Thirst and Other One-Act Plays* (1914).

39. Raymond Sovey (1897–1966) began his theatrical career as an actor but became one of the most successful American set designers of the mid-twentieth century. Carol M. Sax (1885–1961) was a costume designer who went on to become a director and producer. He founded the Vagabond Theatre in Baltimore and became director of the Romany Theatre at the University of Kentucky. Robert Garland (?–1955) became a well-known theater critic for the *New York World-Telegram* and other newspapers. Robert Williams Wood (1868–1955), an American physicist and inventor, is best known for his work on ultraviolet light.

40. Mencken's play *The Artist: A Drama Without Words* was published in 1912.

41. Hippolyte Havel (1871–1950) was a Czech anarchist and close associate of Emma Goldman's as well as a friend of the Provincetown Players group. He is the model for the character Hugo Kalmar in O'Neill's *The Iceman Cometh.*

42. Michael or Mike Gold was the pen name for Itzok, Isaac, or Irwin Granich (1894–1967), who is best known for his novel *Jews Without Money* (1930). He had

three plays produced by the Provincetown Players, *Money* (1920), *Ivan's Homecoming* (1917), and *Down the Airshaft* (1917).

43. Louise Bryant (1890–1936) was a journalist known for her beauty and bohemian ways when she lived in Greenwich Village with John Reed. She toyed with O'Neill in a well-known love triangle, which informs the relationships among Nina, Sam, and Ned in *Strange Interlude*.

44. For Agnes Boulton, see chapter 26.

45. Christine Ell was the cook at Polly Holladay's restaurant, where the Provincetown Players gathered. O'Neill was drawn to the vital spirit she showed despite a very difficult upbringing. She is generally considered to be the model for Josie Hogan in *A Moon for the Misbegotten*.

46. [Virginia Gardner's note] Interviews with Dorothy Day, 1969–1978.

47. Gold's *Down the Airshaft* was part of the third bill of the 1916–1917 Provincetown season, opening on December 28, 1917.

48. Maxwell Bodenheim (1893–1954) was a writer and Greenwich Village character who descended into alcoholism and panhandling after a successful period in the 1920s and 1930s. He had two plays produced by the Provincetown Players, *The Gentle Furniture Shop* (1917) and *Knot-Holes* (1917).

49. It was actually Baudelaire's English translator, Frank Pearce Sturm (1879–1942), who referred to Baudelaire's taking the downward path that leads to salvation in "Charles Baudelaire: A Study," which serves as the introduction to his collected translations of Baudelaire's poetry, *The Poems of Charles Baudelaire* (1906). Baudelaire wrote several poems about cats.

50. O'Neill's *Fog* was produced in January 1917.

51. Alfred Francis Kreymborg (1883–1966), poet, novelist, playwright, puppeteer, editor, and anthologist, saw his play *Lima Beans* produced by the Provincetown Players on a bill with O'Neill's *Before Breakfast* and Neith Boyce's *The Two Sons*, in December 1916. His autobiography, *Troubadour*, was published in 1925.

52. Mina Loy (1882–1966) was an artist, poet, playwright, and novelist.

53. William Zorach (born Zorach Gorfinkel, in Lithuania) (1887–1966) was an American sculptor, painter, printmaker, and writer. He and his wife, Marguerite, designed several of the Provincetown Players' most experimental plays, including Alfred Kreymborg's *Lima Beans* (1916) and Louise Bryant's *The Game* (1916).

## Part 3

1. Hawthorne seems to have misremembered this poem. The *Masses* ceased publication in 1917.

2. In the spring and summer of 1918, Agnes Boulton published "To Have Your Cake and Eat It," *Breezy Stories* (May 1918): 311–17; "The Primrose Path," *Breezy Stories* (June 1918): 112–17; "The First Stone," *Young's Magazine* (July 1918): 63–75; and "Harry and George," *Young's Magazine* (September 1918): 368–79. No story from that year has been found in *Ainslee's*.

3. James Joyce's *Dubliners* was first published in the United States by B. W. Huebsch in 1915.

4. For James O'Neill Jr., see the Biographical Sketches of Important Names in this volume.

5. Mary MacLane's *I, Mary MacLane: A Diary of Human Days* (1917) was called a "sensational confession of egoism" by the *Los Angeles Times* (20 May 1917): III: 24.

6. James O'Neill died of intestinal cancer on August 10, 1920.

7. For Shane O'Neill, see the Biographical Sketches of Important Names in this volume.

8. The reference is to Fifine Clark, Shane's beloved nanny, sometimes called "Gaga," who also served as cook and housekeeper for the O'Neills in Provincetown and was with the family until she died in 1929.

9. Agnes's sister Cecil Boulton (1898–1983) married the painter Edward Fisk (1886–1944), who was a friend of O'Neill's in Greenwich Village before he married Agnes.

10. For Harry Kemp, see headnote to chapter 17.

11. Norman Matson (1893–1966) was a writer with two films to his credit, *I Married a Witch* (1942) and *He Couldn't Say No* (1938). He had a long relationship with Glaspell after the death of her husband, George Cram Cook, but they never married. He collaborated with her on the Broadway play *The Comic Artist* (1933). Charles Kaeselau (1889–1972) was a Swedish artist who studied in Paris and Chicago and settled in Provincetown, where he was one of the first directors of the Provincetown Art Association.

12. Harlan Edward "Harl" Cook (1910–1959) was the son of George Cram Cook (see headnote to chapter 14) and his second wife, Mollie Price. He was born in Iowa but, after his parents' divorce, spent much of his life on Cape Cod, where his father spent his summers.

13. Harry Weinberger (1888–1944) was indeed Eugene O'Neill's lawyer, an often difficult and trying job that he took on in the early 1920s when he was involved with the Provincetown Players. He handled O'Neill's divorce from Agnes Boulton as well as many other matters, often going beyond the normal attorney–client relationship. Weinberger was one of the few O'Neill friends from the 1920s who remained close to him throughout his life.

14. Walter Stiff's photograph of the house about to slide into the ocean was made into a postcard.

15. John Dos Passos (1896–1970) is best known for his novels, particularly the trilogy *U.S.A.* (1937) and *Manhattan Transfer* (1925).

16. "Bunny" was Edmund Wilson's nickname.

17. Charles Demuth (1883–1935) was a well-known modernist painter, part of the Alfred Stieglitz (1864–1946) group in New York. He was an original member of the Provincetown Players and knew O'Neill as early as 1916.

18. Mary Blair (1895–1947) was Edmund Wilson's first wife, and an actor with

the Provincetown Players. She originated the roles of Emma Crosbie in O'Neill's *Diff'rent* in 1920 and Ella Downey in *All God's Chillun Got Wings* in 1924.

19. Thomas Craven (1888–1969) studied art in Paris and settled in Greenwich Village, where he roomed with Thomas Hart Benton (1889–1975) and was friendly with the objectivist painters. He made his name as an antimodernist art critic, making a particular stir with the article "Have Painters Minds?"

20. In the early 1920s, F. Scott Fitzgerald (1896–1940) had published *This Side of Paradise* (1920), *The Beautiful and Damned* (1922), and *The Great Gatsby* (1925).

21. *The World's Illusion* (1919), a novel by Jakob Wassermann (1873–1934).

22. "*Anna Christie*," directed by John Griffith Wray and starring Blanche Sweet as Anna, William Russell as Matt Burke, and George F. Marion as Chris Christopherson, was released in November 1923.

23. O'Neill's stepdaughter was Agnes Boulton's daughter, Barbara Burton (1914–2009).

24. For Kenneth Macgowan, Robert Edmond Jones, and Cleon Throckmorton, see the Biographical Sketches of Important Names in this volume.

25. Eugene O'Neill, "Are the Actors to Blame?" from the Provincetown Players playbill for *Adam Solitaire*, November 6, 1925, in Helen Deutsch and Stella Hanau, *The Provincetown: A Story of the Theatre* (1931), 198.

26. W. S. Gilbert and Arthur Sullivan's *Patience* was revived at the Provincetown Playhouse by the Experimental Theatre, Inc., and directed by Robert Edmond Jones. It opened on December 29, 1924, and ran until the following March. Juliet Brenon played one of the Rapturous Maidens.

27. For Eugene O'Neill Jr., see the Biographical Sketches of Important Names in this volume.

28. O'Neill suffered from "an idiopathic form of late-onset cerebellar cortical atrophy" (B. H. Price and E. P. Richardson Jr., "The Neurological Illness of Eugene O'Neill—A Clinicopathological Report," 1130) and not from Parkinson's disease, with which he had been misdiagnosed during his lifetime. It caused a progressive loss of control of his muscles, beginning with a tremor in his hands, which made it very difficult and finally impossible for him to write.

29. For Carlotta Monterey O'Neill, see the Biographical Sketches of Important Names in this volume.

30. Lawrence Langner gave O'Neill a Dictaphone at one point, hoping that he would be able to dictate his work, but as far as is known, this was never successful.

31. Charles Webster Hawthorne (1872–1930), an American portrait and genre painter, founded the Cape Cod School of Art in 1899 and was a founding member of the Provincetown Art Association in 1914.

32. This is a reference to *Part of a Long Story* (1958). See chapter 26.

33. Sophocles (c. 496–406 BC) was one of the dramatists O'Neill's most revered. The so-called Theban plays, which focus on the house of Atreus, include *Oedipus Rex* (undated) and *Antigone* (undated) as well as *Oedipus at Colonus* (401 BC).

34. Trixie Friganza (Delia O'Callaghan) (1870–1955) began her career in the choruses of musical comedies and worked her way up to having her own vaudeville act. She was a successful comic actor both on the stage and on screen, appearing in a number of films, including *Gentlemen Prefer Blondes* (1928) and *A Star Is Born* (1937).

35. This is a reference to O'Neill's marriage to Carlotta Monterey in 1929 and his move to California in 1936.

36. James Joseph "Jimmy" Collins (1870–1943) broke into Major League Baseball in 1895 with the Boston Beaneaters. He played until 1908, with the Boston Americans and the Philadelphia Athletics as well as the Beaneaters. In his fourteen-year career, he batted .294, with 1,999 career hits and a .928 fielding percentage.

37. The Brooklyn Dodgers were lovingly referred to as "Dem Bums" by many of their fans. The New York Yankees defeated the Dodgers in the 1947 World Series, four games to three.

38. Thomas Mitchell (1892–1962) was an actor, playwright, director, and screenwriter, the first actor to win an Oscar, a Tony, and an Emmy. He is best known for his roles as Gerald O'Hara in *Gone with the Wind* (1939) and Uncle Billy in *It's a Wonderful Life* (1946). He replaced Lee J. Cobb (1911–1976) as Willy Loman in the original production of *Death of a Salesman* (1949). In 1918 he directed O'Neill's *The Moon of the Caribbees* for the Provincetown Players.

39. O'Neill had an orchard and some farm animals at Tao House in California. Mitchell had lived in California since the mid-1930s.

40. The reference is to Sugar Ray Robinson (Walker Smith Jr.) (1921–1989), considered by many to be the greatest boxer of all time. He died in poverty after fighting more than two hundred times in his nearly twenty-six-year career in pro boxing.

41. Gene Buck (1885–1957) was a songwriter, known for "In the Cool of the Evening" (1912), and the chief writer for Florenz Ziegfeld's "Ziegfeld Follies" (1912–1926) and writer and director for his "Midnight Frolics" (1914–1926). He served as president of ASCAP from 1924 to 1941.

42. Louis Wolheim (1880–1931) was a successful Hollywood character actor who played Yank in the original production of *The Hairy Ape* in 1922. He married the Australian actor Ethel Dane (1886–?) in 1923.

43. James Light (1894–1964) joined the Provincetown Players in 1917 and worked as an actor and director for the Players and for their successor, the Experimental Theatre, Inc. He was a trusted friend and collaborator of O'Neill's, directing or codirecting the premieres of *The Hairy Ape* (1922), *The Ancient Mariner* (1923), and *All God' s Chillun Got Wings* (1924).

44. Edward J. "Ted" Ballantine (1888–1968) was a British actor who came to the United States in 1913 and was a founding member of the Provincetown Players, where he acted and directed. He directed O'Neill's *S. S. Glencairn* in 1929 and appeared in many Broadway plays between 1913 and 1951. His wife, Stella, was the niece of Emma Goldman (1869–1940), a good friend of O'Neill's. Their son Ian Ballantine (1916–1995) was to found Bantam Books and Ballantine Books.

45. Thomas Eakins (1844–1916) was a realist painter, photographer, and sculptor, known for his portraiture. His painting *The Gross Clinic* (1875) is recognized as one of the great American works of art.

46. The Hedgerow temporarily ceased operation as a repertory theater in 1956, ending Deeter's thirty-three-year span as director and a board member.

47. *Exorcism* was resurrected in 2011, when a copy of the play was found in the papers of the screenwriter Philip Yordan and printed in the *New Yorker*.

48. M. Eleanor Fitzgerald (1877–1955) worked for Emma Goldman and Alexander Berkman (1870–1936) on *Mother Earth* and other Anarchist publications before becoming business manager of the Provincetown Players in 1918.

49. O'Neill made a strong effort to stop drinking in 1926 and, for the most part, succeeded, although he continued to have short, intense lapses from sobriety into the 1940s.

50. The first quotation is from *Welded* (*Complete Plays, vol. 2, 1920–1931*, 275). The second is from *The Fountain* (*Complete Plays, vol. 2, 1920–1931*, 231).

51. Doris Keane (1881–1945) was an actor best known for her role as Margherita Cavallini in Edward Sheldon's *Romance* (1913), which she played for five years in the United States and Europe, also playing the role in a film in 1920. She played Eleanor Owen in O'Neill's *Welded* for twenty-four performances in 1924.

52. This line occurs in the first scene of *Welded* (239).

53. The source of the quotation is François VI, duc de La Rochefoucauld (1613–1680). *Ouvres Complètes*, texte etablie et annoté par L. Martin-Chauffier (Paris: Gallimard, 1950), 135.

54. Jean Mounet-Sully (1841–1916) was a celebrated French actor whose best-known role was Oedipus in *L'Oedipe roi* (1881), a French adaptation of Sophocles's play, at the Comédie Française. He often played opposite the equally celebrated Sarah Bernhardt (1844–1923).

55. The Provincetown revived *The Emperor Jones* in May and December 1924, and in February 1926. *Where the Cross Is Made* was revived in May 1928. Cowley's name is not in the cast lists for any of these revivals.

56. *The Lower Depths: Scenes from Russian Life* (1902) is the best-known play by the Russian socialist realist playwright Maxim Gorky (1868–1936). It depicts the lives of impoverished Russians at the turn of the twentieth century. It was first produced in New York in 1923, directed by Constantin Stanislavsky (1863–1938) as part of an American tour by the Moscow Art Theatre.

57. Marguerite Frances Baird (1890–1970) was an American landscape painter. After she divorced her first husband, the poet Orrick Johns (1887–1946), she married Cowley in 1919. When she moved to Mexico to obtain a divorce from Cowley in 1931, she had a romantic affair with the poet Hart Crane, his only documented heterosexual liaison.

58. Cowley refers to *Disguises of Love: Psycho-Analytical Sketches*, a translation by Rosalie Gabler of *Masken der Sexualität* by Wilhelm Stekel (1868–1940).

59. Cowley refers to Ernst Toller (1893–1939), George Kaiser (1878–1945), and

Walter Hasenclever (1890–1940), the major dramatists of the German Expressionist movement.

60. In the winter of 1923, O'Neill was at work on *Desire Under the Elms*, which premiered in November 1924.

61. "With beaded bubbles winking at the brim" is a line from "Ode to a Nightingale" (1819) by John Keats (1795–1821).

62. Niles Spencer (1893–1952) was a Precisionist painter who grew up in Rhode Island, often using its textile mills as his subject. He was a student of Robert Henri (1865–1929) and O'Neill's close friend George Bellows (1882–1925), and a friend of the O'Neills' friend Charles Demuth. During the 1920s, he lived in Provincetown.

63. Grace Edna Hart Crane (1878–1947) was Hart Crane's mother.

64. On February 3, 1924, the Experimental Theatre, Inc.'s revival of *Fashion* (1845) by Anna Cora Mowatt (1819–1870), a surprise hit, opened at the Provincetown Theatre. Claire Eames (1894–1930) played the role of Mrs. Tiffany.

65. Susan Jenkins (1896–1982) married James Light in 1917; they divorced in 1922. Between 1918 and 1922, she worked for the Provincetown Players, later finding work in publishing. As Susan Jenkins Brown, she published *Robber Rocks: Letters and Memories of Hart Crane, 1923–1932* (1969).

66. Claire Eames, an American actor who was married to the playwright Sidney Howard (1891–1939), made her stage debut in 1918 at the Provincetown Theatre in a triple bill that included O'Neill's *Ile*.

67. Richard Waslav Rychtarik (1894–1982) was a set and costume designer of major productions at the Metropolitan Opera and the Columbia Broadcasting System. His first wife was Charlotte E. Rychtarik (1894–1950), an accomplished pianist.

68. Anna Cora Mowatt Ritchie, author, actor, and playwright, was born in France to American parents but raised in the United States. The revival by the Experimental Theatre, Inc. of her play *Fashion* ran for 152 performances.

69. Waldo Frank (1889–1967) was a novelist, social historian, political activist, and literary critic. In 1926 he had recently been named a contributing editor of the *New Republic* and had written his influential study of Spanish culture, *Virgin Spain* (1926). He and Hart Crane shared an interest in the mystical theories of George Gurdjieff (1866–1949), which they applied to their writing about the United States, but Frank later repudiated them.

70. Horace Liveright (1883–1933) was the partner of Albert Boni in the Greenwich Village publishing firm Boni & Liveright, which founded the Modern Library and published many contemporary literary writers in the 1910s and 1920s. Otto Hermann Kahn (1867–1934) was a banker, railroad organizer, philanthropist, and patron of the arts. He supported composers and poets, including Hart Crane.

71. Boni & Liveright published Frank's *Virgin Spain* and *Rahab* in 1926, but no book of poems with a preface by O'Neill. When they published Crane's *White Buildings* (1926), Allen Tate (1899–1979), supplied the foreword.

72. Allen Tate, an American poet, literary critic, biographer, and teacher, was a

member of the Fugitive Poets (later called the Southern Agrarians), a group of social thinkers connected at various times to Vanderbilt University.

73. Robert Hobart ("Bob") Davis (1869–1942) was editor-in-chief of the Munsey Magazines, and a powerful figure in the publishing industry.

74. Grover Cleveland (1837–1908) was elected to two nonconsecutive terms (1885–1889 and 1893–1897) as president of the United States.

75. Manuel Komroff (1890–1974) was a writer, translator, and editor. He edited the Modern Library Series for Boni & Liveright in the 1920s before joining the expatriate writers in Paris. He wrote more than forty novels, the best known of which is *Coronet* (1929).

76. Katharine Cornell (1893–1974) is considered by many to be one of the best American theater actors of the twentieth century. Her most famous role was as Elizabeth Barrett Browning in *The Barretts of Wimpole Street* (1931), but she also popularized the plays of Shakespeare and George Bernard Shaw (1856–1950) on the American stage.

77. William Somerset Maugham (1874–1965) and John Galsworthy (1867–1933) were British contemporaries of O'Neill's who wrote both plays and novels. Galsworthy won the Nobel Prize for Literature in 1932, four years before O'Neill.

78. More than 100,000 boxing fans witnessed the fight between Gene Tunney (1897–1978) and Jack Dempsey (1895–1983) on September 22, 1927, at Soldier Field in Chicago. It was the occasion of the notorious "long count," which enabled Tunney, who had been knocked to the canvas in the seventh round, to get back up and defeat Dempsey in ten rounds.

79. O'Neill left Bermuda for New York in August 1927. He returned to Bermuda for a brief visit in October but was back in New York at the Hotel Wentworth by the end of the year. He did not return to Bermuda. Hoffman was born on November 1, 1905, and would have been twenty-two in early 1928.

80. Lawrence Langner (1890–1962) was one of the founders of the Washington Square Players, which became the Theatre Guild, the preeminent Broadway producing organization for drama of literary quality. The Guild produced seven of O'Neill's plays, starting with *Marco Millions* in 1928 and ending with *The Iceman Cometh* in 1946.

81. Eugene O'Neill's father, James, had actually paid for the printing of the volume.

82. The quotation is from *The Great God Brown*, Act IV, scene 1 (*Complete Plays, vol. 2, 1920–1931*, 528).

83. Conrad Aiken (1889–1973) was a prolific American writer of poetry and fiction, who wrote or edited more than fifty books. He did indeed live above the Grolier Poetry Book Shop, on Harvard Square in Cambridge, Massachusetts, which was established in 1927. It claims to be the oldest continuous poetry bookshop in the United States, and has hosted many literary figures.

84. O'Neill did not have Parkinson's disease. For the details of his illness, see note 28 (part 3).

85. *Strange Interlude* opened on January 30, 1928. O'Neill and Carlotta Monterey left for Europe on February 10.

86. Eugene O'Neill Jr. was actually found dead in his cottage in Woodstock, New York, on September 25, 1950. His wrist and ankle had been slashed with a razor.

87. Actually, O'Neill died at the Shelton Hotel in Boston, November 27, 1953.

88. These lines are from Hugh Holland's elegiac sonnet "Upon the Lines and Life of the Famous Scenicke [*sic*] Poet, Master William Shakespeare" included in the First Folio edition of Shakespeare's plays, *Mr. William Shakespeares Comedies, Histories, & Tragedies, Published according to the True Original Copies* (1623).

89. To the previously identified Sophocles, Christopher Marlowe, and William Shakespeare on this list of eminent playwrights, Hoffman adds Aeschylus (525–456 BC), Euripides (480–406 BC), and Pierre Corneille (AD 1606–1684).

## Part 4

1. During the fall and winter of 1928, O'Neill had become ill with influenza during a trip to Saigon, had been hospitalized in Shanghai, and had resumed drinking and been separated briefly from Carlotta. They were reconciled in Egypt in January 1929 and returned to Europe early in 1929. It was presumably during this return journey that the O'Neills became acquainted with Fladger.

2. The O'Neills were actually living in the Château du Plessis, in St. Antoine-du-Rocher, near Tours, France.

3. Joseph Kramm's *The Shrike* ran on Broadway from January 15 to May 31, 1952 and won the Pulitzer Prize for Drama.

4. A revival of *Desire Under the Elms* ran at the ANTA Playhouse from January 16 to February 23, 1952. Celeste Holm (1917–2012) played Anna Christie in a revival that ran from January 23 to February 3, 1952.

5. Greta Garbo was nominated for a Best Actress Oscar for her portrayal of Anna in the 1930 film adaptation of *"Anna Christie,"* directed by Clarence Brown. Her first film with sound, it is famous for the advertising slogan "Garbo talks!"

6. William Harrison "Sparrow" Robertson (1859?–1941) was a popular columnist for the *Paris Herald*, known for his scrambled syntax and his heavy drinking. For twenty years, he haunted the bars on Paris's Right Bank and was said to subsist mainly on the hard-boiled eggs he swiped.

7. Horace Liveright died in 1933.

8. Arthur Pell, the treasurer of Boni & Liveright, had advised against selling the Modern Library to Cerf and Donald Klopfer.

9. Robinson Jeffers (1887–1962) was known for his nature poetry about the California coast. Samuel Hopkins Adams (1871–1958) was best known for his investigative journalism. His exposé of the patent medicine business was a catalyst for the creation of the FDA.

10. For information on Carl Van Vechten, see the headnote to chapter 62.

11. *A Moon for the Misbegotten* was not part of the nine-play cycle. The 1947 premiere production of this play by the Theatre Guild closed out of town in St. Louis before it had a chance to reach New York. Its Broadway premiere was on May 2, 1957.

12. Ralph Barton (1891–1931) was an artist and illustrator, best known for his *New Yorker* cartoons and caricatures of celebrities. Suffering from bipolar disorder, he shot himself at the age of thirty-nine.

13. Although she started living with him in 1923, Carlotta was actually only married to Ralph Barton from 1925 until she divorced him in 1926.

14. In its article on Barton's death, the *New York Times* (21 May 1931: 1) reported that it had been unable to reach either Carlotta Monterey or Eugene O'Neill, and their hotel reported that they had gone out of town.

15. Maxwell Anderson (1888–1959) and Laurence Stallings's (1894–1968) play about World War I soldiers, *What Price Glory?* (1924), starred William Boyd as Sergeant Quirt and Louis Wolheim as Captain Flagg. The 1926 film starred Edmund Lowe and Victor McLaglen. John Ford's 1952 remake starred James Cagney and Dan Dailey. Wolheim played Robert "Yank" Smith in both the Provincetown and the Broadway productions of *The Hairy Ape* in 1922. Carlotta Monterey replaced Mary Blair, who originated the role of Mildred Douglas. It was during this production that she met Eugene O'Neill.

16. For information on Saxe Commins, see the headnote to chapter 51.

17. George Michael Cohan (1878–1942), actor, writer, and producer, is known as the father of American musical comedy, creating and producing more than fifty shows between 1904 and 1920. He wrote immensely popular musical shows that included such songs as "Over There" and "Give My Regards to Broadway," as well as straight plays and many lyrics.

18. Mabel Dodge (1878–1962) was a wealthy socialite who took an interest in the arts. In 1912 she started a salon in New York that became famous for bringing members of the avant-garde art world, intellectuals, labor leaders, and politicians together for conversation. She had a very public affair with John Reed and renovated the former life-saving station at Peaked Hill Bar in Provincetown that eventually became the home of Eugene O'Neill and his second wife, Agnes Boulton.

19. The Washington Square Players' production of *In the Zone* premiered on October 31, 1917.

20. Albert Lewis (1885–1978), the partner of Max Gordon (1892–1978), was a veteran of burlesque and vaudeville as well as a successful producer. Gordon and Lewis were responsible for booking O'Neill's *In the Zone* into the Orpheum Circuit of vaudeville houses in 1918.

21. Jacob Ben-Ami (1890–1977) began his career in the Yiddish theater and participated in it throughout his life. Beginning in 1920 he also appeared on Broadway and performed in Chekhov with Eva La Gallienne (1899–1991) and acted and directed for the Theatre Guild. In 1924 he played Michael Cape in the Experimental Theatre, Inc.'s production of O'Neill's *Welded.*

22. This is a reference to the Experimental Theatre, Inc.

23. The Theatre Guild produced the American premiere of George Bernard Shaw's lengthy comedy *Back to Methuselah,* which ran for twenty-five performances, beginning February 27, 1922.

24. The actor was Katharine Cornell, who rejected the play in order to do Somerset Maugham's *The Letter* in September 1927 (Gelb, *O'Neill*, enl. ed., 633).

25. Langner is correct that O'Neill was thirty-eight years old in the spring of 1927.

26. Philip Moeller (1880–1958) was a respected stage director, playwright, and songwriter as well as one of the founding directors of the Theatre Guild. Besides *Strange Interlude*, he also directed *Mourning Becomes Electra* and *Ah, Wilderness!* for the Guild.

27. This is a reference to Betts Academy, which O'Neill attended from 1902 to 1905.

28. Carlotta Monterey O'Neill, who grew up in Oakland, California, often claimed to have spent her youth in European convent schools.

29. Armina Marshall (1895?–1991) was a cofounder of the Theatre Guild, along with her husband, Lawrence Langner, and Theresa Helburn. With her husband she coauthored seven plays, including the 1933 hit *Pursuit of Happiness*.

30. The reference was to the O'Neills' rented home, the Château du Plessis, near Tours, France.

31. Langner describes O'Neill's plan for the ambitious cycle of plays, "A Tale of Possessors Self-Disposessed," eventually numbering nine, which he hoped would be his great work. Of these plays, only *A Touch of the Poet* (1958) and the posthumously reconstructed *More Stately Mansions* (1967) survive. O'Neill, unable to finish them because of his diminished physical capacity, and unwilling to have them produced in unfinished form, enlisted his wife, Carlotta, to help destroy them toward the end of his life. See chapter 56.

32. *The Forsyte Saga* (1906–1921) by John Galsworthy is a series of three substantial novels and two "interludes" about several generations of the Forsyte family.

33. Sir Cecil John Rhodes (1853–1902) is the English-born South African businessman who founded the De Beers diamond company, the state of Rhodesia (now Zambia and Zimbabwe), and the Rhodes Scholarship.

34. James O'Neill may have been a partner in his friend James P. Sullivan's Buick dealership, which was first called the Monte Cristo Garage and later changed to Buick Sales and Service (George Monteiro, "James Tyrone's 'Packard' in *Long Day's Journey into Night*").

35. George Bernard Shaw's *The Quintessence of Ibsenism* appeared in 1891.

36. The British writer Charles Algernon Swinburne (1837–1909) is best known for his "decadent" sexual poetry. His *Poems and Ballads*, published in 1866, caused a sensation as much for its explicit themes as for its author's poetic skill. O'Neill also has Jamie Tyrone quote Swinburne in *Long Day's Journey Into Night*.

37. Omar Khayyám (1048–1131) was the Persian polymath whose poems have been frequently translated into many languages, most famously (into English) as the *Rubáiyát of Omar Khayyám* (beginning in 1859) by Edward FitzGerald (1809–1883)

38. Oscar Fingal O'Flahertie Wills Wilde (1854–1900) was a poet, playwright, and novelist. Among his best-known works are *The Picture of Dorian Gray* (1891), *The Importance of Being Earnest* (1895), and *The Ballad of Reading Gaol* (1898). In 1895 he was convicted of "gross indecency" with men and served two years at hard labor.

39. Atkinson did not know about O'Neill's brother Edmund, who died in 1885 before his second birthday.

40. *Porgy* by Dubose Heyward (1885–1940) and Dorothy Heyward (1890–1961) ran from October 1927 to August 1928 at the Guild Theatre. O'Neill's *Marco Millions* ran from January to March 1928.

41. Lee Simonson (1888–1967) was a major American scene designer during the twentieth century. He designed more than thirty Broadway productions, mostly for the Theatre Guild, including O'Neill's *Marco Millions*, *Dynamo*, and *Days Without End*.

42. Max Reinhardt (1873–1943) was a German director and producer of plays and films, known for his development of "the New Stagecraft," which aimed to synthesize all the elements of production into an organic work of art. Alexander Woollcott (1887–1943) was a highly respected theater critic for the *New York Times* and the *New Yorker* magazine, and a member of the Algonquin Round Table.

43. Kublai, the Great Kaan was played by McKay Morris (1891–1955).

44. Mamoulian directed *Summer Holiday* (1948), which featured Mickey Rooney (1920–2014) as Richard Miller and Gloria DeHaven (1925–2016) as Muriel McComber.

45. Mai-mai Sze (1910–1992) was a writer and painter, the daughter of a Chinese ambassador to the United States. Her drawing of O'Neill appeared in the program of *The Iceman Cometh* and on the cover of *Newsweek* on June 17, 1957.

46. Born in 1916, Eric Bentley taught at Columbia University for many years. A drama critic, editor, and playwright, he is best known for books such as *A Century of Hero-Worship* (1944), *The Playwright as Thinker* (1946), and *Brecht Commentaries* (1981) and his reviews for the *New Republic*. His "Trying to Like O'Neill," which describes his approach to directing *The Iceman Cometh* by cutting out vast amounts of dialogue that he considered repetitive, is well known.

47. *Volpone* (1606), a play by Ben Jonson (1572–1637), was produced by the Theatre Guild in 1928 under Moeller's direction.

48. O'Neill, who was traveling with Carlotta Monterey and trying to secure his divorce from Agnes Boulton at this time, was angered by what he saw as Agnes's unreasonable demands and a newspaper interview she gave in which she discussed the separation.

49. Claudette Colbert (1903–1996), a French-born American actor of stage and screen, made her debut at the age of fifteen in *The Widow's Veil* (1919) at the Provincetown Playhouse in New York and played Ada Fife in *Dynamo*. Her films include *It Happened One Night* (1934), for which she won an Oscar, *Private Worlds* (1935), and *Since You Went Away* (1944).

50. Bernard Augustine DeVoto (1897–1955), a historian and literary and cultural critic, became an authority on the American West and on Mark Twain. From 1935 until his death he wrote "The Easy Chair," a column in *Harper's Magazine*. The reference is to articles by Helburn and DeVoto in 1936: Theresa Helburn, "O'Neill: An Impression," and Bernard DeVoto, "Minority Report."

51. The announcement that O'Neill was awarded the Nobel Prize was made on

November 12, 1936. O'Neill sent a statement to the newspapers on November 14 that he would be unable to travel from Seattle to Sweden in time for the ceremony. His speech was read in absentia at the awards ceremony on December 10. His appendix was removed on December 29.

52. Kurt Weill (1900–1950), a German composer, was best known in the United States for his collaboration with German playwright Bertolt Brecht on musicals such as *The Threepenny Opera* (1928) and *The Rise and Fall of the City of Mahagonny* (1927).

53. Richard Charles Rodgers (1902–1979) was an American composer and songwriter for Hollywood and the Broadway musical theater, who collaborated with Lorenz "Larry" Milton Hart (1895–1943) on numerous movies and Broadway shows, including, among the latter, *Babes in Arms* (1937), *The Boys from Syracuse* (1938), and *Pal Joey* (1940).

54. George Francis Abbott (1887–1995), sometimes referred to as "Mr. Broadway," was for nine decades active as a Broadway theater producer, director, and playwright, as well as a Hollywood screenwriter, director, and producer. The musical was probably *The Boys from Syracuse* (1938), on which Abbott collaborated with Rodgers and Hart.

55. Oscar Greeley Clendenning Hammerstein II (1895–1960) was an American librettist and theatrical producer of Broadway musicals who collaborated with numerous composers, most notably Richard Rodgers. Among Rogers and Hammerstein's hit musicals are *Oklahoma!* (1943), *South Pacific* (1949), and *The Sound of Music* (1959).

56. Jerome David Kern (1885–1945) was a composer for the musical theater and a prolific writer of popular songs, whose most famous work is *Show Boat* (1927), an adaptation with Oscar Hammerstein II of Edna Ferber's 1926 novel of the same name. The *Marco* musical never materialized.

57. Albert Coates (1882–1953) studied in Russia, Germany, and England and conducted at Covent Garden and the Royal Opera House in London before becoming conductor of the London Symphony Orchestra in 1919, a post that he held until 1923. He wrote seven operas and worked mostly as a guest conductor after 1923.

58. *Porgy and Bess* (1935) was an opera based on DuBose Heyward's novel *Porgy*, with music by George Gershwin (1898–1937), libretto by Heyward, and lyrics by Ira Gershwin (1896–1983) and Heyward.

59. Westport Country Playhouse, in Westport, Connecticut, was founded by Lawrence Langner and Armina Marshall Langner in 1931.

60. Katharine Houghton Hepburn (1907–2003) was an American actor in movies, theater, and television whose many films include *The Philadelphia Story* (1940), *The African Queen* (1951), *Guess Who's Coming to Dinner* (1967), and *On Golden Pond* (1981).

61. Louis Burt Mayer (1874–1957) was a Hollywood film producer, who for many years headed the MGM (Metro-Goldwyn-Mayer) studio.

62. *Mourning Becomes Electra* was filmed in 1947 by RKO and was directed

by Dudley Nichols (1895–1960), with Rosalind Russell (1907–1976) as Lavinia Mannon.

63. *The Cabinet of Dr. Caligari* (1920) was a German expressionist film directed by Robert Wiene (1873–1938).

64. *The Long Voyage Home*, directed by John Ford (1894–1973), was released in November 1940. It starred John Wayne (1907–1979) as Olson, Thomas Mitchell as Driscoll, Barry Fitzgerald (1888–1961) as Cocky, and Ian Hunter (1900–1975) as Smitty. It was adapted by Dudley Nichols from the one-act plays *The Moon of the Caribbees*, *In the Zone*, *Bound East for Cardiff*, and *The Long Voyage Home*, which also form the cycle of plays known as the *S. S. Glencairn*.

65. The 1944 film adaptation of *The Hairy Ape*, directed by Alfred Santell (1895–1981) and starring William Bendix (1906–1964) and Susan Hayward (1917–1975), departed notoriously from O'Neill's play.

66. The 1932 film adaptation of *Strange Interlude* was directed by Robert Z. Leonard (1889–1968) (uncredited) and starred Norma Shearer (1902–1983), Clark Gable (1901–1960), Alexander Kirkland (1901–1986), and Ralph Morgan (1883–1956).

67. *The Iceman Cometh* premiered on October 9, 1946, running for 136 performances in New York. *A Moon for the Misbegotten* was first performed in Columbus, Ohio, on February 20, 1947. The production closed before it reached New York.

68. The story of O'Neill's expulsion from Princeton, which he helped to perpetuate, is apocryphal. O'Neill was not expelled from Princeton but was suspended for low grades and poor attendance and never returned (see chapter 2).

69. "The man who laughs."

70. For information on Sean O'Casey, see the headnote to chapter 46.

71. Henri-René Lenormand (1882–1951) was a French playwright whose work was deeply influenced by Freudian psychological theory.

72. This could be a reference to *Mourning Becomes Electra*, a draft of which O'Neill sent to Nathan for his opinion in April 1931. More likely, however, it refers to *Dynamo*, *Days Without End*, and a play O'Neill tentatively entitled "It Cannot Be Mad," which he conceived of as "a trilogy that will dig at the roots of the sickness of today as I feel it—the death of the old God and the failure of Science and Materialism to give any satisfying new One for the surviving primitive religious instinct to find a meaning for life in, and to comfort its fears of death with" (O'Neill to George Jean Nathan, 26 August 1928, *Selected Letters of Eugene O'Neill* 311).

73. Sinclair Lewis was an American writer, best known for his novels *Main Street* (1920) and *Babbitt* (1922). He won the Nobel Prize in Literature in 1930.

74. Phil Baker (1896–1963) was a popular comedian and songwriter who played the accordion in the vaudeville act "Bernie and Baker."

75. Kalak was a bottled "medicinal water" sold by the Kalak Water Company of New York, Inc., which was located in Brooklyn. Its label was registered in 1915.

76. Jimmy Beith's suicide is a real-life parallel to the suicide of Don Parritt in *The Iceman Cometh*.

77. O'Neill's suicide attempt was an autobiographical source for the events in his one-act play *Exorcism* (1920).

78. Samuel Merritt Hospital in Oakland, California, opened in 1909, along with the new Samuel Merritt School of Nursing, which became Samuel Merritt University in 2009. Merritt Hospital merged with other institutions to eventually become the Alta Bates Summit Medical Center in 1999. O'Neill was a patient there in December 1936, when he had his appendix removed.

79. [Brewer's note] Dr. Charles Caldwell, husband of Myrtle Caldwell, and father of Jane Caldwell, was the physician in charge of the emergency room at Kaiser Foundation Hospital, Walnut Creek, in the 1960's. My friend, Winifred Tharsing, whose husband was a first cousin of Carlotta's, has told me that Dr. Caldwell was reminded of Carlotta by the children of Winifred and Howard who showed up in the Emergency Room for something or other. I'm sorry that when I was aware of Dr. Caldwell's being in Walnut Creek that I was not also aware of the connection with Jane Caldwell.

## Part 5

1. Fetzer reports the community's impression that "he had a car, but did not drive it and got around on foot or with a driver, a fortunate choice as he was usually drunk. His only known contact with the town was at Elliott's Bar, his choice among the two available (Root's the other. Shady Way was too far). Actually, he had no real neighbors. His large and luxurious home was on a wooded hillside overlooking the San Ramon valley with its lush orchards and ranches and a spectacular view of Mt Diablo." It's possible that O'Neill's physical instability was mistaken for drunkenness, but the neighbors' view of him is clear.

2. In the original production of *Mourning Becomes Electra* by the Theatre Guild, which opened on October 26, 1931, Christine Mannon was played by Alla Nazimova (1879–1945), Lavinia Mannon by Alice Brady (1892–1939), and Orin Mannon by Earle Larimore (1899–1947).

3. O'Neill owned a Bugatti car when the O'Neills lived at Le Plessis. The words "(check spelling)" were present in the original interview transcript.

4. This is a reference to Sarah Sandy (1854?–?), who was O'Neill's nursemaid from the time of his birth until he was seven years old. She was thirty-four years old when he was born.

5. In Cambridge, O'Neill boarded with the Ebel family at 1105 Massachusetts Avenue.

6. O'Neill's father, James, actually arrived in the United States at age nine. After spending a short time in Buffalo, the family settled in Cincinnati. James's father, Edward O'Neill, quickly deserted the family and returned to Ireland, where he died soon afterward.

7. In 1956 Marilyn Monroe (1926–1962) was America's sex symbol. She was also a more successful actor than Carlotta Monterey, having already received great

praise for her performances in *Niagara* (1953), *Gentlemen Prefer Blondes* (1953), and *The Seven-Year Itch* (1955).

8. Carlotta O'Neill (Hazel Tharsing) was actually educated in the public schools of Oakland, California, where she was living with an aunt and uncle, and then at St. Gertrude's convent school in Rio Vista, California. According to her cousin Frank Shay, it was her uncle who was a great reader, and the Shay house was well stocked with the English and American classics. Her parents were divorced when she was about three years old, and she seldom saw her father, Chris Tharsing.

9. O'Neill's piece "The Last Will and Testament of Silverdene Emblem O'Neill" was written as consolation when the dog's death was imminent. It was published by Yale University Press in 1956.

10. The Irish poet William Butler Yeats (1865–1939) was a favorite of O'Neill's.

11. Born Joseph Goucher in Woonsocket, Rhode Island (Dowling was his mother's maiden name), Eddie Dowling (1895?–1976) was an actor, director, producer, playwright, and songwriter. His most famous role was that of Tom Wingfield in the Broadway production of Tennessee Williams's play *The Glass Menagerie*, which Dowling produced in Chicago and brought to Broadway in 1945.

12. Bergman refers to the Modern Language Association annual convention in 1978, where she appeared in a panel discussion with Jason Robards Jr. and others sponsored by the Eugene O'Neill Society.

13. Karl Ragnar Gierow, the director of Sweden's Royal Dramatic Theatre, had, with Carlotta O'Neill's permission, constructed a version of *More Stately Mansions* from fragmentary manuscripts he had found in the O'Neill Collection in Yale's Beinecke Library. This was the version performed in Sweden in 1962. Ingrid Bergman played Deborah in the American premiere of the play, directed by José Quintero (1924–1999) in 1967. Quintero presumably refers to the 1964 Yale University Press version of the text, edited by Donald Gallup.

14. [Floyd's note] O'Neill makes similar comments to Lawrence Langner in a letter dated August 16, 1941, urging the Theatre Guild producer to attend a performance of the play in anticipation of an *"Anna Christie"*–Bergman road tour and New York presentation: "We had her out to lunch—and like her a lot. No ham stuff about her. She struck me as intelligent, ambitious, loving her work and willing to work her head off for it, either for films or stage."

Carlotta O'Neill also wrote to Langner (August 10, 1941) praising Miss Bergman.

> "I went yesterday, to the matinee of *"Anna Christie."* (God, what torture, to sit through one of Gene's plays and watch *what* they'll do next!)
>
> To put it in a few words—I liked Bergman & O'Flynn. Bergman was excellent when she had to dig in and work, &, at all times, I felt her the *woman*, not an actress acting! She is good property for any producer.
>
> Bergman can *act*, is beautiful & a *woman*—None of *these damned* silly affectations!
>
> (Eugene O'Neill Collection, Yale)

15. Daks was a brand of trousers sold by Simpson's of Piccadilly in London, beginning in the early 1930s. They were innovative in that, with their self-supporting waistband, they did not require suspenders.

16. Elmer Rice (1892–1967) was an American playwright with leftist political leanings. His best-known plays are the expressionistic *The Adding Machine* (1923) and the realistic *Street Scene* (1929), which won the Pulitzer Prize and was adapted as an opera by Kurt Weill, Rice, and Langston Hughes.

17. Otto Brandstädter was a leftist German writer, editor, and translator of O'Casey's works, among others.

18. Eric Arthur Blair (George Orwell) (1903–1950) was a British writer, best known for his novels *Animal Farm* (1945) and *Nineteen Eighty-Four* (1949).

19. O'Casey refers to Senator Joseph Raymond ("Joe") McCarthy (1908–1957), whose name became synonymous with the anti-Communist witch hunts of the 1950s.

20. O'Casey's son Niall had died of leukemia earlier that month.

21. James "Big Jim" Larkin (1876–1947) founded the Irish Transport and General Workers' Union, the Irish Labour Party, and the Workers Union of Ireland. He is best known for his central role in the 1913 Dublin Lockout.

22. This is a reference to George Jean Nathan's wife, the actor Julie Haydon (1910–1994).

23. The Irish Academy of Letters was founded in 1932, largely through the efforts of Yeats and George Bernard Shaw. O'Neill was a founding member, proposed by Yeats, and supported the Academy with annual donations until his death (Gelb, *O'Neill*, enl. ed., 527).

24. This is a quotation from "Auld Lang Syne" (1788) by Robert Burns (1759–1796).

25. [Krause's note] A copy of this letter was printed in the *New York Times*, 19 November 1959. Mr. Lester Osterman, owner of the newly named Eugene O'Neill Theatre, 230 West 49th Street, New York, had asked for O'Casey's comment on the occasion. The theater had previously been called the Coronet Theatre, and was originally the Edwin Forrest Theatre.

26. Passed in 1896 by the New York state legislature, the Raines Law prohibited the sale of alcohol on Sundays, except by hotels, and then only to guests at meals or in their rooms. Saloons that got around the law by adding furnished rooms and securing a hotel license became known as "Raines hotels."

27. O'Neill refers to several radical groups of the 1910s with whom O'Neill mixed in his Greenwich Village days. The Anarcho-Syndicalists were a branch of the Anarchist movement that focused on the labor movement. "Wobblies" was a nickname for the International Workers of the World, a radical leftist labor union.

28. Joseph Heidt (1910–1952), a friend of O'Neill's who, according to his *New York Times* obituary, accompanied O'Neill to hockey games and bicycle races, was a press agent for the Theatre Guild for a dozen years and the publicity director for more than 150 shows, including *The Philadelphia Story* (1939), *Oklahoma!* (1943), and *Carousel* (1945), as well as *The Iceman Cometh*.

29. *Sister Kenny* (1946), an RKO movie starring Rosalind Russell, Alexander Knox

(1907–1995), and Dean Jagger (1903–1991), tells the story of Elizabeth Kenny, the Australian who devised a treatment for polio.

30. Norman Lewis Corwin (1910–2011) was an American writer, screenwriter, producer, essayist and teacher, who in the 1930s and 1940s was best known as a pioneer in radio broadcasting for CBS, dramatizing episodes of American history, adaptations of literary works, and dozens of original radio plays.

31. Charles Sidney Gilpin (1878–1930) played the title role in *The Emperor Jones* (1920), and in 1920 was the first African American actor to receive the Drama League of New York's annual award.

32. O'Neill expressed these ideas several times as the theme of his never-finished nine-play cycle.

33. This is a reference to the Packard, a boardinghouse run by James and Helen Rippin, who had emigrated from England to New London. O'Neill stayed there in the winter of 1913–1914.

34. The quotation is from "Gunga Din" (1890) by Rudyard Kipling (1865–1936).

35. On September 9, 1931, Benjamin P. Collings of Stamford, Connecticut, was killed aboard his small cruiser *Penguin* in Long Island Sound. His widow insisted that he was attacked by two "pirates," who hit him over the head and threw him overboard. The assailants were never found, and the unsolved mystery was avidly followed in the newspapers.

36. [Dorothy Commins's note] O'Neill later called one of Cornelius Melody's grandsons—a character in *More Stately Mansions*—Honey Harford.

37. [Dorothy Commins's note] Playwright Sheldon, author of *Salvation Nell*, *The Boss*, and *Romance*, suffered for the last thirty years of his life—he died at sixty—from acute arthritis and total blindness. During that period he regularly received visitors and carried on his business lying completely immobilized on a sort of catafalque in his penthouse apartment at Eighty-Fourth Street and Madison Avenue. Carlotta had visited Sheldon on several occasions.

38. Walter "Ice" Casey, employed for the most part as a desk clerk in third-rate New York hotels, was a friend of O'Neill's from his New London days.

39. Dr. Shirley Carter Fisk (1910–1979) received his medical degree from Columbia in 1935 and specialized in internal medicine. He was the top-ranked medical official in the Department of Defense from 1963 to 1967 and later served as a dean at Columbia University's medical school.

40. [Dorothy Commins's note] O'Neill was also fearful that, as he put it to Saxe, "Carlotta in her frenzy might do with my manuscripts what she did with the only picture I had of my mother and myself as a baby." She had destroyed the picture.

41. Harold Willis Dodds (1889–1980) was president of Princeton University from 1933 to 1957.

42. [Dorothy Commins's note] *Basic Writings of George Washington*, edited and with an introduction by Saxe Commins (New York: Random House, 1948). Saxe's inscription reads, "Gene, through all the years with unchanging love and devotion, always Saxe, July 1948."

43. [Dorothy Commins's note] Robert Haas, who had joined Cerf and Klopfer as Random House partners.

44. [Dorothy Commins's note] Once O'Neill and Carlotta were reunited, after his stay in the hospital and move to Boston, Saxe was barred from O'Neill's life by Carlotta. Saxe, knowing that she would intercept any birthday greeting from him, had Dorothy send one in her own name. O'Neill's birthday was October 16.

45. [Dorothy Commins's note] Casa Genotta, built in the depth of the Depression with nonunion help, cost about $100,000 (today it would take several million for such a residence); Tao House, including house, some 150 acres, swimming pool and road building, also came to almost $100,000. The Marblehead place, relatively small and ordinary, cost so much, nearly $90,000, not only because home-building costs soared after World War II but because the O'Neills were in a hurry to move in, something that led to extra expense for overtime labor.

46. This is, of course, Cerf's opinion. The reasons for O'Neill's abandonment of his children were complex. At least at first, O'Neill strongly disapproved of Oona's marriage to Charlie Chaplin, a close friend of Carlotta O'Neill's former husband, Ralph Barton, and a man who was thirty-six years older than Oona. Although he never reconciled with her, there is some evidence that his attitude toward her softened later in his life (see chapter 58).

47. For information on Russel Crouse, see the headnote to chapter 61.

48. Irving Berlin (1888–1989) was one of the greatest American songwriters of the twentieth century. He wrote an estimated 1,500 songs and nineteen Broadway shows. Among his best-known songs are "White Christmas" (1941), the best-selling single record of all time, and "God Bless America" (1938). Ellin Mackay Berlin (1903–1988) was Berlin's second wife, a well-known society heiress.

49. Burl Ives (1909–1995) made his reputation as a folk singer before he was cast in Tennessee Williams's *Cat on a Hot Tin Roof* (1955), which began a successful stage and film career as an actor.

50. Crabtree refers to three musicals. Two are by Richard Rodgers (1902–1979) and Oscar Hammerstein II (1895–1960): *Oklahoma!* opened March 31, 1943, and ran for 2,212 performances on Broadway; *Carousel* opened April 19, 1945, and ran for 890 performances. *Annie Get Your Gun* by Irving Berlin, Dorothy Fields (1905–1974), and Herbert Fields (1897–1958) opened May 16, 1946 and ran for 1,147 performances.

51. William Saroyan (1908–1981), a fiction writer and playwright, began his theater career with the Group Theatre's production of *My Heart's in the Highlands* (1939). His most successful play, the Pulitzer Prize–winning *The Time of Your Life* (1940), which was produced by the Theatre Guild, is a likely influence on O'Neill's *The Iceman Cometh* (1946). He wrote *Elmer and Lily* in 1939. The American Negro Theatre was formed in Harlem in 1940.

52. This is a reference to O'Neill's third wife, Carlotta Monterey O'Neill.

53. Tom Pedi (1913–1996) played the bartender Rocky Pioggi in the Theatre Guild production of *The Iceman Cometh.*

54. In the Theatre Guild production, Pearl was played by Ruth Gilbert (1912–

1993), Harry Hope by Dudley Digges (1879–1947), Larry Slade by Carl Benton Reid (1893–1973), Theodore Hickman (Hickey) by James Barton (1890–1962), and Willie Oban by E. G. Marshall (1910–1998).

55. Robert Edmond Jones was the scene designer for *The Iceman Cometh.* For more information on him, see Biographical Sketches of Important Names.

56. The publication of *The Iceman Cometh* was announced in February 1946. The play premiered on October 9.

57. James Barton was a well-known vaudevillian and character actor. He was fifty-six when he played Hickey in *The Iceman Cometh.*

58. Joseph Marr (1916–1998) was a British actor. He played the bartender Chuck Morello in *The Iceman Cometh.*

59. Earle Larimore had a long and distinguished career as an actor, including several important roles in the Theatre Guild's productions of O'Neill's plays: Sam Evans in *Strange Interlude* (1928), Marco Polo in a revival of *Marco Millions* (1930), Orin Mannon in *Mourning Becomes Electra* (1931), and John in *Days Without End* (1934). He replaced E. G. Marshall as Willie Oban in *The Iceman Cometh* when Marshall replaced James Barton as Hickey. He died October 22, 1947.

60. The Theatre Guild's 1947 production of *A Moon for the Misbegotten* closed before it reached New York.

61. James Howard Dunn (1901–1967), who played Jim Tyrone in the Theatre Guild's 1947 production of *A Moon for the Misbegotten,* was mainly a film actor best known for his role as the feckless father in *A Tree Grows in Brooklyn* (1945), a performance that won him an Academy Award as Best Supporting Actor.

62. The play *Tobacco Road* (1933) was adapted by Jack Kirkland from the Erskine Caldwell (1903–1987) novel by the same name (1932). When the play closed in 1941, after more than three thousand performances, it was the longest-running play in the history of the Broadway theater up to that time. The poor Irish American farmers in *A Moon for the Misbegotten* seem to have been viewed by some audiences as a New England analogue for the notoriously degenerate poor white Southerners in Kirkland's play.

## Part 6

1. Feodor Ivanovich Chaliapin (1873–1938) was a Russian opera star known for his powerful and expressive bass voice.

2. The English translation of the Latin phrase is "Hail and farewell."

3. Merrill Moore (1903–1957) was a prominent psychiatrist practicing in Boston. He was well known as a prolific poet, one who, it is speculated, wrote as many as fifty thousand sonnets.

4. [Dorothy Commins's note] Random House published *A Moon for the Misbegotten* in 1952. After O'Neill's death Carlotta gave the publication rights of *A Touch of the Poet* and *Long Day's Journey Into Night* to Yale University, and they were published in 1957 and 1956, respectively, by Yale University Press.

5. Melville Henry Cane (1879–1980) was a poet as well as a lawyer specializing

in copyright law. A number of writers, including Sinclair Lewis, William Saroyan, and Thomas Wolfe (1900–1938), trusted him with their legal affairs.

6. Earlier in the interview, Carlotta had shown Peck the inscription that was to be published with the play: "For Carlotta, on our 12th Wedding Anniversary. Dearest: I give you the original script of this play of old sorrow, written in tears and blood. A sadly inappropriate gift, it would seem, for a day celebrating happiness. But you will understand. I mean it as a tribute to your love and tenderness which gave me the faith in love that enabled me to face my dead at last and write this play—write it with deep pity and understanding and forgiveness for *all* the four haunted Tyrones. These twelve years, Beloved One, have been a Journey into Light—into love. You know my gratitude. And my love!"

7. Carlotta O'Neill's account is contradicted by a letter she wrote to Russel Crouse's wife, Anna Erskine Crouse (1916–2014), shortly after O'Neill's death: "I have but one reason to live & that is to carry out Gene's wishes. I have my Eugene O'Neill Collection to put in order. What I call the 'twenty-five-year box' is the most interesting part of it— all personal except *Long Day's Journey Into Night*— & not to be opened until twenty-five years after Gene's death" (Louis Sheaffer, *O'Neill: Son and Artist*, 635).

8. Peck refers to the suicide of Eugene O'Neill Jr., and the alienation of Shane and Oona O'Neill, whom O'Neill cut out of his life in the 1940s.

9. The O'Neill's lawyer at the time was William Aronberg. See chapter 55 for Saxe Commins's account of this call.

10. Jean M. Welton was O'Neill's nurse and Carlotta's confidante during the years in Boston.

11. The funeral director, J. S. Waterman on Kenmore Square, was indeed only two blocks from the Shelton Hotel.

12. For a detailed explanation of the negotiations over the production and publication of *Long Day's Journey Into Night*, see Brenda Murphy, *O'Neill: Long Day's Journey Into Night*, 2–11. In a letter to Cerf on June 13, 1951 (after Eugene Jr.'s death), O'Neill reiterated his wish that *Long Day's Journey Into Night* was "to be published twenty-five years after my death—but never produced as a play" (*Selected Letters of Eugene O'Neill*, ed. Travis Board and Jackson R. Bryer, 589).

13. Approximately a thousand volumes from the Eugene and Carlotta O'Neill personal library are located at the B. Davis Schwartz Memorial Library of the C. W. Post Campus of Long Island University in Brookville, New York.

14. *O'Neill*, by Arthur Gelb (1924–2014) and Barbara (Stone) Gelb (b. 1926), was published in 1962.

15. An autopsy performed on Eugene O'Neill revealed that he indeed did not have Parkinson's disease, but cerebellar cortical atrophy (see part 3, note 28).

16. Robert Lee Patterson Jr. (1907–1994), a graduate of the Harvard Medical School in 1932 who trained at the Harvard teaching hospitals, was an orthopedic surgeon in New York City. He was surgeon-in-chief at the Hospital for Special Surgery from 1963 until his retirement in 1972.

17. This was probably Saxe Commins. See chapter 55.

18. Henry Leo Kozol (1906–2008), a neurologist whose work helped to establish the fields of forensic psychiatry and neuropsychiatry, practiced at Massachusetts General and Boston City Hospitals and saw patients until he was eighty-four years old. He became widely known for his examination of Albert DeSalvo (1931–1973), the so-called Boston Strangler, and his expert testimony at the 1976 trial of Patty Hearst (b. 1954).

19. This is a reference to O'Neill's day nurse at Salem Hospital, Mrs. Claire Bird.

20. WQXR is a classical music station in New York City.

21. Howard and Dorothy are Crouse's partner Howard Lindsay and his wife, Dorothy Stickney, (1896–1998), who played the leading roles in *Life with Father*. There is a fuller account of this party in chapter 52.

22. *Annie Get Your Gun*, the hit musical with lyrics and music by Irving Berlin, and starring the singer and actor Ethel Merman (1908–1984), fictionalizes the biography of the legendary sharpshooter Annie Oakley (1860–1926) and her husband, Frank Butler. It opened at the Imperial Theatre on May 16, 1946.

23. For a fuller account of this party, see chapter 52.

24. Born in 1947, Timothy Crouse is a journalist and writer for, among other journals, *Rolling Stone, Esquire,* the *New Yorker*, and the *Village Voice*. He is the author of the well-known satiric account of the journalists who covered the 1972 United States presidential campaign, *The Boys on the Bus* (1973). In 1987 he and John Weidman revisited the original collaboration of Russel Crouse and Howard Lindsay on *Anything Goes*, revising the libretto for a production that ran for 784 performances at Lincoln Center.

25. Sardi's is a fabled restaurant in Manhattan's theater district, located at 234 West 44th Street since its founding in 1927.

26. Joseph Hamilton Basso (1904–1964) was an American novelist and journalist. His most famous novel, *The View from Pompey's Head* (1954), was on the *New York Times* best-seller list for forty weeks. It is believed by some that its portrait of a writer is based on O'Neill. Basso wrote a profile of O'Neill, "The Tragic Sense."

27. Doctors Hospital was at 170 East End Avenue, between 87th and 88th Streets, New York City.

28. Mostly likely, Crouse's wife, Anna Erskine Crouse.

29. Charles O'Brien Kennedy. See chapter 25.

30. Queries in the October 4 and October 17 entries appear in the typescript.

31. Robert Whitehead (1916–2002) was a Broadway producer known for his high literary standards, producing many plays by Arthur Miller and Tennessee Williams, as well as Eugene O'Neill's *A Touch of the Poet* in 1958 and *Marco Millions* in 1964. With director Elia Kazan (1909–2003), he founded the first theater company at Lincoln Center.

32. O'Neill's play *Days Without End* was produced by the Theatre Guild, premiering January 8, 1934.

33. In *Days Without End*, Elsa Loving walks out into the cold with the hope of

literally catching her death by pneumonia after she discovers her husband's infidelity. Although she does catch pneumonia, there is no indication that she dies. It is not clear why the Catholic writers would have wanted her to die.

34. *The Prescott Proposals*, by Howard Lindsay and Russel Crouse, played in Boston from November 16 until November 30, 1953.

35. Elisabeth "Bessie" Marbury (1856–1933 ) was a literary and theatrical agent from a prominent family who lived openly for twenty years in what was generally viewed as a lesbian relationship with socialite Elsie de Wolfe (1865–1950). Carlotta was staying with her in Maine when she became reacquainted with Eugene O'Neill in 1926.

36. Carlotta Monterey divorced her second husband, Ralph Barton, in 1926.

37. This is a reference to McLean Hospital in Belmont, Massachusetts, where Carlotta was committed in 1951.

38. Van Vechten is referring to *Ah, Wilderness!*, in which Cohan made a hit as Nat Miller.

39. Australian-born Dame Judith Anderson (1898–1992) was one of the most highly respected English actors of the twentieth century. She replaced Alice Brady as Lavinia Mannon in the Theatre Guild's New York production of *Mourning Becomes Electra* on May 9, 1932.

40. Carlotta Monterey O'Neill's rewritten diaries are in the Beinecke Rare Book and Manuscript Library, Yale University.

41. Lawrence Langner wrote about O'Neill in his memoir (see chapter 37). It is not the kind of affidavit that Van Vechten describes.

# Works Cited


Aristophanes. *Lysistrata*. London: L. Smithers, 1896.

Atkinson, Brooks. Journal Entry. Typescript. Louis Sheaffer Collection of Eugene O'Neill Materials, Department of Special Collections, Charles E. Shain Library, Connecticut College, New London.

———. "O'Neill Off Duty." *New York Times* 8 October 1933: X1.

Baker, George Pierce, ed. *Modern American Plays*. Boston: Little, Brown, 1915.

Basso, Hamilton. "The Tragic Sense." *New Yorker* 24 (28 February 1948), 34–45, (6 March 1948) 34–49, (13 March 1948), 37–47.

Baudelaire, Charles. *The Poems of Charles Baudelaire*. Trans. F. P. Sturm. London: Walter Scott, 1906.

Beach, Lewis. *The Goose Hangs High*. New York: Samuel French, 1924.

———. *A Square Peg*. Boston: Little, Brown, 1924.

Bentley, Eric. *The Brecht Commentaries*: 1943–1986. New York: Grove, 1987.

———. *A Century of Hero Worship: A Study of the Ideal of Heroism in Carlyle and Nietzsche*. Philadelphia: Lippincott, 1944.

———. *The Playwright as Thinker: A Study of Drama in Modern Times*. New York: Reynal & Hitchcock, 1946.

———. "Trying to Like O'Neill." *Kenyon Review* 14 (July 1952): 476–92.

Black, Stephen. *Eugene O'Neill: Beyond Mourning and Tragedy*. New Haven: Yale UP, 1999.

Boulton, Agnes. "The First Stone." *Young's Magazine* (July 1918): 63–75.

———. "Harry and George." *Young's Magazine* (September 1918): 368–79.

———. *Part of a Long Story: Eugene O'Neill as a Young Man in Love*. London: Peter Davies, 1958.

———. "The Primrose Path." *Breezy Stories* (June 1918): 112–17.

———. "To Have Your Cake and Eat It." *Breezy Stories* (May 1918): 311–17.

Bowen, Croswell, assisted by Shane O'Neill. *The Curse of the Misbegotten: A Tale of the House of O'Neill*. New York: McGraw-Hill, 1959.

Braggiotti, Mary. "Little Girl with a Big Ideal." *New York Post* 20 December 1946: 6.

Brewer, Thalia. Interview Notes with Maxine Edie Benedict, 18 October 1977. Louis Sheaffer Collection of Eugene O'Neill Materials, Department of Special Collections, Charles E. Shain Library, Connecticut College, New London.

Brown, Susan Jenkins. *Robber Rocks: Letters and Memories of Hart Crane, 1923–1932*. Middletown, CT: Wesleyan UP, 1969.

Burlingame, Michael. *Abraham Lincoln: A Life*. Baltimore: Johns Hopkins UP, 2008.
———. *The Inner World of Abraham Lincoln*. Urbana: U of Illinois P, 1994.
———. *Lincoln and the Civil War*. Carbondale: Southern Illinois UP, 2011.
———. "O'Neill Recalled Warmly." *Day* [New London] 21 July 1988: E1.
Burnett, Frances Hodgson. *Little Lord Fauntleroy*. New York: Scribner's, 1919.
Cargill, Oscar, ed. *O'Neill and His Plays: Four Decades of Criticism*. New York: New York UP, 1961.
Cerf, Bennett. *At Random: The Reminiscences of Bennett Cerf*. New York: Random House, 1977.
Clark, Barrett H. *Eugene O'Neill: The Man and His Plays*. 1926. New York: Dover, 1946.
———. *European Theories of the Drama*. Cincinnati: Stewart & Kidd, 1919.
Clark, Barrett H., ed. *Representative One-Act Plays by British and Irish Authors*. Boston: Little, Brown, 1921.
Clark, Barrett H., and George Freedley. *A History of Modern Drama*. New York: Appleton-Century, 1947.
Cobb, Irvin S. *Exit Laughing*. New York: Garden City, 1942.
Coleridge, Samuel Taylor. "The Rime of the Ancient Mariner." William Wordsworth and Samuel Taylor Colderidge. *The Lyrical Ballads*. London: T. N. Longman, 1798. 1–51.
Commins, Saxe. *"Love and Admiration and Respect": The O'Neill-Commins Correspondence*. Ed. Dorothy Commins. Durham: Duke UP, 1986.
Conrad, Joseph. *Lord Jim*. London: Blackwood, 1900.
Corbett, Scott. *The Sea Fox*. New York: Crowell, 1956.
Corelli, Marie. *Wormwood, a Drama of Paris*. London: Bentley, 1890.
Cowley, Malcom. *Blue Juniata*. New York: J. Cape and H. Smith, 1929.
———. *Exile's Return: A Narrative of Ideas*. New York: Norton, 1934.
———. *The Viking Portable Faulkner*. New York: Viking, 1946.
———. "A Weekend with Eugene O'Neill." *Reporter* 5 September 1947: 33–36.
Crane, Hart. *The Bridge*. New York: H. Liveright. 1930
———. *The Letters of Hart Crane 1916–1932*. Ed. Brom Weber. Berkeley: U of California P, 1965.
———. *White Buildings: Poems by Hart Crane*. New York: Boni & Liveright, 1926.
Craven, Thomas. "Have Painters Minds?" *American Mercury* March 1927: 257–62.
Crawford, F. Marion. *The White Sister*. New York: Macmillan, 1909.
Crawford, F. Marion, and Walter Hackett. *The White Sister: A Romantic Drama in Three Acts*. New York: Dramatists Play Service, 1937.
Crouse, Russel. "Extracts from the Diaries of Russel Crouse: Eugene O'Neill." Typescript. Eugene O'Neill Collection, Beinecke Rare Book and Manuscript Library, Yale University, New Haven, Connecticut.
Day, Dorothy. *The Long Loneliness: The Autobiography of Dorothy Day*. New York: Harper, 1952.
Deutsch, Helen, and Stella Hanau. *The Provincetown: A Story of the Theatre*. New York: Farrar and Rinehart, 1931.

De Polo, Harold. "Meet Eugene O'Neill—Fisherman." *Outdoor America* May 1928: 5–8.

DeVoto, Bernard. "Minority Report." *Saturday Review of Literature* 21 November 1936: 3.

Dos Passos, John. *Manhattan Transfer*. New York: Harper, 1925.

———. *U. S. A.* New York: Modern Library, 1939.

Dowling, Robert. *Eugene O'Neill: A Life in Four Acts*. New Haven: Yale UP, 2014.

Elkins, Felton B. *Three Tremendous Trifles*. New York: Duffield, 1919.

"Eugene O'Neill Friendship Formed by West Hartford Man while on Shipboard." *Hartford Courant* 14 October 1929: 14.

Fechter, Charles. *Monte Cristo*. 1883. Ed. Anne Dhu McLucas. New York: Garland, 1994.

Ferber, Edna. *Showboat*. New York: Grosset & Dunlap, 1926.

Fitzgerald, F. Scott. *The Beautiful and Damned*. New York: Scribner's, 1922.

———. *The Great Gatsby*. New York: Scribner's, 1925.

———. *This Side of Paradise*. New York: Scribner's, 1920.

Floyd, Virginia. *Eugene O'Neill: A World View*. New York: Frederick Ungar, 1979.

Frank, Waldo. *Rahab*. 1922. New York: Boni & Liveright, 1926.

———. *Virgin Spain: Scenes from the Spiritual Drama of a Great People*. New York: Boni & Liveright, 1926.

Galsworthy, John. *The Forsyte Saga*. New York: Scribner's, 1922.

Gardner, Virginia. *"Friend and Lover": The Life of Louise Bryant*. New York: Horizon, 1982.

———. *The Rosenberg Story*. New York: Masses and Mainstream, 1954.

Gelb, Arthur and Barbara. *O'Neill*. New York: Harper, 1962.

———. *O'Neill*. Enl. ed. New York: Harper and Row, 1973.

———. *O'Neill: Life with Monte Cristo*. New York: Applause, 2000.

Glaspell, Susan. *The Complete Plays*. Ed. Linda Ben-Zvi and J. Ellen Gainor. Jefferson: McFarland, 2010.

———. *The Road to the Temple*. New York: Frederic A. Stokes, 1927.

Goethe, Johann Wolfgang von. *Die Leiden des jungen Werthers*. Leipzig: Weygandschen Buchhandlung, 1774.

Gold, Michael. *Jews without Money*. New York: H. Liveright, 1930.

Gordon, Max, with Lewis Funke. *Max Gordon Presents*. New York: Bernard Geis, 1963.

Hamilton, Clayton. *Conversations on Contemporary Drama*. New York: Macmillan, 1925.

———. "A Shelf of Printed Plays." *Bookman* April 1915: 178–84.

———. *"So You're Writing a Play!"* Boston: Little, Brown, 1935.

———. *The Theory of the Theatre, and Other Principles of Dramatic Criticism*. New York: H. Holt, 1910.

Hapgood, Hutchins. *An Anarchist Woman*. New York: Duffield, 1909.

———. *A Victorian in the Modern World*. New York: Harcourt, Brace, 1939.

Hastings, Warren H., and Richard F. Weeks. "Episodes of Eugene O'Neill's Undergraduate Days at Princeton." *Princeton University Library Chronicle* 293 (Spring 1968): 208–15.

Hawthorne, Hazel. *Salt House*. New York: Frederick A. Stokes, 1934.

———. *Three Women*. New York: E. P. Dutton, 1938.

Helburn, Theresa. "O'Neill: An Impression," *Saturday Review of Literature* 21 November 1936: 10.

———. *A Wayward Quest: The Autobiography of Theresa Helburn*. Boston: Little, Brown, 1960.

Hoffman, Calvin. *The Man Who Was Shakespeare*. London: M. Parrish, 1955.

———. "Of Eugene O'Neill Remembered." Typescript. Louis Sheaffer Collection of Eugene O'Neill Materials, Department of Special Collections, Charles E. Shain Library, Connecticut College, New London.

Holland, Hugh. "Upon the Lines and Life of the Famous Scenicke [*sic*] Poet, Master William Shakespeare." *Mr. William Shakespeares Comedies, Histories, & Tragedies, Published according to the True Original Copies*. London: Isaac Laggard and Ed Bount, 1623.

Howard, Bronson. *Shenandoah: A Military Comedy in Four Acts*. New York: Samuel French, 1897.

*I'll Take My Stand: The South and the Agrarian Tradition*. By Twelve Southerners. New York: Harper and Row, 1930.

Joyce, James. *Dubliners*. London: G. Richards, 1914.

Kemp, Harry. "O'Neill as an Actor Is Recalled by One Who Saw Him in '17." *New York Herald Tribune* 17 March 1929, sec. 7: 5.

———. "O'Neill of Provincetown." *Brentano's Book Chat* May–June, 1929: 45–47.

———. *Tramping on Life: An Autobiographical Narrative*. New York: Boni & Liveright, 1922.

Kennedy, Charles O'Brien, ed. *American Ballads: Naughty, Ribald, and Classic*. New York: Fawcett, 1952.

———. "Eugene O'Neill." *Lambs' Script* March & April 1954: 1–4.

King, William Davies. *Another Part of a Long Story: Literary Traces of Eugene O'Neill and Agnes Boulton*. Ann Arbor: U of Michigan P, 2010.

Komroff, Manuel. *Coronet*. New York: Coward-McCann, 1929.

Kreymborg, Alfred. *Lima Beans: A Scherzo Play in One Act*. New York: Samuel French, 1925.

———. *Troubadour*. New York: Boni & Liveright, 1925.

Langner, Lawrence. *The Magic Curtain: The Story of a Life in Two Fields, Theatre and Invention, by the Founder of the Theatre Guild*. New York: E. P. Dutton, 1951.

Lardner, John. *The John Lardner Reader: A Press Box Legend's Classic Sportswriting*. Ed. John Schulian. Lincoln: U of Nebraska P, 2010.

———. "O'Neill's Back." *Look* 26 February 1952.

La Rochefoucauld, François VI, duc de. *Ouvres Complètes*. Texte etablie et annoté par L. Martin-Chauffier. Paris: Gallimard, 1950.

Latimer, Frederick P. "Eugene Is beyond Us." *Day* [New London] 15 February 1928: 2.

Lewis, Sinclair. *Babbitt*. New York: Harcourt Brace, 1922.

———. *Main Street*. New York: Harcourt Brace, 1920.

Loving, Pierre. "Eugene O'Neill." *Bookman* August 1921: 511–13.

———. *Monsieur de Balzac Entertains a Visitor*. Seattle: U of Washington Bookstore, 1929.

———. *The Stick-Up: A Rough-Neck Fantasy*. Cincinnati: Stewart Kidd, 1922.

MacLane, Mary. *I, Mary MacLane: A Diary of Human Days*. New York: F. A. Stokes, 1917.

Manners, J. Hartley. *Peg O' My Heart: A Comedy of Youth*. New York: Grosset and Dunlap, 1913.

Masefield, John. *Salt-Water Poems and Ballads*. 1916. New York: Macmillan, 1936.

Masters, Edgar Lee. *Spoon River Anthology*. New York: Macmillan, 1944.

Maugham, W. Somerset. *Caesar's Wife: A Comedy in Three Acts*. London: Heineman, 1922.

McGinley, Arthur B. "Columnist Recalls Eugene O'Neill as Dreamy Reporter in New London." *New Haven Evening Register* 28 November 1953: 48.

Mencken, H. L. *The Artist: A Drama without Words*. Boston: J. W. Luce, 1912.

———. *A Book of Burlesques*. 1916. New York: Knopf, 1921.

Monteiro, George. "James Tyrone's Packard in *Long Day's Journey Into Night*." *Notes on Contemporary Literature* 42 May 2012: 4–6.

Murphy, Brenda. *O'Neill: Long Day's Journey Into Night*. Cambridge and New York: Cambridge UP, 2001.

Nathan, Adele. Letter to the Editor. "Eugene G. O'Neill: 1916." *New York Times Magazine* 6 October 1946: 18.

Nathan, George Jean. "The Bright Face of Tragedy." *Cosmopolitan* August 1957: 66–69.

———. *The Intimate Notebooks of George Jean Nathan*. New York: Alfred A. Knopf, 1932.

O'Casey, Sean. *The Letters of Sean O'Casey*. Vols. III–IV. Ed. David Krause. Washington, DC: The Catholic U of America P, 1989–1992.

———. *Mirror in My House: The Autobiographies of Sean O'Casey*. New York: Macmillan, 1956.

———. *Rose and Crown*. New York: Macmillan, 1952.

"O'Neill Bad Actor, Stage Hand Recalls." *Hartford Courant* April 3, 1929: 18.

O'Neill, Eugene. "Are the Actors to Blame?" Helen Deutsch and Stella Hanau. *The Provincetown: A Story of the Theatre*. Farrar and Rinehart, 1931. 198.

———. *Complete Plays*. Ed. Travis Bogard. 3 vols. New York: Library of America, 1988.

———. *Eugene O'Neill at Work: Newly Released Ideas for Plays*. Ed. Virginia Floyd. New York: Frederick Ungar, 1981.

———. *Exorcism*. *New Yorker* 17 October 2011: 72–80.

———. *The Last Will and Testament of Silverdene Emblem O'Neill*. New Haven: Yale UP, 1956.

———. *The Lost Plays of Eugene O'Neill*. New York: Citadel, 1963.

———. *More Stately Mansions*. Shortened from the author's partly rev. script by Karl Ragnar Gierow and edited by Donald Gallup. New Haven: Yale UP, 1964.

———. *Poems 1912–1944*. Ed. Donald Gallup. Boston: Ticknor & Fields, 1980.

———. *Selected Letters of Eugene O'Neill*. Ed. Travis Bogard and Jackson R. Bryer. New Haven: Yale UP, 1988.

———. *"The Theatre We Worked For": The Letters of Eugene O'Neill to Kenneth Macgowan*. Ed. Jackson R. Bryer, with the assistance of Ruth M. Alvarez and introductory essays by Travis Bogard. New Haven: Yale UP, 1982.

———. *Thirst, and Other One-Act Plays*. Boston: Gorham P, 1914.

———. *Work Diary 1924–1943*. Ed. Donald Gallup. 2 vols. New Haven: Yale U Library, 1981.

Peck, Seymour. Excerpts from an Interview with Carlotta Monterey O'Neill. 2 October 1956. Transcript in Louis Sheaffer Collection of Eugene O'Neill Materials, Department of Special Collections, Charles E. Shain Library, Connecticut College, New London.

———. "Talk with Mrs. O'Neill." *New York Times* 4 November 1956. Proquest Historical Newspapers, 141.

Price, B. H., and E. P. Richardson Jr. "The Neurological Illness of Eugene O'Neill—A Clinicopathological Report." *New England Journal of Medicine* 342 (13 April 2000): 1126–33.

Rand, Ayn. *The Night of January 16th*. New York: Longman, Green, 1936.

Reed, John. *Ten Days That Shook the World*. New York: Boni & Liveright, 1919.

Ryan, Paul. "Eugene O'Neill: A Hundred Years On." *Drama: The Quarterly Theatre Review* 4 (1988): 27–30.

Shakespeare, William. *Mr. William Shakespeares Comedies, Histories, & Tragedies, Published according to the True Original Copies*. London: Isaac Laggard and Ed Bount, 1623.

Schriftgiesser, Karl. "The Iceman Cometh." *New York Times* 6 October 1946: X1, 3

———. *Families: From the Adamses to the Roosevelts*. New York: Howell, Soskin, 1940.

———. *The Lobbyists: The Art and Business of Influencing Lawmakers*. Boston: Little, Brown, 1951.

———. *This Was Normalcy: An Account of Party Politics during Twelve Republican Years, 1920–1932*. Boston: Little, Brown, 1948.

Sheaffer, Louis. Notes from interviews with Kathleen Pitt-Smith, Mrs. Mabel Haynes, Manuel Zora, Rouben Mamoulian, Karl Schriftgiesser, Sallie Coughlin, Carl Van Vechten, Beatrice Ashe Maher, Dorothy Day, Dr. Frederic B. Mayo, Paul Crabtree, and Russel Crouse in the Louis Sheaffer Collection of Eugene O'Neill Materials, Department of Special Collections, Charles E. Shain Library, Connecticut College, New London.

———. *O'Neill: Son and Artist*. Boston: Little, Brown, 1973.

———. *O'Neill: Son and Playwright*. Boston: Little, Brown, 1968.

Sheldon, Edward. *The Nigger: An American Play in Three Acts*. New York: Macmillan, 1915.

Stekel, Wilhelm. *Disguises of Love: Psycho-Analytical Sketches*. Trans. Rosalie Gabler. London: Paul, Trench, Truber, 1922.

Stoeckel, Herbert J. "Memories of Eugene O'Neill." *Hartford Courant* 6 December 1953, Sunday Magazine: 3, 16.

———. *The Strange Story of John Hanson, First President of the United States.* Hartford: Hanson House, 1956.

Sullivan, Dan. "Friend of Eugene O'Neill Tells of Dramatist's Tie to Brother." *New York Times* 31 July 1967: 21.

Throckmorton, Juliet. "As I Remember Eugene O'Neill." *Yankee Magazine* August 1968: 85, 93–95.

Tyler, George C., in collaboration with J. C. Furnas. *Whatever Goes Up.* Indianapolis: Bobbs-Merrill, 1934.

Van Vechten, Carl. *Letters of Carl Van Vechten.* Ed. Bruce Kellner. New Haven: Yale UP, 1987.

Vorse, Mary Heaton. *Time and the Town: A Provincetown Chronicle.* New York: Dial, 1942.

*Washington Square Plays 1.* Garden City: Doubleday, 1916.

Wassermann, Jakob. *The World's Illusion.* Trans. Ludwig Lewisohn. New York: Harcourt, Brace and Howe, 1920.

Weaver, John V. A. "I Knew Him When—." *New York Sunday World* 26 February 1926. Rpt. *O'Neill and His Plays: Four Decades of Criticism.* Ed. Oscar Cargill, N. Bryllion Fagin, and William J. Fisher. New York: New York UP, 1961.

Welch, Mary. "Softer Tones for Mr. O'Neill's Portrait." *Theatre Arts* May 1957: 67–68.

Werner, Hazel Hawthorne. "Recollections." Typescript. Louis Sheaffer Collection of Eugene O'Neill Materials, Department of Special Collections, Charles E. Shain Library, Connecticut College, New London.

Wilde, Oscar. *Salome.* London: E. Mathews & J. Lane, 1894.

Williams, Tennessee. *The Glass Menagerie.* New York: Random House, 1945.

Williams, William Carlos. Letter to Louis Sheaffer, 19 April 1957. Louis Sheaffer Collection of Eugene O'Neill Materials, Department of Special Collections, Charles E. Shain Library, Connecticut College, New London.

Wilson, Edmund. *The Twenties: From Notebooks and Diaries of the Period.* Ed. Leon Edel. New York: Farrar, Straus and Giroux, 1975.

Woodworth, Robert A. "The World's Worst Reporter." *Providence Journal* 6 December 1931, Sunday Magazine: 3.

Woolf, S. J. "Eugene O'Neill Returns after Twelve Years." *New York Times Magazine* 15 September 1946: 6.

Young, Stark. "Eugene O'Neill: Notes from a Critic's Diary." *Harper's Magazine* June 1957: 66–71, 74.

———. *So Red the Rose.* New York: Scribner's, 1934.

# Index


Abbey Theatre, xviii, 215
Abbott, George Francis, 47, 172, 340n54
Abercrombie and Fitch, 284
*Abortion* (O'Neill), 49, 327n22
*Abraham Lincoln: A Life* (Burlingame), 283
Academy Awards, 31, 347n61
Academy of Design, 224
Achilles (heel), 137
Adams, Major, 195, 196
Adams, Samuel "Sam" Hopkins, 147, 336n9
Aeschylus, 139, 235, 336n89
*Ah, Wilderness!* (O'Neill), xvii, xviii, 36, 91, 103, 141, 149, 155, 158–60, 163, 169, 350n394
Aiken, Conrad, 136, 335n83
*Ainslee's* (magazine), 80
Alta Bates Summit Medical Center, 342n78
"Alexander's Ragtime Band," 250
*All God's Chillun Got Wings* (O'Neill), xvi, 50, 90, 119, 190, 191, 314
Allen, Viola, 37, 325n32
*Allison's House* (Glaspell), 51
ALS (illness), 224
America (American, Americans, Americana), 115, 119, 132, 134, 138, 148, 151, 152, 157, 163, 165, 176, 177, 188, 191, 196, 201, 204, 213, 214, 215, 217, 218, 219, 221, 229, 235, 257, 261, 282, 295, 305
*American Ballads: Naughty, Ribald, and Classic* (Kennedy), 92
American Field Service, 110
American Negro Theatre, 252, 346n51
American Theater (St. Louis, Missouri), 20
*An Anarchist Woman* (Hapgood), 56
Anarchists, 221, 344n27
Anarcho-Syndicalists, 344n27
Ancient Mariner (character), 35
Anders, Glen, 154
Anderson, Judith, 304, 350n39
Anderson, Maxwell, 148, 337n15
Anheuser-Busch, 187
*Animal Farm* (Orwell), 344n18
*"Anna Christie" (Anna Christie)* (O'Neill), xv, xvii, 29, 32, 49, 50, 77, 84, 85, 113, 114, 118, 132, 144, 146, 173, 195, 212, 213, 322n9, 323n17, 331n22, 343n14
*Anna Christie* (film), 336n5
*Annie Get Your Gun* (Berlin, Fields and Fields), 252, 296, 300, 301, 346n50, 349n22
Anthony, Dion (character), 134, 135
*Anything Goes* (Lindsay and Crouse), 295, 349n24
*Anything Goes* (Lindsay and Crouse; revision by Timothy Crouse and John Weldman), 295, 349n24
Arc de Triomphe (Paris), 196
Arlington National Cemetery, 45
Aronberg, W. E., 266, 267, 269, 288, 298, 300, 348n9
Art Association, 83
Art Students League (New York), 53
Arthur B. McGinley Award for Service to Profession and Community, 36
*The Artist* (Mencken), 68, 328n40
"Ashcan School" (painting), 321n3
Ashe (Maher), Beatrice, xiv, 3, 43, 45–46, 323n20, 325n3, 326n5
Astor, Nancy (character in *Winston Churchill*), 211
Atkinson, Justin Brooks, 130–31, 141, 158–60, 216, 218, 280, 339n39
Atkinson, Oriana, 218

Atlantic House, 55
"Auld Lang Syne" (Burns), 344n24
*Austin Statesman* (newspaper), 198
Avellar (Mrs.), 99

B. Davis Schwartz Memorial Library of the C. W. Post Campus of Long Island University (Brookville, New York), 348n13
*Back to Methuselah* (Shaw), 152, 337n23
Badger, Richard, 30, 135
Baird, Marguerite Frances ("Peggy"), 113, 116, 333n57
Baker, George Pierce, 4, 30, 31, 43, 45, 47–49, 165, 206, 313. *See also* Drama 47 Workshop (Baker's Harvard Workshop)
Baker, Phil, 193, 341n74
Ballantine, Stella, 100, 332n44
Ballantine, Edward J. ("Ted"), 100, 332n44
Ballard, John Frederick, 47, 326n13
Baltimore (Maryland), 66, 68
Barclay (Hotel Barclay), 163, 237, 239
Barkan, Hans (Dr.), 199
Barnard College, 28
Barnum, P. T., 79
Barret House, 233
Barry, Philip, 258
Barrymore, Ethel, 258
Barrymore, John, 92, 326n13
Barrymore, Lionel, 92
Barton, James, 255, 346–47n54, 347n57, 347n59
Barton, Ralph, xvii, 148, *182*, 301, 304, 305, 314, 337n12, 337n13, 337n14, 346n46, 350n36
*Basic Writings of George Washington* (Dorothy Commins), 345n42
Basques (Basque country), 167, 192
Basso, Joseph Hamilton, 296, 349n26
Baudelaire, Charles, 22, 73, 329n49
Beach, Lewis, 47, 326n15
Beachcombers Club, 83
Beardsley, Aubrey, 45, 325n2
Beatty (nurse), 293
Beauvais, Gaston (character), 321–22n4
Bedini, Vincent, 113, 115, 116
*Before Breakfast* (O'Neill), 58, 64–65, 328n32
Beinecke Rare Book and Manuscript Library, 350n40
Beith, Jimmie, 195, 196, 341n76
Belgrade (Belgrade lakes) (Maine), 122, 124, 127–28, 192, 314–15
Bellevue (hospital), 196
Ben-Ami, Jacob, 151, 337n21
Bendix, William, 341n65
Benedict, Maxine Edie, 141, 198–99
Benedictine (drink), 195
Bennett, Richard, 23
Bennie (husband of Maxine Edie Benedict), 199
Bentley, Eric, 166, 339n46
Benton, Thomas Hart, 331n19
Bergman, Ingrid, 3, 4, 201, 212–14, 343n12, 343n13, 343n14
Berlin, Ellin Mackay, 295, 346n48
Berlin, Irving (Irving Berlins), 250, 295, 301, 346n48, 349n22
Bermuda, xvi, 77, 85, 86, 94, 95, 121, 132, 133, 136, 137, 138, 151, 152, 153, 165, 192, 316, 327n27, 335n79
Betts Academy (Stamford, Connecticut), 154, 234, 338n27
Betty (character in *Threepenny Opera*), 211
*Beyond the Horizon* (O'Neill), xv, 23, 30, 50, 71, 77, 86, 94, 103, 118, 128, 146, 191, 322n9
*The Big Idea* (Hamilton), 28
Bird, Claire, 293, 349n19
Black, Stephen, 2
Blair, Eric Arthur (George Orwell). *See* Orwell, George (Eric Arthur Blair)
Blair, Mary, xvi, 5, 84, 86, 89, 90, 328n32, 330–31n18, 337n15
Blemie (dog), xviii, 209, 343n9
*Blood and Sand*, 161
"Blow the Man Down," 112–13
*Blue Juniata* (Cowley), 110
Bodenheim, Maxwell, 72, 329n48
Bogard, Travis, 45
bohemian (bohemians), 35, 59, 60, 194, 234, 241, 242, 316, 329n43
Boulton, Agnes. *See* O'Neill, Agnes Boulton
Boulton, Cecil, 81, 330n9

Boulton, Edward W., 94, 101
Boni & Liveright (Albert Boni and Horace Liveright), xv, xvi, 46–49, *182*, 237, 334n71, 335n75, 336n8
Book-of-the-Month Club, 282
Booth, Edwin, 36, 324n23
Boothe, Clare, 229
*The Boss* (Sheldon), 345n37
Boston (Massachusetts) (Bostonians), xvi, xx, 30, 36, 48, 105, 135, 143, 203, 220, 236, 238, 247, 263, 269, 271–72, 275, 278, 279–80, 281, 283, 284, 286, 287, 290–93, 296–302, 327n20, 332n36, 336n87, 346n44, 347n3, 348n10, 349n18, 350n34
Boston City Hospitals, 349n18
Boston Strangler. *See* DeSalvo, Albert
*Boston Transcript* (newspaper), 220
*Bound East for Cardiff* (O'Neill), 21, 32, 51, 53, 56, 65, 67–68, 191, 195, 235, 322n8, 323n17, 341n64
Bowen, Crosswell, 1, 114
Bowery (New York), 111
Boyce, Neith, 56, 57, 329n51
*The Boys on the Bus* (Timothy Crouse), 349n24
*Boys Will Be Boys: A Comedy of the Soul of Man Under Prosperity* (Kennedy), 92
Brady, Alice, 204, 227, 342n2, 350n39
Brandstädter, Otto, 216, 344n17
Brecht, Bertolt, 340n52
Breese, Edmund, 37
*The Bridge* (Crane), 118
Broadhurst Theatre, 173
Broadway, xiv, xv, xvi, xviii, 3, 9, 15, 23, 28, 43, 47, 57, 71, 77, 92, 94, 102, 103, 112, 114, 138, 144, 146, 147, 150, 158, 161, 165, 201, 203, 211, 227, 233, 252, 257, 295, 314, 316, 323n22, 324n25, 325n35, 325–26n4, 326nn13–15, 327n23, 330n11, 332n44, 335n80 336n3, 336n11, 337n15, 337n17, 337n21, 339n41, 340nn53–56, 343n11, 346n48, 346n50, 347n62, 349n31
Brook Farm (Ridgefield, Connecticut), 95, 113, 117, 151
Brooklyn (New York), 70, 92
*Brooklyn Daily Eagle*, 18
Brooklyn Dodgers (Beloved Bums), 92, 252, 332n37
Brooks Bros., 254
Broun Jr., Heywood Campbell, 37, 325n31
Brown, Bill (character), 135
Bryan, William Jennings, 79
Bryant, Louise, xiv, 67, 71, 72, 329n43
Bryer, Jackson R., 45, 314
Buck, Gene, 93, 332n41
Buenos Aires (Argentina), 22, 187
Bugatti (racer) (Begotti), 205, 342n3
Buick, 158
Buick Sales and Service. *See* Monte Cristo (car agency)
Buner, P., 299
Bureau of Missing Persons, 117
Burlingame, Michael, 283
Burns, Ric, 2
Burns, Robert, 344n24
Burt, Frederic (Frederick, Fred, Freddie), 51, 53, 327n23
Burton, Barbara, 85, 331n23
Butler, Frank, 349n22
Byron, 173
Byron, Lord, 13

*The Cabinet of Dr. Caligari* (Wiene), 175, 341n63
Cabot, Ephraim (character), 134, 160
Caldwell, Charles (Dr.), 199, 342n79
Caldwell, Erskine, 347n62
Caldwell, Jane, 199, 342n79
Caldwell, Myrtle, 198, 342n79
California, 11, 90, 141, 148, 163, 201, 203, 211, 217, 224, 237, 238, 249, 274, 277, 303
Caliglia (character), 134
*Call* (newspaper), 70
Calvin & Rose G. Hoffman Marlowe Memorial Trust, 132
Camblos, Henry, 19
Camblos, Katie Shaw, 18–19
Cane, Melville Henry, 273, 274–75, 347–48n5
Cape, Michael (character), 337n21

Cape Cod (Massachusetts), 66
Caprimulgi, 158
Carbone, Inc., 283, 284, 286
Caribbean series, 49
Carlin, Terry, xiv, 43, 51, 53, 56, 57–58, 60, 61, 70, 72, 83, 111, 313
Carlyle Hotel, 281
*Carousel* (Rodgers and Hammerstein), 161, 164, 165, 252, 346n50
Caruso, Enrico, 46, 325n6
Casa Genotta (Sea Island, George), xvii, xviii, 154, 155, 169, 303, 315, 346n45
*Casablanca*, 212
Casey, Walter "Ice," 242, 243, 244, 296, 345n38
*Cat on a Hot Tin Roof* (Williams), 346n49
*Catholic Worker* (newspaper), 70
Catholic Writers Guild, 300
Catholicism (Catholics), 12, 37, 70, 73, 148, 286, 349–50n33
*Le Cavalier Polonais* (Rembrandt Harmenszoon van Rejn), 34, 323n19
Cavallini, Margherita (character), 107, 333n51
Cave, M., 299
Cedar Rapids (Iowa), 303
Cellar Players of the Hudson Guild, 66
Cerf, Bennett Alfred, xviii, 2, 3, 141, 146–49, 173, 201, 247, 249–51, 263, 270, 271, 272–73, 275, 281–82, 293, 294, 296, 336n8, 346n43, 346n46, 348n12
Cerf, Phyllis, 250, 270, 281, 282, 296
Chadwick, George Whitefield, 46, 526n8
Chaplin, Charles (Charlie), xix, 1, 138, 285, 304, 313, 346n46
Charles E. Shain Library (Connecticut College), 18
Charles River (Massachusetts), 263
Château du Plessis ("Le Plessis"), xvii, 141, 155, *184*, 188, 195, 206, 315, 336n2, 338n30, 342n3
Chaucer, Geoffrey, 13
Chekov, Anton, 67, 337n21
Chicago (Illinois), 10, 18, 49
*Chicago American* (newspaper), 303
*Chicago Tribune*, 71
Chaliapin, Feodor Ivanovich, 265, 347n1
China (Chinese), 59, 61–62, 141, 167, 168, 193, 212, 224, 239
*Chris* (O'Neill), 9
*Chris Christophersen* (O'Neill), xv, 9, 323n17
Christie, Anna (character), 212, 336n4
Christopherson, Chris (character), 195
Churchill, Winston, 224
City College of New York, 203, 224
Civil War, 169
Clan Chiefs (Irish), 218
Clark, Barrett H., 1, 34, 194, 231
Clark, Fifine ("Gaga"), 58, 81, 114, 116, 327–28n31, 330n8
classics (academic discipline), 109, 265, 315
Cleveland (Ohio), 187, 206, 262
Cleveland, Grover, 124, 335n74
Clytemnestra (character), 191
Coates, Albert, 173, 340n57
Cobb, Irvin Shrewbury, 8, 31–32
Coca-Cola, 193, 194
Cocky (character), 341n64
Cohan, George Michael, 149, 158, 159, 229–30, 304, 337n17, 350n38
Colbert, Claudette, 168, 339n49
Coleridge, Samuel Taylor, 323n21
Collings, Benjamin P. (Collings case), 235–36, 345n35
Collins, James Joseph ("Jimmie"), 92, 332n36
Columbia School of Journalism, 146
Columbia University, 28, 104, 146
Columbus, Ohio, 261, 262
Comédie Française, 109
*comédie humaine* (Balzac), 169, 170. *See also* "A Tale of Possessors Self-Dispossessed" (nine-play cycle) (O'Neill)
Commins, Dorothy, 247, 248, 296, 345nn36–37, 345n40, 345n42, 346nn43–45, 347n4
Commins, Saxe, xiv, 2–3, 149, 201, 237–48, 263, 265–75, 282, 296, 300, 345n42, 346n44, 348n9, 349n17
*Common Clay* (Kinkead), 47, 326n14
"The Commons" (Princeton University), 12–13
Connecticut, xiii, xiv, xv, 7, 90, 113, 159,

231, 232–33, 234, 235, 236, 313, 316, 340n59, 345n35
Connecticut College, 45, 283
Connecticut Sportswriters Alliance, 36
Connecticut State House of Representatives, 33
Connolly, Marc, 9
Conrad, Joseph, 30, 323n14
Cook, George Cram (Jig), xiv, 37, 51, 54, 56, 57, 61, 67, 313, 324n27, 327n24, 330nn11–12
Cook, Harland Edward "Harl," 82, 330n12
Cooks (George and Susan), 53
Cooper, Gary, 162
Cora (character), 211
Corbett, Scott, 88
Corelli, Marie, 16, 321–22n4
Corneille, Pierre, 139, 336n89
Cornell, Katherine, 130, 335n76, 338n24
Cornell University, 187
Corwin, Norman Lewis, 226, 345n30
Coughlin, Sally, 2, 3, 263, 290–94
*The Count of Monte Cristo* (Charles Morey), 11, 20–21, 37, 65, 106, 225, 233, 324n25. *See also* Monte Cristo (character)
Cowley, Malcolm, 3, 77, 110, 333n57
Crabtree, Paul, 3, 4, 201, 252–56, 346n50
Crane, Grace Edna, 118, 120, 334n63
Crane, Harold Hart, 3, 77, 95, 113–20, 333n57, 334n69
*The Crime in the Whistler Room* (Wilson), 89
Craven, Thomas, 85, 331n19
Crillon, 295
Crouse, Anna Erskine, 297, 299, 301, 302, 348n7, 349n28
Crouse, Russel, xviii, 3, 250, 263, 269, 281, 282, 295–302, 348n7, 349n21, 349n24, 349n28, 350n34
Crouse, Timothy, 296, 349n24
the Crucifixion, 167
Cupid, 196
*The Curse of the Misbegotten: A Tale of the House of O'Neill* (Bowen), 1

*The Daily Princetonian*, 12
*Daily Worker* (newspaper), 71
Daks (trousers), 215, 217, 244n15
Danville (California), 141, 198
Davis, Robert Hobart ("Bob"), 121–22, 123, 124, 127, 129, 335n73
*The Day* (newspaper), 33, 39, 283
Day, Dorothy, 3, 70–73, 121
*Days Without End* (O'Neill), xviii, 22, 37, 141, 149, 155, 158, 159, 160, 300, 304. 339n41, 341n72, 347n59, 349n32, 349–50n33
De Beers (company), 338n33
De Polo, Harold, 4, 71, 77, 95, 121–29, 327n27
*Death Valley Days*, 252
Debelleville, Frederick, 37, 324n25
Deborah (character), 343n13
Deeter, Jasper, 77, 102–3
DeHaven, Gloria, 339n44
Dempsey-Tunney (fight), 131, 335n78
Demuth, Charles, 83, 330n17
Denmark (Danish), 154, 208, 286
the Depression, 146, 169, 176, 204, 346n45
DeSalvo, Albert, 349n18
*Desire Under the Elms* (O'Neill), xvi, xvii, 40, 50, 87, 117, 122, 123, 132, 134, 144, 159–60, 191, 314, 334n60, 336n4
Detroit (Michigan), 261–62
DeVoto, Bernard Augustine, 171, 339n50
Dickinson College, 102
*Die Leiden des jungen Werthers* (Goethe), 323n18
*Diff'rent* (O'Neill), 23, 50, 84, 90, 92, 122
Digges, Dudley, 255, 346–47n54
*The Disguises of Love* (Stekel), 114
"Doc" Boyce's (bar), 15
Doctors' Hospital, xx, 164, 244, 245, 269–70, 274, 281, 290–91, 293, 296, 297–98, 349n27
Dodds, Harold Willis, 245, 345n41
Dodge, Mabel, 94, 150, 337n18
*Dodsworth* (Lewis), 229
Dollar Line (steamship company), 143
Dos Passos, John, 82, 330n14
Douglas, Mildred (character), 203
Douglaston (Queens, New York), 18
Dowling, Eddie (Joseph Goucher), xix, 211, 253, 254, 343n11

Dowling, Robert, 2
*Dr. Jeykll and Mr. Hyde*, 161, 324n25
Drama 47 Workshop (Baker's Harvard Workshop), 47, 165, 206
Drama League of New York, 345n31
*Drama Review* (journal), 211
Dreiser, Theodore, 37, 67, 328n36
Driscoll, 195
Driscoll (character), 195, 341n64
*Dubliners* (Joyce), 80, 330n3
*Dulcy* (Kaufman and Connolly), 9
Dunes (Provincetown), 58, 59, 60, 77, 79, 81, 84, 97, 99–100, 150, 151, 324n27
Dunn, James Howard, 260, 261, 347n61
Durgin and Parks (restaurant), 49, 327n20
Dutch, 154, 208
*Dynamo* (O'Neill), xvii, 20, 141, 167–68, 189, 191, 339n41, 339n49, 341n72

Eakins, Thomas, 101, 333n45
Eames, Claire, 119, 334n64, 334n66
East Eighty-Seventh Street (New York), 244, 250, 260
East River (New York), 270
Eastman, Max, 67
Eastman School of Music, 161
Ebel (family), 342n5
Electra (character), 191
Elkins, Felton Broomall, 48–49, 326n11
Elkins-Widener family, 47, 326n11
Ell, Christine, 71, 80–81, 329n45
Ellsworth, Mark, 37, 324n25
*Elmer and Lily* (Saroyan), 252, 346n51
Emmy Award, 212
Emperor Jones (character), 81, 224, 345n31
*The Emperor Jones* (O'Neill), xv, xvii, 22, 23, 32, 40, 50, 54, 57, 81, 84, 85, 102, 110, 114, 118, 224, 227, 313, 316, 323n17, 325n35, 327n30, 333n55, 345n31
*Encyclopaedia Britannica*, 113
*Enemies* (Boyce and Hapgood), 56
England (English, British), xvi, 89, 94, 99, 115, 123, 154, 161, 192, 194, 205, 208, 235, 322n4, 338n33, 340n57, 343n8, 345n33, 350n39
Esteban (toy monkey), 199
*Ethan Frome* (Davis), 229
Etoile (Paris), 196
*Eugene O'Neill: Beyond Mourning and Tragedy* (Black), 2
*Eugene O'Neill: A Documentary Film* (Burns), 2
*Eugene O'Neill: A Life in Four Acts* (Dowling), 2
Eugene O'Neill Foundation, 198
*Eugene O'Neill: The Man and His Plays* (Clark), 1, 231
Eugene O'Neill National Monument Association, 198
"Eugene O'Neill Returns After Twelve Years," 66
Eugene O'Neill Society, 343n12
Eugene O'Neill Theatre, 219, 344n25
Euripides, 139, 336n89
Europe (European), 34, 77, 115, 141, 143, 166, 176, 190, 192, 193, 215, 304
*European Theories of the Drama* (Clark), 34
Evans, Sam (character), 347n59
*Exile's Return* (Cowley), 110
*Exorcism* (O'Neill), 102, 333n47, 342n77
Experimental Theatre, Inc., 77, 104, 337nn21–22

Fairleigh-Dickinson College, 265, 315
*Families: From the Adamses to the Roosevelts* (Schriftgiesser), 220
*Fashion* (Mowatt), 119
Faulkner, William, 110, 237
*Faust* (Goethe), 323n18
Federal Theatre Project (New Jersey), 66
Ferber, Edna, 340n56
Fernandez, Willie, 112
Fetzer, Claudia Andreasen, 201, 342n1
Fields, Dorothy, 346n50
Fields, Herbert, 346n50
Fife, Ada (character), 339n49
Fifth Avenue (New York), 243, 274
Fisk, Edward, 81
Fisk, Shirley Carter (Dr.), 243–44, 269, 345n39
Fitzgerald, Barry, 341n64
FitzGerald, Edward, 338n37

Fitzgerald, F. Scott, 85, 331n20
Fitzgerald, M. Eleanor (Fitzi), 104, 240–41, 242, 333n48
Fladger, Louis, 141, 143, 336n1
Florida, 33, 158
*Fog* (O'Neill), 323n15
Folkard and Lawrence, 11
Fonda, Henry, 224
Fontanne, Lynn, 165
Ford, John, 341n64
Forest Hill Cemetry, 279
*The Forsyte Saga* (Galsworthy), 156, 338n32
Fort Wayne (Indiana), 187
Forty Third Street (New York), 227, 233
*The Fountain* (O'Neill), 50, 122, 151, 333n50
The Four Hundred, 49, 327n21
Fourth Street (New York), 70, 110
France (French), 29, 86, 109, 115, 138, 141, 144, 188, 193, 203, 204, 205, 208, 214, 239, 274, 303
Francis, John, 60, 94, 99
Francis, John (Mrs.), 99
Frank, Waldo, 119–20, 334n69
French, Samuel, 92
French Syndicalists, 221
French-Canadian (nurse), 144
*A Friend Indeed* (Hamilton), 28
Friganza, Trixie (Delia O'Callaghan), 90, 332n34
Fulton, Robert, 193

Gable, Clark, 341n66
Gaelic, 209, 215, 218
Gallup, Donald, 343n13
Galsworthy, John, 131, 156, 335n77, 338n32
Garbo, Greta, 144, 174, 336n5
Gardner, Virginia, 71, 329n46
Garland, Robert, 68
Gaul, Harriet, 79, 80
Gaul, Harvey, 79
Gaylord Farm Sanatorium (Wallingford, Connecticut), 7, 234–35
Gelb, Arthur, 2, 19, 284, 302, 322n6, 348n14
Gelb, Barbara (Stone), 2, 284, 322n6, 348n14
Georgia, 141, 147, 169, 171, 193, 203, 217, 303
German Expressionists, 114
*German Submarines in Yankee Waters* (James), 54
Germany (German), 29, 114, 192
Gershwin, George, 340n58
Gershwin, Ira, 340n58
Gierow, Karl Ragnar, 343n13
Gilbert, Ruth, 346–47n54
Gilhooley's, 253, 255
Gilpin, Charles Sidney, 227, 345n31
*Give Your Heart to the Hawks* (Jeffers), 149
Glaspell, Susan Keating (Mrs. Cook), xiv, 3, 37, 43, 51–52, 54, 67, 68, 79, 81, 100, 151, 313, 324n27, 327n24, 328n33, 330n11
*The Glass Menagerie* (Williams), 343n11
*Glencairn Cycle* (O'Neill), 54, 327n25, 341n64
"God Bless America" (Berlin), 346n48
Goddard Seminary, 220
*Gods of the Wild*, 128
Goethe, Johann Wolfgang von, 33, 323n18
*Gold* (O'Neill), 191
Gold, Michael, 70, 72, 328–29n42
Golden Rule, 233
Golden Theatre, 138
Golden Swan. *See* "Hell Hole" (Golden Swan saloon)
Gordon, Max, 115, 229–30, 337n20
Gorky, Maxim, 333n56
Goucher College, 66
Granada (Spain), 193
Grand Central Station (New York), 269
Great Britain, 29, 150
*The Great God Brown* (O'Neill), 4, 50, 132, 134, 135, 136, 191, 227, 314, 335n82
"Great God O'Neill," 50, 128
Greece (Greek), 51, 54, 109, 138, 169, 191, 265
Greek tragedy, 89, 258, 261
Greeley, Horace, 79
Greene, John M, 232
Greenwich Village (New York), xiv, xvi, 4, 5, 16, 22, 43, 51, 53, 59, 70, 72, 73,

74, 77, 79, 84, 89, 94, 110, 111, 112, 118, 121, 138, 194, 224, 229, 322n5
Greenwich Village Theatre, 9
Grolier Poetry Bookshop, 135–36, 335n83
Group Theatre, 346n51
Guéthary (Basque country), 192
Guild Theatre, 339n40
"Gunga Din" (Kipling), 345n34

Haas, Robert, 247, 346n43
*The Hairy Ape* (film), 341n65
*The Hairy Ape* (O'Neill), xv, xix, 40, 48, 50, 57, 93, 113, 132, 138, 148, 160, 173, 175, *186*, 203, 217, 234, 313, 337n15
Hamilton, Clayton, 8, 28–30, 323n15, 323n16
Hammerstein II, Oscar Greeley Clendenning, 173, 340n55, 346n50
Hapgood, Hutchins, 3, 43, 56–58, 100
Harford, Honey (character), 238, 345n36
Harlem, 303
Harlem Division, 113
Harlem Renaissance, 303
Harris, Jed, 47
Harry Hope (character), 111, 221, 254, 346–47n54
Harry Hope's ("No Chance Saloon," "Bedrock Bar," "End of the Line Café,""Bottom of the Sea Rathskeller") (saloon), 111, 211, 221, 254, 256
Harrisburg Community Theatre, 102
Hart, Lorenz 'Larry" Milton, 172, 340n53, 340n54
Hartford (Connecticut), 36, 46, 143, 231
*The Hartford Courant* (newspaper), 232, 235
Hartford History Center of the Hartford Public Library, 231
*Hartford Times*, 33, 36
Hartley Manners-Laurette Taylor (combination), 46, 326–26n4
Harvard Club, 299
Harvard Medical School, 348n16
Harvard University, 30, 31, 43, 45, 47, 56, 110, 130, 135, 206, 211
Hasenclever, Walter, 114, 334n59
Hastings, Warren, 3, 7, 11–17
Havel, Hippolyte, 70, 72, 111, 328n41
Hawthorne, Charles Webster, 88, 331n31
Haydon, Julie (Mrs. George Nathan), 217, 344n22
"Haymarket" (New York), 15, 321n3
"The Haymarket" (O'Neill), 321n3
Haymarket martyrs (Chicago), 70
Haynes, Mabel, 3, 8, 25–27
Hayward, Susan, 341n65
Hearst, Patty, 349n18
Hedgerow Theatre, 102, 333n46
Heidt, Joseph, 222, 232, 234, 236, 344n28
Helburn, Teresa, 3, 141, 150, 161, 165–77, 252, 253, 338n29, 339n50
"Hell Hole" (Golden Swan saloon), xiv, 43, 54, 70–71, 110–12, 117, 195, 322n5
"Hell-on-Wheels," 63
Hepburn, Katherine Houghton, 174, 175, 340n60
Hercules (Herculean), 266
Heyward, Dorothy, 339n40
Heyward, Dubose, 339n40, 340n58
Hickman, Theodore "Hickey" (character), 254, 255, 256, 346–47n54, 347n57, 347n59
"High Dive," 234
Hill, Beatrice, 46
Hindu, 107
*History of Modern Drama* (Clark), 34
Hoboken (New Jersey), 193
Hoffman, Calvin (Leo Hochman), 3, 77, 132–39, 335n79
Hogan, Josie (character), 257–61, 329n45
Holder Hall (Princeton University), 12
Holladay, Louis, 16–17, 322n5
Holladay, Paula "Polly," 322n5, 329n45
Holland, Hugh, 336n88
Hollander, 22
Hollywood, 135, 174–76, 213, 224, 226, 252, 295, 332n42, 340nn53–54, 340nn61–62
Holm, Celeste, 144, 336n4
Holmes, Oliver Wendell, 224
Home for the Aged and Infirm, 172
*l'homme qui rit*, 188
Honduras, xiii, 7, 18, 19

Hornsby, Rick, 72
Hospital for Special Surgery, 348n16
Hotel Cadillac, 233
"The Hound of Heaven" (Thompson), 70, 71, 73
Hudson Dusters (Dusters) (West Side gang), 111–12
Hudson River, 116
Hughes, Langston, 344n16
*Hughie*, xviii, 201, 272
*The Hunted* (O'Neill), 175. See also *Mourning Becomes Electra* (O'Neill)
Hunter, Ian, 341n64
Hunter, Kim, 257

Ibsen, Henrik, 232
*The Iceman Cometh* (O'Neill), xviii, xix, 3, 18, 66, 69, 111, 150, 166, 174, 177, 201, 211, 216, 220–22, 224, 227–28, 231–33, 250, 252, 253, 255–56, 277, 284, 296, 313, 328n41, 335n80, 339nn45–46, 341n67, 341n76, 344n28, 346n51, 346n53, 346–47n54, 347nn55–59
*I'll Take My Stand* (Southern Agrarians), 104
Ilsa (character in *Casablanca*), 212
Imperial Theatre, 349n22
*Inheritors* (Glaspell), 51
*The Inner World of Abraham Lincoln* (Burlingame), 283
International Workers of the World, 344n27
Invitation to Learning, 266
*In the Zone* (O'Neill), xiv, 150, 151, 195, 229, 327n25, 337nn19–20, 341n64
Irish (Ireland, Irishman), 51, 65, 70, 93, 103, 111, 113, 116, 138, 150, 204, 215, 216, 217, 218, 219, 251, 257, 259
Irish Academy of Letters, 218, 344n23
Irish-American, 156, 347n62
Irish Citizen Army, 215
"It Cannot Be Mad" (O'Neill), 341n72
Italy (Italian), 143, 253
Ives, Burl, 250–51, 296, 346n49

Jagger, Dean, 344–45n29
James, Henry J., 54
James, William, 56
Japan (Japanese), 297
Jeffers, Robinson, 147, 149, 336n9
Jenkins, Charles E., 18
Jenkins, Kathleen. *See* O'Neill, Kathleen Jenkins (Pitt-Smith)
Jenkins (Brown), Susan, 118, 119, 334n65
Jerusalem, 215
Jimmie the Priest's (saloon), 111, 137, 193, 195–96
Jo (character in *Little Women*), 257
John (character), 347n59
John Francis' General Store, 60
John Francis House (John Francis's "flats"), 79, 94
John Golden Theatre (New York), 154
*John Lardner Reader* (Schulian), 144
John the Baptist (biblical), 45
Johnson, Earle F., 263, 283–86
Jones, Margo, 299
Jones, Robert Edmond (Bobby Jones), 77, 85, 86, 104, 105, 107, 113, 119, 150, 167, 254, 256, 314, 347n55
Jonson, Ben, 167, 339n47
Joseph (biblical), 48
Joyce, James, 80, 330n3
*The Joyous Season* (Barry), 258
*Juno and the Paycock* (O'Casey), 215

Kaeselau, Charles, 81, 330n11
Kahn, Otto Hermann, 119, 334n70
Kaiser, George, 114
Kaiser Foundation Hospital, 342n79
Kalak, 194, 341n75
Kalmar, Hugo (character), 111
Kaufman, George S., 9, 229
Kazan, Elia, 349n31
Keane, Doris, 107–8, 333n51
Keats, John, 13, 334n61
Keefe and Keefe (ambulance), 243
Kemp, Harry ("the poet of the dunes"), 37, 43, 53, 59–65, 81, 91, 324n27, 328n33
Kennedy, Charles O'Brien, 77, 92–93, 297, 349n29
Kenny, Elizabeth, 344–45n29
Kern, Jerome David, 173, 340n56
Khan, Kublai (character), 162, 339n43

Khayyam, Omar, 159, 338n37
Kinkead, Cleves, 47, 326n14
Kipling, Rudyard, 13, 30, 235, 323n14, 345n34
Kirkland, Alexander, 341n66
Kirkland, Jack, 347n62
Klan (Ku Klux Klan; KKK), 59, 119
Klopfer, Donald, 146, 247, 336n8, 346n43
Knights of Labor, 221
Knopf, Alfred A., 305
Knox, Alexander, 344–45n29
Komroff, Manuel, 130, 335n75
Kozol, Dr Henry Leo, 292, 298, 299, 301, 349n18
Kramm, Joseph, 336n3
Krause, David, 216, 344n25
Kreymborg, Alfred, 74, 329n51

La Gallienne, Eva, 337n21
Lafayette (California), 198
Lafayette Hotel, 86
Lambs Club, 31
Langner, Lawrence (the Langners, Mrs. Langner), 3, 134, 141, 150–57, 161, 163, 165, 169, 173, 174, 232, 249, 252–55, 263, 267, 269, 288, 293, 296, 297, 300, 302, 304, 305, 331n30, 335n80, 338n25, 338n29, 338n31, 340n59, 343n14, 350n41
Larchmont Yacht Club (Westchester, New York), 18
Lardner, John Abbott, 141, 144–45
Lardner, Ring, 144
Larimore, Earle, 154, 204, 256, 342n2, 347n59
Larkin, James "Big Jim" ("Irish Labor Leader"), 216–17, 344n21
de La Rouchefoucauld, 108, 333n53
"The Last Will and Testament of Silverdene Emblem O'Neill," xviii, 343n9
Latimer, Frederick Palmer (Judge Latimer), 4, 7, 33–35, 323n21, 325n34
*Lazarus Laughed* (O'Neill), 33, 103, 130, 134, 189, 191
Le Plessis, 195
Lee, William, 3, 7, 20–21
Leeds, Nina (character), 135
LeHand, Marguerite "Missy" (character in *Sunrise at Campobello*), 257
Leland, 301
Lenorman, Henri-René, 190, 341n71
Leonard, Robert Z., 341n66
*The Letters of Sean O'Casey*, 216
Lewis, Albert "Al," 151, 229, 337n20
Lewis and Gordon, 229, 337n20
Lewis, Sinclair, 193, 216, 237, 341n73, 347–48n5
Library of Congress, 303
*Life with Father* (Lindsey and Crouse), 295, 349n21
Life of O'Neill, 218
Life-Saving Station (Coast Guard Station) (O'Neill's house, Provincetown), xv, 58, 62, 63–64, 80–82, 85, 88, 94, 150, 151, *181*, 337n18
Light, James, 95, 118, 119, 314, 328n32, 332n43, 334n65
Light, Susan (Sue). *See* Jenkins (Brown), Susan
Lily (character), 159
*Lima Beans* (Kreymborg), 74, 329n51, 329n53
Lincoln, Abraham, 283
Lincoln Center, 349n31
*Lincoln and the Civil War* (Burlingame), 283
Lindsay, Dorothy, 296, 349n21
Lindsay, Howard, 295, 296, 301, 349n21, 349n24, 350n34
Little Theatre movement, 66–67
*Little Women*, 257
Liveright, Horace, 119, 146, 334n70
Living Theater, 74
*The Lobbyists* (Schriftgiesser), 220
Lodge, Henry Cabot, 220
Loew's Theater (St. Louis, Missouri), 20
London (England), 107, 189, 192, 215
*Long Day's Journey Into Night* (O'Neill), xviii, xix, xx, 1, 3, 18, 25, 91, 103, 137, 201, 207, 209, 217, 234, 272–75, 277–78, 282, 322n9, 315, 316, 322n9, 324n24, 338n34, 338n36, 347n4, 348nn6–7, 348n12
Long Island (New York), 204, 231–32, 234, 235

*The Long Voyage Home* (O'Neill), 69, 175, 191, 341n64
*Lord Jim* (Conrad), 323n14
Lord's Prayer, 114, 286
*The Loretta Young Show*, 252
*Lost in the Stars*, 161
*Love 'Em and Leave 'Em* (Weaver and Abbott), 47, 50
Louisville, Kentucky, 18
Loving, Elsa (character), 349–50n33
Loving, Pierre, 7, 22–24
*The Lower Depths: Scenes from Russian Life* (Gorky), 112, 333n56
Loy, Mina, 74, 329n52
Lunt, Alfred, 165
Lyman, David Russell (Dr.), 235

McCarthy, Joseph Raymond "Joe," 216, 344n19
McComber, Muriel (character), 339n44
McGinley, Art, 4, 7, 36–38
McLean Hospital (Boston), 287, 301, 350n37
*Macbeth* (Shakespeare), 9
Macdougal Street (New York), 23, 43, 57, 58, 74, 327n30
Macgowan, Kenneth, xv, 77, 85, 104, 107, 314
MacLane, Mary, 81, 330n5
Madden, Richard, 147, 148–49, 229–30, 265
Madison Avenue (New York), 217, 269, 271
Madison Hotel (Hotel Madison), 148, 217, 304
Madison Square Garden, 156, 188
Maeterlinck, Maurice, 33, 323n18
*Magda* (Sudermann), 9
Maher, Beatrice Ashe. *See* Ashe (Maher), Beatrice
Maher, James E., 45
Main Street (New London), 27, 36, 281
Maine, 81, 122, 125, 127, 136, 192, 293
Malvolio (character), 24, 323n11
Mamoulian, Azalea, 164
Mamoulian, Rouben, 3, 141, 161–64, 339n44
*The Man Who Was "Shakespeare"* (*The Murder of the Man Who Was "Shakespeare"*), 132
Manges, Horace, 272
Manners, J. Hartley, 46, 32526n4
Mannon, Christine (character), 191, 342n2
Mannon, General (character), 175
Mannon, Lavinia (character), 160, 175, 191, 340–41n62, 342n2, 350n39
Mannon, Orin (character), 175–76, 191, 342n2, 347n59
Mannons (characters), 4, 169, 191
Mansfield, Richard (Meridan Phelps), 37, 324n25
Manufacturers Trust Company, 274
*Many Loves* (Williams), 74
Maplewood (New Jersey), 212
Marblehead (Massachusetts), 2–3, 138, 199, 203, 236, 247, 263, 266, 267, 276, 281, 283–87, 290, 297, 298, 302
Marblehead Neck, 236, 247, 248, 287, 297, 346n45
Marbury, Elisabeth "Bessie," 301, 350n35
*Marco Millions* (O'Neill), xvi, 3, 77, 103, 150, 152, 153, 161, 165, 172–73, 191, 335n80, 339nn40–41, 340n56, 347n59, 349n31
Marinoff, Fania, 147, 154, 155, 303, 304
Markham, Marcella, 4, 201, 211
Marlowe, Christopher, 132, 139
Marr, Joseph, 256, 347n58
Marsden, Charles (character), 135
Marshall (Langner), Armina, 154–56, 173, 258, 302, 338n29, 340n59
Marshall, E. G., 346–47n54, 347n59
Martin, John, 127–29
Masefield, John, 23, 30, 323n14
Massachusetts General Hospital, 277, 288, 349n18
*The Masses* (magazine), 53, 67, 70, 80–81
Massey, Edward, 47, 326n10
Masters, Edgar Lee, 48, 326–27n17
Matson, Norman, 81–82, 330n11
Maugham, William Somerset, 131, 190, 335n77, 338n24
Maurin, Peter, 70
Mayer, Louis Burt, 174, 340n61

Mayo, Dr. Frederic Breed, 2, 263, 269, 287–89
Mechanicsburg (Pennsylvania), 102
Medan (Sumatra), 158
Melody, Cornelius (character), 238, 345n36
Melrose (Massachusetts), 130
Mencken, H. L., 37, 67, 68–69, 187, 234, 324–25n29, 325n30, 328n36, 328n40
Mennonite (family), 206
Merman, Ethel, 300, 301, 349n22
*Merton of the Movies* (Kaufman and Connolly), 9
Metro-Goldwyn-Mayer (MGM), 163, 174, 340n62
Metropolitan Museum of Art, 239
Mexican War, 233
Meyer, Frank, 266–67
Michelangelo, 162
*The Mighty Nimrod* (Kennedy), 92
Miller, Arthur, 3, 349n31
Miller family (characters), 159
Miller, Nat (character), 159
Miller, Richard (character), 159, 339n44
Milton, John, 14
*Mirror in My House* (O'Casey), 215
Mitchell, Thomas, 92–93, 332n38, 341n64
Modern Language Association, 343n12
Modern Library (book series), 146, 237, 246, 291, 336n8
Moeller, Philip, 150, 154, 161, 165, 167, 338n26, 339n46
Molière (Jean-Baptiste Poquelin), 67, 328n35
Molnár, Ferenc, 67, 328n35
Monroe, Marilyn, 208, 342–43n7
Mont Blanc, 124
Monte Cristo (car agency), 158, 338n34
Monte Cristo (character), 11, 20–21, 31, 37, 48, 58, 65, 75, 91, 206
Monte Cristo Cottage, 7, *178*, *179*, 283, 284, 324n24
Monterey, Carlotta. *See* O'Neill, Carlotta Monterey (born Hazel Tharsing)
*A Moon for the Misbegotten* (O'Neill), xviii–xix, xx, 148, 177, 201, 218, 224, 232, 256, 257, 261, 296, 299, 336n12, 341n67, 347n60, 347n61, 347n62, 347n4
*The Moon of the Caribbees* (O'Neill), xiv, 32, 72, 191, 195, 323n17, 341n64
*The Moon of the Caribbees and Six Other Plays of the Sea* (O'Neill), xiv–xv, 146
Moore, Dr. Merrill, 267, 268, 270, 298–301, 347n3
*More Stately Mansions*, xviii, 213–14, 272, 338n31, 343n13, 345n36
Morello, Chuck (character), 347n58
Morgan, Ralph, 341n66
Morris, McKay, 339n43
Mounet-Sully, Jean, 109, 333n54
Mount Sinai Hospital, 241
*Mourning Becomes Electra* (O'Neill), xvii, 3, 4, 40, 109, 141, 155, 160, 168–69, 172, 174–76, 191, 204, 227, 234, 235, 314, 338n26, 340–41n62, 341n72, 342n2, 347n59, 350n39
*The Movie Man* (O'Neill), 327n22
Mowatt (Ritchie), Anna Cora, 119, 334n64, 334n68
Murphy, Brenda, 348n12
Museum of the City of New York, 224, 305
*Music After the Great War* (Van Vechten), 303
*My Heart's in the Highlands* (Saroyan), 346n51

Nassau (Long Island), 156, 232
*Nassau Daily Review-Star* (newspaper), 231–32
Nassau Inn, 15
Nathan, Adele Gutman, 43, 66–69, 319
Nathan, George Jean, xv, 3, 5, 37, 68, 141, 187–97, 215, 217, 219, 234, 293, 325n30, 328nn35–37, 341n72, 344n22
National Historic Site, 198
Nazimova, Alla, 204, 227, 342n2
Nazism, 216
Negro (Negroes), 111, 230, 238, 260, 304
Nembutal, 299
New England, 114–15, 156, 204, 228, 232–34, 247, 248, 259, 290
"New England Interiors" (Johnson), 283
New Jersey, 18, 70, 74, 94, 203, 212, 265, 270

New London, Connecticut, xiii, xiv, 3, 7, 8, 25, 27, 28, 29, 30, 33, 35–37, 39, 40, 43, 45, 55, 158, 159, 206, 222, 233–35, 242, 247, 283, 292
*New London Telegraph*, 4, 7, 33–34, 36, 39–40, 235, 321n3, 323n13
New Orleans (Louisiana), 21, 249
*New Republic* (magazine), 104
New School for Social Research, 265
New York, xiii, xiv, xv, xvii, xviii, xix, xx, 7, 9, 11, 15–17, 20, 21, 23, 31, 36, 37, 43, 51, 53, 56, 57, 74, 75, 77, 82, 84, 85, 86, 104, 107, 110, 114, 116, 117, 118, 132, 133, 134, 137, 141, 146–49, 153, 158, 165, 166, 169, 170, 187, 188, 192, 193, 199, 201, 203, 204, 210, 212, 215, 217, 220, 224, 227, 231, 232, 234, 237, 238, 248, 250, 253, 257, 260, 261, 265, 266, 268–71, 274, 275, 277, 281, 288–89, 295, 299, 300, 301, 303, 304, 305
*New York Evening Mail*, 33
*New York Evening Post*, 20
New York Giants, 252
*New York Herald Tribune*, 198
*New York Journal American*, 234
New York Public Library, 45
*New York Times*, 130, 195, 198, 203, 219, 220, 222, 284, 303, 344n25, 344n28
New York Yankees, 92, 252, 332n37
*New Yorker* (magazine), 148, 314, 333n47, 337n12, 339n42, 349n24
New York-Chicago Supply Company, 322n7
Nichols, Dudley, 34041n62, 341n64
*Nigger Heaven* (Van Vechten), 303
*Nineteen Eighty-Four* (Orwell), 344n18
Nobel Prize for Literature, 3, 66, 134, 141, 157, 171, 176, 196, 201, 220, 335n77, 33940n51
North Shore (Massachusetts), 234, 235, 283

O'Brien, Joe, 53
O'Casey, Sean, xviii, 3, 9, 190, 201, 215-19, 233, 344n17, 344n19, 344n25
O'Flynn, 343n14
*O'Neill* (Gelbs), 2, 284, 322n6, 348n14
*O'Neill: Life with Monte Cristo* (Gelbs), 2
*O'Neill: Long Day's Journey Into Night* (Murphy), 348n12
*O'Neill: Son and Artist* (Sheaffer), 2, 18
*O'Neill: Son and Playwright* (Sheaffer), 2, 18
O'Neill, Agnes Boulton, xiv, xvii, 3, 43, 58, 71, 73, 77, 79, 80–82, 85, 88, 89, 94–101, 108, 113, 114, 116, 117, 121, 123, 125, 128–29, 138, 141, *182*, 203, 313, 316, 327n27, 329n2, 330n9, 330n13, 331n23, 337n18, 339n48
O'Neill, Carlotta Monterey (born Hazel Tharsing), xvi, xvii, xix–xx, 1–4, 77, 80, 93, 94, 121, 138, 141, 143, 147, 148, 154–58, 163–64, 167, 169–71, *184*, *186*, 193, 197, 198, 199, 201, 203–10, 211, 212, 213, 215, 217, 218, 222–24, 232, 234, 236, 238–48, 249–51, 255, 259, 260, 261, 263, 266–75, 276–80, 281–88, 290–305, 314, 337n15, 338n27, 338n31, 339n48, 342n79, 34243n7, 343n8, 343n13, 343n14, 345n37, 345n40, 346n44, 346n46, 346n52, 347n4, 348n6, 348n7, 348n10, 348n13, 350nn35–37, 350n40
O'Neill, Edmund, 315, 339n39
O'Neill, Edward, 342n6
O'Neill, Eugene Gladstone, *184*; broken arm episode (1948), 243–44, 263, 274, 287–88, 296; broken leg episode (1951), xix–xx, 2, 203, 263, 267–69, 276–77, 281, 287, 290, 293; childhood of, xiii, 9–10, 33, *178*, *180*; death and burial of, xx, *186*, 276–77, 279–80, 286; and drinking, xiv, xvi, 1, 7, 12, 14–17, 48, 54, 57–58, 70, 79, 81, 83, 88, 90, 94–96, 105, 111, 115–17, 137, 147, 153, 163, 193–94, 206, 234, 296, 304, 333n49, 336n1; in Sea Island, Georgia, xvii, xviii, 147, 154, 169, 171, *183*, 193; in Greenwich Village, 4–5, 23, 43, 70, 72, 89–90, 110–11, 224–25, 229; at Harvard, xiv, 30–31, 47–50, 206; humor of, 5, 38, 50, 58, 122, 209, 225, 227, 233, 252–53, 256, 261, 274; love of popular music, 46, 86, 199, 229–30, 249–50, 295–

96, 304, 325n3; in Marblehead, xix, 2, 203, 236, 247, 267, 276, 281, 283–85, 287; in New London, xiii, xiv, 7, 28–29, 33–41, 45–46, 158–59, 206–7, 233–35, 247, 292; at New London *Telegraph*, xiii, 7, 33–41; in Park Avenue apartment, 239–44; and Parkinson's disease, xix, 1, 136, 174, 211, 230, 240, 243, 249, 259, 268, 270–72, 276, 288–89, 291, 331n28; and Nobel Prize, xviii, 1, 3, 66, 134, 157, 171, 176, 196, 339n51; at Peaked Hill Bar, xv, 80, 84–86, 96–100, 181–82; and pets, 113, 116, 189, 193, 205, 209, 343n9; physical descriptions of, 4, 11, 29, 33, 35, 49, 56, 61, 73, 84, 103, 127, 133–34, 147, 150, 153, 160, 162, 213, 215, 221, 225; at Princeton, xiii, 1, 11–17, 48, 187, 206; at Provincetown, xiv–xvi, 22–23, 37, 43, 50–54, 56–57, 64–65, 67–68, 70, 74–75, *181*; and sex, 72, 89, 114, 138; as sports fan, 5, 91, 92, 131, 144–45, 156, 180, 238, 252, 260, 344n28; spousal abuse, 80, 83, 101, 242, 251, 279; suicide attempt, xiii, 102, 196, 342n77; and swimming, 28, 54, 85, 86, 97, 98, 100, 136–37, 147, 150–51, 152, 155–56, 158, 168, 192, 193, 208, 247, 325n1; at Tao House, xviii, xix, 175, 199, 201, 205, 212, 299, 325n3, 346n45; tuberculosis of, xiii, xiv, 7, 54, 112, 234, 235; writing habits of, 9699, 114, 164–68, 194, 207–8, 222, 227, 249

O'Neill Jr., Eugene, xiii, xviii, xix, 1, 7, 18, 19, 86, 138, 250, 265, 266, 267, 277–78, 285, 304, 315, 336n86, 348n8, 348n12

O'Neill family, 25–26, 37, 234

O'Neill Jr., James (Jamie), xiii, 1, 11, 12, 14–15, 17, 26–27, 37, 40, 77, 80–81, 102–3, 113, 159, *180*, 188, 218, 283, 304, 315–16, 325n35

O'Neill Sr., James, xiii, 1, 4, 7, 8, 9, 11, 12, 18, 20–21, 26, 30, 31–33, 36–37, 40, 43, 48, 55, 58, 65, 74–75, 81, 91–92, 102, 103, 106, 159, *180*, 188, 196, 206, 225, 233, 235, 247, 285, 315, 316, 324nn23–26, 330n6, 335n81, 338n34, 342n6

O'Neill, Kathleen Jenkins (Pitt-Smith), xiii, 3, 7, 18–19

O'Neill, Mary Ellen (Ella) Quinlan, xiii, xiv, xv, 1, 3, 7, 8, 9–10, 11, 12, 25–27, 37, *179*, 187, 233, 242, 285, 315

O'Neill, Nance, 37

O'Neill (Chaplin), Oona, xvi, xix, 1, 2, 77, 94, 125, 138, 250, 265, 271, 272, 278, 285, 288, 291, 313, 346n46, 348n8

O'Neill, "Red," 45, 325n1

O'Neill, Shane, xiv, xix, 1, 2, 58, 77, 81, 85, 86, 94, 101, 138, *182*, 199, 250, 265, 272, 278, 285, 291, 299–300, 304, 316, 327–28n31, 330n8, 348n8

Oakland (California), 198, 224, 314, 338n28, 343n8

Oakley, Annie, 349n22

Oates, Whitney J., xviii, 265

Oban, Willie (character), 256, 346–47n54, 347n59

*The Obituary* (Commins), 237

Oedipus (character), 89, 108–9, 333n54

*Oedipus at Colonus* (Sophocles), 89, 331n33

*Oedipus Rex* (Sophocles), 108–9, 331n33, 333n54

Off-Broadway, 3, 130

"The Old Bean," 194–95

*Oklahoma!* 161, 164, 165, 252, 340n55, 344n28, 346n50

Old Testament, 191–92

Old Vic, 108

Olson (character), 341n64

Orestes (character), 191

Orpheum Circuit, 229

Orwell, George (Eric Arthur Blair), 216, 344n18

Osterman, Lester, 216, 219, 344n25

*Othello* (Shakespeare), 229, 324n23

Packard (boarding house), 345n33

Paine's Fireworks,

*Paradise Lost* (Milton), 14

Paris (France), 110, 141, 144, 168, 190, 196, 244, 303, 315, 321–22n4, 330n11, 331n19, 335n75, 336n6

*Paris Herald* (newspaper), 144, 190
Parkinson's (disease), xix, 1, 136, 174, 211, 230, 240, 243, 249, 259, 268, 270–71, 276, 288, 289, 291, 331n28, 335n84, 348n15
Parritt, Don (character), 3, 252, 253, 255, 341n76
*Part of a Long Story* (Agnes Bolton), 331n32
*Patience* (Gilbert and Sullivan), 86, 331n26
Patterson Jr., Dr. Robert Lee, 291, 298, 348n16
Payton, Corse, 37, 324n26
Peaked Hill Bar, xv, 77, 79, 80, 81, 82–83, 84, 87, 89, 94–97, 100, *181*, *182*, 337n18. *See also* Life-Saving Station (Coast Guard Station) (O'Neill's house, Provincetown)
Pearl (character), 254, 346–47n54
Peck, Seymour, 3, 201, 203, 263, 276, 278, 348n8
Pedi, Tom, 253, 346n53
Pell, Arthur, 336n8
*Penguin* (boat), 236, 345n35
Peninsular Wars, 238
Pequot Avenue (New London), 206–7, 324n24
Pequot Summer Colony, 37
Pernod, 144
Philadelphia, Pennsylvania, 9, 90, 94, 102, 169, 256
Philips Academy, Andover, 283
Pinehurst (Provincetown), 57
Pioggi, Rocky (character), 346n53
Pitt-Smith, George, 18
Pittsburgh, Pennsylvania, 110, 156, 262
Playwrights Company, 173
*Plots and Playwrights* (Massey), 47
*The Plough and the Stars* (O'Casey), 9, 215
*PM* (newspaper), 203
Poe, Edgar Allan, 4, 13, 225, 238
Point O'Rocks Lane (Marblehead Neck, Massachusetts), 248
Polo, Marco (character), 347n59
Pond's Extract, 196
Pope Francis, 70
*Porgy* (Dubose and Dorothy Heyward), 161, 339n40, 340n58
*Porgy and Bess*, 161, 173, 340n58
Potiphar's Wife (biblical), 48
Power, Tyrone, 37; father of, 324n25
Powers, Tom, 154
*Prescott Proposals* (Lindsey and Crouse), 301, 302, 350n34
*President Monroe* (ship), 143
Price, Mollie, 330n12
Princeton University, xiii, 1, 7, 11–13, 15–17, 21, 48, 89, 187, 206, 245, 246, 265, 283, 305, 315, 321nn1–2, 321–22n4, 322n7, 327n18, 341n68, 345n41
Prohibition, 111
Providence (Rhode Island), 36, 39
*Providence Journal-Bulletin*, 39
Provincetown (Massachusetts), xiv, xv, xvi, 3, 4, 19, 37, 38, 43, 50, 51, 53, 54, 56, 57, 59–62, 64, 66, 67, 71, 77, 79, 82, 84, 88, 89, 94, 111, 121, 150, 192, 313, 316, 324n27, 327nn28–29, 327–28n31, 330n8, 330n11, 334n62, 337n18
Provincetown Players, 22–23, 37, 43, 51, 53, 56–57, 59, 61–62, 70, 72, 74, 77, 79, 84, 85, 89, 92, 102, 104, 106, 107, 110, 112, 118, 119, 133, 138, 151, 153, *181*, 237, 313, 314, 316, 322n5, 322n8, 323n17, 324n27, 327nn23–24, 327nn28–30, 328nn32–33, 328n41, 328–29n42, 329n45, 329n47–48, 329n51, 329n53, 330n13, 330n17, 330–31n18, 332n38, 332nn43–44, 333n48, 333n55, 334n64–65, 337n15
Provincetown Playhouse, 22–23, 43, 58, 70, 74, 77, 89, 104, 106, 107, 112, 138, 153, 331n26, 339n49
Provincetown Theatre (New York), 85, 118–19, 133
Pulitzer Prize, xv, xvii, 2, 18, 21, 30, 51, 77, 141, 146, 220, 272, 322n9, 344n16, 346n51
*Punch* (magazine), 123
Puritan (Puritans), 105, 115, 156, 191, 194
Purdy's Station, 113, 117
*Pursuit of Happiness* (Lawrence Langner and Armina Marshal), 338n29
Pyne, Mary, 53, 58

Quintero, José, 3, 214, 343n13
*The Quintessence of Ibsenism* (Shaw), 159, 338n35

Rabelais, 188
Radio City (New York), 232
Raines Law, 110, 221, 344n26
Random House, xviii, xix, xx, 141, 146, 149, 237, 244, 246, 271, 272–73, 275, 277, 282, 346n43, 347n4
*Rangely* (skiff), 123
Rauh, Ida (Mrs. Max Eastman), 37, 324n27
Red Inn (Provincetown), 84
Reed, John (Jack), xiv, 54, 67, 71, 327n26, 337n18
Regent Nursing Home, 297
Reid, Carl Benton, 255, 346–47n54
Reinhardt, Max, 161, 314, 339n42
Rembrandt Harmenszoon van Rejn Reid, 323n19
*Representative One-Act Plays by British and Irish Authors* (Clark), 34
Revelation (scripture), 32122n4
Revolutionary War, 151
Rhodes Scholarship, 338n33
Rhodes, Sir Cecil John, 158, 338n33
Rice, Elmer, 216, 344n16
Ridgefield (Connecticut), xv, xvi, 77, 86, 94, 95, 113, 116, 117, 118, 151, 313, 316
"The Rime of the Ancient Mariner" (Coleridge), 323n21
Rippin, Helen, 345n33
Rippin, James, 345n33
Ritz-Carlton Hotel, 247, 284
Robards Jr., Jason, 343n12
Robeson, Paul, xvi, xvii, 90
Robertson, Sparrow, 141, 144–45, 190, 336n6
Robinson, Sugar Ray (Walker Smith Jr.), 93, 190, 332n40
Rodgers, Richard Charles, 172, 340n53, 340nn54–55, 346n50
Rogers, Will (35), 32324n22
Roma (restaurant), 49
*Romance* (Sheldon), 107, 333n51, 345n37
Rooney, Mickey, 339n44
*Rose and Crown* (O'Casey), 215
*The Rosenberg Story* (Gardner), 71
"Rosie" (player piano), 249–50, 304, 325n3
Roosevelt, Franklin Delano, 147
Roosevelt, Theodore, 224
"Rosie, You Are My Posy," 193
Rowland (Mrs.) (character) 65
Royal Dramatic Theatre, 343n13
*Rubáiyát of Omar Khayyám*, 338n37
Rubin, Jane, 265
Russell, Rosalind, 340–41n62, 344n29
Russia (Russian), 161, 190, 303, 327n26, 333n56, 340n57, 347n1
Rutgers University, 90
Rutherford (New Jersey), 74, 265
Ryan, Paul Ryder, 211
Rychtarik, Charlotte E., 119, 334n67
Rychtarik, Richard Walter, 119, 334n67
Rye (New York), 211

*S. S. Glencairn*. See *Glencairn Cycle* (O'Neill)
*The Saint* (Young), 104
Saint Antoine du Rocher (Touraine), 187
*Saint Joan* (Shaw), 167
St. Louis (Missouri), 20, 201, 262
Salem (Massachusetts), 267, 268, 269–70, 297, 300
Salem Hospital, xx, 3, 267, 287, 288, 290, 297, 301, 349n19
Salome (biblical), 45, 325n2
*Salt House* (Werner), 79, 80
*Salt-Water Poems and Ballads* (Masefield), 323n14
Salvation Army, 284
*Salvation Nell* (Sheldon), 345n37
Samuel Merritt Hospital (Oakland, California), 198, 342n78
Samuel Merritt School of Nursing (Oakland, California), 198, 342n78
Samuel Merritt University, 342n78
*San Antonio Express*, 198
San Francisco (California), 141, 143, 198, 201, 212, 224, 234, 249, 280
Sandy, Sarah, 342n4
Santell, Alfred, 341n65
Sardi's (restaurant), 296, 349n25
Saroyan, William, 252, 346n51, 347–48n5

*Saturday Review of Literature* (magazine), 171
Savoy Plaza, 301
Sax, Carol, 68
Scandinavia, 92, 286
Schnitzler, Arthur, 67
Schriftgiesser, Karl, 201, 220–23
Schulian, John, 144
Schwab, Dr. Jacob, 288
Scriptures (Biblical), 132, 156
*The Sea Fox* (Corbett), 88
Sea Island (Georgia), xvii, xviii, 141, 147, 148, 154–57, 158, 169, *183*, 193, 249, 315
Seattle (Washington), 141, 224
*The Second Engineer* (O'Neill), 49
The Second Mate (character), 322n8
*Selected Letters of Eugene O'Neill* (Bogard and Bryer), 45
*The Shadow of a Gunman* (O'Casey), 215
Shakespeare, William, 13, 14, 36, 132, 138, 139, 229, 315, 323n11, 324n25, 325n32, 335n76, 336nn88–89
Shaw, George Bernard (G.B.S.), 9, 13, 150, 151, 153–54, 165, 166, 167, 224, 227, 335n76, 337n23, 338n35, 344n23
Shay, Frank, 343n8
Sheaffer, Louis (Louis Slung), 2, 3, 18, 43, 46, 71, 74, 88, 161, 216, 222, 263, 276, 287, 290, 303
Shearer, Norma, 341n66
Shelley, Percy Bysshe, 13
Sheldon, Edward Brewster, 47, 107, 239, 140, 326n12, 345n37
"A Shelf of Printed Plays" (Hamilton), 323n16
Shelton (Connecticut sanatorium), xiii, 7
Shelton Hotel (Boston, Massachusetts), xx, 263, 271–72, 279, 280, 286, 299, 300, 336n87, 348n11
Shotgraven, Amelia (character in *Solid Gold Cadillac*), 257
*Show Boat* (Kern and Hammerstein), 340n56
*The Shrike* (Joseph Kramm), 144, 336n3
*The Silver Tassie* (O'Casey), 215
Simeon (character), 123
*The Silver Whistle*, 252
Simonson, Lee, 161, 339n41
*Sister Kenny* (movie), 226, 344–45n29
Sixth Avenue (New York), 23, 70, 110, 111
Slade, Larry (character), 111, 254, 256, 313, 346–47n54
Sloan, John, 321n3
*The Smart Set*, 68, 187
Smith, Joe, 195
Smithers (character), 102
Smitty (character), 341n64
Smollett, Tobias, 13
Snail Road (Provincetown), 81
*So Red the Rose* (Young), 104
*"So You're Writing a Play!"* (Hamilton), 28
*The Solid Gold Cadillac* (Teichman and Kaufman), 229
"Songs of Araby," 46, 326n7
Sophocles, 89, 108, 139, 144, 331n33
*The Sound of Music* (book, Crouse), 295, 340n55
*South Pacific*, 340n55
Southern Agrarians, 104
Sovey, Raymond, 68, 328n39
Spaeth, J. Duncan, 13, 321n1
Spain (Spanish), 168, 169, 187, 188, 193, 334n69
Spencer, Niles, 116, 334n62
Spithead (Bermuda), 85
*Spoon River Anthology* (Masters), 48, 326–27n17
Stallings, Laurence, 148, 337n15
Stamford (Connecticut), 159, 234. *See also* Betts Academy (Stamford, Connecticut)
Star (drugstore), 26
*State of the Union* (book, Crouse), 295
Steele, Wilbur Daniel, 37, 67, 324n27
Stein, Gertrude, 237
Stekel, Wilhelm, 114, 333n58
Stella (character in *Streetcar Named Desire*), 257
*The Stick-Up* (Loving), 22
Stickney, Dorothy, 349n21
Stiff, Walter, 82, 330n14
Stockholm, 171, 275
Stoeckel, Herbert J., 4, 201, 231–36
Stonehenge, 215

*Strange Interlude* (film), 341n66
*Strange Interlude* (O'Neill), xvi, xvii, 3, 20, 40, 77, 103, 130, 134, 138, 141, 147, 152–53, 154, 160, 165–68, 172, 175, 176, 189, 204, 322n9, 329n43, 335n85, 338n26, 341n66, 347n59
*The Strange Story of John Hanson, First President of the United States* (Stoeckel), 231
*The Straw* (O'Neill), xv, 9, 50, 191
Strindberg, August, 67, 73, 91, 232, 239
Sturm, Frank Pearce, 329n49
Sullivan, James P., 338n34
*Summer Holiday,* 163, 339n44
*Suppressed Desires* (Glaspell and Cook), 68
Sweden (Swedish), 171, 214, 286
Swinburne, Algernon Charles, 13, 159, 338n36
Switzerland, 176, 291
Sze, Mai-mai, 164, 339n45

*Taking Chances*, 203
"A Tale of Possessors Self-Dispossessed" (nine-play cycle) (O'Neill), xviii, 141, 147, 157, 171–74, 201, 207, 213, 223, 278–79, 336n11, 338n31, 345n32
Tammany Hall, 221
Tao House, xviii, xix, 141, 175, 198, 199, 201, 205, 212, 299, 315, 325n3, 332n39, 346n45
Tate, Allen, 120, 334n71, 334–35n72
Taylor, Laurette, 46
Teichman, Howard, 229
"Tenderloin" (New York), 15, 321n3
*"Texas, Li'l Darlin',"* 252
Tharsing, Chris, 343n8
Tharsing, Hazel. *See* O'Neill, Carlotta Monterey (born Hazel Tharsing)
Tharsing, Winifred, 342n79
*The Theory of the Theatre* (Hamilton), 28
*Theatre Arts* (magazine), 104
Theatre Guild, xvi, xvii, xviii, xix, 3, 20, 77, 114, 134, 141, 150–53, 158, 161–62, 165–67, 170–73, 176–77, 201, 211, 229, 231, 232, 238, 249, 250, 252–54, 256, 257–58, 259–61, 267, 277, 295, 299, 304, 314, 335n80, 336n11, 337n21, 337n23, 338n26, 338n29, 339nn40–41, 339n47, 342n2, 343n14, 344n28, 346n51, 346n53, 346–47n54, 347nn59–n61, 349n32, 350n39
Theatre de Lys, 211
Thebes, 108
*Thirst* (O'Neill), xiv, 65, 323n15, 327n29
*Thirst and Other One Act Plays* (O'Neill), xiv,135, 323n15
*This Was Normalcy* (Schriftgiesser), 220
Thompson, Francis, 70, 73
*Three Women* (Werner), 79
*The Threepenny Opera*, 211, 340n52
*Three's a Crowd*, 229
Throckmorton, Cleon, 84, 85, 86, 316
Throckmorten, Juliet Brenon, 4, 77, 84–87
Tiffany & Company, 19
*Time and the Town* (Vorse), 53–55
*The Time of Your Life* (Saroyan), 346n51
Times Square (New York), 232, 233
*Tobacco Road* (Jack Kirkland), 262, 347n62
Toller, Ernst, 114
Tony (Antoinette Perry) Awards, 203, 212
*A Touch of the Poet* (O'Neill), xviii, xix, 156, 170, 213, 224, 232, 238, 272, 279, 338n31, 347n4, 349n31
Touraine (France), 187, 193
Tours (France), 141, 195, 303
*The Tragedian's Tragedy*, 138.
"The Tragic Sense" (Basso), 349n26
*Tramping on Life: An Autobiographical Narrative* (Kemp), 59
*A Tree Grows in Brooklyn* (Betty Smith), 347n61
*Trifles* (Glaspell), 51, 54, 68
Truman, Harry S., 224
Twain, Mark, 224, 339n50
"'Twas Christmas in the Harem," 193
*Twelfth Night* (Shakespeare), 323n11
Tyler, George, 3, 7, 9–10
Tyrone, Edmund (character), 1
Tyrone, James (character), 261, 315, 338n34, 347n61
Tyrone, Jamie (character), 1, 316, 338n36
Tyrone, Mary (character), 315
Tyrone family (characters), 25

Ufford, Celian, 79
Ulster (Ireland), 218
Union Square Stock Company, 233
United States (U.S.A.), 59, 66, 88, 102, 141, 146, 150, 161, 167, 187, 192, 233
United States Conference of Catholic Bishops, 70
United States Congress, 70
University Hall (Princeton University), 12, 16
University Library (Princeton University), 13
University Place (Princeton, NJ), 12, 13
"Upon the Lines and Life of the Famous Scenicke Poet, Master William Shakespeare" (Hugh Holland), 138, 336n88

Vagabond Players, 66, 67, 69
van Dyke, Henry Jackson, 14, 321n2
Van Vechten, Carl, 3, 147, *184*, *185*, 263, 303–5, 350n38, 350n41
*Variety* (magazine), 173
*The Verge* (Glaspell), 51
*Victoria* (Furness Bermuda liner), 133
*A Victorian in the Modern World* (Hapgood), 56
*The View from Pompey's Head* (Basso), 349n26
*Viking Portable Faulkner* (Cowley), 110
*Volpone* (Jonson), 167, 339n47
Volstead Act (National Prohibition Act), 23, 323n10
Vorse, Albert White, 53
Vorse, Mary Heaton, 3, 37, 43, 53, 100, 324n27

Wagnerian opera, 176
Waldorf, 298
Wallingford (Connecticut), 7, 234–35
Ware, Helen, 37, 324n28
*Warnings* (O'Neill), 323n15
*Washington Post* (newspaper), 220
Washington Square (New York), 50, 67, 90
Washington Square Players, xiv, 150, 151, 229, 326n10, 335n80, 337n19
Wassermann, Jakob, 85, 331n21
Waterman, J. S., 348n11
Wayne, John, 341n64
Weaver, John Van Alstyn, 4, 43, 47–50, 326n9
Weeks, Richard F., 3, 7, 11–17
Weill, Kurt, 172, 340n52, 344n16
Weinberger, Harry, 82, 330n13
Welch, Mary, 4, 201, 257–62
Welch, Tom, 13
*Welded* (O'Neill), 50, 107, 108, 151, 189, 333n50, 333n52, 337n21
Wellington (Duke of), 238
Welton, Jean M., 280, 348n10
Wentworth Hotel (Hotel Wentworth) (New York), 133, 162
Werner, Hazel Hawthorne, 3, 77, 79–83
Werner, Morris Robert, 79, 81
Westley, Helen, 150, 165
Westport Country Playhouse, 173, 340n59
Westport (Connecticut), 204, 256
Wharf Theater (Provincetown), 53, 67, 327n28
*What Price Glory?* (Anderson and Stallings), 148, 337n15
*Where the Cross Is Made* (O'Neill), xiv, xv, 110, 191, 333n55
"Whiskey for My Johnnie," 112
"White Christmas" (Berlin), 346n48
Whitehead, Robert, 349n31
Whitman, Walt, 233, 234
*White Buildings* (Crane), 118, 120
"White Hat" club (Princeton University), 13
*The White Sister* (F. Marion Crawford and Walter Hackett), 37, 48
White, Robert, 299
Wiene, Robert, 341n63
Wilde, Oscar Fingal O'Flahertie Wills, 13, 45, 67, 159, 338n38
Williams, Tennessee, 3, 130, 343n11, 346n49, 349n31
Williams, William Carlos, 3, 43, 74–75
Wilson, Edmund ("Bunny"), 3, 4–5, 77, 80, 81, 82, 89–91, 330n16, 330n18
Wilson, Woodrow, 1, 16, 48, 187, 321n2, 327n18
Wingfield, Tom (character), 343n11
*Winston Churchill*, 211

*Within the Gates* (O'Casey), 215
Wobblies, 221, 344n27
de Wolfe, Elsie, 350n35
Wolfe, Thomas, 347–48n5
Wolheim, Louis, 95, 148, 175, 332n42, 337n15
Woman's Peace Party, 53
*The Women* (Boothe), 229
Wood, Peggy, 47
Wood, Robert Williams (Dr.), 68
Woodstock (New York), 116, 118, 266
Woodworth, Robert, 4, 7, 39–41
Woolcott, Alexander, 161, 339n42
Woolf, Samuel Johnson (S. J.), 4, *185*, 201, 224–28
World Series, 92
*The World's Illusion* (Wassermann), 85
World War I (First World War), 89, 110, 115, 143, 233, 295
World War II, 220, 346n45
*Wormwood, a Drama of Paris* (Corelli), 16, 321–22n4

Yale University, xviii, 138, 187, 265, 277, 284, 295, 305, 313, 315, 347n4, 350n40
Yale University Library, 275
Yale University Press, xx, 275, 282, 343n13, 347n4
Yank (Robert "Yank" Smith) (character), 51, 175, 327n19, 337n15
*Yankee Magazine*, 84
Yeats, William Butler, 209, 218, 343n10, 344n23
Young, Stark, 3, 4, 77, 104–9

Zeus, 162, 164
Zora, Manuel ("Manny"), 3, 77, 88
Zorach, Marguerite, 329n53
Zorach, William, 74, 83, 329n53